GREEK PEOPLE

FOURTH EDITION

Robert B. Kebric

University of Louisville

Boston   Burr Ridge, IL   Dubuque, IA   Madison, WI   New York   San Francisco   St. Louis
Bangkok   Bogotá   Caracas   Kuala Lumpur   Lisbon   London   Madrid   Mexico City
Milan   Montreal   New Delhi   Santiago   Seoul   Singapore   Sydney   Taipei   Toronto

For Judy

Higher Education

GREEK PEOPLE, FOURTH EDITION

Published by McGraw-Hill, a business unit of The McGraw-Hill Companies, Inc. 1221 Avenue of the Americas, New York, NY, 10020. Copyright © 2005, 2001, 1997, 1989 by The McGraw-Hill Companies, Inc. All rights reserved. No part of this publication may be reproduced or distributed in any form or by any means, or stored in a database or retrieval system, without the prior written consent of The McGraw-Hill Companies, Inc., including, but not limited to, any network or other electronic storage or transmission, or broadcast for distance learning.

Some ancillaries, including electronic and print components, may not be available to customers outside the United States.

ISBN 0-07-286903-8

1 2 3 4 5 6 7 8 9 0 DOC/DOC 0 9 8 7 6 5 4

Editor-in-chief: *Emily Barrosse*
Publisher: *Lyn Uhl*
Sponsoring editor: *Monica Eckman*
Development editor: *Kirsten Mellitt*
Marketing manager: *Katherine Bates*
Production services manager: *Jennifer Mills*
Production service: *Fairplay Publishing Service*
Manuscript editor: *Margaret Moore*

Art director: *Jeanne M. Schreiber*
Design manager: *Kim Menning*
Cover designer: *Lisa Adamitis*
Interior designer: *Wendy LaChance*
Art manager: *Robin Mouat*
Photo researcher: *LouAnn Wilson*
Illustrator: *Martha Gilman Roach*
Production supervisor: *Rich DeVitto*

The text was set in 11.5/13.5 Adobe Garamond by Thompson Type and printed on acid-free 45# New Era Matte by RR Donnelley, Crawfordsville.

On the cover: The Acropolis at Athens. 1846 by Leo von Klenze. © Joachim Blauel/Artothek. Courtesy Bayerische Staatsgemäldesammlungen, Neue Pinakothek, Munich.

On the half-title page: Female figures form the east pediment of the Parthenon, by the sculptor Phidias. (See page 170 of the text.) Photo by author.

On the chapter openers: The coin shown on the chapter opening pages is the reverse side of a tetradrachm of Alexander the Great (336–323 B.C.). It shows a seated Zeus holding a scepter and eagle. Alexander's name appears in Greek characters on the right. Author's collection.

The credits for this book begin on page C-1, a continuation of the copyright page.

Library of Congress Cataloging-in-Publication Data
Kebric, Robert B.
    Greek people / Robert B. Kebric.—4th ed.
        p. cm.
    Includes bibliographical references and index.
    ISBN 0-07-286903-8 (sc)
    1. Greece—Biography.   I. Title.
DF208.K4 2005   2004046547

Preface

The Individual in History

People make up societies, comprise civilizations. We may formulate and embrace as many theories and compile as many timetables or lists of significant events as we wish to help us understand the past, but we must always return to the simple reality that people are at the foundation of our inquiries.

So often in studies of eras before our own, people have been forced into the background, assigned a role secondary to theories and events. Their humanness has been forgotten. We tend to race over their names—especially if they sound or appear foreign—to discover what happened. Who they were as individuals within the context of their times has mostly gone unnoticed.

No "great people" theory or biographical approach to history is being argued here. There have, of course, always been the Pericleses and Alexanders; they are too closely tied to the events of their times not to have been given extensive coverage. But most modern texts have developed little more than their political *personas,* and, as for the less prominent individuals in ancient society, we have seldom heard of them at all. Characters of lesser note are nonetheless still important for whatever contribution they made to their society. The study of people from many walks of life adds depth to our understanding of the ancient Greeks and, ultimately, of ourselves.

Audience and Approach

In today's society, there is a greater interest in individuals and groups of individuals. For insight into the world of Ancient Greece, *Greek People* will help satisfy that interest. It should prove a useful alternative to more traditional event-and-theory books and be another option for those who have had previous positive response to the few modern works that have emphasized people and the Greek biographies of Plutarch.

Intended for anyone interested in ancient Greek society, *Greek People* attempts to present the ancient Greeks as they were—not cardboard figures who lived in a past so distant that it seems they could never have any meaning for us today. The general historical background necessary to understand developments in antiquity is provided—but the emphasis is on people. The choice of the men and women presented here is necessarily limited. Our knowledge of the past extends only as far as our surviving sources allow. Some of the names will be familiar; others will be more obscure.

Some eras provide more interesting personalities than others, and matching the peculiar circumstances of a particular period with an individual who might best represent some historical or cultural aspect of that period can be a challenge. Nevertheless, each figure selected illustrates an aspect of human activity or behavior within his or her society that might have been neglected or only touched upon in a more general text. In the process, a more "humanistic" view of civilization should evolve.

Many quotations and extracts from ancient writers—sometimes the subjects themselves—have been incorporated so that the people, as much as possible, can tell their own stories. Other interesting individuals who have relevance in a particular chapter are included at appropriate places in boxed-off sections. These brief glimpses should further enrich the reader's appreciation of the "ancient personality." Numerous pedagogical aids, such as maps, illustrations, a chronological table, and a glossary and pronunciation guide, also make *Greek People* a more useful work.

I have selected translations that may not be the most literal but that are, generally, what I feel to be the most readable without losing accuracy. To avoid confusion for the general reader, Latin transliterations have usually been substituted for Greek transliterations in translations where the latter have been used. In maps that have been reproduced from other sources, Greek transliterations of the place names have been retained.

A Concluding Observation

When human beings began to keep track of themselves, the question they first asked was "Who am I?" and then—"What did I do?" Their own individual existence was foremost in their thoughts. In our complex and, some would say, impersonal society, the "doing" often seems to take precedence over the "being." *Greek People* tries to keep both in mind—the person *and* his or her accomplishments. It offers the lives and the world of a few people from the distant past in the hope that the gulf of years that separates us from Ancient Greece will begin to diminish.

The Second Edition and Acknowledgments

I have been pleased at the generally positive reception of *Greek People*—not only by historians and humanists but also by members of the legal and scientific communities and other interested readers at large—and welcome the opportunity for a second edition.

Inevitably, the modern publishing process and all its ramifications contributes to error, and I have attempted to correct and revise any portion of the text that needed such, remaining grateful to those who pointed out any oversight by me or the publisher. There has been an explosion of bibliography since *Greek People* first appeared in 1989, and where appropriate, suggested readings at chapter ends have been significantly enlarged. Additions have also been made to the Chronology, and an expanded illustration program, including many new photos uniquely suited to this book and a geographical map of Greece, has been included. There is added information on Alexander and his father Philip, as some readers requested, along with supplemental sections on women, the role of wife and husband in Ancient Greece, humor, old age, and other social topics. All in all, I hope this is now a book that will remain a useful gauge of the Ancient Greeks through the turn of the century.

I reiterate my appreciation to Professors Thomas W. Africa, Erich S. Gruen, and Frank W. Walbank for reading the original draft of *Greek People;* to Professors Julian Archer, Charles Daniel, Ruth Pavlantos, Paul Properzio, and William H. Stiebing for reviewing the manuscript for Mayfield; and to my previous editor, Lansing Hays. Special thanks go to users of the first edition. For the second edition, I would like to express my gratitude once again to Professor Walbank, whose additional comments and encouragement were very welcome. I would also like to thank the following reviewers selected by Mayfield for their input, which, while remarkably varied, did provide some helpful suggestions: Eugene N. Borza, Penn State University; Douglas Domingo-Forasté, California State University, Long Beach; Radd K. Ehrman, Kent State University; Richard C. Frey, Southern Oregon State College; R. L. Hohlfelder, University of Colorado at Boulder; John H. Kroll, The University of Texas at Austin; and C. Renaud, Carthage College. I also thank Dennis Korbylo for additional photographic work; Mayfield Publishing Company for the opportunity to revise *Greek People;* my editor, Holly Allen, who has overseen the preparation of the new edition; my production editor, April Wells-Hayes; and my wife, Judith Kebric, for her assistance and support through both editions.

I am grateful to the various authors, presses, museums, and other photo sources for their permission to use copyrighted material. Specific acknowledgments for translations and the full references for all photos, maps, and other illustrations are listed at the end of the book.

Finally, I wish to thank all the others who in some way assisted me in the preparation of *Greek People*.

The Third Edition and Acknowledgments

Recently, while the downstairs of our house was being finished, I mentioned to the carpenter, Jim Lund, that he had done such a good job that he should "sign" his work somewhere. To my surprise, he answered that he already had—in the interior of the casing of one of the ceiling beams he had constructed. He also said that he had written the date, mentioned the weather, and left a dollar bill in it. When I asked him why he had done so, he replied that when the house was remodeled or torn down in the future (hopefully, the not-too-present future!), the person doing the work would know he was the one who had built it, the date, what kind of day it was, and would also have something personal of his from the time to hold. He then told me that he had begun the practice because when he was young, he used to accompany his father, also a carpenter, on his projects. Whenever they did remodeling jobs in older neighborhoods on houses built in the early part of the century, they would find the same kind of messages. He said he was fascinated to find the name of a carpenter like himself from the 1920s, or that on a particular date the weather had been "sunny," or a penny or nickel put there by someone now long dead. In that manner, he added, with a touch of emotion, he felt a kinship with that person and that his profession was literally being passed down from generation to generation to craftspeople who had preceded him. Now he wanted to be remembered in the same way fifty or seventy-five years down the road. I told him that without really knowing it, he was unconsciously enacting what history is really all about: who I am, what I did, and how I pass on information about my own time to those in the future. I can think of no more apt example to convey, simply, what history is all about than this one that just "fell into my lap." People seem to have the idea that the study of history is something separate from what they do every day—when, in fact, like Jim, they are exercising the historical process with everything they do. It was with this kind of thought in mind that I originally set out to write this volume, and I am gratified that it continues to attract new readers and keep previous ones interested. I am pleased to prepare a third edition.

I have added an appendix on the people of the Lost Continent of Atlantis because of the fascination their story continues to provide, and I hope my conclusions have put the legend in a rational perspective. The same can be said for a new discussion of the famed Marathon runner, who supposedly brought Athens the news of its victory over Persia at Marathon and whose effort ultimately prompted the modern marathon race. A more sober treatment of Semonides' long poem on women and an insight into the text and times of the Rosetta Stone, the Ptolemaic inscription that provided the key to deciphering the Egyptian hieroglyphs, complete the major text additions. I have also added new photographic material, much of it about women, and recent supplemental bibliography, which has been appended to the end of existing bibliographical sections.

Most of those who have assisted me in the past with the creation and production of this volume have already been mentioned in previous prefaces. I thank them again and express my appreciation. I also add specific thanks to Sarah B. Pomeroy for comments about Semonides' poem on women. I mention Glenn Bugh, Virginia Technical Institute and State University; Kevin Carroll, Arizona State University; Robert L. Hohlfelder, University of Colorado at Boulder; and Myra Levin, Towson State University as readers for this edition and am grateful for their input. I also wish to thank Nikki Lewis and Gene Johnson for their assistance in preparing additional photographs. I remain indebted to the various authors, presses, museums, and all others who have contributed in some way to the success of this work—and especially to my wife, Judith.

The Fourth Edition and Acknowledgments

For the fourth edition, I have reduced the bibliography. It was expanding too fast and was never intended as a primary purpose of the book. High permission fees for visual material have required that some illustrations be eliminated—but much of interest has also been added from personal photo archives. I have also removed some individual boxes in the text in order to make room for new material without significantly increasing the size of the volume. Selecting what to omit was not easy, and I hope the deleted selections do not inconvenience anyone who had found them useful (all is not completely lost, for I have included short references to the excised material where appropriate in the text). In their place, I have added a series of *"Reel" Looks,* which deal with how Greece and Greek people have been treated in Hollywood. As modern society continues to become more visually oriented, historical films have emerged as a primary influence in shaping public perceptions about history. Since Hollywood's fascination with Greece has lately renewed and popular interest increased, these short glimpses from well-known epics will establish how poorly Greek history has been served by them. Finally, I have added a brief glimpse at slavery in Athens, focusing on the story of a former slave named Pasion, who rose from the slave block to freedom, wealth, and citizenship.

I reiterate my thanks to past individuals and institutions, whose assistance in the preparation of this and previous editions is greatly appreciated. I add specific recognition to Harlan J. Berk, Ltd., of Chicago, who generously supplied numerous coin images for this edition, and John Hale for providing the latest information about Delphi. I thank the following reviewers of this edition and am appreciative to those who offered constructive input:

J. Donald Hughes, University of Denver
Glenn R. Bugh, Virginia Tech
Sarah Stever, University of Detroit
Glee E. Wilson, Kent State University

I also wish to thank Nikki Bronke, Christine Howard, Jessica Spayd, Dennis Korbulo, Steven Villwock, and Gene Johnson for their assistance in the preparation of additional photographic material. Monica Eckman, my editor, has done all she could to make my transition to McGraw-Hill a good experience. As ever, I remain grateful to Frank Walbank, Tom Africa, Joe Slavin, and most especially, my wife Judith. Belated recognition goes to Professors Marvin Berry, Saul Levin, and Michael Mittelstadt.

About the Author

Professor Kebric teaches Greek and Roman History, History of the Olympic Games, and the Humanities at the University of Louisville. He is the author of a number of books and articles, including *Roman People,* the companion volume of *Greek People.* He was born in Palo Alto, California, and attended the University of Southern California, where he was Phi Beta Kappa and a Woodrow Wilson Fellow. He received his M.A. and Ph.D. from Binghamton University in New York. He has been historical consultant to Time-Life Books and is a published photographer. He has directed and lectured in programs in Greece, Italy, Egypt, Turkey, and Israel, and spends extended periods in England, Australia, and Hawaii. He lives with his wife, Judith Hartung Kebric, and four basenjis in Louisville, Kentucky. Contact him at robert. kebric@louisville.edu.

Contents

Chapter 4   Eros Unchained

Chapter 5   The Problem with Persia

Chapter 6   A Gilded Edge for a Golden Age

Chapter 7   Rowdies, Rogues, and Robbers

Illustrations and Maps

Figures

Maps

Chronology

The following chronology emphasizes the major events and people discussed in this volume.

Date	Events and People
c. 3000 B.C.	Beginnings of non-Greek Minoan civilization on Crete.
c. 2200–1500	Height of Minoan civilization.
c. 2100	Greek-speaking peoples begin arriving and settling on the Greek mainland. Cultural interchange with the more advanced Minoans begins.
2000	
c. 1600–1100	Period of Achaean, or Mycenaean, Greek civilization in Greece.
c. 1450	Achaeans extend their influence to Crete and dominate Aegean. Minoans begin to disappear as autonomous people.
c. 1400–1200	Period of widespread destruction of sites on Crete and in Greece.
c. 1250	Trojan War.
c. 1100	Dorian pressures; collapse of Achaean civilization; end of Bronze Age in Greece.
c. 1100–750	Greek Dark Age: Breakdown of organization and literacy; mainland migrations to Aegean islands and coast of Asia Minor; Greece enters the Iron Age.
1000	
776	Olympic Games begin.
c. 750–500	Archaic Age: The Greek Renaissance; the revival of trade and commerce ("Commercial Revolution"); return of literacy; age of colonization, tyranny, and the lyric poets.
c. 750	Homer (*Iliad* and *Odyssey*).
735	Naxos, first Greek colony in Sicily, founded; Syracuse established in 733.

720	Sybaris founded in southern Italy; colonization spreading to northern Greece and the Hellespont.
c. 700	Hesiod (*Works and Days* and *Theogony*) (Chapter 2). Hoplite warfare introduced.
c. 650	Archilochus (Chapter 1); ?"Lycurgan" reform at Sparta.
625–585	Tyranny of Periander at Corinth.
	Arion (Chapter 2).
621	Law code of Draco in Athens.
c. 600	Sappho (Chapter 4).

600 . . . .

594	Solon's reforms in Athens.
585	First Greek philosopher, Thales of Miletus, active (Chapter 2).
582–573	Other athletic "circuit" games established: Pythian Games at Delphi (582), Isthmian at Isthmia (581), and Nemean at Nemea (573).
566	Panathenaic festival at Athens reorganized.
561–527	Period of Pisistratus' tyranny at Athens (firmly entrenched by 546).
560–546	Croesus, king of Lydia (Chapter 3).
536	Milo of Croton's first Olympic victory (Chapter 3).
c. 532–522	Polycrates, tyrant of Samos (Chapter 2).
	Eupalinus' tunnel (Chapter 2).
527	Hippias succeeds his father, Pisistratus, as tyrant of Athens.
514	Harmodius and Aristogiton assassinate Hipparchus (Chapter 4).
508	Cleisthenes' democratic reforms in Athens.

500 . . . .

	Westward expansion of the Persian Empire had encompassed the Greeks of Asia Minor. Athens and Sparta have emerged as leading powers on the mainland.
	Height of Phayllus' athletic career (Chapter 3).
493–c. 471	Themistocles as a major political force in Athens.
490–479	Persian Wars with Greek victories at Marathon (490), Salamis (480), Plataea and Mycale (479).
487	Ostracism introduced in Athens.
484	Initial victory of Aeschylus, Athens' first great tragedian.
480–476	Theagenes' Olympic victories (Chapter 3); the poet Pindar's first *Olympian Ode* (476).
478	Delian League founded with Athens as its leader.

469	Cimon's victory at the Eurymedon River (Chapter 5).
468	Sophocles' first dramatic victory over Aeschylus.
460s	Height of Polygnotus' artistic career, *Iliupersis* and *Nekyia* at Delphi; *Iliupersis* in Stoa Poikile in Athens (Chapter 5).
462	Anaxagoras becomes first philosopher to reside in Athens (Chapter 6).
461	Cimon's ostracism and Pericles' ascendancy to power.
460	. . . .
456	Death of Aeschylus.
455	Euripides' first dramatic competition (first victory 441).
454	Athens defeated in Egypt by Persians. Pericles moves Delian League treasury from Delos to Athens for "protection."
450/449	Cimon's ostracism over; dies during campaign in which his forces defeat the Persians at Cyprus. "Peace of Callias" ends hostilities with Persia.
445	Thirty Years Peace between Athens and Sparta.
441–439	Samos crushed by Pericles after rebellion against Athenian Empire; Sophocles' *Antigone*.
440s–430s	Height of the "Golden Age" of Pericles in Athens. Parthenon and other buildings on the Acropolis built; Aspasia, Phidias, Socrates, Sophocles, Euripides, and the sophists are active (Chapter 6).
431–404	Peloponnesian War between Athens and Sparta.
430	Plague, described by the historian Thucydides, strikes Athens (Chapter 6).
429	Death of Pericles.
427–388	Career of Aristophanes, Athens' greatest comic playwright.
421	Peace of Nicias brings temporary end to Peloponnesian War.
420	. . . .
	Trial of the "Poisonous Stepmother" (Chapter 7).
415–413	Athenian expedition to Syracuse in Sicily, which ends in disaster.
414	Peloponnesian War resumes.
406	Deaths of Sophocles and Euripides.
405	Spartan naval victory at Aegospotami brings Peloponnesian War to a close the following year.
400–360	Greece thrown into confusion as a result of the Peloponnesian War. Pasion active (Chapter 7).
c. 400	Trial of Euphiletus for killing the adulterer Eratosthenes; trial of Diogeiton the embezzler (Chapter 7).
399	Trial and death of Socrates.

c. 288   Theophrastus' *Characters* (Chapter 7).

272–146   Hellenistic civilization reaches its peak.

c. 270   Aristarchus of Samos (Chapter 8).

200 . . . .

146   Rome completes its conquest of Macedonia and Greece.

146–30   The great Hellenistic monarchies end as provinces of the Roman Empire.

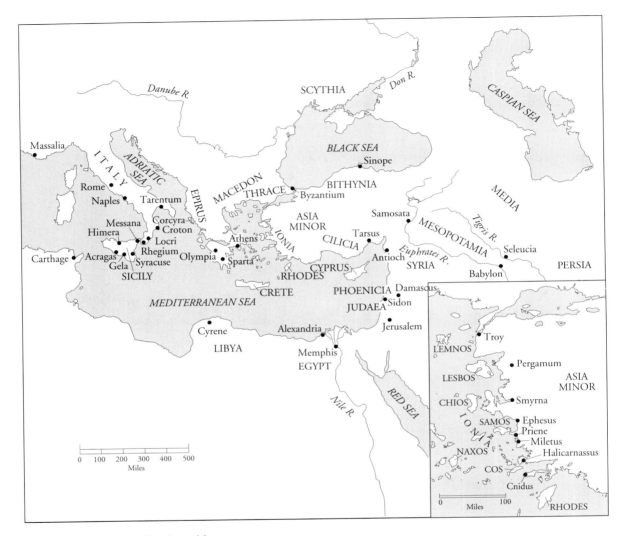

Map 1 *The Ancient Greek world*

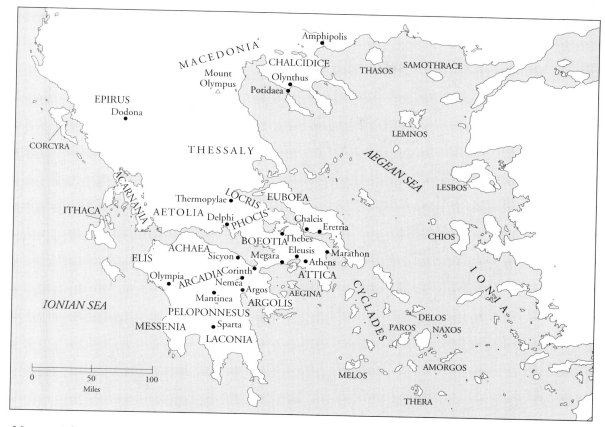

Map 2   The Greek mainland

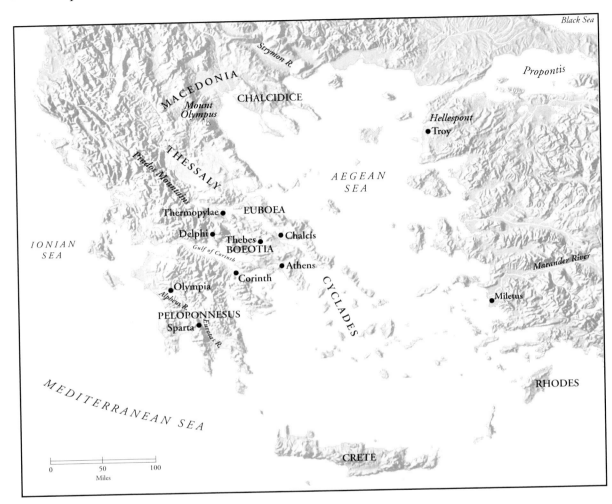

Map 3   *Geographical map of Greece*

1

After Homer

A New Age Finds Its Voice—
Archilochus of Paros, Poet,
Soldier, Illegitimate Son

The fox knows many tricks, the hedgehog only one.
One good one.
(Lattimore, *Greek Lyrics,* "Archilochus" 17)

Homer's "People"

It is in the pages of Homer's *Iliad* and *Odyssey* that the first notable personalities in the Greek tradition come to life. Although quasi-historical at best,
figures such as Agamemnon, Achilles, Odysseus, Ajax, Menelaus, and Helen
have taken on individual personalities. Stories of their exploits beneath the
walls of Troy have inspired readers and listeners for more than twenty-six
centuries, providing fascinating fare for scores of generations. They have
fired the imagination of countless writers, poets, dramatists, artists, and
composers and have enriched our vocabulary with terms such as *odyssey,*
Achilles' heel, and *Trojan horse.*

There is a natural tendency for us to want to believe the tales of heroic
men and women from the remote past, but when placed under the scrutiny
of modern scholarship, the Homeric tradition has not held up well. Agamemnon, Achilles, and the others may have been real people at one time, but the
actual circumstances of their lives are unknown, and descriptions of their
glorious deeds probably belong more to the realm of folktale, myth, and saga
than to fact. Although Homer harks back to a thirteenth-century B.C. world

Figure 1.1 *An idealized representation of Homer (British Museum, London)*

1

Figure 1.2
*Artist's rendition of
Troy in the early
thirteenth century* B.C.

Figure 1.3   *The remains of the walls of Troy, level VI. Chronologically, the Trojan War had to have occurred
c. 1250* B.C. *If so, this was the city that immediately preceded the one involved in the war (VIIA). Scholars have
suggested that the Troy pictured here was destroyed by an earthquake, but some recent arguments contend that this
was the Troy of the Trojan War (see Figure 1.2).*

of Achaean warrior-kings and nobles living in fortified strongholds, clad in gleaming bronze, and brandishing weapons of same, his poems actually reflect a much later period of Greek history—most likely the tenth and ninth centuries B.C. and perhaps slightly afterward.

To most classical Greeks, however, Homer's poems *were* accurate accounts of the Trojan War. They were an important part of the common heritage of Greece, and their content was not to be doubted. In the fifth century B.C., for example, the historians Herodotus and Thucydides felt no reason to question the Homeric version of events at Troy. Later, Alexander the Great traced his ancestry to Achilles, modeled himself on his exploits, and carried a copy of the *Iliad* (or excerpts from it) with him on campaign. Greek children were nurtured on the stories, and many were made namesakes of the godlike heroes. These epic poems were continually combed for suitable parallels and instructional material to fit contemporary situations. The impact of Homer's epics on ancient Greek society was so great that it may not be an exaggeration to say that they had an effect not unlike that which the Bible has had on Judeo-Christian society.

Homer, in fact, lived long after the events he purports to describe—probably in the eighth century B.C. Hundreds of years had passed since his Bronze Age heroes boarded their ships to fight at Troy around 1250 B.C. (traditionally dated 1194 B.C.). Achaean society had crumbled and fallen,

Figure 1.4
The walls of the Achaean citadel of Mycenae, traditionally home of Agamemnon, leader of the Greeks at Troy

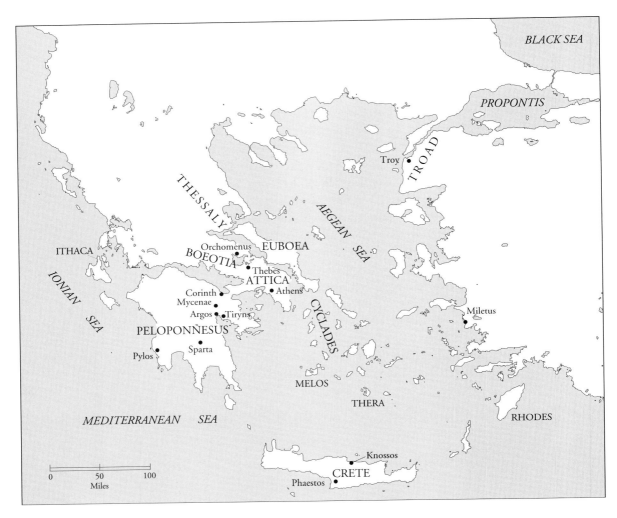

Map 4
The Achaean world

just as the Minoans, the advanced pre-Greek civilization on the island of Crete, had earlier disappeared. The Minoans had been among the most sophisticated people in the world, reaching their zenith at about the same time Achaean civilization was developing on the Greek mainland. Living in large urban areas dominated by huge palace complexes such as the one at Knossos on the northern coast of Crete, the Minoans had developed a vast trading network (one of their islands, Thera, may be the origin of the story of the lost continent of Atlantis; see the Appendix, p. 276) and passed on their knowledge of architecture, art, writing, and seamanship to the cruder, more warlike Greeks in the north. They eventually fell victim to their aggressive neighbors and were swallowed up by greedy warlords from Mycenae or elsewhere. The subsequent demise of the Achaeans themselves was the result, perhaps, of the weakening effects of a war at Troy, internal struggles, invasions, or all three.

A "Dark Age," beginning about 1100 B.C., descended on the land—literacy disappeared for an extended time, and the quality of life declined for most Greeks. Many uprooted themselves and migrated elsewhere, a large number moving eastward across the Aegean. When the difficulties had passed and the Archaic Age (c. 750–500 B.C.) began, Homer, a bard living in Ionia on the central coast of Asia Minor, wove his tales about the "Wrath of Achilles" and the "Return of Odysseus" from a tangled collection of orally transmitted stories that had been corrupted, interpolated, and embellished over the centuries. He gave life to characters he knew nothing about, and he immortalized a war that was as remote to him as the Columbus story is to us today. Homer himself, like his characters and poems, in many ways remains a question mark.

Growing Pains and Problems

Before we can flesh out the earliest personalities of real substance among the Greeks, we must attempt to learn something about the conditions of the times that produced them. At best, it is a difficult task, since sources are scant and insights are few.

From the Achaean beginnings to Homer (c. 1600–750 B.C.), the major form of government in Greece had been kingship. During the Bronze Age, some kings (often nothing more than chieftains) had been powerful, judging from the traditions and ruins of citadels like Mycenae. Even so, their control, as well as their territory, was limited, and continual struggles among neighboring monarchs probably hastened the collapse of Achaean society. Certainly, there would be few "Agamemnons" or "Achilleses" in the centuries that followed, and the petty kings who ruled the world Homer depicted did not long survive the recovery from the Dark Age.

That problems had been brewing for these kings may be reflected in the *Odyssey,* in which Homer makes clear Odysseus' limited power, describing the contempt with which the princely suitors of his wife held the family and household of the long-overdue king of Ithaca. Most Greek kings had disappeared by the early seventh century B.C. They had become so unimportant that no tradition about their overthrow was preserved—unlike the Romans, who continued to celebrate the toppling of their monarchy in 509 B.C. for centuries.

The kings were eventually replaced by local nobles, who organized themselves, although not formally, into small ruling cliques or oligarchies. Few in number, their status had originally been gained through accumulation

A "Reel" Look at Greek People I: *Helen of Troy* or Helen of Hollywood?

THIS IS THE FIRST of several short glimpses that will focus on how Hollywood has portrayed Greek people. Film has become such an influential medium that movies with historical themes are the standard by which many today view history. For that reason alone, it is beneficial to consider here relevant aspects of several Hollywood epics. They are, in chronological order, *Alexander the Great* (1955), *The 300 Spartans* (1962), *Jason and the Argonauts* (1963), and *Helen of Troy* (2003). As these brief portraits will demonstrate, while films do generate widespread interest in Greece, their purpose remains entertainment. Generally, they are a poor guide by which to judge historical accuracy.

After about a half century, one would expect a remake of the 1955 epic, *Helen of Troy,* to surpass the original in every way. Instead, the audience learns up front what to expect from the much touted television miniseries *Helen of Troy* (2003) when the voice of Menelaus, brother of Agamemnon, warns what we may have heard about Helen and the Trojan War is "not the way it happened." "Let me tell you the real story," he offers, "I know. . . . I was there." He is certainly right about one thing—this was *not* the way it happened, and both Homer and history have been grossly disserved by this updated version of the venerable story.

Appropriate for such fare, the new *Helen* premiered on Easter eve on the U.S.A. Cable Entertainment channel opposite the *Ten Commandments* on network television, though it has nothing to do with Judeo-Christian tradition. Apparently, that no longer matters in these days of ratings wars when the philosophy of studio heads seems to be "if it is ancient, it must be Easter." Despite their protestations about painstaking accuracy in preview trailers for the piece, John Kent Harrison's direction and Ronni Kern's screenplay are more suited to *Hercules: The Legendary Journeys* or MTV than serious historical drama. The Tro-

jans appear to be the good guys and the Greeks the bad, and Kern has decided to retell the story of Helen and Troy mostly around sister and brother teams—the Greeks represented by Helen and Clytemnestra and Agamemnon and Menelaus; the Trojans, Paris and Hector. Just about everyone still ends up dead but not exactly how or when they do according to Homeric tradition. Hector, distracted during a contrived duel, is speared through by an unethical Achilles. Agamemnon is murdered in his bath by his wife, Clytemnestra, but not at Mycenae in Greece. She somehow shows up at Troy and kills him for not only sacrificing their daughter but also for raping Helen and other poolside debaucheries she observes. Paris is curiously stabbed (fruitlessly reaching out to the gods, as if they were going to help, as he expires) while rescuing Helen from Agamemnon and the Greek mob, and for all their efforts, the couple must ultimately be content with only a brief surreal reunion—the kind between dead lovers that show up so often in films today. With no one left to help her, Helen inevitably trudges off through a ruined Troy behind her estranged husband, Menelaus. "I will follow," she says reluctantly. "I accept," returns Menelaus. The miniseries ends at this point with a woman's voice mournfully singing what sounds like "Terriblo . . . Terriblo." She was right. It was "Terriblo."

The casting of the major characters for *Helen of Troy* is generally disappointing when compared with Homer. The central figure is, of course, Helen. Sienna Guillory, the actress who portrays her, is fresh and pretty but certainly unrepresentative of Marlowe's famous line about the face that "launched a thousand ships." In fact, we see so many shots of her bare backside during the film that one might surmise it was more in honor of that part of her anatomy for which the ships were launched. Particularly egregious is the representation of Achilles. In the *Iliad,* he is distinguished by epithets such as "swift footed" and "fair haired."

The Achilles in *Helen of Troy* bellows loudly but does not appear especially fleet of foot—nor does he have any hair at all. His appearance is more appropriate for television wrestling spots, as is his gear, which is not armor at all but mostly a series of straps. Useless in battle as this armor was, his mother Thetis need not have wasted her time securing for him a new suit of it from Hephaestus, as she does in the *Iliad,* if this fellow were her son. No wonder Paris so easily disposes of him in the miniseries. Considering the design of Achilles' ill-crafted chariot, he probably would have eventually died of embarrassment, anyway.

There is also little of the *Iliad*'s "shining helm" about other armor in the film, a concoction running over a thousand-year period from pseudo-Mycenaean boar's tusk helmets, in this case fashioned in metal, to reproductions of first-century A.D. Celtic shields and helmets from the British Museum. In an apparent attempt to ape the successful film *Gladiator,* a makeshift "arena" before the walls of Troy plays host to contrived "dagger duels," with weapons that bear no resemblance to surviving period specimens. The same can be said for other arms, especially the ridiculously tiny spears; and the soldiers' greaves are so ill fitting that they look tied on with twine.

More historical surprises await us. We learn, for instance, that the real reason for the Trojan War was not to retrieve Helen but to secure the "silks and spices of Byzantium"—not that any were available at Troy. Troy was actually a commercial center that appears to have specialized mostly in spun yarn or textiles and in the breeding and exporting of horses. It is not clear exactly what caused the real war, but it likely had something to do with who controlled the Dardanelles, the waterway leading into the Black Sea area, rich in gold and grain. Troy also had nothing to do with Byzantium (the eventual location of Constantinople), which was not even founded by Greeks until the seventh century B.C.—600 years

after the Trojan War! We visually stride through a Trojan marketplace reminiscent of one seen in *Conan the Barbarian* (1982) (or, more recently, *The Scorpion King* [2002]) and inexplicably gaze up at Minoan columns with flutes in them, while being passed by people dressed in button-down tunics, turbans, and oriental garb (perhaps they brought the silk to Troy). A belly dancer adds to the wholly inappropriate atmosphere.

Meanwhile, to the west across the Aegean, a much oversized, formerly landlocked Sparta has been situated directly above the sea, apparently so that Paris can intercede at the last moment to save Helen. Forced to marry Menelaus, a man she does not love, she was about to fling herself into the watery depths below in a scene reminiscent of Rose and Jack on the fantail in *Titanic* (1997). Troy, too, sits closer to the sea, only a stone's throw from the Greeks and their fleet, whose "strong benched" vessels in the *Iliad* hardly look the part. Little room is left for the troops to camp and maneuver, so one is not surprised to find disguised Greeks showing up in the Trojan market undetected. The Trojan Horse, too, a worthy effort though perhaps not within the technological capabilities of the day, simply appears before the city gates unnoticed until a perceptive child stumbles upon it. The "traitor," Sinon, who is left to deceive the Trojans and convince them to pull the horse within their walls, looks more swami than Greek, and why he is buried up to his neck (*Scorpion King*?) when the Trojans discover him is anyone's guess. The actual historical tradition is suspect, anyway, since the best explanation for the "Trojan Horse" is that it actually symbolized an earthquake which destroyed portions of the walls of Troy close to the time of the war. Poseidon, the god of earthquakes as well as the sea, was sometimes represented as a horse. Consequently, the entire tradition, albeit a

(continued)

A "Reel" Look at Greek People I: *Helen of Troy* or Helen of Hollywood? (continued)

wonderful one, may be merely a personification of Poseidon crumbling the walls at Troy with one of his earthquakes.

All in all, it appears that the main reason for making *Helen of Troy* was to capitalize on the rejuvenation of epic movies along ancient lines, begun so surprisingly by the success of *Gladiator* in 2000.

The bigger-budget epic, *Troy* (which probably should have been called *Achilles* and may satisfy Brad Pitt fans), was released as this edition went to press. Although the film deals with a difficult historical period to reconstruct, one does not know what to make of its amalgamation of erroneous detail. The movie so distorts the poetic tradition it purports to follow that it is a stretch even to say that the story was "inspired" by Homer (as the film credits do). This Helen remains a somewhat lackluster substitute for the traditional beauty and is seldom seen; the Trojan Horse, however, does look more appropriately homemade (though one wonders why no one saw anybody inside through the cracks). And, oh yes . . . the now familiar "ancient world" mournful background wailing turns up again here.

Figure 1.5   The south, or main, gate of Troy VI, flanked by the remains of a major tower (see Figure 1.2, far left, for reconstruction). Was this inspiration for the "Scaean Gate" in Homer (and "great tower of Ilios"), where Helen traditionally would have entered Troy?

of wealth, prowess in war, wisdom in counsel, religious authority, and less honorable avenues, all sanctified by the passage of time and reaffirmed by a lineage that typically began at some god's loins. This elite lorded over the small, disorganized urban centers that at this juncture were merely fledgling city-states, collections of villages still in search of an identity. In addition to these nobles, who were gradually evolving into a true aristocracy, was a larger group of not-so-well-born or wealthy citizens who were nonetheless supportive of aristocratic values. Together they controlled the productive land, defended the community from attack, and made all the important political decisions. There were no law codes: Whatever aristocrats said *was* law for those not of their position.

Homer may have unintentionally provided us with the earliest example of the beginnings of a challenge to this traditional aristocratic authority. Many portions of his *Iliad* reflect a society closer to Homer's own time, and in a long passage involving a man named Thersites (*Iliad* 2.211–277), the latter challenges the princely words of his overlords at Troy. In return, he receives a proper rebuke for his impertinence and is painfully reminded of his place. While set within the heroic framework of the Trojan War centuries earlier, the episode may, in reality, have been inspired by more contemporary dissatisfaction with aristocratic rule. Be that as it may, aristocracies were quick to quell any signs of insubordination. The perpetuation of their hereditary power was all-important. They were always divided by jealousies among the great families, but the one thing that kept them unified was the protection of their privileged status from "contamination" by interlopers such as Thersites, who may even have had some credentials to do what he did—but not the *right* ones!

Aristocrats remained in virtual control of Greek society until the effects of the "Commercial Revolution," which followed the Dark Age, began to be felt. Trade between Greeks and outsiders had never completely halted after the Achaean collapse, but economies had contracted and become localized. During the eighth century B.C., however, these local economies began to be affected by a recovering and growing Mediterranean economy, and the accompanying changes were destined to have a deleterious effect on the aristocracy's hold on society.

Ironically, it was primarily men of aristocratic background who were the first to take advantage of the new economic situation. Practiced in overseas piracy and having obtained by barter what they could not seize by force, they were the only ones who had the requisite ships and foreign contacts—guest-friendships and the like—to make long-distance trade feasible and who had a surplus of goods to exchange in the new markets. They were also the first in the post–Dark Age period to learn how to write (an important tool whose use they would have to restrict if they hoped to retain their absolute supremacy in the new world), since the revival of trade necessitated a means to keep track of it.

However, with the continued growth of trade and the eventual establishment of colonies throughout the Mediterranean, nonaristocratic elements increasingly took advantage of the new economic opportunities at home and abroad. These opportunities eventually contributed to the rise of an entirely new, at least semiliterate, segment of Greek society that had never been present before—a "middle class" of sorts, between the peasant farmers and shepherds and the aristocrats. It was made up of successful farmers with a healthy sprinkling of merchants, tradesmen, mercenaries, artisans, and craftsmen; and its emergence hastened the development of the city-states into true urban and commercial centers.

The radical changes brought on by the Commercial Revolution ultimately proved distasteful to many aristocrats. Since their power base remained essentially local, they could not prevent an increase in the numbers and prosperity of the new business class. They soon found their wealth being rivaled by that of the most prominent nonaristocrats. Not wishing to compete with people they considered inferior or even undesirable (to be sure, many of the early participants in this revolution must have been adventurers, thieves, the disinherited, and those not bound by convention), the most conservative aristocrats began to withdraw from the world of commerce. Their alienation only invited future economic (and political) disaster. They also found that their own growing needs in the new world were stimulating the success of the very people they abhorred, making them increasingly dependent on the latter. Consequently, the more practical aristocrats continued to expand their commercial interests. If pressed, they were even willing to sacrifice a little of their "blue blood" to marry into the wealthiest of the new families, who were anxious for such unions to add prestige and political power to their wealth.

By the mid–sixth century B.C., money—in the form of electrum, gold, silver, and, later, bronze and copper—had come into use. Although money may not have been as important a factor in the economic growth of Greece as once believed, it still had the impact of further facilitating trade, providing a new fluidity that guaranteed an even greater distribution of wealth. Certainly, the Commercial Revolution had an equalizing effect on some portions of Greek society.

Another consequence of the Commercial Revolution that weakened the traditional position of the aristocracy was a change in warfare that had taken place by about 700 B.C. Previously, aristocrats had prided themselves on being the defenders of the homeland (although it is clear from Homer's *Iliad,*

A "Reel" Look at Greek People II: *Jason and the Argonauts—* A "Golden Fleecing" of the Epic

THE TRADITION OF THE *Argonautica,* or *The Voyage of Argo,* was already firmly established before Homer made reference to Jason in the *Iliad* and *Odyssey.* No poet could weave the rich but difficult variations of the old story into lasting form until Apollonius of Rhodes penned his definitive version of the Argonauts' quest for the "Golden Fleece" in the third century B.C. By the time Apollonius wrote during the Hellenistic period, Homeric heroes who had achieved their goals through brute strength, prowess, and the will of the gods were no longer convincing. The gods themselves were neither revered nor respected as much as they had been in Homer's day, and living myth was a thing of the distant past. People were more skeptical and not content to believe that gods alone controlled Jason's fate and were interactive in all matters. Apollonius, himself an academic and once head of the Great Library at Alexandria, had to take a more realistic view, regarding the gods as something of a curiosity. The story still demanded their presence, but they became more symbolic or ornamental than effectual, since everything could happen with or without their intervention. Audiences remained enraptured by a good adventure and fascinated by the mythic tradition, but most saw workman-like abilities and one's own resourcefulness as more credible means toward achieving one's desires. What Homer could do with the sweep of a god's hand, Apollonius had to explain more fully in rational, contemporary terms—although the workings of magic, strongly embraced throughout the Greek world, were always an acceptable alternative and often employed in the *Argonautica.*

Apollonius, of course, already differed from Homer in that his *Argonautica* was meant to be read, not recited. Nonetheless, five centuries after Homer, he was still expected to deal with material in the same epic framework while making it relevant to his audience. The process might be compared to authoring a Shakespearean play today that would still appeal to a modern general reader. Romantic love was also required, and there is nothing in Homer remotely close to Medea's passionate desire for Jason in the *Argonautica.* The result for Apollonius is a literary product that included all that was expected in an epic tale—the Golden Fleece, the serpent who guarded it, the Clashing Rocks, the Harpies, the fire-breathing bulls, the earthborn men, and Talos the bronze giant—but we also have a hero, Jason, who is not particularly heroic. He knows what he must do, but he cannot do it without the help of those around him. He has a marvelous ship called the *Argo* built under Athena's watchful eye, an accomplished sorceress and lover to protect him in Medea, and a remarkable crew with extraordinary powers—but even they appear able to contribute their talents only in specific situations, much like teams of specialists we enjoy watching today in classic films like *The Magnificent Seven, The Guns of Navarone, The Professionals,* and *The Dirty Dozen.* Their abilities usually stretch the imagination—but not so much as to completely outstrip the sensibilities of the day.

Apollonius has attracted both ancient and modern critics. He was certainly no Homer, but there are flashes of brilliance in his poetry. In his contrast of Medea's uncontrolled longings for Jason with her absolute confidence as a great sorceress, it is difficult to find fault. Apollonius set himself a formidable task and while not entirely successful in combining all the diverse elements

(continued)

A "Reel" Look at Greek People II: *Jason and the Argonauts—* A "Golden Fleecing" of the Epic (continued)

of the *Argonautica* into a seamless whole, the proof of his achievement lay in the fact that it is his version of the epic which has endured. It is the one that Vergil, considered an eminently more accomplished poet, later used as inspiration for portions of his *Aeneid*—especially the love of Dido for Aeneas. Hollywood, too, was quick to seize upon the appeal of Apollonius' epic saga but, predictably, recast the classic tale in its own image.

Known more popularly today as the adventure of *Jason and the Argonauts,* Hollywood produced a film by that name in 1962 and capitalized on Apollonius' original theme of romance and adventure—especially the quest for the "Golden Fleece." Rather than attempt to represent the tale faithfully, however, the subject was chosen primarily to act as a vehicle for another of special-effects wizard Ray Harryhausen's cult fantasies. *Jason and the Argonauts* has taken its place alongside Harryhausen's *The 7th Voyage of Sinbad* and other Sinbad adventures, as well as helped inspire another popular classic with a mythological theme, *Clash of the Titans.* In *Jason and the Argonauts,* the bronze giant, Talos, the serpent (in this case, a multi-headed hydra) who guards the Fleece, and the skeleton warriors who rise from the ground to challenge Jason and his men, have all become "fantasy convention" draws and legendary examples of the Harryhausen craft in predigital days. The special effects are mostly all

Figure 1.6   Athena (left) supervising the building of Argo. *Terra-cotta panel found near Porta Latina, Rome. First century A.D. (?). (British Museum, London)*

that viewers remember about the film. Although still fascinating fare on its own, the picture has omitted entire episodes and altered or changed the story line so much that only a faint echo remains of Jason's original adventure in the *Argonautica*. The return home, most of Book IV in the epic, never made the script, and, of course, the filmmakers chose an "all live happily ever after" ending with Jason securing the Fleece—and Medea's love.

It is the Fleece, itself, however, that provides the most interestingly topic for discussion here. While often regarded as little more than an imaginary symbolic panacea, the "Golden Fleece" was quite real—in a practical sense. In fact, there have been countless "golden" fleeces over the millennia used by countless individuals, although few as illustrious as Jason, and demonstrations of their "magical" powers still continue today. The story arose originally, as the ancient Greek geographer Strabo attests (11.2.19), from a mining procedure employed by people in the Black Sea area, where Colchis, the traditional location of the Golden Fleece, was situated. As streams ran down from the Caucasus Mountains, presently in the area of the Republic of Georgia (formerly Soviet Georgia), they brought with them nuggets and flakes of gold. Prospectors pegged a fleece, or sheepskin, on a board which was then submerged in an opportune spot to collect the gold carried by the water that passed over it. The gold was trapped in the wool, and when it was removed from the water, the fleece had indeed become "golden." Widespread use of the process continued until the 1930s when it was no longer considered a feasible method by which to mine gold. It was the area's richness in gold in antiquity, as well as the age-old belief that the precious metal was the "cure-all" for any ills, which probably first started the story about the wondrous powers of a "Golden Fleece" and guaranteed it a shining spot in Greek heroic tradition.

at least, that personal glory often took precedence over civic responsibility). The important fighting, it seems, consisted mostly of personal duels between enemies of equal status. If Homer is to be believed, an entire aristocratic code of conduct accompanied these duels, which included among other things an inquiry into each other's genealogy (one would not want to injure a distant relative or obscure family friend!) before they proceeded to bash in each other's heads. The fight was usually to the death, and the victor, after giving a triumphal war cry, gathered up his conquered foe's armor, took it back to camp, and piled it in a corner of his tent as a trophy. If this description approximates standard Dark Age military procedure, then it changed completely with the introduction of "hoplite warfare."

The hoplite soldier's equipment included a helmet (see Figure 1.8, page 15), greaves on his lower legs, a shield worn on the left arm that protected his body from his neck to his knees, a small sword, a long pike, and a chest

Figure 1.7
A representation of hoplites in action (from the Nereid Monument from Xanthos in Lycia, c. 400 B.C.). (British Museum, London)

protector. Since he fought in a formation called the "phalanx," which was several ranks deep, he was less vulnerable than an individual warrior fighting by himself. It follows, then, that he did not need as much protection as his aristocratic predecessors and that his armor, although still heavy and substantial, was probably now slightly more affordable for a large number of wealthy nonaristocrats. (Advances in metallurgy and metalworking at about the same time also must have made military equipment somewhat more cost-effective and probably enhanced its reusability.) Soldiers, not the state, provided their own equipment, and although hoplite armor was far more expensive than what they had previously worn as support troops, their improved status as first-line heavy infantry made most members of the newly wealthy families willing to absorb the cost.

Phalanxes could be adjusted in size and organization, and on level ground at least, they had a decided advantage over less sophisticated modes of warfare. Most early battles—pushing and shoving matches where pikes usually prevailed over swords—would be won when one phalanx broke and drove the other from the field. A passage preserved by Plutarch about the Euboeans' fighting prowess may be the earliest reference to hoplite warfare:

> Indeed there will be no longer many bows stretched
> nor will slings be frequent when Ares brings together
> the crush of battle in the plain;

Figure 1.8
Greek hoplite helmets.
(Olympia Museum,
Greece)

It will be work for swords, causing much grief; for they
are experts in that (kind of) battle, the lords of Euboea
who are famous with their spears.
(*Theseus* 5.3 quoting Archilochus)

Precisely what led to this new form of warfare is not clear, but it is unrealistic to believe that the art of war would have remained static in a rapidly changing society. City-states had developed into institutions that, although still small, were now becoming too organized for the old ways of war to remain practical. Wars between city-states necessitated the involvement of greater numbers of combatants, and, for the first time, aristocrats were not the only ones who chanced to gain or lose through them. The opportunity for an immediate increase in personal wealth did not go unnoticed by prosperous nonaristocrats, nor did the fact that their own possessions needed protection. Thus, a new kind of fighting evolved that provided an organized way of attacking as well as defending against enemies. Aristocrats and non-aristocrats alike took their position in the phalanx.

Figure 1.9
A bronze statuette from Tarentum of a Greek cavalryman, c. 550 B.C. This warrior once held a spear and shield, and his helmet was topped by a crest that ran sideways. (British Museum, London)

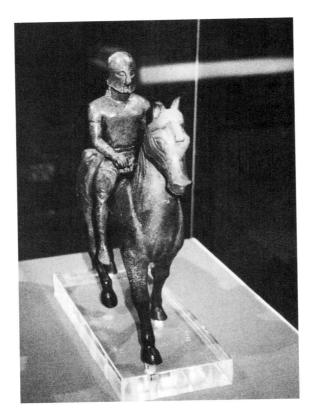

Since the pikes and swords of nonaristocratic hoplites cared little for genealogies, aristocratic codes of conduct soon became only memories. Numbers alone made the phalanx style of fighting more suitable to the new wealthy. There also may have been incentives or concessions offered by the aristocrats to guarantee the participation of the new "hoplite class" in battle, for they could no longer survive militarily without them. As a result, the aristocracy quickly lost its monopoly on warfare. It may not be coincidence that at about the same time the hoplite formation was introduced, weapons, previously symbols of status, began to disappear from contemporary burials of aristocrats (although, surely, part of this disappearance had to do with the realization that burying expensive implements of war was not a profitable practice).

The greatest of the aristocratic families attempted to salvage some of their flagging military prestige by continuing to participate as cavalrymen whose effectiveness, depending on a region's geographical suitability for horsemanship (for example, Thessaly) and tradition, ranged from decorative to fully functional. Only the grandest of landholders could afford to raise horses on acreage that was always strained to produce anything. However, they were

Figure 1.10
This early and exaggerated representation appears, from its extended prow, to be a warship and its oarsmen. It is contemporary with the developing Greek phalanx and cavalry. (British Museum, London)

fighting a losing battle. As the new farming and commercial families continued to gain influence through accumulation of wealth and their greater role in the protection of the state, they soon demanded a role in government.

Some of these changing attitudes toward aristocrats and the self-centered world they monopolized can be seen firsthand in the contemporary poetry of Archilochus of Paros, who was active c. 680–640 B.C.

Archilochus Challenges the "Establishment"

"I am two things," Archilochus of Paros flatly states: "A fighter who follows the Master of Battles, and one who understands the gift of the Muses' love." So speaks one of the earliest Greek voices after Homer, a voice that, unlike the latter's, also has a legitimate personality we can attach to it—usually dissatisfied or contemptuous.

Unfortunately, it is also a voice that has stirred much controversy, for it is not always clear in his poetry when Archilochus is speaking about himself, indulging in poetic license, or being metaphorical rather than historical. The meaning, intent, and characters in his poems have all been interpreted variously, and even the authorship of some of the lines attributed to him is disputed. Consequently, Archilochus has been seen as everything from a "restless merchant aristocrat" who writes a calculated and traditional kind of poetry, to an impoverished mercenary of questionable aristocratic background who spills forth poetry from the soul.

The truth probably lies somewhere in between. However, the fragmentary nature of his poems, the mythical, anecdotal, heroic, and religious tradition that grew up around him in later centuries, and the fact that he lived in an obscure period of Greek history—all combine to frustrate our inquiries into Archilochus' life. The story of how he supposedly became a poet is ample evidence of the problems:

> They say that when Archilochus was still a little boy he was sent into the country by his father Telesicles, in order to bring a cow down to be sold. And so he got up very early and set off while it was still night, though the moon was shining, and fetched the cow to take her to town. When he got to the place called Lissides, he thought he saw a company of women, and supposing them to be country girls on their way from work, going to town for a holiday, he began to tease them. They responded with jokes and foolery, and then they asked him if he meant to sell his cow. When he said yes, they answered that they would give him a fair price for it, but as soon as these words were spoken, both they and the cow disappeared. All the frightened boy could see was a lyre, lying at his feet, but in a little while he came to his senses and understood that these were the Muses who had appeared to him, and that this was their gift. He picked up the lyre and went on into town, where he told his father all that had happened to him, and Telesicles, hearing the tale and seeing the instrument, was filled with astonishment. The first thing he did was to make a search for the cow, throughout the length and breadth of the island, but no trace of it could be found. Later, when he was sent to Delphi by his fellow citizens, along with Lycambes, to ask for oracular guidance, he went the more willingly because he wished to ask about this adventure, and when they arrived, and entered the sanctuary, the god spoke this prophecy to Telesicles:
>
> > Deathless that son is to be, o father Telesicles,
> > famous in song among men, he who first gives you speech
> > on your return from this shrine, into your native land.
>
> And when they got back to Paros, Archilochus was the first of his sons to meet and to greet his father.
> (*Mnesiepes Inscription* E[1] II 22–54)

Archilochus was born of an aristocratic father named Telesicles, who had founded a Parian colony on Thasos. His mother was said to have been a slave named Enipo. Recent attempts to dismiss this tradition as a later biographer's creation—the name Enipo was conveniently derived from *enipe,* or "child of abuse," which is how Archilochus may have described himself in a lost poem—have not been entirely successful. The name may be explained away, but not the stigma of slavery attached to his mother, whose real name may never have been known. Other explanations have also failed to eliminate convincingly the tradition of "illegitimacy," a situation that no doubt contributed to Archilochus' chaotic life and unsettled status.

From the clues he gives about himself in his poetry, there is enough to convince us that Archilochus rightly deserves to be identified (from our distant viewpoint) as the first "individual" in Greek history. He stands precisely between the old world of aristocratic domination and the new, more democratic world of changing values, of which he is the primary spokesman. As one scholar has observed, "Seldom has a frontier society had a man of such genius to represent its life to itself and to posterity" (Rankin, *Archilochus of Paros,* 97).

Although Hesiod (see Chapter 2) is our earliest example of a notable Greek whose life—somewhat freed from the kind of myth and tradition that so completely obscures Homer—can be recounted to some extent, it is Archilochus who first provides glimpses into his affairs that reveal a complete individual. He loves, he hates; he is sad, he is happy; he knows victory, he has tasted defeat; he laughs, he cries; he has seen all that life can offer, he knows death. There seems to be little that he has not experienced.

Initially at least, Archilochus appears to have been one of the earliest amateur poets, writing not for profit or a livelihood but because he had to write. Writing provided a kind of therapy for Archilochus, a way to release his emotions. However, it is clear that there was also a professional aspect to his work, for he wrote paeans to Apollo and dithyrambs to Dionysus (and protodramas), which were performed publicly and probably had official sanction. Nonetheless, it was always the "personal" tone of his poetry that shone through most clearly, a characteristic that Critias, a high-minded ancient critic of the fifth century B.C., thought revealed too much:

> For if he had not published [he says] such a reputation of himself amongst the Greeks, we would not have learned that he was the son of Enipo who was a slave-woman; or that he left Paros through poverty and lack of means and went to Thasos; or that when he arrived he was hostile to the people who were there, speaking ill impartially of both friends and enemies. Nor would we have known, in addition to these facts, that he was an adulterer, had we not learned it from himself; nor that he was a sex maniac and a rapist; nor (what is even more disgraceful than this), that he threw away his shield. So Archilochus did not prove to be a good witness in his own cause, leaving such a fame and repute behind him.
> (Critias in Aelian, *Varia Historia* 10.13)

If contemporaries—and later critics—often found the tone and themes of Archilochus' poetry unheroic or common, Archilochus' behavior in war, the second of his admitted preoccupations, also shocked through its lack of an aristocratic stamp. He was a battle-wearied veteran who had little time for histrionics and knew what it took to survive. His name literally means "captain of a company," which he, in fact, appears to have been—more probably a general like his friend Glaucus, whom he often addresses in his poems. It is unlikely that Archilochus "grew into" such a prophetic name; rather, he must have adopted it once his life became primarily a military one. Whatever the case, he knew not to put his trust in some inexperienced aristocratic dandy whose genealogy was longer than his time spent in battle:

> I don't like the towering captain with the spraddly length of leg,
> one who swaggers in his lovelocks and cleanshaves beneath the chin.
> Give me a man short and squarely set upon his legs, a man
> full of heart, not to be shaken from the place he plants his feet.

To Archilochus, war was not a glorious pursuit in which honor, prestige, and reputation were put on the line. People could get killed, and they often did. In his view, there was no substance in the time-honored aristocratic ideals about death in battle: "No man is respected, no man spoken of, when he is dead by his townsmen. All of us, when still alive, will cultivate the live man, and thus the dead will always have the worst of it."

Consequently, Archilochus was not going to charge into the fray and chance losing his life just because some age-old tradition dictated he should. "Let him go ahead," he recommends, probably referring to some eager aristocrat. "Ares [the god of war] is a democrat. There are no privileged people on a battlefield."

Figure 1.11
A hoplite soldier bids farewell to his family as he departs for war. The emotion of the moment is clear as his father and mother (or wife) know his future is uncertain. The addition of the faithful household dog adds poignancy to the scene. Note the handshake, evidence that it was already a time-honored practice. Stamnos, Athens, mid–fifth century B.C. (British Museum, London)

It also meant absolutely nothing to Archilochus to run when the going got tough, a fact of which, to the chagrin of most aristocrats, he boasted openly:

> Some barbarian is waving my shield, since I was obliged to
>   leave that perfectly good piece of equipment behind
> under a bush. But I got away, so what does it matter?
>   Let the shield go; I can buy another one equally good.

Such thinking was certainly not the "right stuff" in the view of a privileged warrior caste that had always demanded that its members return from battle "with their shield—or upon it!" These warriors viewed a soldier without a shield as a coward who must have thrown down his equipment to run.

Archilochus apparently not only did not care if he left his shield behind but also speaks lightly of the time-honored piece of equipment—long viewed as a status symbol among the aristocracy. For Archilochus, one might just as well pick up another shield any time at the local "thieves' market" (an indication that reinforces the notion of more widespread availability of weapons during this period). This one passage probably did more to disturb aristocrats of his own generation—and later—than any other he wrote. It was also largely responsible for the tradition about his verse being banned at Sparta, where his ideas were considered seditious.

Because of the frequent references to war and battle in his poetry, some have concluded that Archilochus must have been a mercenary, one who earned his living by selling his fighting skills. At times, he even appears to refer to himself as such. It does seem that he is involved in wars much too frequently to be only a member of a citizen militia, but he certainly does not appear to have been a simple mercenary. As mentioned previously, one of his companions was Glaucus, a noteworthy individual in the early history of Thasos, where Archilochus was often in battle. Mercenaries would have to have been of a very high caliber, indeed, if these two companions are any indication, and it is strange that Archilochus warns his friend about depending too much on mercenaries, if that were their own profession.

Also, his activities in defending Thasos from enemies in Thrace and from Naxos appear to go much deeper than any mercenary role would require and tend to indicate his close connection with the government of Paros. "Soldier of fortune" might be a better way to describe his habits, although there is still an implied responsibility in his actions and words. Wealth could accrue from spoils of fighting, and battle itself appears to have filled a need for Archilochus. But he was too literate, moved in circles too high, and was too much a part of the symposia scene (the most appropriate setting for drinking and reciting his verse) to be more than a common paid soldier.

Achilles, the Reluctant Warrior—The Human Cost of Valor

ALTHOUGH THERE HAVE BEEN times in history when a glorious death in battle has been regarded as desirable, generally, the horrors of war and the loss of life that accompanies it have never been an easy burden to bear—no less in antiquity than today. With the stroke of a sword or the thrust of a spear, parents might be deprived of the son who was to care for them in old age, a young wife could become a widow, and children, fatherless. Too many people, it seems, had experienced what the fifth-century B.C. tragedian, Aeschylus, so vividly verbalized:

> Those they sent forth they knew;
> now, in place of the young men
> urns and ashes are carried home
> to the houses of the fighters.
> (*Agamemnon* 433–436)

In his play *Lysistrata,* set in Athens during the Peloponnesian War (431–404 B.C.), the comic poet Aristophanes turns serious for a moment and succinctly sums up the fear of every mother when he has his women express their heartfelt concern: "We give you sons and you send them off to fight," and "We give birth to men and you make them die."

Although few would argue with such sentiments, the frequency of war in Ancient Greece, both domestic and foreign, practically guaranteed the probability of military action at least once in a lifetime—more if one lived in a major city. The defense of the community had to take precedence over pleas like those expressed by Aristophanes' mothers. Citizen militias were usually enough to handle most emergencies, and military training was a part of a young man's (ages 18–20) education in the majority of cities. In Sparta, it was a way of life. The emphasis on honorable behavior in battle was too strong to overlook, for every soldier knew what had been expressed in an early martial poem from the seventh century B.C., attributed to Tyrtaeus of Sparta: "It is a shameful sight when a dead man lies in the dust there, driven through from behind by the stroke of an enemy spear." Even worse than the death of a loved one was the knowledge that he had died a dishonorable death, an embarrassment with which his family had to live.

As might be expected, not everyone went off to war willingly, and Athenians who avoided military service (or were cowards or deserters) apparently were excluded from the Agora, or marketplace, or at least were restricted from entering sacred areas or shrines. Aristophanes refers, not infrequently, and sometimes by name, to "draft dodgers" and those who shirked their duty to their country for whatever reason. In his play *The Wasps* (1117–1119), for example, the chorus speaks these lines: "But our greatest vexation is . . . a NON-VETERAN slacker, whose hand never knew oar, nor lance, nor blister upraised in his Country's defense."

In Athens, there is also the story about Meton the astrologer, who, upset by signs that the Athenian expedition to Sicily (415–413 B.C.) would end in disaster, feigned madness and burnt his house down to evade service, although others say he did it to make the Athenians feel sorry for him and excuse his son from the expedition (Plutarch, *Nicias* 13.5–6). In Rome, too, we find similar examples of reluctance on the part of many recruits. Riots broke out in the late 150s B.C. over recruiting for an unpopular war in Spain. The first Roman emperor, Augustus, reputedly had to resort to extreme measures to "scare up" some replacements for an army annihilated in Germany.

We even find reticence in places where we expect it least, as in the Greek heroic tradition. Of the heroes who traditionally fought at Troy, for instance, Achilles was by far the greatest and most easily recognized. He had only to give his war cry and the Trojans would flee the battlefield, and his withdrawal from the fighting could cause the Greek war effort to collapse completely. Perhaps no other figure in literature so epitomizes brute strength and warlike prowess as Achilles. Thus, it is somewhat surprising to find, tucked away in the same tradition that made him the mightiest of the warlords at Troy, a story that related how he was missing and unaccounted for when the call first went out to gather for the great expedition.

In the *Iliad* (21.110–113), while at Troy, Achilles had already resigned himself to his fate to live a short but glorious life when he said to Lycaon:

> Yet even I have also my death and my strong destiny, / and there shall be a dawn or an afternoon or a noontime / when some man in the fighting will take the life from me also / either with a spearcast or an arrow flown from the bowstring.

Achilles' mother, the sea nymph Thetis, knew that her son was fated to die at Troy, so like any concerned mother, she had tried to prevent his being drafted for the expedition. The various strains of the story of her efforts have been summarized by Robert Graves (*The Greek Myths,* Vol. 2, 280):

> Now, Thetis knew that her son would never return from Troy if he joined the expedition, since he was fated either to gain glory there and die early, or to live a long but inglorious life at home. She disguised him as a girl, and entrusted him to Lycomedes, king of Scyros, in whose palace he lived under the name of Cercysera, Aissa, or Pyrrha; and had an intrigue with Lycomedes' daughter Deidameia, by whom he became the father of Pyrrhus, later called Neoptolemus. . . .

When the heroes were called to gather for the expedition and no one could locate Achilles, Odysseus was one of the ones sent to search for him. Odysseus, too, had originally been a reluctant participant and pretended he had gone mad so he would not have to go to war:

> Now, Odysseus had been warned by an oracle: "If you go to Troy, you will not return until the twentieth year, and then alone and destitute." He therefore feigned madness, and Agamemnon, Menelaus, and Palamedes found him wearing a peasant's cap shaped like a half-egg, ploughing with an ass and an ox yoked together, and flinging salt over his shoulder as he went. When he pretended not to recognize his distinguished guests, Palamedes snatched the infant Telemachus from Penelope's arms and set him on the ground before the advancing team. Odysseus hastily reined them in to avoid killing his only son and, his sanity having thus been established, was obliged to join the expedition. (Graves, 2, 279)

Odysseus then headed a search party to locate the missing Achilles, for it had been prophesied that the Greeks could never conquer Troy without his aid:

> Odysseus, Nestor, and Ajax were sent to fetch Achilles from Scyros, where he was rumored to be hidden. Lycomedes let them search the palace, and they might never have detected Achilles, had not Odysseus laid a pile of gifts—for the most part jewels, girdles, embroidered dresses and such—in the hall, and asked the court-ladies to take their choice. Then Odysseus ordered a sudden trumpet-blast and clash of arms to sound outside the palace and, sure enough, one of the girls stripped herself to the waist and seized the shield and spear which he had included among the gifts. It was Achilles, who now promised to lead his Myrmidons to Troy. (Graves, 2, 280–281)

It is indeed ironic that the Greeks chose the great Achilles for this role of draft dodger. Inevitably, he would die at Troy as was fated. An arrow shot by Paris and guided by Apollo struck him in his one point of vulnerability, his heel. Perhaps Greek families found some consolation in the knowledge that even divinities such as Thetis were sometimes as helpless as humans to prevent the death of their children in battle.

As already mentioned, Archilochus was most likely the son of an aristocratic father and a slave mother. There seems to be no compelling reason not to accept this situation, since offspring from such relationships were common in early Greece. Such a birth need not have been a major hindrance for Archilochus, since all his father had to do was declare him legitimate to confirm his status and rights as an aristocrat. Whether his father had been willing to do so, we cannot tell (the tradition that Telesicles had been informed by the oracle at Delphi that his son was to be "immortal" is a late one and would have had no bearing on his decision), but an incident in the *Odyssey* may provide a clue.

Odysseus, recently returned to his native kingdom of Ithaca after a twenty-year absence, was disguised as a beggar by the goddess Athena to protect him from the hostile suitors who had been wooing his wife. Arriving at the hut of his old swineherd, Eumaeus, Odysseus did not wish to reveal his true identity, so when the latter inquired of his origins, the wily hero simply made up a story. He tells Eumaeus that his father was a wealthy man from Crete but that his mother, unfortunately, was a slave. Consequently, when his father died, he inherited little—in this case, a humble dwelling and some other belongings—since most of the property was divided among the legitimate sons produced by proper wedlock. His share had not been enough to support him, so he was forced to make his own way in the world, eventually becoming a beggar.

It appears from Odysseus' yarn that although there was little social stigma attached to being illegitimate, someone of this background was still "second-class" in terms of inheritance—provided for only after the legitimate sons had received their share. Sometimes, there were even too many legitimate sons, and the younger ones, although properly bred, were often left with nothing but a name. Perhaps Archilochus' troubles had arisen from a similar set of circumstances. In many ways, he strikingly resembles Odysseus—a noble, a fighter, a wanderer, one who knows the sea and its dangers, one who has lost friends and relatives, a lover of many women (but especially one), and a man who survives by his wits. If Archilochus felt a certain identification with the hero, then Odysseus' beggar story may have made that identification even more complete.

In one poem, Archilochus implies (if he is referring to himself) that he once did have "wealth" but that he lost it in a shipwreck. Whether he is speaking metaphorically or actually referring to a fortune lost, we have no way of knowing. If the latter is correct, it need not represent any family inheritance but could be simply an investment of his own earnings in a trading venture that ended in catastrophe. There are other indications of lost wealth, but the following poem, presumably autobiographical, speaks de-

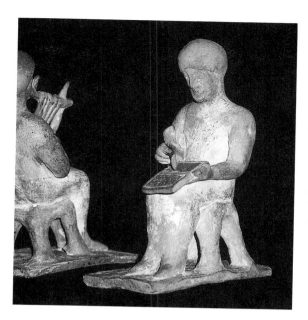

Figure 1.12
These miniature terra-cottas from Thebes showing one figure writing and another holding a lyre, date from the end of the age of the "lyric" poets and reflect, generally, both the creative and performing process of Archilochus and his fellows. (Louvre, Paris)

spairingly about his general condition (which seems to include poverty at the time of composition):

> To the gods all things are easy. Many times from circumstance
> of disaster they set upright those who have been sprawled at length
> on the ground, but often again when men stand planted on firm feet,
> these same gods will knock them on their backs, and then the evils
>   come,
> so that a man wanders homeless, destitute, at his wit's end.

If Archilochus was ever involved in politics—and it seems unlikely that he could have avoided it entirely—he appears to have had little taste for it. A poem he composed about the contemporary king of Lydia, Gyges, provides such an indication:

> Nothing to me the life of Gyges and his glut
> of gold. I neither envy nor admire him, as
> I watch his life and what he does. I want no pride
> of tyranny; it lies far off from where I look.

One tradition has it that Archilochus left Paros in poverty to seek a new life on Thasos, a wild and unsettled island off the inhospitable Thracian coast. His family had established the Parian colony there, so perhaps he hoped for a chance to start anew and even become politically active. However, his knack for making enemies got him into trouble on Thasos as well, indicating that popularity was never one of his assets.

Another tradition, presumably referring to the same departure from Paros, says that Archilochus did not leave but was banished because he tried to involve the citizens in some lewd form of Dionysiac worship. (The god supposedly struck the males of the island impotent because of their treatment of Archilochus.)

Perhaps the reason for the variant stories about Archilochus' departure from Paros is that later biographers did not really know why he went to Thasos. He appears glad to have left Paros, but since his own poetic references to Thasos are mostly military and he had high-ranking friends there like Glaucus, he may have been on an official mission to protect Parian interests in local gold mines. Those gold mines would have been crucial for Paros. Conditions on Thasos were probably not as bad as Archilochus would have us believe, and, also, the opportunities for increasing his own wealth would not have been lost on this soldier-poet.

Archilochus' poetry was not always directed against aristocrats, their ideals, and war. Other interests included drinking, old age, and some of the earliest examples of beast fables, and he makes the first conscious, deliberate use of sexuality as a main poetic theme. He even refers to an eclipse of the sun, probably on April 6, 648 B.C., which, if accurate, would be the first precise date in Greek history. It is his love poems, however, that are of particular interest.

Archilochus' Love for Neobule

Unlucky at life, Archilochus also appears to have been unlucky at love. At least once in his chaotic existence, he found love—not the kind of coarse, momentary sexual gratification stolen from a well-worn whore in the sweaty backrooms of the counterculture world Archilochus seems to have known so well, nor the pleasures he found in the pampered parlors of long-haired courtesans or in the seduction of an innocent. What he found, it seems, was the kind of romantic love that every poet's soul desires and seldom finds. Her name was Neobule, and she was the daughter of a prominent Parian named Lycambes.

Here we see a different Archilochus, one who reveals a tenderness behind the thick hide he had worked so hard to develop. "O that I might but touch Neobule's hand," he yearns in a wistful moment. We catch an unguarded glimpse of the vulnerability of the professed adulterer, who also composed these lines, perhaps for his sweetheart:

> Such is the passion for love that has twisted its way beneath
>   my heartstrings
> and closed deep mist across my eyes
> stealing the soft heart from inside my body. . . .

Archilochus must have fallen hard, and there appears to have been an engagement, but the marriage never took place. Lycambes, who must have been the same man who accompanied Archilochus' father to Delphi and was an associate in the founding of the colony on Thasos, broke it off, although we do not know why. It may be that Neobule's mother, Amphimedo, rather than Lycambes, was the one who favored the match. Her death is referred to by Archilochus, who calls her a "decent woman," in a poem composed after the breakup. It may be that when she died, her husband no longer saw any reason to embrace Archilochus as his son-in-law. It could also be that Archilochus' status as the son of a slave woman ultimately so distressed Lycambes that he no longer considered the marriage a suitable one. This reasoning especially seems to hold true if the former had recently suffered a major financial loss, as he seems to indicate in his poetry, and relied mostly on his soldiering skills for support.

Perhaps some of the poet's cruder, more graphic verses—for example, "fall forcefully on her body, and press belly to belly and thighs to thighs"— made the prospective father-in-law wince and take another look at the vulgar suitor when he realized he would be tying a man of such reputation permanently to his family. Or there could have been political differences that placed a strain on the relationship of the two families that could not be overcome, as there often were between members of leading families. (Was Archilochus' reference to an oracle advising to "Reign with absolute power" just poetic license on his part?)

Whatever the case, Archilochus' rebuff was apparently total, and we must believe him when he tells us: "One sizable thing I do know: How to get back my own with a man doing me wrong," and, "I know how to love those who love me, how to hate. My enemies I overwhelm with abuse. The ant bites!" He turned to his poetry to vent his wounded pride:

What a burden off my neck!
What a joy to escape marriage!
Another time, Lycambes,
    father-in-law almost.
I can't bring you to your knees.
Honor presupposes a sense of shame,
And that you haven't got.

Surprisingly, Neobule also becomes the target of Archilochus' wrath. Was it she who destroyed his ego and spurned him? (Was she the one who considered him "lazy" in one of his poems?) Or did his rejection by her father simply poison him against her also? Certainly, he was none too complimentary toward the woman he had previously wanted to marry:

Neobule I have forgotten, believe me, do.
Any man who wants her may have her.
Aiai! She's past her day, ripening rotten.

The petals of her flower are all brown.
The grace that first she had is shot.
Don't you agree that she looks like a boy?

A woman like that would drive a man crazy.
She should get herself a job as a scarecrow.
I'd as soon hump her as [kiss a goat's butt].

In the same poem, Archilochus describes his seduction of a young girl who seems to be Neobule's younger sister. Such action could have been his ultimate form of revenge (although, interestingly, he does not appear to complete the act), but we must wonder whether the episode actually happened or if it was poetic fantasy. It seems odd that he would have been able to approach the younger sister so freely—and she receive him so willingly—when he had been rejected by the family and become so hostile toward them. The alleged seduction also raises the interesting possibility that Archilochus may have previously approached the younger sister (it certainly would not have been out of character) while engaged to Neobule and thus earned the wrath of both Neobule and Lycambes.

The tradition indicates that Archilochus' satiric attacks on the Lycambid family were unceasing and became so abusive that, ultimately, father and daughters all committed suicide. We tend to want to dismiss the story out of hand as a later accounting of how Archilochus finally got his revenge—it fits well with the popular concept of his venomous personality. We probably should dismiss it because the poetry that remains which berates the family is hardly worthy of anyone's suicide. However, the tradition is a strong one, and in a society that still retained elements of a "shame" culture, honor was of paramount importance (and curses were not regarded lightly). The Lycambid family's "dirty linen" aired in public by a man as ruthless as Archilochus may have had an effect difficult for us to calculate. One study has suggested that the suicides may have been the actual reason behind Archilochus' exile from Paros. Another states that we should dismiss the tradition entirely and denies that there was ever a romance between Archilochus and Neobule.

Archilochus' End

A love lost, a wandering existence, a familiarity with the sea, friends lost in battle and drowned (apparently even a brother-in-law), cautious words about the tenuousness of life, contempt for practically everyone, a tainted birth, and a mocking indifference for age-old aristocratic values—all took their toll on Archilochus. The following poem, couched, not surprisingly, in military terms, probably best sums up his philosophy of life:

> Heart, my heart, so battered with misfortune far beyond your
>   strength,
> up, and face the men who hate us. Bare your chest to the assault
> of the enemy, and fight them off. Stand fast among the beamlike spears.
> Give no ground; and if you beat them, do not brag in open show,
> nor, if they beat you, run home and lie down on your bed and cry.
> Keep some measure in the joy you take in luck, and the degree
> you give way to sorrow. All our life is up-and-down like this.

It is perhaps no surprise to find that the strongest tradition about Archilochus' death has him killed in battle—at the hands of Calondas of Naxos, also known as "the Crow." A popular story had Apollo so angry at Calondas for killing his favorite (as seen earlier, Archilochus' family probably had connections with Apollo at Delphi) that even though Calondas pleaded he had killed Archilochus in a fair fight, he was driven from the god's temple.

That Archilochus was killed in battle by a Naxian is not impossible, since we know he was involved in wars with Naxos. The assertion that he was killed by "the Crow," however, may be more difficult to accept. For someone who wrote beast fables to have met his end at the hands of a crow, when he had apparently referred to himself elsewhere on occasion as an insect called the cicada, shapes up more as a metaphorical meal in the animal world concocted by a later biographer than an actual historical incident. Consequently, Calondas' responsibility for the deed cannot be assumed with any certainty.

The Parians established a hero-cult for Archilochus. Some of his quotations became sayings that were popular throughout the Mediterranean world. He was linked forever with Apollo, Dionysus, and Demeter. Every schoolboy in Greece and Rome who studied Greek knew about Lycambes' broken word. With Homer and Hesiod, as one of the originators of the Greek poetic tradition, Archilochus' work had great influence and was admired (or vilified) for centuries to come. The great comic playwrights of fifth-century B.C. Athens looked back to him as the father of satire. And even the Church Fathers found him useful to quote (although usually in a negative way) as late as the sixth century A.D.

"There is in him the utmost vigor of language, thoughts forcible, concise, and lively, and abundance of life and energy," remarked Quintilian about seven hundred years after the poet's death. But, he continues, some think "he is inferior to any writer whatever," owing his success "to his

Some Funny Folk—An Insight into Greek Humor: "Homeric" Frogs and Mice, King Agesilaus and Queen Gorgo of Sparta, and Diogenes the Cynic

WE HAVE SEEN IN this chapter how the *Iliad* and *Odyssey* of Homer were held sacred by many Greeks, but we have also seen that there were always a few, like Archilochus, who found such esteemed writings and the ideals encompassed in them ripe for attack: Homer wrote of the "stuff" from which heroes are made while Archilochus "unstuffed" them. Archilochus also liked "beast" fables (and, metaphorically, appears later to have become part of one himself—see p. 29), so he would have appreciated the following spoof of the *Iliad,* attributed to a certain Pigres of Caria and dated to the early fifth century B.C. Instead of Greeks and Trojans squaring off, we have the great armies of the Frogs and Mice, who have come to blows after the Frog king, Puff-jaw, accidentally drowned the noble Mouse, Crumb-snatcher, in the lake. This will cause, as the "poet" reminds us in his invocation to the Muse, "that awful strife, that clamorous deed of war," when "the Mice proved their valor on the Frogs. . . . Thus did the war begin."

The Mice, after the proper inflammatory speeches, armed themselves:

First they fastened on greaves and covered their shins with green bean-pods broken into two parts which they had gnawed out. . . . Their breastplates were of skin stretched on reeds, skillfully made from a ferret they had flayed. For shields each had the center-piece of a lamp, and their spears were long needles all of bronze, the work of Ares, and the helmets upon their temples were nut shells.

Meanwhile, the Frogs (following proper exhortations)

covered their shins with leaves of mallows, and had breastplates made of fine green beet-leaves, and cabbage leaves, skillfully fashioned, for shields. Each one was equipped with a long, pointed rush for a spear, and smooth snail-shells to cover their heads. Then they stood in close-locked ranks upon the high bank, waving their spears, and were filled, each of them, with courage.

The narrative continues:

Then gnats with great trumpets sounded the fell note of war, and Zeus the son of Cronos thundered from heaven, a sign of grievous battle.

First Loud-croaker wounded Lickman in the belly, right through the midriff. Down fell he on his face and soiled his soft fur in the dust; he fell with a thud and his armor clashed about him. Next Troglodyte shot at the son of Mudman, and drove the strong spear deep into his breast; so he fell, and black death seized him and his spirit flitted forth from his mouth. Then Beety struck Pot-visitor to the heart and killed him, and Bread-nibbler hit Loud-crier in the belly, so that he fell on his face and his spirit flitted forth from his limbs. Now when Pond-larker saw Loud-crier perishing, he struck in quickly and wounded Troglodyte in his soft neck with a rock like a mill-stone, so that darkness veiled his eyes. Threat Ocimides was seized with grief, and struck out with his sharp reed and did not draw his spear back to him again, but felled his enemy there and then. And Lickman shot at him with a bright spear and hit him unerringly in the midriff. And as he marked Cabbage-eater running away, he fell on the steep bank, yet even so did not cease fighting but smote that other so that he fell and did not rise again: and the lake was dyed with red blood as he lay outstretched along the shore, pierced through the guts and shining flanks. Also he slew Cheese-eater. . . . But

Reedy took to flight when he saw Ham-nibbler, and fled, plunging into the lake and throwing away his shield. Then blameless Pot-visitor killed Brewer and Water-larker killed the lord Ham-nibbler, striking him on the head with a pebble, so that his brains flowed out at his nostrils and the earth was bespattered with blood. Faultless Muck-coucher sprang upon Lick-platter and killed him with his spear and brought darkness upon his eyes: and Leeky saw it, and dragged Lick-platter by the foot, though he was dead, and choked him in the lake. But Crumb-snatcher was fighting to avenge his dead comrades, and hit Leeky before he reached the land; and he fell forward at the blow and his soul went down to Hades. And seeing this, Cabbage-climber took a clod of mud and hurled it at the Mouse, plastering all his forehead and nearly blinding him. Thereat Crumb-snatcher was enraged and caught up in his strong hand a huge stone that lay upon the ground, a heavy burden for the soil: with that he hit Cabbage-climber below the knee and splintered his whole right shin, hurling him on his back in the dust. But Croakerson kept him off, and rushing at the Mouse in turn, hit him in the middle of the belly and drove the whole reed-spear into him, and as he drew the spear back to him with his strong hand, all his foe's bowels gushed out upon the ground. And when Troglodyte saw the deed, as he was limping away from the fight on the river bank, he shrank back sorely moved, and leaped into a trench to escape sheer death. . . .

Now there was one among the Mice, Slice-snatcher, who excelled the rest, dear son of Gnawer the son of blameless Bread-stealer. He went to his house and bade his son take part in the war; but he himself stood exulting by the lake. This warrior threatened to destroy the race of Frogs utterly, and splitting a chestnut-husk into two parts along the joint, put the two hollow pieces as armor on his paws: then straightway the Frogs were dismayed and all rushed down to the lake, and he would have made good his boast—for he had great strength—had not the Son of Cronus, the Father of men and gods, been quick to mark the thing and pitied the Frogs as they were perishing. . . .

(*Battle of Frogs and Mice,* lines 5–6, 8, 124–131, 161–167, 199–250, 259–270, and 302–303)

Zeus ended the mighty struggle and saved the Frogs by first warning the indefatigable Mice with a thunderbolt, and, that failing, he launched an army of crabs (an armored division) upon the hapless rodents, who turned and fled: "Already the sun was set, and so came the end of the one-day war."

While the comedies of Aristophanes (quoted throughout this text) immediately come to mind when one mentions Ancient Greek humor, the Spartans usually do not. They certainly did not like anything about "flip" people like Archilochus, whose writings were banned at Sparta and whose advice—to throw away one's shield and run when the fighting got tough—they countered with the exhortation "Come back with your shield—or on it!"—that is, victorious or dead. Spartans are not typically known for being "funny," but, as Plutarch notes in his life of the Spartan lawgiver, *Lycurgus* (20.5), they did have a particular kind of humor, which, like their speech, was short and to the point. He lists a number of their sayings in his *Moralia.* The following are attributed to King Agesilaus (444–360 B.C.); Queen Gorgo, the wife of King Leonidas

(continued)

Some Funny Folk—An Insight into Greek Humor (continued)

(who died at Thermopylae in 480 B.C.—see page 127); and anonymous Spartan women:

Agesilaus:

> When someone praised an orator for his ability in making much of small matters, Agesilaus said that a shoemaker is not a good craftsman who puts big shoes on a small foot.
> (*Moralia* 208c)

> Seeing in Asia a house roofed with square beams, he asked the owner if timber in that country grew square. And when the man said, "No, but round," he said, "Well, then, if they were square, would you finish them round?"
> (210e)

> When he was invited to hear the man who imitated the nightingale's voice, he begged to be excused, saying, "I have heard the bird itself many times."
> (212f)

Queen Gorgo:

> Being asked by a woman from Attica, "Why is it that you Spartan women are the only women that lord it over your men?" she said, "because we are the only women that are mothers of men."
> (240e)

Anonymous Spartan women:

> A Spartan woman, in answer to her son who said that the sword which he carried was short, said, "Add a step to it."
> (241f)

> A Spartan woman, being asked if she had made advances to her husband, said, "No, but my husband has made them to me."
> (242c)

> A Spartan woman (being sold as a slave after being taken captive), asked by a man if she would be good if he bought her, said, "Yes, and if you do not buy me."

Finally, Diogenes (c. 400–325 B.C.), founder of the Cynic philosophy, was known for his eccentricity. Consequently, stories, many of them anecdotal or apocryphal, abound about his off-beat activities. In his *Lives of Eminent Philosophers*, Diogenes Laertius (third century A.D.) has attributed the following sayings to Diogenes the Cynic:

> Plato had defined Man as an animal, biped and featherless, and was applauded. Diogenes plucked a chicken and brought it into the lecture-room with the words, "Here is Plato's man."
> (6.40)

> A eunuch of bad character had inscribed on his door the words, "Let nothing evil enter." "How then," Diogenes asked, "is the master of the house to get in?"
> (6.39)

> When he was sunning himself . . . Alexander [the Great] came and stood over him and said, "Ask me any boon you like." To which Diogenes replied, "Stand out of my light."
> (6.38)

Figure 1.13
Ionic capital from c. 550 B.C. found on Paros. It apparently supported a portrait of Archilochus and was part of his memorial. The inscription (in fourth-century B.C. characters) reads "Archilochus of Paros, son of Telesicles, rests here; Docimus, son of Neocreon, set up this memorial." (Paros Museum)

subjects, not to his genius" (*Institutio oratoria* 10.1.60). Pro or con, one thing is clear: Whenever people heard Archilochus' name, their thoughts were probably close to the sentiments that inspired this false epitaph:

> This tomb by the sea is the grave of Archilochus . . .
> Pass softly by, good wayfarer, or you'll rouse the wasps
> that settle on it.
> (*Palatine Anthology* 71)

Violent, passionate, sensitive, and irreverent, Archilochus was one of Greece's earliest artists. But just as important, he was the first individual we know of to use his writings to puncture the previously secure world of the aristocracy, a world, ironically, of which he was still a part. The ideals he attacked would continue to flourish, but his contemptuous voice was symptomatic of the growing troubles between aristocrats and the new forces that had arisen in Greek society.

Suggestions for Further Reading

Homer's *Iliad* and *Odyssey* are obvious starting places. Their actual historical setting is characterized best by M. I. Finley in *The World of Odysseus* (New York: The New York Review Books, Incorporated, [reprint] 2002). For the earlier Minoans, see J. W. Graham, *The Palaces of Crete* (Princeton, N.J.: Princeton University Press, [revised edition] 1987); on Thera, D. A. Hardy et al., *Thera and the Aegean World III*, Vols. 1–3 (London: The Thera Foundation, 1990). J. Chadwick's *The Mycenaean World* (New York: Cambridge University Press, 1976) and *The Decipherment of Linear B* (1960) provide a useful introduction to the Achaeans, the Bronze Age inhabitants of Greece who traditionally fought at Troy. Readers interested in the Trojan War will find fascinating fare in D. Page, *History and the Homeric Iliad* (Berkeley and Los Angeles: University of California Press, 1966). A useful supplement intended for general audiences and based on the T.V. series is M. Wood's *In Search of the Trojan War* (New York: Facts on File, 1985), which is well illustrated and presents the reader with the major issues and evidence. Also on Troy, see V. Tolstikov and M. Treister, *The Gold of Troy: Searching for Homer's Fabled City* (New York: Abrams, 1996); J. V. Luce, *Celebrating Homer's Landscapes: Troy and Ithaca Revisited* (New Haven, Conn.: Yale University Press, 1998); and S. H. Allen, *Finding the Walls of Troy: Frank Calvert and Heinrich Schliemann at Hissarlik* (Berkeley and Los Angeles: University of California Press, 1999). Readers desiring a short overview of the state of knowledge and scholarship about Troy and Bronze and Dark Age Greece up until 1993 will profit by consulting C. G. Thomas's *Myth Becomes History; Pre-Classical Greece. Publications of the Association of Ancient Historians,* No. 4 (Claremont, Calif.: Regina Books, 1993). See also O. Dickenson, *The Aegean Bronze Age* (Cambridge: Cambridge University Press, 1994); R. Drews, *The Coming of the Greeks: Indo-European Conquests in the Aegean and the Near East* and *The End of the Bronze Age* (Princeton, N.J.: Princeton University Press, 1993 and 1995); J. Hooker, *The Coming of the Greeks* (Claremont, Calif.: Regina Books, 1999); and C. G. Thomas and C. Conant, *Citadel to City-State: The Transformation of Greece 1200–700 B.C.* (Bloomington: Indiana University Press, 1999). C. Starr's *The Economic and Social Growth of Early Greece 800–500 B.C.* (New York: Oxford University Press, 1977) and A. Snodgrass's *Archaic Greece, The Age of Experiment* (Berkeley and Los Angeles: University of California Press, 1980) will familiarize readers with the problems, controversies, and nature of the Archaic period. Starr's *Individual and Community: The Rise of the Polis 800–500 B.C.* (New York: Oxford University Press, 1986) is the culmination of many years of study on the period (cf. also Starr's *Origins of Greek Civilization 1100–650 B.C.,* reissued in 1991 as a Norton paperback); see also *The Aristocratic Temper of Greek Civilization* (New York: Oxford University Press, 1992). A. R. Burn's *The Lyric Age of Greece* (New York: St. Martin's Press, 1968) remains a useful overall survey of the period, and O. Murray's *Early Greece* (Stanford, Calif.: Stanford University Press, 1983) is also a worthwhile introduction. Differing views of Archilochus and his poetry can be found in A. J. Podlecki's competent and sober *The Early Greek Poets and Their Times,* Chapter 2 (Vancouver: University of British Columbia Press, 1984); in A. Rankin's appraisal, *Archilochus of Paros* (Park Ridge, N.J.: Noyes Press, 1977); and A. P. Burnett's *Three Archaic Poets: Archilochus, Alcaeus, and Sappho* (Cambridge, Mass.: Harvard University Press, 1983), a dramatically different and studied interpretation of Archilochus. Collected fragments of Archilochus in translation are in R. Lattimore, *Greek Lyrics,* "Archilochus" (Chicago & London: The University of Chicago Press [revised and enlarged second edition], 1960), and G. Davenport's *Archilochus, Sappho, Alkman: Three Lyric Poets of the Late Greek Bronze Age* (Berkeley and Los Angeles: University of California Press, 1980).

On warfare, see V. D. Hanson, editor of *Hoplites* (New York: Routledge, 1991) and author of *The Western Way of War: Infantry Battle in Classical Greece* (New York: Oxford University Press, 1990), and *Warfare and Agriculture in Classical Greece* (Berkeley and Los Angeles: University of California Press, 1998); and P. Connolly, *Greece and Rome at War* (London: Greenhill Books, 1998). For Greek cavalry, L. J. Worley's *Hippeis: The Cavalry of Ancient Greece* (Boulder, Colo.: Westview Press, 1994) and I. G. Spence's *The Cavalry of Classical Greece* (New York: Oxford University Press, 1996) are informative. Also useful are J. Rich and G. Shipley, *War & Society in the Greek World* (New York: Routledge, 1995); M. Sage, *Warfare in Ancient Greece: A Sourcebook* (New York: Routledge, 1996); and P. B. Kern, *Ancient Siege Warfare* (Bloomington: Indiana University Press, 1999). Other works of interest for Chapter 1 are T. Severin, "Sailing in Jason's Wake," *National Geographic,* Vol. 168, No. 3, 1985, 406–420; J. Solomon, *The Ancient World in Cinema* (New Haven: Yale University Press [revised and expanded edition], 2001) although often careless; D. W. Tandy, *Warriors into Traders: The Power of the Market in Early Greece* (Berkeley and Los Angeles: University of California Press, 1997); K. Shipton and A. Meadows (eds.), *Money and Its Uses in the Ancient Greek World* (New York: Oxford University Press, 2001); P. Cartledge et al., *Money, Labour and Land in Ancient Greece: Approaches to the Economics of Ancient Greece* (New York: Routledge, 2002); D. Ogden, *Greek Bastardy in the Classical and Hellenistic Periods* (New York: Oxford University Press, 1996); and D. L. Cairns, *Aidos: The Psychology and Ethics of Honor and Shame in Ancient Greek Literature* (New York: Oxford University Press, 1993).

General Reading

Some useful general works are J. Boardman, *The Oxford History of Greece and the Hellenistic World* (New York: Oxford University Press, 1991); N. G. L. Hammond, *History of Greece to 322 B.C.* (Oxford: Oxford University Press, 1986); S. Pomeroy et al., *Ancient Greece: A Political, Social, and Cultural History* (New York: Oxford University Press, 1999); T. Martin, *Ancient Greece: From Prehistoric to Hellenistic Times* (New Haven, Conn.: Yale University Press, 1996); R. Osborne, *Greece in the Making 1200–479 B.C.* (New York: Routledge, 1996); C. Freeman, *The Greek Achievement: The Foundation of the Western World* (New York: Viking Penguin, 1999); N. F. Jones, *Ancient Greece: State and Society* (Upper Saddle River, N.J.: Prentice-Hall, 1997); and D. Nardo (ed.), *The Complete History of Ancient Greece* (San Diego, Calif.: Greenhaven Press, 2001). F. Frost's *Greek Society,* 5th ed. (Boston: Houghton Mifflin, 1997) is more in line with the content of this volume and has attracted a large following over the years.

For reference works, atlases, literary, and other studies of interest, *The Oxford Classical Dictionary* is the standard English reference work for the Classical world. See also S. Hornblower and A. Spawforth (eds.), *The Oxford Companion to Classical Civilization* (New York: Oxford University Press, 1998); D. Sacks et al., *A Dictionary of the Ancient Greek World* (New York: Oxford University Press, 1995); and D. Bowder, *Who Was Who in the Greek World, 776 B.C.–30 B.C.* (Ithaca, N.Y.: Cornell University Press, 1982). P. Connolly's *The Ancient City: Life in Classical Athens and Rome* (New York: Oxford University Press, 1998) is an invaluable aid, while L. Adkins and R. A. Adkins, *Handbook to Life in Ancient Greece* (New York: Oxford University Press, 1997), and R. Garland's *Daily Life of the Ancient Greeks* (Westport, Conn.: Greenwood Press, 1998) are also useful. R. J. A. Talbert (ed.), *Barrington Atlas of the Greek and Roman World* (Princeton, N.J.: Princeton University Press, 2000), is definitive on the Classical world. P. Levi's *Atlas of the Greek World* (New York: Facts on File, 1980) and R. Morkot's *The Penguin Historical Atlas of*

Ancient Greece (New York: Penguin Books, 1996) are less formal, contain many illustrations, and are directed more at the general reader. On literature, see A. Dihle, *A History of Greek Literature from Homer to the Hellenistic Period* (New York: Routledge, 1994), and A. Lesky, *A History of Greek Literature* (New York: Crowell, 1966). E. R. Dodds's *Greeks and the Irrational* (Berkeley and Los Angeles, 1960) is the classic work on the ancient Greek mentality. See also J. Brunschwig and G. E. R. Lloyd (eds.), *Greek Thought: A Guide to Classical Knowledge* (Cambridge, Mass.: Harvard University Press, 2000); *Human Landscape in Classical Antiquity* (New York: Routledge, 1996), edited by J. Salmon and G. Shipley; M. R. Lefkowitz and G. M. Rogers, *Black Athena Revisited* (Chapel Hill: University of North Carolina Press, 1996); M. R. Lefkowitz, *Not Out of Africa* (New York: Basic Books, 1997); and *Greek Gods, Human Lives* (New Haven, Conn.: Yale University Press, 2003).

2

A World of Iron and Tyrants

Hesiod the Bard, Polycrates of Samos, and Eupalinus the Engineer

I wish I were not counted among the fifth race of men,
but rather had died before, or been born after it.
This is the race of iron.
(Hesiod, *Works and Days* 174–176)

Social and Economic Changes

Despite the changes in Archaic Greek society, articulated in part by Archilochus, the aristocracy had no intention of voluntarily allowing their favored position to slide. The poet Alcaeus (c. 600 B.C.) of Mytilene, for example, seems to vow in one of his poems that he will fight for the values he treasures. In another, he reflects on the turmoil in his homeland by representing his state as a ship being tossed about in a storm. However, the world *was* changing, and a half-century later, the poet Theognis of Megara bitterly described how far the cause of the "nouveau riche" had progressed by his day:

> Those who before knew nothing of lawsuits, nothing of laws,
> who went about in goatskins flapping over their shoulders,
>   who lived on the ranges, far out from the town, like wild deer,
> these are now the Great Men. . . . Our former nobles
>   are Rabble now. Who could endure it when things are so?
> They swindle each other, they mock at one another, and meanwhile
>   understand nothing at all of what good and bad men think.
> (Lattimore, Theognis ff., *Greek Lyrics*)

and

> Never yet . . . was a city destroyed by its nobles,
>   but only after base men take to disorderly ways,
> and debauch their own people and give rights to the unrighteous
>   for the sake of their own money and power; and when this is so,
> hold no hope for such a city to remain unshaken
>   for long, although for the time it rides on a tranquil keel,
> not when such activities have tempted the base men
>   and private advantage comes with public disaster. For this
> breeds civil discord and men's blood shed by their fellow-citizens,
>   and monarchies. But pray that our city may never be such.
> (Lattimore, 39 ff.)

Not all nonaristocrats, however, benefited from the effects of the Commercial Revolution described in Chapter 1. It may have advanced the cause—economically, militarily, and politically—of members of the new "middle class," who raised the ire of Alcaeus and Theognis, but this group constituted only a small segment of society. The majority of Greeks remained what they had always been, poor peasant farmers, and their lot went from bad to worse.

"There's no poor man who's known as good or valued much," concluded Alcaeus, and few aristocrats would have argued. While economies had remained local, there probably existed a small measure of interdependency between the poor and their overlords. The poor had been able to eke out a living, enough to support their families in meager fashion and still have some left for the next year's planting and the marketplace. However, this situation changed as they were completely dislocated by the new, rapidly developing Mediterranean economy.

The business mentality that characterized the new age made these unfortunate farmers easy prey for aristocrats and the recently emerged wealthier nonaristocratic families with farming and commercial interests. The emphasis on gain and profit outweighed whatever "community spirit" had existed. Even time-honored common memberships in basic kinship, religious, and political groups, which were at the foundation of primitive society, provided little, if any, relief for the poor. Many poor farmers were forced to put themselves and their families up as collateral for whatever assistance they did receive, and debt-slavery was the predictable result. This quickly grew into a most lucrative enterprise, for a small loan to a struggling farmer could ultimately lead to a nice profit for the lender. In addition, there seems to have been little reluctance on the part of most creditors to take advantage of their less fortunate fellow citizens and sell them.

As more and more families were split up and sold in their native cities and elsewhere in Greece and the Mediterranean, farmers facing debt-slavery understandably reacted violently to protect themselves and their loved ones.

They had little alternative, since the corruption and lack of concern of most local administrators drove the poor farmers to toss aside caution and the awe in which they had previously held their "betters." The extent to which the poor were vulnerable is made perfectly clear by the situation in which the bard Hesiod found himself around 700 B.C.

Gods and Justice: Hesiod Speaks Out

After Homer, Hesiod is the next great figure in Greek literature. In fact, they are usually spoken of together. Sandwiched between Homer and Archilochus, Hesiod produced two major epics—the *Theogony* (literally, "Birth of the Gods") and the *Works and Days*. The former is the first systematic attempt to catalogue the various major and minor divinities. It describes their origins, relationship to one another, characteristics, and duties, as well as presenting a version of the Greek cosmogony—from the beginnings of the universe to the time when Zeus established his authority on Mt. Olympus. The *Works and Days* is a farmer's almanac of sorts that contains basic information on farming, homespun advice, folk wisdom and maxims, and even a word or two on seamanship. Both works provide details about Hesiod's life.

Hesiod's profession as a bard, or singer of tales, seems to have come about mostly by accident. Like Homer, Hesiod was born in Asia Minor, where his father was involved, apparently without much success, in sea trade. "Grim poverty" forced the family to move from Cyme in Aeolia to the central mountainous pasturelands of Greece in Boeotia. There they established a household in the "worthless village" of Ascra, "a place bad in winter, worse in the summer, never good," near Mt. Helicon. Hesiod tended sheep, a tedious pursuit at best, and apparently the bard-to-be whiled away the hours of boredom singing and composing poems.

Pastoral societies are understandably ones in which visions of and visitations from gods are most frequent. Thus, perhaps not surprisingly, Hesiod tells us he was with his sheep, alone, probably struggling to keep his senses about him on a hot afternoon, when the "Muses of Olympus" first spoke to him:

> "Listen, you country bumpkins, you swag-bellied yahoos,
> we know how to tell many lies that pass for truth,
> and we know, when we wish, to tell the truth itself."
> So spoke Zeus' daughters, masters of wordcraft,
> and from a laurel in full bloom they plucked a branch,
> and gave it to me as a staff, and then breathed into me
> divine song, that I might spread the fame of past and future,
> and commanded me to hymn the race of the deathless gods,
> but always begin and end my song with them.
> (*Theogony* 26–34)

Although poetry now became an important part of Hesiod's life, he probably still had not had much chance to refine his lyrics and songs before his father died. He mentions a victory "in a song contest" at Chalcis in Euboea at the funeral games of one Amphidamas (an event at which later tradition would also place Homer—sometimes even identified as Hesiod's cousin!—so that he might compete with his famous rival), but it likely dates from a later time, for Hesiod would have been too unknown to have been invited to such an important event at this juncture (Amphidamas is almost certainly the prominent leader who we know was killed during the Lelantine War about 700 B.C.). Also, if Hesiod were already famous, his father's death would not have had the dramatic impact on his future that it obviously did.

Up to that time, the fledgling poet's existence had been hard, but not as difficult as that of most of the peasants among whom he lived. His father had apparently been more successful in Boeotia, because Hesiod clearly expected to receive an inheritance that would make his life more tolerable. It is doubtful he foresaw that he would actually have to make a living from his poetic talents. Unexpectedly, his brother, Perses, appears to have conspired with local authorities, "bribe-devouring princes," to cheat Hesiod out of most of his inheritance. This behavior was clearly not what Hesiod anticipated from those who ruled, as is indicated by this idealized passage from the *Theogony:*

> And if the daughters of great Zeus honor a king
> cherished by Zeus and look upon him when he is born,
> they pour on his tongue sweet dew
> and make the words that flow from his mouth honey-sweet,
> and all the people look up to him as with straight justice
> he gives his verdict and with unerring firmness
> and wisdom brings some great strife to a swift end.
> This is why kings are prudent, and when in the assembly
> injustice is done, wrongs are righted
> by the kings with ease and gentle persuasion.
> When such a king comes to the assembly he stands out;
> yes, he is revered like a god and treated with cheerful respect.
> Such is the holy gift the Muses give men . . .
> kings are from the line of Zeus.
> (81–96)

The treatment Hesiod received from the princes who cheated him was a far cry from this model; consequently, he appears to have ended with little to live on. It was most likely this situation that forced him to study in earnest the craft of the rhapsode. His talent was enough to make him the most successful, best-known member of the profession during his period.

Hesiod would aim the *Works and Days* specifically at his conniving brother, an appeal of sorts, urging Perses to give back what he had so wrongfully taken and to earn an honest living by the "sweat of his brow." He set out everything Perses would need to know to profit in work and in life, and in case his brother failed to take him seriously, he warns that Zeus is a god of justice and would somehow punish his underhanded dealings if he did not make amends.

"Perses," he says, "obey justice and restrain reckless wrongdoing." "The road to fair dealings is the better one. Justice is the winner in the race against insolent crime. Only fools need suffer to learn. . . . Justice howls when she is dragged about by bribe-devouring men whose verdicts are crooked when they sit in judgment." "Men," he continues, "whose justice is straight know neither hunger nor ruin, but amid feasts enjoy the yield of their labors. . . . But far-seeing Zeus, son of Kronos, is the judge of wanton wrongdoers who plot deeds of harshness."

Hesiod's belief that the gods were just and moral was an idea that was relatively new, having been set forth so forcefully only once before in Book 24 of Homer's *Odyssey*. In any primitive society, the poets are to a large extent responsible for shaping the character and behavior of the gods of that society. Hesiod was in the forefront of that process among the Greeks.

The World in Decline

Hesiod's brother, of course, paid no heed, although the poet probably held little hope of "rehabilitating" him, for his bitterness was already apparent in the *Works and Days*. Hesiod is sometimes referred to as the West's first "prophet of doom," because he described, in declining order, the "Five Ages of Man." The first was a beautiful Age of Gold, a time when the gods ruled justly, when everything was perfect and no problems existed. This period was followed by a lesser Age of Silver, during which mortals offended Zeus, who buried them and created a third age—this time, of bronze. The Age of Bronze was inferior to the first two, being much coarser and more destructive, but when this period, too, had ended, a ray of hope returned during the fourth age: the Age of Hero-Men. This was a better and more just age that momentarily halted the decline of the world, thought Hesiod, who stood in awe of the heroes who fought at Troy and at Thebes and peopled the world during this period. But alas, the fifth and final age, Hesiod's own, he considered the worst of all ages, equating it with iron:

> I wish I were not counted among the fifth race of men,
> but rather had died before, or been born after it.
> This is the race of iron. Neither day nor night
> will give them rest as they waste away with toil
> and pain. Growing cares will be given them by the gods,
> and their lot will be a blend of good and bad.

Zeus will destroy this race of mortals
when children are born gray at the temples.
Children will not resemble their fathers,
and there will be no affection between guest and host
and no love between friends or brothers as in the past.
Sons and daughters will be quick to offend their aging parents
and rebuke them and speak to them with rudeness
and cruelty, not knowing about divine retribution;
they will not even repay their parents for their keep—
these law-breakers—and they will sack one another's cities.
The man who keeps his oath, or is just and good,
will not be favored, but the evil-doers and scoundrels
will be honored, for might will make right and shame will vanish.
Base men will harm their betters with words
that are crooked and then swear they are fair.
And all toiling humanity will be blighted by envy,
grim and strident envy that takes its joy in the ruin of others.
Then Shame and Retribution will cover their fair bodies
with white cloaks and, leaving men behind,
will go to Olympos from the broad-pathed earth
to be among the race of the immortals, while grief and pain
will linger among men, whom harm will find defenseless.
(*Works and Days* 174–201)

Certainly, Hesiod was disappointed and was never able to forget the wrongs done to him, though, ironically, it was his brother who was indirectly responsible for his fame. But if Hesiod could be so easily abused— and he was a man of somewhat more substance than the typical Greek—then it is clear that most peasant farmers were virtually helpless against the stronger and wealthier in society.

With so many farmers facing debt-slavery and crying out for social justice and equality, and with animosity growing stronger between the new wealthy families, who were demanding political equality, and the established aristocracy, it is no surprise that tensions increased dramatically in the small city-states of Greece. Add to this disputes over property rights, a clamoring for redistribution of land, the probable strain of an increasing population, and the migration of impoverished farmers from country to city, and the potential for civil discord and violence became very real.

Colonization and the Rise of Tyrants

In an attempt to relieve the many pressures facing their small city-states, the Greeks began sending out colonies to other parts of Greece and the Mediterranean. Evidence suggests that colonists from at least one mother-city were

Figure 2.1
A seventh-century B.C.
terra-cotta statuette
of a farmer with his
plough and team
from Boeotia, the
area of Greece in
which Hesiod lived
c. 700 B.C. *(Louvre,*
Paris)

selected by lot and that they faced death and confiscation of property if they refused to go. This compelling evidence indicates that the colonies were not, as some believe, primarily economic ventures.

Many colonists, however, certainly would have left voluntarily, viewing the opportunity to begin a new life as an attractive alternative to what they had at home. A farmer facing debt-slavery, for example, had nothing to lose by going. Members of newly prosperous families seeking political power might find it in a new city. Even disinherited aristocrats probably recognized the opportunities for gaining the wealth and power they needed to match their prestigious but bankrupt names.

A small army would secure the site for the colony, usually preapproved by the oracle at Delphi (see Chapter 3) or some other shrine where the will of the gods could be divined. Once established, the colonists owed no allegiance to the mother-city, although family and religious ties, as well as the potential for future economic benefits, usually guaranteed some continued relationship. Eventually, after about two centuries of colonization, Greek cities stretched as far east as the Black Sea and as far west as Spain. But the main concentration was in the area from southern Italy and Sicily to the coast of Asia Minor.

The establishment of colonies, however, could not eliminate the many problems facing the Greeks. They were half-measures at best, providing only short-term relief. In time, a new governmental institution—tyranny— would grow out of the social, economic, and political difficulties of the day.

Today, the word *tyrant* carries with it many negative connotations that were not implied in the original Greek usage, at least not before the fourth century B.C. To the Greeks, a tyrant was simply one who had seized or been

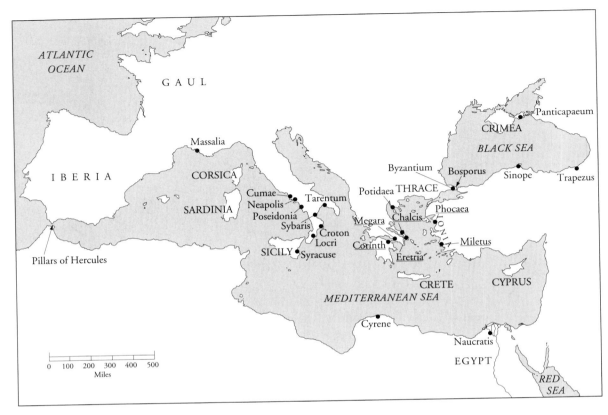

Map 5
Major colonies
and mother-cities
(underlined)

given power in an irregular fashion, contrary to any constitutional process. "Tyrant" was never either a formal title or an official position. Archilochus appears to have introduced the word when speaking of Gyges of Lydia. He regarded it as synonymous with "king," a tradition followed by later poets. In many ways, tyranny represented a revival of monarchy, but "dictator" or "strongman" is probably the more accurate rendering.

Tyrants usually, but not always, held their position by force. They took over when the existing aristocratic governments could not cope successfully with society's problems—to provide a more effective rule. However, balancing public necessity with personal ambition was not always a major concern, and many tyrants became oppressive. They could be cruel or kind, competent or incompetent. They came in all shapes and sizes. The only aspect they all shared was that they had aristocratic backgrounds.

Tyrants took advantage of the factionalism within some of the city-states to establish their power. There must have been a connection between their

rise and the rise of hoplite warfare, because the two are essentially contemporary and tyrants often had hoplite support. Tyrants mostly represented a revolution against the aristocracy, although conceivably they could find their support anywhere—even among their fellows, who often needed leadership in fighting nonaristocratic challengers. The latter group also might place their hopes in one man. Sometimes, the various quarreling factions might even agree to confer power on an acceptable individual, who, during a specified period, was to settle a city-state's problems. Most tyrants, however, received their support from the masses, and for this reason—although it may seem a contradiction in terms—the institution of tyranny must be viewed ultimately as a step toward popular government in Greece.

The Age of Tyrants did not last long, most tyrannies having disappeared by 500 B.C. Tyrannies were largely family affairs, and seldom did they extend past the tyrant's son, grandson, or other male relative, although the city of Sicyon experienced such rule for a century. One person's lifetime could encompass much of most cities' experience with the institution, as

Figure 2.2
Remains of the Greek colony of Poseidonia (later called Paestum) in Italy, founded in the mid–seventh century B.C. by the existing Greek colony of Sybaris. In the foreground is the interior of the Basilica of Hera (mid–sixth century B.C.), the best-preserved Archaic temple in the Greek world. Beside it in the background is the Temple of Neptune (mid–fifth century B.C.), also remarkably preserved.

A Revolution in Thought—Thales of Miletus, the First Greek Philosopher

TRADITIONAL SOCIAL AND POLITICAL beliefs and values changed rapidly between the eighth and sixth centuries B.C. Thus, it should come as no surprise that the time-honored explanations of the nature of the universe and the gods, best represented in the works of Homer and Hesiod, should also come under close scrutiny. It was in Ionia in the sixth century that the earliest philosophers (their numbers never large, their ideas never widely embraced—nor understood) became dissatisfied with the traditional religio-mythological explanations for why things happen and looked for more rational answers. The first of these men was Thales of Miletus, who was active about 585 B.C. and is generally regarded as the "Father of Western Philosophy."

It is appropriate that in a time of political change and commercial opportunity the man who began the "Greek Enlightenment," the inquiry into knowledge, would traditionally be involved in politics and be an entrepreneur of the first rank. In respect to the latter pursuit, Aristotle, who wanted to see Thales' moneymaking ability only in terms of a philosophical exercise, describes Thales' astuteness as follows:

> There is the anecdote of Thales the Milesian and his financial device, which involves a principle of universal application, but is attributed to him on account of his reputation for wisdom. He was reproached for his poverty, which was supposed to show that philosophy was of no use. According to the story, he knew by his skill in the stars while it was yet winter that there would be a great harvest of olives in the coming year; so, having a little money, he gave deposits for the use of all the olive-presses in Chios and Miletus, which he hired at a low price because no one bid against him. When the harvest-time came, and many were wanted all at once and of a sudden, he let them out at any rate which he pleased, and made a quantity of money. Thus he showed the world that

philosophers can easily be rich if they like, but that their ambition is of another sort.
> (*Politics* 1, 1259a)

If Thales had, indeed, cornered the olive oil market, it is doubtful that he did it merely to make a philosophical point!

The rational examination of the world that Thales began was continued by others at Miletus, and from there it spread into the Mediterranean world, often taking on more metaphysical aspects. Because he was the first, Thales was immortalized by the ancients as one of the "Seven Sages" of Greece and was credited with many philosophical and scientific achievements that were not his. The most famous of these was the prediction of the solar eclipse of May 28, 585 B.C., an impossible feat given the state of knowledge at that time. The resultant attempts at biography provide a mish-mash of detail, as the following excerpt from Diogenes Laertius in the third century A.D. attests:

> Herodotus, Duris and Democritus are agreed that Thales was the son of Examyas and Cleobulina, and belonged to the Thelidae [Nelidae?] who are Phoenicians, and among the noblest of the descendants of Cadmus and Agenor. As Plato testifies, he was one of the Seven Sages. He was the first to receive the name of Sage, in the archonship of Damasias at Athens, when the term was applied to all the Seven Sages, as Demetrius of Phalerum mentions in his *List of Archons*. He was admitted to citizenship at Miletus when he came to that town with Nileos, who had been expelled from Phoenicia. Most writers, however, represent him as a genuine Milesian and of a distinguished family.
>
> After engaging in politics he became a student of nature. According to some he left nothing in writing. . . . But according to others he wrote nothing but two treatises, one *On the Solstice* and one *On the Equinox*, regarding all other matters as incognizable. He seems by some accounts to have been the first to study

astronomy, the first to predict eclipses of the sun and to fix the solstices. . . . And some . . . declare that he was the first to maintain the immortality of the soul. He was the first to determine the sun's course from solstice to solstice, and according to some the first to declare the size of the sun to be one seven hundred and twentieth part of the solar circle, and the size of the moon to be the same fraction of the lunar circle. He was the first to give the last day of the month the name of Thirtieth, and the first, some say, to discuss physical problems.

Aristotle and Hippias affirm that, arguing from the magnet and from amber, he attributed a soul or life even to inanimate objects. Pamphilia states that, having learnt geometry from the Egyptians, he was the first to inscribe a right-angled triangle in a circle. . . . Others tell this tale of Pythagoras. . . . Thales is also credited with having given excellent advice on political matters. For instance, when Croesus sent to Miletus offering terms of alliance, he frustrated the plan; and this proved the salvation of the city when Cyrus obtained the victory. Heraclides makes Thales himself say that he had always lived in solitude as a private individual and kept aloof from State affairs. Some authorities say that he married and had a son . . . others that he remained unmarried and adopted his sister's son, and that when he was asked why he had no children of his own he replied "because he loved children." The story is told that, when his mother tried to force him to marry, he replied it was too soon, and when she pressed him again later in life, he replied that it was too late. Hieronymus of Rhodes . . . relates that, in order to show how easy it is to grow rich, Thales, foreseeing that it would be a good season for olives, rented all the oil-mills and thus amassed a fortune.

His doctrine was that water is the universal primary substance, and that the world is animate and full of divinities. He is said to have discovered the seasons of the year and divided it into 365 days.

He had no instructor, except that he went to Egypt and spent some time with the priests there. Hieronymus informs us that he measured the height of the pyramids by the shadow they cast, taking the observation at the hour when our shadow is of the same length as ourselves. He lived . . . with Thrasybulus, the tyrant of Miletus.
(1.22–27)

What *is* clear from the preceding passage is that Thales believed water to be the basic substance from which all solids, liquids, and gases were formed. (He also believed that the earth was a disk floating on water, a situation that conveniently explained earthquakes.) Simple observation revealed the omnipresence of water (Miletus itself looked out over the vast sea), and water's life-giving properties for humans, animals, and plants were no secret to anyone. Although such rational inquiries may make Thales appear to be questioning the existence of the gods, just the opposite is true, for in his own view the world was animate and "full of divinities."

Thales' conclusions would be challenged immediately by members of his own Milesian school of thought. Anaximenes rejected water as the basic element and offered air. Thales' kinsman Anaximander rejected both ideas and held that all living things inhabiting the earth, a drum hanging free in space, were generated from moisture (semen). Anaximander also appears to have produced the first map of the earth, postulated an evolutionary theory, and believed that the universe was governed by what he termed the "Infinite," which was divine, immortal, and the origin for everything.

Radical ideas such as these became another thread in the fabric that was to clothe a new world, which, intellectually, would reach its peak in the works of Plato and Aristotle in the fourth century B.C.

evidenced by this tomb inscription of a member of a family of tyrants, Archedice of Athens:

> This dust hides Archedice, daughter of Hippias, the most important man in Greece in his day; but though her father, husband, brothers, and children were tyrants, her mind was never carried away into arrogance.
> (Thucydides 6.59)

One obvious reason for the rapid demise of tyranny was that tyrants were easy targets for assassins: A government could be overthrown by killing one person. However, the main explanation for the rise and fall of the institution in such a short period of time was the simple fact that the circumstances in society that produced tyranny soon passed. Tyrants filled a gap between the time when the old order was breaking down and a new order had not yet been established.

There would be another Age of Tyrants in the Greek West, which, because of its later foundation through colonization, lagged behind developments in the East; but ultimately, both East and West would advance to more sophisticated and stable forms of government—among them, democracy.

Polycrates of Samos

Of the many tyrants who ruled during the seventh and sixth centuries B.C., the greatest was probably Polycrates of Samos. During his reign (c. 532–522 B.C.), he established Samos, a large and wealthy Ionian island, as a major commercial center and one of Greece's first great naval powers, extending its influence over neighboring islands, the coast of Asia Minor, and elsewhere. He also supported artists and poets and made the island an important cultural center. One ancient writer, although not always reliable and often concerned with lost morals and excess, gives us this appraisal of Polycrates' rule:

> Alexis in the third book of his Samian Annals says that Samos was adorned by Polycrates from (the resources of) many cities. He introduced Molossian and Lacedaemonian hounds, goats from Scyros and Naxos, cattle from Miletus and Attica. Alexis also says that he summoned craftsmen at very high rates of pay. Having had fashioned for himself, before his tyranny, expensive couches and drinking-cups, he gave them over for the use of those becoming married or engaging in very large festivities. Because of all this there is good reason to marvel at the fact that the tyrant is not mentioned as having sent for women or boys from anywhere, despite his passion for liaisons with males; for he was even a jealous rival for the love of Anacreon the poet, when he cut off in anger the hair of his lover. Polycrates was the first man to build ships and name them "Samian" after his country. But Clearchus says that Polycrates, the tyrant of

luxurious Samos, was destroyed because of the intemperance of his ways by cultivating the Lydian effeminacies. It was for this reason that he set up the Samian bazaar in the city to vie with the one known in Sardis as Sweet Embrace [brothel quarter]; and as against the "flowers of the Lydians" he constructed the notorious "flowers of the Samians." Of these (neighborhoods), the Samian bazaar was an alley (of) courtesans. The alley truly filled Hellas with every food tending towards enjoyment and incontinence.
(Athenaeus 540d–f)

Polycrates came from a prominent family, and his father, Aeaces, was a man of some influence. The general circumstances that led to his rise as tyrant are not clear, but Samos' fortunes had probably been declining recently because of Persian pressures. About 532 B.C., the story goes, he seized control with the aid of only fifteen hoplites and appears to have ruled with his two brothers until he executed one and exiled the other.

As sole ruler, Polycrates' power expanded rapidly, and few could challenge his fleet of 100 Samian warships and 1,000 archers. Although some critics styled Polycrates a pirate, his actions reveal him to be much more than a random raider. The wars he waged and his interference with shipping, friend and foe, in the area were chiefly designed to keep Samos atop the commercial world. Naturally, his enemies, particularly the nearby mainland city of Miletus, with whom Samos was usually at war, would squawk. On one occasion, he defeated a fleet from Lesbos that had come to the aid of Miletus and put the prisoners to work digging a moat around his city wall.

Polycrates' greatest enemy was the nearby Persian Empire, and in his dealings with it, as in his other actions, he predictably chose to pursue the dangerous course. Unwilling to become a Persian dependent, he determined, instead, to be the champion of Persian resistance. Although the Persians may have felt that Samos lay within their sphere of influence, Polycrates' fleet was too formidable for them to challenge, and they had to leave him alone, a fact that was said to have caused embarrassment to Oroites, the Persian governor of the area nearest the island. At the same time, Polycrates was never foolish enough to push the Persians too far, and he even cooperated with them when it was to his benefit.

Polycrates' desire to expand trade and his general anti-Persian attitude led him into an association with Amasis, king of Egypt, who had his own doubts about Persian intentions. The friendship apparently was at the root of a popular story told about Polycrates by Herodotus.

Generally regarded as the first historian, Herodotus was no fan of Polycrates. Although born at Halicarnassus, he had fled tyranny there and moved to nearby Samos, where he lived for a time. Consequently, he was very familiar with the island's history. The combination of his dislike for tyrants and a sympathy with whatever anti-Polycrates tradition remained in the first half of the fifth century B.C. resulted in his portraying an end for Polycrates that resembles a Sophoclean tragedy.

Herodotus still believed that the gods would punish human beings for their "hubris," or overweening pride. In his minitragedy about Polycrates, he has the tyrant progress through the same steps that similarly doomed tragic figures on the stage would go through. According to Herodotus, Amasis became alarmed at the unceasing good fortune of Polycrates and cautioned him that the gods would notice his success. Amasis told Polycrates that before he offended the gods and earned their wrath, he should demonstrate his humility by throwing away his most prized possession. Polycrates proceeded to toss an emerald and gold ring into the sea—but it was already too late.

A few days later, a fish was caught, its size and markings so striking that it was brought before the tyrant as a special gift. Polycrates was delighted, but his initial joy soon turned to dismay when he cut open the fish and found his ring in its belly. His offering had not been accepted, and the gods were already moving to bring about his ruin. Amasis, knowing that his friend was doomed, renounced his dangerous friendship with him.

The story, although entertaining, has its shortcomings. It was Polycrates, *not* Amasis, who broke the friendship. In fact, Amasis did not outlive the wily tyrant, who, at about the time of his former friend's death, had found it opportune to aid the Persians when they invaded and conquered Egypt in 525 B.C.

Polycrates' "betrayal" of Egypt did not, however, end in the expected benefits. The contingent of forty ships he had sent was manned by political enemies, whom he expected would not return from the expedition. Return they did—with the intention of overthrowing the tyrant—and they rallied the Spartans and Corinthians, who had gripes against Polycrates. Polycrates was hard-pressed but survived a forty-day siege and successfully defended the city.

Ultimately, the tyrant's phenomenal luck ran out. He supposedly was tricked into a secret meeting with the Persian governor, Oroites, who apparently whetted Polycrates' appetite with promises of treasure in return for his assistance, and was unceremoniously crucified about 522 B.C.

Eupalinus the Engineer

The cultural heritage left by Polycrates was impressive. Poetic talents included the likes of Anacreon and Ibycus, whose choral lyrics made him one of the most important forerunners of Greek tragedy. Polycrates' most famous artist in residence was Theodorus, who, among other things, had fashioned his patron's fateful emerald ring. Interestingly, Polycrates was unable to retain the services of the son of another one of his artisans—Pythagoras, the philosopher, who could have been the brightest star in the tyrant's court had he not fled to Italy about 530 B.C.

Among the projects completed on Samos during Polycrates' administration, three stand out as exceptional: a temple to the goddess Hera that was the largest such structure of its day and probably the model for all Ionic temples built afterward; an impressive mole (breakwater) that protected the harbor at Samos and, according to Herodotus, ran some 400 yards in water 120 feet deep; and a tunnel that was constructed through a hill to bring water to the city. Herodotus, who had undoubtedly seen and inspected the tunnel himself, gives the following account:

> I have dwelt the longer on the affairs of the Samians, because three of the greatest works in all Greece were made by them. One is a tunnel, under a hill 900 feet high, carried entirely through the base of the hill, with a mouth at either end. The length of the cutting is almost a mile—the height and width are each eight feet. Along the whole course there is a second cutting, thirty feet deep and three feet broad, whereby water is brought, through pipes, from an abundant source into the city. The architect of this tunnel was Eupalinus, son of Naustrophus, a Megarian.
> (3.60)

Although Herodotus was mistaken about the length of the tunnel—it was actually about 3,300 feet long—its execution certainly ranks among the most brilliant engineering feats in antiquity, and its creator, Eupalinus of Megara, deserves a high place in the history of civil engineering. To accomplish such a feat at this time was nothing less than astounding, and because we have no information concerning the methods by which Eupalinus constructed the tunnel, modern scholars have tried to theorize how he did it. What makes the feat especially amazing is that tunnels were apparently begun simultaneously on either side of the mountain, and with only slight adjustment, they actually met in the middle! How Eupalinus was able to maintain the alignment of the tunnels through the center of a mountain is certainly a question worth pursuing.

The presence for a while of Pythagoras on Samos at about the same time Eupalinus was building his tunnel has led some scholars to speculate that he provided the engineer with a version of the "Pythagorean theorem" to help guide the course of the tunnels. This idea, however, has been dispelled by ground surveys around the hill in question—the terrain is much too uneven for any kind of geometric scheme ever to have been successfully applied.

A more reasonable explanation for how the square-sectioned tunnel was cut through solid rock in complete darkness has since been offered, and it concerns the use of mirrors. It is a well-known practice in Egypt today, for

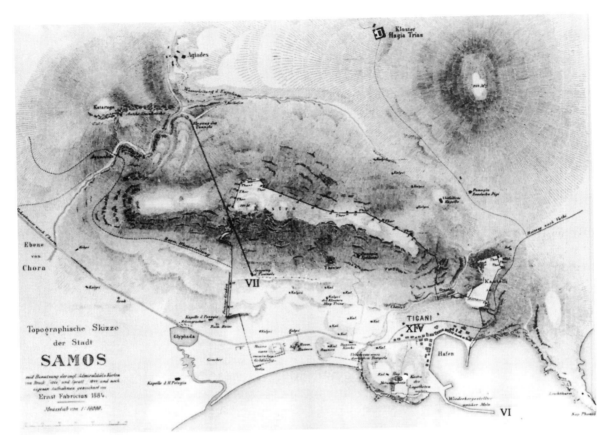

Figure 2.3

Nineteenth-century plan (in German) showing ancient Samos and Eupalinus' tunnel. The tunnel cut through Mt. Castro and emerged at point VII, bringing water to the city below. XIV marks the center of the old city. The great harbor mole of which Herodotus speaks is at VI.

instance, to illuminate the tombs of ancient Egyptians buried across the Nile from Thebes by utilizing mirrors. One person will catch a beam of sunlight on a mirror and direct it at the mirror of another person standing below at the entrance to a tomb. That person can then aim the reflected light inside the tomb—to someone else, if necessary—and by this relay, even the innermost recesses of a tomb can be lighted.

A similar system probably guided the work crews in Eupalinus' tunnel. A short distance in from the south entrance, before what was the ancient doorway into the tunnel proper, there is a vertical light shaft that emits a blinding ray of sunlight into an otherwise dark interior. A large mirror, probably on a fixed base with a fixed angle, could have been at the bottom of the shaft to catch the light. As the light poured in, it was thrown forward down the tunnel in a precise beam for the workmen to follow. The single light source could not have remained an effective guide over a long distance inside the hill. Thus, we might surmise, as in the case of the Egyptians, that

Arion—A Musician Sings for His Life

TYRANTS LIKE POLYCRATES WERE always on the lookout for new talents to adorn their courts. It was not so much that they were patrons of the arts (although some certainly were) as it was that they wished to add to their prestige by showing up their rivals with a better collection of reigning "stars" in residence. In the seventh century B.C., the great tyrant of Corinth, Periander, had attracted to his service the most renowned lyre player and singer of the day, Arion of Methyma.

Arion was one who did benefit from the new economic opportunities of this period, and his talents took him from his native island of Lesbos to audiences all over the Mediterranean. His specialty was the dithyramb, or choral ode to Dionysus (from which tragedy would eventually evolve), and his performances made him a wealthy man. However, Arion's story also reflects a darker side of the Commercial Revolution. Gain outweighed morality not only in regard to debt-slavery but also in other ways, and the dangers of plying the trade routes by sea were not always restricted to storms.

Herodotus tells the story of how Arion barely escaped with his life when the crew of the ship transporting him decided he was worth more to them dead than alive:

> Arion, they say, who was spending the greater part of his time at the court of Periander, was seized with a longing to sail to Italy and Sicily; but when he had made a great deal of money there, he wanted to come home to Corinth. So he set sail from Tarentum, and, as he trusted no people more than Corinthians, he hired a boat of men from Corinth. But when they were out to sea, those Corinthians plotted to throw Arion overboard and take his money. When he understood what they would be at, he begged for his life at the sacrifice of the money. However, he could not prevail on them, and they, who were his ferrymen, bade him either kill

Figure 2.4 Periander, tyrant of Corinth (Vatican Museums, Rome)

> himself—that he might have a grave when he was landed—or straightaway jump into the sea. So, penned in helplessness, Arion besought them, since they were so determined, to stand by and watch him while he sang, standing with all his gear on him on the poop deck of the ship; he promised, once he had sung, to make away with himself. They for their part thought what a pleasure it would be for them to hear the greatest singer in the world, and so they retreated from the stern of the boat to amidships. He put on all his gear, took his lyre in his hand, and taking his stance on the poop went through the High Shrill Song [a special and well-known

(continued)

Arion—A Musician Sings for His Life (continued)

song in honor of Apollo], and, when it was finished, cast himself into the sea, just as he was,
with all his gear. Away they sailed to Corinth;
but, says the tale, a dolphin picked Arion up on
his back and brought him back to Taenarum.
He disembarked from the dolphin and went to
Corinth (with all his gear) and, on his coming,
told all that had happened to him. Periander—
for he didn't believe him—held Arion under
guard, suffering him to go nowhere else at all,
and kept vigilant watch for his ferry men. When
they came, they were summoned to his presence
and asked if they had any news of Arion. Yes,
they said, he must be safe somewhere in Italy,
since they had left him prospering in Tarentum.
At that moment Arion appeared before them
just as he was when he had leaped into the sea;
whereupon they, in their utter confusion, were
unable to deny what was brought home to
them. This is what the Corinthians and Lesbians say, and there is at Taenarum a small ded-
icatory offering of Arion, made of bronze and
figuring a man riding upon a dolphin.
(1.24)

How Arion actually made it safely to shore
(Herodotus—and Periander—were skeptical)
cannot be known. Many stories of friendly relations between humans and dolphins circulated
in antiquity, one even involving Alexander the
Great, and modern research attests to the intelligence of the creature and its affinity to people.

Figure 2.5
*This fourth-century B.C. coin from Tarentum
attests to the popularity of the "boy on a dolphin"
theme in that city. Interestingly, it was also from
Tarentum that Arion had set sail and encountered
the dolphin which, as in the image above, saved
his life by picking the musician up on his back.*

The fact, however, that Tarentum, the city from
which Arion set sail on his fateful voyage, symbolized Taras (Tarentum) riding atop a dolphin
on its coinage (see Figure 2.5) in the same fashion Arion did, makes this episode a little too co-
incidental to be factual. Perhaps he was rescued
by Tarentines, and the story inevitably developed
along the lines it did. The dolphin's role in Arion's story was also a natural since the singer and
musician was under the protection of Apollo, to
whom the dolphin was sacred.

some effective system of relay mirrors was set up as the tunnel progressed,
carefully maintaining the original direction.

Such a process and the use of, perhaps, something like a simple water
level were basically all that was needed to ensure that both tunnels met in
the middle of the mountain. Small variations in the tunnel wall are mostly
the result of the workmen having to follow the natural "give" of the rock as
they were cutting, but they always returned to their original course. Fortu-

Figure 2.6
The tunnel of
Eupalinus, one of
the great engineering
feats of antiquity

nately, there are many sunny days in this part of the world, for an overcast sky would certainly have impeded progress.

The basic premise of the mirror theory has been tested with success in the tunnel itself, and since mirrors, some gifts from King Amasis, have been found on Samos dating from Polycrates' time, there is no question that they were available. Only one vertical light shaft has been discovered, but it seems safe to assume that there was also something similar for the north tunnel, although a second shaft may not have been necessary if light could have been reflected directly into the tunnel by some other method.

Reflections from mirrors viewed at a distance—just as modern Samian children play the light off mirrors on passing ships at sea—probably also helped Eupalinus ascertain the correct starting places for the tunnels on either side of the hill. Consequently, what at first appears to have been an extremely complex problem was, it seems, solved in rather simple fashion. We who are used to technologically advanced methods sometimes forget how much can be accomplished with the fewest of resources.

Suggestions for Further Reading

Works by Podlecki, Starr, Snodgrass, Burn, and Murray cited in Chapter 1 remain useful. A. N. Athanassakis's *Hesiod: Theogony, Works and Days, Shield* (Baltimore: The Johns Hopkins University Press, 1983) is a good translation (with commentary) of Hesiod's work. See, too, M. R. Lefkowitz on Hesiod in *The Lives of the Greek Poets* (Baltimore: The Johns Hopkins University Press, 1981), Chapter 1. T. J. Figueira and G. Nagg's *Theognis of Megara: Poetry and the Polis* (Baltimore: The Johns Hopkins University Press, 1985) highlights the work of Theognis. A. Andrewes, *The Greek Tyrants* (New York: Harper & Row, 1963), is the best starting place for discussions of Greek tyranny, and J. Boardman's *The Greeks Overseas: Their Early Colonies and Trade* (London: Thames & Hudson, 1980) is equally pertinent for colonization. Cf. also A. J. Graham, *Colony and Mother City in Ancient Greece* (Chicago: Ares Publishers, 1983). Two specific works on Eupalinus' tunnel are J. Goodfield and S. Toulmin, "How Was the Tunnel of Eupalinus Aligned?" *Isis* 56 (1965), 46–55; and H. Baker, "The Tunnel of Eupalinus," *MQR* 15 (1976), 53–63. Other useful general studies are L. G. Mitchell and P. J. Rhodes (eds.), *The Development of the Polis in Archaic Greece* (New York: Routledge, 1997); C. Dougherty and L. Kurke (eds.), *Cultural Poetics in Archaic Greece: Cult, Performance, Politics* (New York: Oxford University Press, 1993); L. H. Jeffery's *Archaic Greece: The City-States c. 700–500 B.C.* (New York: St. Martin's Press, 1976); R. J. Hopper's *The Early Greeks* (New York: Barnes & Noble, 1976); and G. L. Huxley's *The Early Ionians* (New York: Humanities Press, 1966).

For other topics touched on in this chapter, see A. Burford, *Land and Labor in the Greek World* (Baltimore: The Johns Hopkins University Press, 1993); S. Isager and J. E. Skydsgaard, *Ancient Greek Agriculture: An Introduction* (New York: Routledge, 1992); R. Sallares, *The Ecology of the Ancient Greek World* (Ithaca, N.Y.: Cornell University Press, 1991); and J. D. Hughes, *Pan's Travail* (Baltimore: The Johns Hopkins University Press, 1996). On religion and philosophy, see W. Burkert, *Greek Religion* (Cambridge: Harvard University Press, 1987); G. S. Kirk and J. E. Raven, *The Presocratic Philosophers,* 2nd ed. (New York: Cambridge University Press, 1983); and E. Hussey, *The Presocratics* (New York: Scribner, 1972). Also of interest are Burkert's *The Orientalizing Revolution: Near Eastern Influence on Greek Culture in the Early Archaic Age* (Cambridge: Harvard University Press, 1992) and *Ancient Mystery Cults* (Harvard, 1987); R. Parker's *Athenian Religion: A History* (New York: Oxford University Press, 1996); and S. Price's *Religions of the Ancient Greeks* (Cambridge: Cambridge University Press, 1999). On music, see W. D. Anderson, *Music and Musicians in Ancient Greece* (Ithaca, N.Y.: Cornell University Press, 1995); M. L. West, *Ancient Greek Music* (New York: Oxford University Press, 1992); and J. G. Landels, *Music in Ancient Greece and Rome* (New York: Routledge, 1998).

3

The Panhellenic Games

Phayllus of Croton—An Early Sports Hero

. . . there is no greater glory for a man while he lives
than that which he gains through the speed of his feet
or the strength of his hands.
(Homer, *Odyssey* 8.147–148)

The Rise of the City-States

The Archaic Age was witness to many changes and new ideas, but unquestionably, the rise and growth of the city-state, or *polis,* was the most significant development to come out of the Dark Age. Clusters of villages, often geographically isolated in a mountainous country, usually with a common kinship base, gradually emerged out of the previous centuries of chaos as bona-fide small urban centers. Fiercely independent and autonomous, each had its own political system, chief deity, "national" identity, and territory.

Relations between these city-states were frequently strained, eventually prompting alliances to arise between the larger ones jockeying for power and smaller ones looking for protection. The historical Greeks would mature as a disunified people with no federal or centralized government—a concept difficult for us to understand since we are used to thinking in terms of unified countries with specific borders, governed from capital cities.

The colonization movement, mentioned in Chapter 2, provided further disunity, as city-states were established all over the Mediterranean world. Consequently, it might be correct to say that the "borders" of ancient Greece were anywhere that Greeks resided in number. Their main concentration outside the Greek peninsula and islands was in southern Italy and Sicily in the West and on the coast of Asia Minor in the East. This broad area, more than any other geographical designation, constituted ancient Greece (called "Hellas" by the Greeks, who also referred to themselves as "Hellenes").

Despite the fact that the Greeks were so politically disunified and spread over such a large portion of the Mediterranean world, they did, nonetheless, share a number of things in common. Just as we would not lose our identity

Croesus of Lydia: Riddles and Ruin—A Foreign King Consults the Oracle of Apollo at Delphi

THE GREEKS NEVER WISHED to make an important decision without first obtaining some indication from the gods as to whether they would be successful. One of the places they could go to consult the gods directly was Delphi, the shrine of Apollo, located on the slopes of Mt. Parnassus above the Gulf of Corinth. (See Figure 5.14 for a model of Delphi.)

Delphi was regarded as the center of the earth and had long been a sacred area, even before Apollo took over the site. Already by the Archaic period, the oracle had emerged as the premier shrine for such consultations, and even non-Greeks like Croesus, king of Lydia in Asia Minor, sought advice there.

Inquirers, of course, did not confront the god directly but received answers to their questions from a Pythia, a woman who prophesied under divine inspiration. Replies to important queries were often in the form of a riddle, or at least ambiguous, since straight answers would have disgruntled distinguished customers and quickly impugned the shrine's efficacy. Even so, reinterpretations were not uncommon, and it appears Delphi was never able to fully recover from its failure to predict the Greek victory in the Persian Wars.

According to ancient sources, the Pythia worked herself into a mediumistic trance by sitting on a tripod and inhaling a "pneuma," or breath that rose from a cleft in the earth. This ex-

halation had a sweet smell and could rise either as a free gas or from the waters of the sacred spring Kassotis. This ancient tradition, although attested by the well-known second-century A.D. biographer and moralist, Plutarch, who was also priest of Apollo at Delphi, was rejected in the twentieth century when archaeologists failed to find a large chasm under the Temple of Apollo. Scholars also assumed that such an intoxicating emission could be produced only in a volcanic area, which Delphi is not. But recent investigations by a team of archaeological and scientific specialists, including Professor John Hale, have shown that the Temple of Apollo was deliberately constructed over a spot where two geological faults cross and a seasonal spring rises to the surface. Laboratory analyses of the rock and water in the sanctuary detected the presence of petrochemicals including ethylene, a sweet-smelling gas that can induce both mild "out-of-body" trances as well as the occasional violent delirium. According to Professor Hale, these scientific results vindicate the accuracy of the ancient writers. As for the religious side of the trance, Plutarch himself said that the "pneuma" was just a trigger: the most important source of the woman's oracular power was her spiritual preconditioning and her physical rituals of purification. Some have suggested the Pythia may also have chewed laurel leaves and drank from the nearby sacred spring. In this altered state, she be-as Americans if the artificial borders surrounding our country were removed, the Greeks, borders or no, were bound together ethnically, linguistically, and culturally—no matter where they lived. They identified with the Homeric poems, for example, which they considered their common heritage. They shared the same religion and gods, as well as prominent shrines like the oracle of Apollo at Delphi. In addition, there were also the Panhellenic athletic contests.

came the medium through which Apollo supposedly spoke.

Although the shrine was open year-round, Apollo himself was "present" only once a month, nine times a year, so only the most important inquirers had a chance to be admitted on those days. Delphi gave favored status to some cities and individuals, and it also helped to make a large contribution to the shrine beforehand or at the time of inquiry. Details about the procedure of consultation are difficult to reconstruct and will never find complete agreement, particularly for the earliest days of the shrine. Questions, verbal or written, certainly sometimes secret, were regarded as sacred and given to the priest beforehand, probably to allow him time to compose a response—though his interpretation of utterances from the Pythia was supposed to be impromptu (and often, apparently, not very good) verse or prose.

After making the required religious offerings, the questioner would be led to an antechamber in the Temple of Apollo, where he probably waited while the priest went to where the entranced Pythia was sequestered and put the question to her. It does not follow that replies by different priestesses could be delivered in any uniform way, since, as Plutarch states (*Moralia* 397c) even centuries after the great days of the shrine, each Pythia responded in accordance with her personal nature and how she was moved by the

god's inspiration. This is consistent with the story preserved by the Delphians themselves (*Moralia* 433cd) about the shepherd who accidentally first discovered the spot where the Pythia eventually sat. He started spewing forth what could only be interpreted as "inspired utterances." Undoubtedly, the once-potent gas emitted from the cleft could be overwhelming, and at the oracle's height, the vapors may have often precluded the Pythia from having any control whatsoever over what she said and how she said it—clearly one reason why, on the day of consultation, two priestesses were required with a third in reserve. Whatever the case, "replies" were certainly confused (but did not exclude poetic language), "understood" only by the priest who, when finished, would inform the client either verbally or in written form of Apollo's response. The consultation was over. No official interpretation was offered, and if one had not brought his own interpreter, there were undoubtedly a number waiting just down the hill or in the inquirer's city. By contrast, Plutarch records that in later years at Delphi, when many other oracles in the Greek world had even ceased functioning, the complaint was that the oracular responses were too simplistic (*Moralia* 409c).

For most Greeks, this was a legitimate and accepted way to learn the will of the gods. Because

(continued)

Croesus of Lydia: Riddles and Ruin (continued)

Figure 3.1   *Remains of the Temple of Apollo at Delphi, site of the Delphic oracle*

it was Apollo's sanctuary, Delphi also served as an international bank, a sure sign that cities felt safe depositing large funds there. The priests, too, operated the shrine, fully believing they were acting as Apollo's instrument. It goes without saying, however, that they could and did manipulate oracles favorably for Delphi and their friends— they influenced events locally and even internationally. Aristophanes, for one, had fun showing the potential misuse and alteration of oracles with his character Paphlagon, meant to represent the devious Athenian demagogue Cleon, in his play *Knights.*

Perhaps the most famous inquiry at Delphi was made by the aforementioned Croesus, whose agents consulted the oracle shortly before 546 B.C. Croesus was concerned about Cyrus the Persian, who was threatening his kingdom. After attempting to make the Delphians well disposed toward him through generous and expensive gifts, he was ready. Herodotus recounts his version of the story:

On those of the Lydians who were to bring these gifts to the shrines Croesus laid command that they should ask the oracles: "Shall Croesus make war on the Persians, and shall he take to himself any allied force?" When the Lydians came to where they were sent and dedicated the offerings, they consulted the oracles, saying: "Croesus, king of the Lydians and other nations, inasmuch as he has come to think that these are the only oracles among mankind, has sent to you gifts worthy of your discoveries; so now it is you he asks if he should make war upon the Persians and if he should take to himself any allied force." That was their question; and the judgment of both oracles came out the same, declaring to Croesus that if he made war on the Persians he would destroy a mighty empire; and they advised him to find out which were the most powerful of the Greek peoples and make them his friends.

When Croesus heard the answers that were returned to him from the god, he was exceedingly pleased at the oracles, expecting of a certainty that he would destroy the kingdom of Cyrus; and he sent to Delphi and paid a fee to the Delphians at two gold staters a man (having found out their number by inquiry). The Delphians in return gave Croesus and the Lydians the right of primacy of consultation of the oracle, remission of all charges, and the best seats at the festivals; and, moreover, anyone of the Lydians who chose to might become a Delphic citizen for all time to come.

So Croesus, having paid this fee to the Delphians, consulted them a third time; for since he had found very truth in the oracle, he was for using it to the fullest. His consultation was now the question: Would his monarchy last long? Whereupon the Pythia gave the following answer:

> Whenever a mule shall become sovereign
> king of the Medians,

Figure 3.2 *Stater issued under Croesus of Lydia. Herodotus indicates that the king distributed many gold staters at Delphi in hopes of a favorable response to his inquiry.*

> then, delicate Lydian, flee by the stone-
> strewn Hermus,
> flee, and think not to stand fast, nor
> shame to be chicken-hearted.

When these words came to Croesus, he was most delighted of all; for he thought that a mule would surely never become king of the Medians instead of a man, and so neither he himself nor his issue would ever be deprived of the power.
(1.53–56)

As might be expected, Croesus' euphoria was premature. He had interpreted the oracle as being favorable to himself (and he had certainly paid enough to expect such an outcome), but he should have also been prepared for the negative side of the riddle. The oracle had stated that if Croesus "made war on the Persians he would destroy a mighty empire." Unfortunately, it did not say whose empire. In 546 B.C., Cyrus, "the mule," referred to by the oracle (because like a mule, he was of mixed stock), overthrew Croesus and destroyed his kingdom. Clearly, one had to be careful when interpreting oracles!

In respect to the latter, the love for sport and individual competition was a distinguishing characteristic of Greek society, a passion that was unrivaled until the nineteenth century of our own era. Of the many athletes who, over the centuries, participated in the Panhellenic Games, few left a reputation equal to that of Phayllus of Croton. The fact that he and others like him came from southern Italy and elsewhere to compete in games on the Greek peninsula is an indication of just how strongly the Greeks who had migrated continued to regard their traditional institutions. The several athletic festivals that together constituted the Panhellenic Games are best exemplified by the ancient Olympics.

The Olympic Games

A religious ceremony dedicated to Zeus, father of the gods, the Olympic Games were the greatest of all the Greek sports festivals. They were held every four years at Olympia, Zeus' sacred precinct on the banks of the Alpheus River in Elis, a rural area in the western Peloponnesus. Although ancient tradition indicates that the site had long been associated with athletic competitions, the Olympic Games did not formally begin until 776 B.C.—the most confirmable early date in Greek history—when Coroebus of Elis was crowned

Map 6
Sites of major Greek games. The Olympics were held at Olympia; the Pythian Games at Delphi; the Isthmian Games near Corinth at Isthmia; and the Nemean Games at Nemea. Together, these four constituted the ancient "circuit" of Greek athletic festivals. The most important local games were held at Athens during the Panathenaic festival.

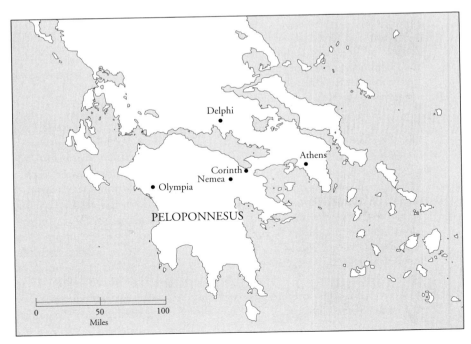

Figure 3.3
The stadium at Olympia, site of the ancient Olympic Games

the first Olympic victor. The Games continued for almost 1,200 years, probably ending when the Christian Roman Emperor Theodosius banned all pagan cults in 393 A.D.

The Olympics had begun rather modestly, with a footrace of about 200 meters as the only event, and it was not until half a century later that the second race, the 400 meters, was added. Before the close of the seventh century B.C., the distance race, the pentathlon (a grueling test of strength and endurance that combined long jumping, throwing the discus and javelin, wrestling, and a 200-meter sprint), wrestling, boxing (which was the most dangerous Olympic sport since competitors wrapped their fists and forearms with heavy leather thongs), single-horse as well as four-horse chariot races, the popular pankration (a combination of wrestling, judo, boxing, and brawling!), and the majority of the boys' contests had all been introduced.

Originally, it is probable that all nonequestrian events took place near the altar of Zeus within the sacred precinct, or Altis. In the sixth century B.C., simple logistics and increasing crowds prompted the laying out of a rather humble facility that would be the first of three stadiums. The same century also witnessed the beginning of a major building program at

Figure 3.4
Athletes preparing to run, wrestling, and with javelin, three events of the pentathlon. Funerary base, c. 510 B.C. (National Museum, Athens)

Olympia, culminating in the great fifth-century B.C. Temple of Zeus that housed the sculptor Phidias' (see Chapter 6) colossal gold and ivory statue of the god, one of the "Seven Wonders of the Ancient World."

In 472 B.C., the Games were expanded to five days, and with the possible exception of the two-horse chariot race, the program of major events had been set. Nevertheless, as the following list (which includes all Olympic events) indicates, additions would continue to be made:

Olympic Event	*Year Introduced*
200-meter race	776 B.C.
400-meter race	724 B.C.
4,800-meter race	720 B.C.
Pentathlon	708 B.C.
Wrestling	708 B.C.
Boxing	688 B.C.
Four-horse chariot race	680 B.C.
Pankration	648 B.C.
Single-horse race	648 B.C.
Boys' 200-meter race	632 B.C.
Boys' wrestling	632 B.C.
Boys' pentathlon	628 B.C. (dropped same year)
Boys' boxing	616 B.C.
Race in armor	520 B.C.

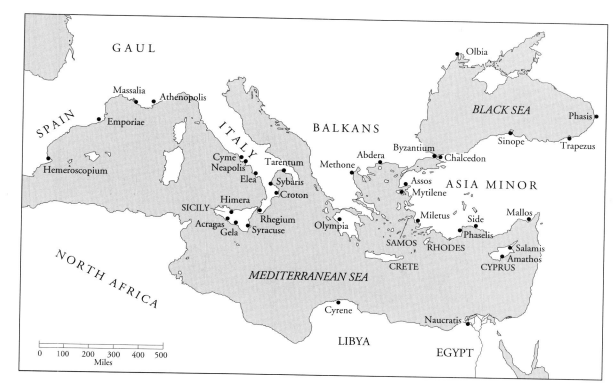

Map 7
Some geographical origins of Greek Olympic athletes. Competitors came from all over the ancient Mediterranean world, especially southern Italy and Sicily.

Mulecart race	500 B.C. (dropped 444 B.C.)
Race for mares	496 B.C. (dropped 444 B.C.)
Two-horse chariot race	408 B.C.
Trumpeter competition	396 B.C.
Herald competition	396 B.C.
Four-horse chariot race (foals)	384 B.C.
Two-horse chariot race (foals)	268 B.C.
Single-horse race (foals)	256 B.C.
Boys' pankration	200 B.C.

Note: No team events such as relay races were introduced in the ancient Olympics, and the marathon is a modern creation.

The schedule of events over the five-day festival cannot be reconstructed with precision, but briefly, the program and its preliminaries probably developed along the following lines: During the summer of an Olympic year, the competitors were required to arrive at Elis, which controlled the proceedings at Olympia, at least one month prior to the start of the Games to train under the watchful eye of ten judges. These judges were chosen from among the

Map 8
Olympia in the fifth century B.C.

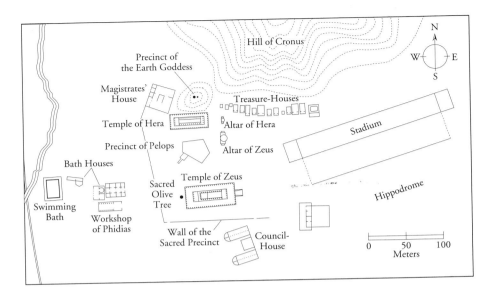

local Elean nobility, who would supervise the festival. They would determine who were the best and most worthy athletes, weeding out the weaker ones, checking matters relating to their citizenship, eliminating those with slave or criminal backgrounds, and making all other necessary decisions. Two days before the Games were to begin, the entourage of qualified athletes, their trainers, and the judges started on their trek to Olympia, where they would arrive on the eve of the festival.

The first day had no scheduled athletic events, but the agenda included general festivities, sacrifices, prayers, and the taking of oaths by both judges and athletes. The second day witnessed the start of the competition with the chariot and horse races in the hippodrome, or racetrack (a flat open area adjacent to the Olympic stadium). The pomp and fuss surrounding the introduction of the entrants in the four-horse chariot race, the most dazzling and expensive event in the Olympics, probably constituted the closest thing the ancient Games had to an opening ceremony. The pentathletes competed in the afternoon of the same day, and although it is not known exactly how a winner was determined, one likely possibility is that the prize was awarded to the competitor who won the majority of the five events. If there was no clear-cut winner, perhaps those still in contention wrestled for the garland of victory.

The third day of the festival, the middle day, was calculated to coincide with the full moon (this could be in either August or September in a given Olympiad) and was the most religious day of the Olympics. The great procession to the altar of Zeus where 100 oxen were sacrificed was by far the

Figure 3.5
Small representation of Zeus in a four-horse chariot (quadriga) *similar to the kind raced at Olympia (British Museum, London)*

most impressive of the public and private religious rites that took place on the morning of this day. The remaining flesh of the sacrificial victims would be consumed later in the day at a great banquet. The afternoon was reserved for the boys' competition. The fourth day consisted of individual races and the body-contact events, with the race in armor closing out the athletics. On the fifth day, most if not all of the victors were crowned, and after more sacrifices and a banquet to honor the winners, the Olympiad ended.

In the Olympics, only one winner was crowned in each event, and at least during historical times, the award was a simple wreath of olive leaves, sacred to Zeus and befitting the religious and physical ideals behind the Games. There were, however, many unofficial benefits that accrued to the Olympic champion. He might, for example, have his feat immortalized in an ode composed and recited by one of the great poets of the day, perhaps Pindar (518– 438 B.C.), who commemorated the victories of numerous successful athletes. Among those he celebrated in his verse was Xenophon of Corinth, about whose remarkable accomplishments in the Olympics of 464 B.C. Pindar sang:

Father Zeus,
ruling with wide sway
from Olympia's height,

Figure 3.6
Pindar. His Odes
celebrated many
Olympic victories.
(Capitoline Museums
[Montemartini],
Rome)

> harbor no envy
>   against my words
>   now or ever.
> Guide this people
>   away from harm,
>   and swell the sails
> of Xenophon's luck.
>   Welcome the revelry
>   due him for his crowns.
> He comes from Pisa's plain, winner—
>   as no mortal before him—
>   in foot race and pentathlon too.
> (*Olympian Ode* 13.24–31)

A statue might be raised to a victorious athlete in the sacred precinct of Olympia, which would be a source of pride for the winner and his family and for visitors from his city for generations to come. Pausanias, the Greek traveler who visited and described Olympia in the second century A.D., provides us with our fullest account of the ancient site (*Description of Greece*, Books 5–6). He saw literally hundreds of such statues made mostly of marble or bronze, although the oldest he observed had been carved out of wood.

An appreciative state might raise another such statue at home, as well as reward their hero with sizable cash payments, free board for life, and other similar honors. Although the tradition that some Greek cities even dismantled a portion of their walls to admit an Olympic victor is, at least during the Classical Age, unsubstantiated, we are, nonetheless, well informed as to the lengths a city would go to celebrate its hero. In 412 B.C., for example, the people of Acragas in Sicily welcomed home their 200-meter champion, Exaenetus, in high fashion, escorting him into the city in a chariot that was attended by 300 other chariots pulled by white horses. In pride and purse, it is clear that the Olympic victor wanted for nothing.

To be an Olympic champion was, of course, the ambition of many, but only a few succeeded. Training began early in life, and before the sixth century B.C., it was rather informal, since there were as yet no gymnasiums or professional trainers to provide formal guidance. Nonetheless, there are indications that athletes were already adopting and sharing training techniques, exercises, and diets that they had found to be successful and were devoting themselves full-time, or nearly so, to developing their athletic skills. Despite arguments to the contrary, there is nothing to demonstrate that early athletes were exclusively aristocrats. In fact, Coroebus, the first Olympic champion, appears to have been a cook. It might be correct to assert that aristocrats were generally in a better position to pursue athletic careers, but the playing field, then as now, also provided an opportunity for nonaristocratic youths to rise socially and economically in their respective cities.

When gymnasiums finally were introduced (most likely out of a need to keep citizen armies physically fit for active service), they quickly became social and religious centers and the focal point for most forms of exercise. This included the training of Greek youths in sports. Professional trainers, former athletes and sometimes victors themselves, were employed by the state (and often by individuals) to supervise the proceedings and to guide those who showed the most promise into athletic careers. Victories in the Games brought prestige and glory to a winner's city, and the Greeks did not compete to lose. Training was serious business—not recreation. Merely to participate meant nothing, and to lose brought the kind of shame that Pindar describes in another of his odes:

> For them was judged no pleasureful trip home. When they
> came back to their mothers, no joy burst forth, none of that
> laughter that gratifies. No. Rather, down back roads, hiding
> from their enemies, they skulk, bitten by their calamity.
> (*Pythian Ode* 8.83–87)

Exercise and practice took place in the nude ("gymnasium" comes from the Greek word *gymnos,* which means "naked") to the accompaniment of music, and tradition, as well as artistic convention, depicts athletes—with the exception of those in the equestrian events—performing naked in formal competition. However, it is clear that in the early days of the Olympics, loincloths were worn, and common sense dictates that in some events this practice would have continued, if only for the protection of the athletes.

Those who did win at Olympia were regarded by many as almost divine. They were as close as any human could come to being a god without offending the gods, and they held a special place in Greek society, venerated in a higher and more idealistic fashion than any of our much-touted athletes today. However, lest the ancient Games and their participants be over-romanticized, it should be noted that many of the same problems afflicting the modern Olympics also plagued them.

The political atmosphere in Greece was highly charged because the major city-states were constantly in competition with one another—not just athletically but militarily and otherwise. These city-states generally could not get along with one another, and about the only thing they could agree on was that a Greek, no matter what his city, was still superior to any non-Greek. This racist attitude usually barred foreigners from participating in the Olympics. However, it should be noted that there were not many peoples outside the Greek world who would have been interested in competing, because few maintained a similar athletic tradition. Should it prove politic to allow some important person to participate who did not have the required pure Greek pedigree, the judges could and occasionally did look the other way.

It would be difficult to believe—despite the religious overtones of the Games—that the bad feelings that existed between various city-states before an Olympiad would be replaced by a spirit of friendly competition during an Olympic truce. Enemies simply expressed their hostilities in a different way. Unlike at today's Games, amity was not a major consideration. Athletes were killed during the competition, and perhaps not all of those deaths were entirely accidental! Consequently, the playing field was, in many respects, a battlefield. Even the possession of Olympia itself might be contested by arms when the Games were taking place, as in 364 B.C. when Arcadian invaders reached the sacred precinct itself.

Military overtones should come as no surprise, since the origins of sport are rooted in war games—games that helped prepare soldiers for the rigors of actual combat. The earliest examples of athletic contests in Western literature appear during the funeral games held by the warrior society depicted by Homer in the *Iliad* and *Odyssey.* Here, there were no athletes who were not also soldiers, and the Greek word for battle and contest is the same: *agon.* Many Olympic events simply grew out of military exercises, such as throwing the javelin or spear, running, hand-to-hand combat (wrestling and boxing), and riding. The race in armor was a constant reminder of the connection between soldier and athlete.

One persistent myth about the ancient Olympics is that the participants were strictly amateurs. This simply is not true. If an amateur is defined as one who does *not* profit from his or her athletic talents, then there were no amateurs in antiquity. The modern concept of amateurism, ironically derived from erroneous nineteenth-century romantic aristocratic notions about Greek athletics, did not exist. Winning an Olympic event was too prestigious an honor to be left to chance. Participants, as well as their trainers, were polished professionals, pampered, subsidized, and nurtured by their city-states. Larger cities even attempted, many times successfully, to lure established champions away from smaller cities with promises of money. Dicon of Caulonia in southern Italy was one who accepted such an offer. After Dicon had won the boys' 200 meters at Olympia in 388 B.C., the Syracusans offered him money to declare and compete for them. It proved a wise investment, for Dicon would continue his winning ways as an adult, and he garnered two victories for Syracuse in the next Olympics. Apparently, Dicon's example proved infectious, for in the same Games of 384 B.C., Sotades of Crete won the distance race but was competing for Ephesus four years later.

Such "goings on" at the Olympics were not unusual, especially after the fifth century B.C., and other examples of "unsportsmanlike conduct" are not difficult to find. Sostratus of Sicyon, a pankratiast during the mid–fourth century B.C. who won three Olympic victories, had the nasty habit of immediately bending back (and apparently breaking) the fingers of his opponents. He was known as "Fingerman." Another pankratiast, Sarapion of Alexandria, ran away when he found the competition too formidable at the 201st Olympiad in 25 A.D. Callipus of Athens "bought off" his opponents in the pentathlon at the 112th Olympiad, and it was revealed that Apollonius Rantes had lied to the judges about his whereabouts when he was late for the Games of 93 A.D.

We also know of men who would lie about their ages so that they might compete in the boys' events (ages 12–18). Since there were no birth certificates, an adult with boyish features might pass himself off as a youngster, hoping to use his maturity to steal a victory. When caught, most errant athletes were subjected to fines or exclusion from the Games. Some were even flogged, an unusual punishment since it was usually reserved for slaves. Because cheating would also bring the fury of Zeus down on the perpetrator, fines were most often spent to erect statues and dedications to the god, a way to appease his wrath and also a warning to others not to be so foolish. Clearly, athletic peccadillos are not just a symptom of our own times. Even city-states could be punished, as when Sparta was excluded and fined for not observing the Olympic truce in 420 B.C.

Athletes' fallibilities, then as now, usually go unnoticed by the general fan, but critics are more merciless in their judgments, and there were those in antiquity who found the mix of unprecedented adulation and unexemplary behavior too much to bear. In their minds, the contributions made by such men to society simply did not justify the praise, prestige, and wealth heaped on them. Euripides, the great Athenian tragic playwright, voiced some of his objections in the *Autolycus,* produced about 420 B.C.:

> Of the thousands of evils which exist in Greece there is no greater evil than the race of athletes. In the first place, they are incapable of living, or of learning to live, properly. How can a man who is a slave to his jaws and a servant to his belly acquire more wealth than his father? Moreover, these athletes cannot bear poverty nor be of service to their own fortunes. Since they have not formed good habits, they face problems with difficulty. They glisten and gleam like statues of the city-state itself when they are in their prime, but when bitter old age comes upon them they are like tattered and threadbare old rugs. For this I blame the custom of the Greeks who assemble to watch athletes and thus honor useless pleasures in order to have an excuse for a feast. What man has ever defended the city of his fathers by winning a crown for wrestling well or running fast or throwing a discus far or planting an uppercut on the jaw of an opponent? Do men drive the enemy out of their fatherland by waging war with discuses in their hands or by throwing punches through the line of shields? No one is so silly as to do this when he is standing before the steel of the enemy.
>
> We ought rather to crown the good man and the wise man, and the reasonable man who leads the city-state well and the man who is just, and the man who leads us by his words to avoid evil deeds and battles and civil strife. These are the things which benefit every state and all the Greeks.
> (Frag. 282)

Others complained that athletes might take advantage of the status gained by their victories to enhance themselves politically. Surely, the four triumphs of Chaeron of Pellene in Olympic wrestling (356–344 B.C.), for example, had more than a passing impact on his rise as tyrant of his city. Still others simply made jokes about athletes:

> Charmus once ran the distance race against five competitors, but came in seventh. You will probably ask, "Since there were six contestants, how could he come in seventh?" The reason was that a friend of his ran onto the track shouting "Go Charmus!" Thus he came in seventh, and if he had five more friends he would have finished twelfth.
> (*Palatine Anthology* 11.82)

Professionalism, politicism, bribery, racism, public adulation, as well as outrage and derision, were as much a part of ancient athletic contests as they are today—perhaps more so. Nonetheless, the Games provided the

Greeks with a great social and religious experience, and in the final analysis, the positive aspects of the competition probably outweighed the negative.

Other Panhellenic and Local Games

In addition to the Olympic Games, important Panhellenic athletic festivals were also held at other locations in Greece (see Map 6). The Pythian Games took place every four years at Delphi and were dedicated to the god Apollo; near Corinth, the Isthmian Games, sacred to Poseidon, were celebrated every two years, as were the Nemean Games at Nemea, where Zeus was again honored. Prizes were a laurel wreath, a crown of pine branches, and a crown of wild celery, respectively, but as at the Olympics, winning athletes could expect more "pocketable" rewards when they returned home. Together the four games formed the "circuit," and they were so arranged that athletes would have at least one of the festivals in which to compete each year. The three "lesser" games may have been useful in helping to eliminate the weaker competitors before the gathering at Olympia.

Many other local sports festivals also existed, and they *did* offer valuable prizes. The most prominent of these was associated with the Panathenaea in

Figure 3.7
The stadium at Delphi, site of the Pythian Games

Figure 3.8
Site of the stadium at Isthmia (Isthmian Games). In the foreground are the remains of the triangular starting blocks. The hole at the right is where the starter stood waist deep. At a signal, he would pull the cords he held in his hands that led to starting gates on each side of him, and the runners would all be released at the same time. The rest of the stadium has been built over or is overgrown with trees and shrubs. The Isthmus of Corinth canal is the waterway in the upper left of the photo.

Figure 3.9
The restored stadium at Nemea, where the Nemean Games were held

Athens, a celebration that honored the city's patron goddess Athena. Here, victories were extremely profitable, and athletes collected amphoras of olive oil for their winning efforts, which were worth small fortunes on the open market. Just how much profit there could be in choosing an athletic career is made startlingly clear by a prize list that survives from one Panathenaic festival held during the first half of the fourth century B.C. David Young (*The Olympic Myth of Greek Amateur Athletics,* 124) has calculated that the winner in the men's 200 meters earned the equivalent of $121,200 if the prize is equated with a modern daily wage of $101. Other victors in these Games picked up equally impressive awards, ranging in the tens of thousands of dollars.

Women's Games

Aside from virgins and a priestess of Demeter, women were excluded from viewing the Olympics, and none could compete. It is interesting to note, however, that even though they could not be present, women were allowed to

---

Some Women Athletes—Three Sisters: Tryphosa, Hedea, and Dionysia

THESE LATER DEDICATIONS AT Delphi from c. 45 A.D. demonstrate that women's athletics had risen in status and were apparently thriving in the Greek half of the early Roman Empire at the Pythian, Isthmian, Nemean, and various local games. The three young women honored here certainly were dominant and ubiquitous in their participation. The fact that they could travel to so many different contests—and win—over a period of several years suggests that they were well funded and certainly not amateurs. (One also notes that the name Antigonus keeps popping up as the director of the festival in which each sister wins the footrace.)

Hermesianax, son of Dionysius, a citizen of Caesarean Tralles [a city in Asia Minor] and of Corinth, put up these statues of his daughters, who held the same citizenships, in honor of Pythian Apollo.

His daughter Tryphosa was winner of the girls' stade race at Delphi in the year when Antigonus was director of the games and again when Cleomachides was director, and then at the next Isthmian Games when Juventius Proclus was director, the first girl to accomplish this.

His daughter Hedea was winner of the race of war chariots at Isthmia when Cornelius Pulcher was director, winner of the stade at Nemea when Antigonus was director, and at Sicyon when Menoites was director. She also won the girls' lyre contest at Athens in honor of the Emperor when Nuvius son of Philinus was director. She was the first girl in a long time to become a citizen of [name lost].

His daughter Dionysia won the stade at [name of festival lost] when Antigonus was director and at the Asclepian Games in sacred Epidaurus, when Nicoteles was director. [W. Dittenberger, *Sylloge Inscriptionum Graecarum* (*Syll³*) 802 (Leipzig, 1924); L. Moretti, *Iscrizioni Agonistiche Greche* (*IAG*) 63 (Rome, 1953); and H. W. Pleket, *Epigraphica II: Texts on the Social History of the Greek World* No. 9 (Leiden, 1969)]

Figure 3.10
A small sixth-century
B.C. *bronze figure of a*
sprinting young female
Spartan (Laconian)
athlete (National
Museum, Athens)

enter chariots (and probably horses, too) in their names at the competition. Cynisca, daughter of King Archidamus II of Sparta, for example, won victories in 396 and 392 B.C. and set up dedications at Olympia to commemorate her triumphs. In later centuries, a few women's events were introduced into the other "circuit" games, but never at Olympia, where chauvinism prevailed. There was, however, a women's "Olympics," which was held separately from the men's and at a different time. Pausanias describes the female Games that honored Zeus' wife Hera and were called the Heraea. Sixteen women chosen from among the women of Elis supervised the proceedings:

> Every fourth year at Olympia the Sixteen Women weave a robe for Hera, and they also sponsor the Heraea competition. This contest is a foot race for virgins who are of different ages. They run in three categories: the youngest first, the slightly older ones next, and then the oldest virgins are the last to run. They run as follows: their hair hangs down on them, a chiton reaches to a little above

Figure 3.11
The Heraea, or
women's "Olympics,"
was dedicated to Hera,
represented here on a
fourth-century coin
issued by Elis, the city
that oversaw the
Olympic Games.

the knee, and the right shoulder is bared as far as the breast. They also use the Olympic stadium, but the track is shortened by one-sixth. The winners receive a crown of olive and a portion of the cow sacrificed to Hera, and they have the right to dedicate statues with their names inscribed upon them. Those who serve the Sixteen Women are, like the sponsors of these games, women. They trace the competition of the virgins also back to antiquity.
(*Description of Greece* 5.16.2–8)

Spectators

Something must also be said about the spectators who came by the thousands to witness the great athletic displays, especially the Olympics. A general truce allowed free movement to Olympia, and probably no other regularly scheduled event in antiquity attracted such crowds of people, a pilgrimage of fans from all over the Greek world heading for the same destination at the same time.

Admission to the Games was free (although contributions were encouraged), but this was probably no real compensation for the hardships endured by those who came to watch. Some undoubtedly felt that they, rather than the athletes, were the ones who deserved the awards. For example, there were no permanent facilities or lodgings at Olympia, which was a sacred precinct—not a city. Spectators had to accommodate themselves as best they could during the five days of the celebration. There were no seats except those for judges and dignitaries, so one had to watch the proceedings in the stadium or hippodrome, sitting or standing wherever one could find a vantage point. There was no adequate water or sanitation system until the second century A.D., and the typical flies, policing problems, and "fast food" were all part of the fabric. In regard to the last, Aristophanes uses an opportunity in *The Clouds* to refer to the cramps and upset stomachs that typically resulted after buying meat stew from vendors at the Panathenaean celebration.

Callipateira of Rhodes—A Daring Mother

THE ANCIENT OLYMPIC GAMES were a male stronghold. But according to tradition, that fact did not stop one enterprising, athletics-minded mother, a widow named Callipateira, from risking certain punishment to help guide her son to victory and share in his moment of triumph. Pausanias, after mentioning the Elean law of throwing off nearby cliffs any woman discovered at or in the vicinity of the Olympic festival, relates the famous story:

> They say that no woman has ever been caught except Callipateira. [Some say that the name of the woman was Pherenice, not Callipateira.]

She had been widowed and, disguised like a male trainer, she took her son to Olympia to compete. When her son Peisirodus won, Callipateira jumped over the fence with which the trainers were restrained, and exposed herself. She was thus discovered to be a woman, but they released her unpunished out of respect for her father, her brothers, and her son all of whom had been victors at Olympia. They passed a law, however, that in the future trainers would have to attend the competition in the nude.
(*Description of Greece* 5.6.7–8)

Figure 3.12 Pankratiast, probably first century A.D. Athletics had become a business during the Roman Empire, and many athletes belonged to guilds. The attitude of this figure would suggest that he was a professional. (Louvre, Paris)

Jostling with crowds to sneak a peak at one's favorite hero in action was probably one of the lesser difficulties spectators had to face, as the Stoic philosopher Epictetus (living in the first–second century A.D.) indicated:

> There are enough irksome and troublesome things in life; aren't things just as bad at the Olympic festival? Aren't you scorched there by the fierce heat? Aren't you crushed in the crowd? Isn't it difficult to freshen yourself up? Doesn't the rain soak you to the skin? Aren't you bothered by the noise, the din and other nuisances? But it seems to me that you are well able to bear and indeed gladly endure all this, when you think of the gripping spectacles that you will see.
> (*Dissertations* 1.6.23–29)

It is also clear that some spectators came more for the festivities surrounding the games than the games themselves: An inscription at Delphi where the Pythian Games took place forbids anyone to bring wine near the stadium track on pain of offending Apollo and also paying a stiff fine!

The Later Years

After the Greek world had succumbed to the Romans, the major games continued to be held, but athletics became more of a business (athletes belonged to guilds) than a pastime. There also had arisen literally hundreds of "prize" and "sacred" games, mostly in the Eastern, or Greek, half of the Empire. The Romans never really warmed sufficiently to their subjects' form of sport, but even so, sensational figures such as the Emperor Nero could not resist

associating themselves with the prestigious Greek festivals. For Nero, they provided a means by which he could reinforce his own inflated estimation of his talents, picking up both athletic prizes and awards in musical competitions and making a mockery of the proceedings in the process. It was he, it is said, who first introduced a music contest at Olympia, a dubious distinction if this anecdotal passage from Suetonius is any indication of audience reaction to a performance by Nero:

> No one was allowed to leave the theater during his performances, however urgent the reason, and the gates were kept locked. There are stories of women in the audience giving birth, and of men being so bored that they would sneak out by jumping off the wall at the back of the theater, or by playing dead and being carried away for burial.
>
> (*Nero 23*)

In the end, it was not the degradations and humiliations of those like Nero that put an end to the Olympics and all the other games, but a new religion, Christianity. Until the day the Games ended, a victory in the Olympics remained the pinnacle of an athlete's career.

Phayllus of Croton

Phayllus of Croton was certainly not the most famous of the Greek athletes who competed during the heyday of the Panhellenic Games, but his story is one of the most interesting and striking. Like many other athletes, especially from Croton, which provided an extraordinary number of Olympic champions before 480 B.C., Phayllus combined his prowess on the playing field with a distinguished military career.

During the Second Persian War, most Greeks in Italy refused to come to the aid of their fellow Greeks on the peninsula who were resisting Xerxes' invasion (see Chapter 5). Phayllus outfitted a ship and brought it to Salamis (an island off the coast of Attica, the district in which Athens was situated), where, in 480 B.C., he helped destroy the Persian fleet. This feat by itself marks him as an unusual personality; indeed, Alexander the Great was so impressed by Phayllus' action that after he had conquered the Persian Empire in the next century, he sent a portion of the spoils to Phayllus' old city as a token of his admiration. Nonetheless, Phayllus is primarily remembered for his skill as a long jumper.

Although never a victor at the Olympics, Phayllus competed in the Pythian Games at Delphi, and early in the fifth century B.C. (before 480), he won two victories in the pentathlon and a first in the 200 meters. It was his performance in one of the pentathlons, however, that is most noteworthy. In that competition, he is said to have recorded the longest jump in human history—an incredible distance of 55 feet! The tradition adds that Phayllus' leap carried him so far that he landed beyond the pit and broke his leg. One has to wonder why that was all that he broke, since his effort propelled him almost 26 feet past the current world record. Physically, it is not possible for a human being to jump so far, and we might simply dismiss the story if it were not for Chionis of Sparta, who supposedly leaped 52 feet in the seventh century B.C. Furthermore, there is evidence that the normal length of ancient long-jump pits was 50 feet!

Perhaps such remarkable distances can be explained by the fact that ancient long jumpers employed hand weights (*halteres*) that weighed two or more pounds. They learned to coordinate the weights with their jumps in the following manner: After a short running approach, the competitor

Milo of Croton

NO ATHLETE IN ANTIQUITY enjoyed greater celebrity than Milo of Croton, whose wrestling prowess endeared him to fans of his own generation and those that followed. He had already helped establish the reputation of Crotonian athletes before Phayllus, and beginning as a youth in 536 B.C., he put together an amazing string of "circuit" victories over a period of almost thirty years. His victories included six triumphs at Olympia, another six in the Pythian Games, ten at Isthmia, and an additional nine at Nemea.

Reputed to be a close friend of the philosopher Pythagoras, Milo apparently found the former's physical and political philosophies appealing. He combined athletics with politics, and he led his city to a crushing defeat of its nearby archrival, Sybaris. Predictably, the magnitude of his feats grew as the centuries passed, and remarkable stories routinely became attached to him. His appetite was a favorite topic: He is said to have eaten 40 pounds of meat and bread in a single sitting and washed it down with 8 quarts of wine. Another story has him parading around the Olympic stadium with a four-year-old bull on his shoulders, which he proceeded to slaughter and devour. Apparently, gobbling up whole bulls or oxen was quite common for Milo (interesting, since Pythagoreans were forbidden to eat flesh), as he did it on other occasions as well!

The actual athletic talents of Milo, although clouded by legend, are beyond doubt. Pausanias preserves some of the less fantastic accounts:

> Milo won six victories in wrestling at Olympia, including one in the boys' category [536 B.C.].

At Delphi he won six times in the men's category and once in the boys'. He came to Olympia to wrestle for the seventh time [in 512 B.C.], but he could not beat his fellow citizen Timasitheus who was younger than he and who refused to come to close quarters with him. It is also said that Milo carried his own statue into the *Altis,* and there are stories about him concerning the pomegranate and the discus. He would grip a pomegranate so that no one could wrest it away and yet not squeeze it so hard as to bruise it. He would stand upon a greased discus and make fools out of those who would rush at him and try to knock him off the discus. There were other things which he did to show off. He would tie a cord around his forehead as if it were a ribbon or a crown. He would then hold his breath until the veins in his head were filled with blood and then break the cord by the strength of those veins. Another story is that he would let his right arm hang down along his side to the elbow, but turn his forearm out at right angles with the thumb up and the fingers in a row stretched out straight so that the little finger was the lowest, and no one could force the little finger away from the other fingers. They say that he was killed by wild beasts. In the land of Croton he happened upon a dried up tree trunk into which wedges had been placed to split it. Milo, in his vanity, stuck his hands into the trunk, the wedges slipped, and Milo was caught in the trunk until wolves discovered him.

(*Description of Greece* 6.14.5–8)

would throw the weights forward as he leaped, then thrust them back to give himself added momentum. The weights were then dropped and the rest of the jump completed without them. It is odd that the concept of using weights had arisen at all, since they would seem to interfere with the natural running and jumping rhythm of an athlete, but we must remember that this event almost certainly originated as a military exercise. The practice may have begun as a training technique to help soldiers become accustomed to managing their hand-held equipment effectively while jumping on the run during combat.

Perfecting this technique undoubtedly took much time, and the fact that an athlete's jump was counted only if he landed upright in the pit is further indication of the event's military background. A soldier who jumped over an obstacle only to fall backward on the ground would have little chance of survival on the battlefield. Eventually, the exercise itself must have become a form of competition, and the training weights remained an integral part of it. The reason that modern athletes have had so much trouble re-creating the ancient technique of long jumping is most likely because using weights is contrary to all that they have learned. For the ancient jumper, however, the event did not exist without the weights, and years of practice resulted in the complete coordination of the latter with body movement. The weights obviously were effective within the context of the event in antiquity—but such weights still could not propel anyone even remotely close to distances of 50 feet or more.

Some have argued that the ancient long jump was something more akin to the event known today as the triple jump and that Phayllus and Chionis reached their fabulous marks in this manner. However, what evidence there is for a triple jump in antiquity is slight and not compelling. Even if its existence could be firmly established, the distances are still too fantastic, for no modern Olympian had triple jumped farther than Phayllus' 55 feet until 1960. Romantics might contend that ancient athletes were capable of equaling and even surpassing the marks of today's athletes, but such a notion is not realistic. Athletes were much smaller in stature, their training techniques would have been vastly inferior, and it is doubtful that people like Phayllus would even have been competitive with their modern counterparts. Furthermore, if jumping weights posed problems in coordination in a single jump, then trying to manipulate them successfully in a triple jump would be virtually impossible.

Finally, there is the suggestion that the event was a standing rather than a running long jump and that a jumper's distance was the result of totaling together a number of short jumps. Several arguments exist against such an idea. First, judging from the modern statistics available, it would take at least five such jumps to travel over 50 feet. Since the awkward nature of the event discourages sizable differences between the jumps of even the best standing long jumpers, the jumps of Phayllus and Chionis would not have stood out or been that much greater than any other athlete's. Consequently,

Figure 3.14
Pottery fragment showing a long jumper in action holding halteres. *The weights apparently enhanced his distance when flung forward at the beginning of his leap and thrust backward before landing. Artistic convention, at least, portrayed ancient athletes as competing in the nude. (Private collection)*

there would not have been much reason to remember their efforts or consider them distinguished. Second, artistic representation of the various stages of long jumping in antiquity clearly indicates a fluidity of movement that would not characterize a standing jump. Third, there is no evidence of a widespread interest in such an event in Ancient Greece. Even its history in the modern Olympic Games was short-lived.

There is, then, no logical explanation for the length of Phayllus' jump, and we are left with two choices: Either accept it as the greatest physical feat in the history of humankind or assign the story to the realm of sports folklore. The latter is, of course, the correct choice, and how such a feat ever became associated with Phayllus will never be known. It should be remembered, however, that his alleged leap took place in the days before Herodotus, the first historian, had written his first word. Much of what had previously passed for history was little more than a hodgepodge of material—some true, much not. The world's second-longest jump, by Chionis, occurred during a much more obscure period in Greek history. When this information is combined with the fact that the ancients—unlike us today—were generally quite careless about noting the marks of their athletes (the *number* of victories was what impressed them), it begins to become clear how Phayllus and Chionis might have "accomplished" their records.

The 50-foot pits? The tradition is just as weak on this point. We do not know if all Greek long-jump pits were typically that long, and in the earlier days of the Games, at least, the pit had to be redug for every competition, usually after the passage of two to four years. To suggest that the length of

Theagenes of Thasos

THEAGENES, A PANKRATIAST, BOXER, distance runner, and contemporary of Phayllus, was another of the lionized sports heroes of Greece. Among ancient athletes, only Milo was perhaps more celebrated than Theagenes, who picked up multiple victories in all the "circuit" games. His exploits predictably, as with Milo and Phayllus, are a mixture of fact and fiction, and as Pausanias notes in the following extract, Theagenes apparently remained a force to be reckoned with even after his death! Successful athletes (his 1,400 victories in all games are considered an exaggeration by most) like Theagenes often became the object of hero cults, and they were also thought, because of their winning ways, to possess magical or healing powers. Pausanias writes:

> They say that when Theagenes was nine years old, as he was going home from school, the bronze statue of some god which stood in the agora caught his fancy, so he picked up the statue, put it on his shoulders, and carried it home. The citizens were outraged by what he had done, but one of their respected elders convinced them not to kill the boy, but to order him to go home immediately and bring the statue back to the agora. He did this and quickly became famous for his strength as his feat was shouted though the length and breadth of Greece. [Pausanias refers to his earlier remarks about Theagenes' boxing victory in the Olympics of 480 B.C., then continues.] . . . At the next festival [476 B.C.], Theagenes won the *pankration*. He also won three times at Delphi in the boxing. His nine victories at Nemea and ten at Isthmia were divided between the boxing and the *pankration*. At Phthia in Thessaly he ceased training for the boxing and the *pankration*, but concentrated upon winning fame

among the Greeks for his running, and he defeated those who entered in the distance race. He won a total of 1,400 victories. After he died, one of his enemies came every night to the statue of Theagenes in Thasos, and flogged the bronze image as though he were whipping Theagenes himself. The statue stopped this outrage by falling upon the man, but his sons prosecuted the statue for murder. The Thasians threw the statue into the sea, following the precepts of Draco who, when he wrote the homicide laws for the Athenians, imposed banishment even upon inanimate objects which fell and killed a man. As time went by, however, famine beset the Thasians and they sent envoys to Delphi. Apollo instructed them to recall their exiles. They did so, but there was still no end to the famine. They sent to the Pythia for a second time and said that, although they had followed the instructions, the wrath of the gods was still upon them. The Pythia responded to them:

You do not remember your great
  Theagenes.

The Thasians were then in a quandary, for they could not think how to retrieve the statue of Theagenes. But fishermen, who had set out for fish, happened to catch the statue in their nets and brought it back to land. The Thasians set the statue back up in its original position, and are now accustomed to sacrifice to Theagenes as to a god. I know of many places, both among the Greeks and among the barbarians where statues of Theagenes have been set up. He is worshipped by the natives as a healing power.
(*Description of Greece* 6.11.2–9)

Figure 3.15
A contemporary representation of Phayllus. Interestingly, this and other existing vase paintings of him indicate he was best known for his skills as a discus and javelin thrower—which is strange if his reputation as a long jumper is a valid one. (Getty Museum, Malibu, Calif.)

pits in various locales always conformed precisely to a specific distance over a period of so many centuries is, judging from the problems in regulating the standards for modern track and field facilities, unrealistic. Furthermore, even if we accept a 50-foot pit, it does not mean that anyone was capable of jumping that far. It should be noted that modern long-jump pits extend much farther than any person could ever leap. What may have happened is that the stories of the incredible marks of Phayllus and Chionis, however they started, were transformed from the realm of myth into history, convincing later Greeks that such distances were possible to achieve. It could happen again, they might argue—if the gods willed it—so they had better be prepared with long pits. Certainly, no one was in any danger of overshooting such a pit, but it may have provided a psychological impetus for the jumpers—that is, "if Phayllus could do it, then. . . ."

One last piece of evidence mitigates against the validity of Phayllus' record. It is the distance recorded for his discus throw, which apparently was in the same pentathlon in which he recorded his remarkable leap. He is reported to have tossed the discus a mere 95 feet, which is almost 150 feet short of the modern record (but, interestingly, is about the same distance

Phidippides—The Marathon Runner Who Never Was

THE MODERN MARATHON RACE is based on one of the most famous and persistent stories from ancient Athenian tradition: about a herald, usually identified as Phidippides, who ran from Marathon to Athens in 490 B.C. to bring news of the startling Greek victory over the mighty Persian army (see Chapter 5). The tradition continues that after proclaiming the victory at Marathon, Phidippides dropped dead from exhaustion—and his name has been celebrated ever since. The distance of the modern marathon, calculated at 26 miles 385 yards, is thought to duplicate the length of Phidippides' run to Athens. Many mistakenly believe the modern race was an ancient athletic event—but it was actually created for the first modern Olympic Games at Athens in 1896. There was no marathon before that date.

In Athens today, one can still become part of the legend of the ancient marathon runner by attending the "Sound and Light" performance illuminating the Acropolis. During the most dramatic moment, the Marathon runner returns from the battle with his immortalized message, mesmerizing the audience as the sound of his footsteps progresses (from one large elevated speaker to another) as he makes his way through the countryside to the city to give his report. The

footsteps become louder and louder, and he appears to come closer and closer. There is no one there, of course, but that does not stop everyone in the audience sitting in the open area that was once the Athenian assembly from unconsciously turning their heads to follow the sound of his progress. Finally, when the runner reaches the last speaker—and, we presume, his imaginary destination—the footsteps stop. He blurts out his message of victory with his last breath and then, with a muffled sound, drops dead. The audience gasps appropriately and leaves, having vicariously lived the legend of the Marathon runner. Unfortunately, a legend is all the story appears to be.

The definitive source for the battle of Marathon is, of course, Herodotus, whom we have already mentioned as the first historian and whose history covered the Persian Wars. While Herodotus does describe the battle and does mention Phidippides (6.105–117), two problems immediately arise. He mentions absolutely nothing about a Marathon runner, and he cites Phidippides only as a professional runner whom the Athenians sent to Sparta *before* the battle of Marathon to request Sparta's aid. Hence, the most contemporary source of information (and Herodotus

Robert B. Garrett, who supposedly had little experience, threw the discus in the first modern Olympics in Athens in 1896). Certainly, we have a right to expect better from one such as Phayllus. Yet, 95 feet *is* a credible distance for an ancient discus thrower (unless he were Odysseus), and because it is such a realistic mark, it further serves to demonstrate the problem with Phayllus' long jump. One does not leap with the gods and throw with the wood nymphs! Even ancient sports enthusiasts must have wondered about the discrepancy.

As Phayllus supposedly jumped five feet past the pit and broke a leg, in the 1928 Winter Olympics, a Norwegian ski jumper overshot the undersized does not miss much that is dramatic) does not know the story. In fact, as W. Sweet indicates (*Sport and Recreation in Ancient Greece,* 34), the first time we hear anything about the Marathon runner is about 600 years later when Plutarch states:

> Heraclides Ponticus reports that Thersippus of [the Attic deme] Eroeadae brought back the news about Marathon; but most declare it was Eucles, who ran in full armor still hot from battle, and burst through the doors of the leading men of state able to say only "Rejoice; we are victorious" before dropping dead.
> (*Moralia* 347c)

Plutarch cites Heraclides Ponticus as his source for the tradition that someone named Thersippus brought back the news about Marathon. Heraclides lived in the fourth century B.C. and is much closer to the event than Plutarch, but he is still more than a century removed from the battle of Marathon. However, Plutarch goes on to say that most authorities (whoever they are) do not agree with Heraclides and identify the runner as a soldier named Eucles, who had apparently participated in the battle. Lucian, the famous satirist who was born about the time

Plutarch died in the second century A.D., writes that the runner's name was "Philippides," which is obviously a confused spelling of the name "Phidippides" that "took over" at a later date. Consequently, after reviewing the pertinent ancient sources, we end up with a confused assortment of detail: There *was* an actual runner named Phidippides—but he had nothing to do with bringing news about the Marathon victory to Athens. How his name became erroneously attached to the story is anyone's guess, and, to make matters worse, later tradition changed his name to Philippides; and at least two other men, Thersippus and Eucles, are said to have performed the same feat. We are left with three men and a misspelling running together to Athens with the same news.

Needless to say, the entire story must be suspect. Sending back heralds in situations such as the one described at Marathon was standard procedure for the Greeks, but, as seen from Herodotus, we cannot be sure any herald was even dispatched to Athens. Also, the distance, time, and circumstances all mitigate against the story of the Marathon runner. First of all, the distance is

(continued)

facility at St. Moritz by 36 feet and was badly injured. This latter story has become nothing more than a minor piece of modern sports trivia. However, if the Norwegian had been living in Phayllus' day and it was not known that the landing area was shorter than the norm, perhaps he, too, like Phayllus (and Chionis), would have soared into the realm of immortality with what *appeared to be* the greatest ski jump in history. It may be that the 50-foot-plus long jumps of antiquity resulted from a similar set of circumstances. Whatever the case, it is clear that Phayllus' feat must be assigned to the realm of fiction, the traditional kind of "sports story" with which ebullient fans of any era celebrate the exploits of their heroes on the playing field.

Phidippides—The Marathon Runner Who Never Was (continued)

Figure 3.16   The plain of Marathon (1994) where the Persians were defeated in 490 B.C. and, supposedly, Phidippides began his run of over 26 miles to bring Athens news of the victory.

only a little over 26 miles. By contrast, Phidippides' run to Sparta was about 145 miles. Herodotus specifically states (6.116) that the Athenians who had fought at Marathon rushed back to Athens as fast as they could to defend it from the Persians, who had boarded their ships and were now sailing round the tip of Attica, hoping to take the city before the troops could arrive back to prevent them. The soldiers moved so fast that they did, in fact, arrive back in time to thwart the Persians. What, then, would be the point in dispatching a runner, who would arrive with his message only a short time before the entire army, which was "rushing with all speed" back to the city? We are only talking about 26 miles, which was not an overwhelming distance to cover—even for tired

men in armor. If Plutarch's account about Eucles has any validity, then it was he, a soldier who had apparently fought in the battle and was still in his armor, who was the first to bring the news about Marathon—and the Persians sailing round. Thus, by this report, it was not a professional herald who brought the news but the earliest of the soldiers who arrived back from Marathon.

Furthermore, Herodotus states (6.115) that pro-Persian sympathizers at Athens gave a pre-arranged signal with "a shield" (presumably flashing it off the sun from high ground) to the Persians once they were out to sea—indication that their "friends" were ready to assist if they could sail round to Athens and take the city before the army returned. While Herodotus dismisses the "slander" that it was a certain prominent Athenian family who was responsible for the signal, he does not disclaim the signal itself. If the Persians had been victorious at Marathon, there would not have been any need for the signal—Athens would have subsequently been overwhelmed by Persian land and sea forces. Consequently, the results of the battle were known by the signaler—and if his signal could be seen by the Persians at sea, then it is likely that it could also be seen by the army at Marathon and by agents of interested parties at Athens. What point would there have been, then, for the Athenian army to send back a runner? The news about Marathon would have preceded him by a large margin, and the runner's message would have been received by a diminished citizenry that included powerful Persian sympathizers, who were prepared to turn the city over to their friends. The more logical strategy would be for the *entire* army to return as quickly as possible to protect their loved ones from envisioned harm and prevent their property (these *were* hoplites) from falling into Persian hands. Such motivations could certainly lighten even 120 pounds of armor—and exhaustion.

Finally, the message itself that Phidippides (or whoever) supposedly carried places the entire episode in doubt. Considering that the Persian naval force with the remains of the army at Marathon were sailing around Cape Sunium and would arrive shortly to take the city, a declaration of victory at Marathon would have meant very little, indeed, to the Athenians. The real message would have to have been "Rejoice; we are victorious . . ." but also "By the way . . . the Persian fleet is anchoring right off shore." If the one who brought *this* message had dropped dead after delivering it, then his body probably would have had on it the footprints of those in the community who were now rushing to defend its walls, for at this juncture it would not have been clear if the Athenians had won anything—the city was still in extreme danger. If the remainder of the 10,000 Athenian hoplites who fought at Marathon had not made it back in time, they would have had nothing to which to return. There certainly would have been no reason to rejoice. Ultimately, however, the soldiers did return to Athens in time, and the Persians, realizing there was nothing to be gained, sailed back to Asia. It was probably not long after that, when the mythology began to cloud the real details about Marathon, that the story of the Marathon runner was first "remembered."

In conclusion, the story of a runner named Phidippides, or any other runner, bringing news of the victory at Marathon to Athens, though a nice tradition (and one that still excites the Greeks), has no basis in fact. The most we can say is that someone could have brought word about the victory to the city; in all likelihood, however, he was one of the first-returning soldiers who had fought there, and his main concern would have been preparing his fellow citizens who wished to fight to defend Athens from the expected Persian attack by sea.

Suggestions for Further Reading

The most comprehensive ancient source is Pausanias' *Description of Greece* (Books 5 and 6), which contains a full discussion of the site of Olympia (in the second century A.D.) and the traditions associated with it. D. Young's *The Olympic Myth of Greek Amateur Athletics* (Chicago: Ares Press, 1984) is the best starting place for interested readers, but H. A. Harris's earlier works, *Greek Athletics and Athletes* (Bloomington: Indiana University Press, [reprint] 1960) and *Sport in Ancient Greece and Rome* (Ithaca: Cornell University Press, 1972), remain useful. A brief well-illustrated introduction is J. Swaddling's *The Ancient Olympic Games,* published by the University of Texas Press (Austin, 1984) in cooperation with the British Museum. W. Sweet's *Sport and Recreation in Ancient Greece* (New York: Oxford University Press, 1987) is the definitive sourcebook for athletic material. Of related interest are S. G. Miller, *Ancient Greek Athletics* (New Haven, Conn.: Yale University Press, 2004); M. Golden's *Sport and Society in Ancient Greece* (Cambridge: Cambridge University Press, 1998) and D. Sansone's *Greek Athletes and the Genesis of Sport* (Berkeley and Los Angeles: University of California Press, 1988). On the oracle at Delphi, see, now, J. Hale et al., "Questioning the Delphic Oracle," *Scientific American,* August 2003 (also *Scientific American.com* version, September 28, 2003); the geological revelations in this article make all previous studies inaccurate.

4

Eros Unchained

Bisexuality Among the Greeks— Sappho of Lesbos, Harmodius and Aristogiton of Athens, Theodotus and His Lovers

Remember that desire is an integral part of all human nature.
(Lysias, *Oration* 3.4)

The Cultural Background for Bisexuality

As seen in previous chapters, the Archaic period witnessed much that was new in Greek society and much that had changed. It was also in this period, by the early sixth century B.C., that homosexuality, or more correctly, bisexuality, had reached maturity as an established and widespread social practice among Greek males. Contemporary poets like Theognis make references to it, and an impressive number of vase paintings represent overtly homosexual acts.

It must be emphasized that not all Greeks were bisexuals, that the practice of homosexual relations was not the same in every Greek city, that it was mostly an elitist, upper-class phenomenon, and that it was subject to the same kinds of social (and sometimes legal) restrictions that affect sexual behavior in any society. Excessiveness and effeminacy were frowned on, as was the prostitution of a *citizen's* body; relationships between partners of the same age and homosexual activities of any sort by older persons were also considered offensive.

The ideal relationship, the noble, educational one—openly encouraged, ritualized, and facilitated by convenient gathering places like gymnasia, where youths exercised naked—was between a young, unmarried man (generally up to about ages 28–30) and a "beardless" youth. This relationship was ostensibly restricted to one stage of life and was supposed to end when marriage turned a male's attraction away from members of his own sex and toward his wife. Former erotic attachments then usually matured into life-long friendships that could prove useful politically, or otherwise, in later years. However, it is clear from a number of examples that just as a husband was free to engage in sexual relations with women other than his wife (slaves, prostitutes, and courtesans—not other married women, except, perhaps, in places like Sparta), many married men and widowers did in fact continue to pursue youths. They relished their relationships and were willing to suffer possible ridicule or embarrassment.

The origins of pederasty, sexual relations between men and adolescents, in Ancient Greece is a confused issue at best. Male bonding in the Dark Age warrior-fraternities of a small, militaristic Greek society—along with admiration for physical prowess and beauty—must have been influential. For example, the military state of Sparta developed institutionalized homosexuality. Perhaps such relationships also arose, in part, from the need to provide a form of guidance for youths who had lost their fathers in battle. Degradation (and fear) of women, who were consciously kept in a subordinate position to males, played a role, as did the complete segregation of the sexes until marriage among the Greek elite and those who modeled themselves on their behavior. Male bonding was further reinforced and misogynic attitudes perpetuated during the Classical Age in the symposia, which were exclusively male entertainments among friends that consisted mostly of drinking, conversation, and pleasurable pursuits—including hired women for some and youths for others. Adult males of comfortable status seem to have regularly attended these gatherings, distant carryovers from the days when warrior-kings whiled away the evening hours in similar pursuits with their battle-hardened nobles.

The Greeks themselves had little clear idea about the origins of pederasty, but they sanctified it mythologically by assigning Zeus an irresistible passion for his youthful cup-bearer, Ganymede, and by making Oedipus' father, Laius, the first mortal to commit a homosexual act (Euripides, *Chrysippus* frag. 840; Plato, *Laws* 836C; Hellanicus F187). Even Achilles and Patroclus, although never described as such by Homer, were later held up as classic examples of martial homosexuality—giving Greek males heroic figures of epic proportions to emulate.

Although there is little concrete evidence available and it is seldom represented in literature or art, female homosexuality also existed. It may have been considered a "taboo" subject in male-dominated Greek society, and whatever evidence remained certainly would not have survived easily in later Christian

Figure 4.1
Large terra-cotta depicting Zeus carrying off Ganymede to Olympus, where the son of the king of Troy would be made cup-bearer of the gods and be given eternal youth. Zeus' passion for Ganymede helped sanctify pederasty in the eyes of many Greeks. (Olympia Museum)

days. Nonetheless, a few examples did manage to slip through. There is, for example, an Attic red-figure wine cup that depicts a woman kneeling before another and touching her genitals (see Figure 4.2); a much older plate from the island of Thera represents two women who seem to be courting. Plutarch, in his life of *Lycurgus* (18.4), mentions that noble women at Sparta had younger maidens as lovers. A Hellenistic poem speaks of two women from Samos who do not play according to the rules of Aphrodite and are chided for their unseemly sexual behavior (ironically, the male poet [Asclepiades 7] responsible for the lines mentions his own homosexual desires!).

Figure 4.2
Attic red-figure wine
cup depicting a
"lesbian" scene, c. 530
B.C. *(Tarquinia*
Museum, Italy)

Restricted, segregated, and often made to feel inferior, young girls had only others of their own sex with whom to express their desires until marriage—usually at puberty or not long thereafter. Therefore, it is no surprise that erotic feelings, love, touching, and caressing would be shared among them. Physical association in groups was not as common as among adolescent males, but it was not infrequent, especially at festivals in the choruses of virgins, who, undoubtedly chosen for their looks, performed maiden songs (composed by males) that spoke, among other things, about their beauty. Since marriage did come so early, there could be no exact parallel to male pederasty (nor would it have been tolerated); nevertheless, as at Sparta, relations did occur between women of "good repute" and virgins. The finest example of

Figure 4.3
Terra-cotta figures of women dancing, perhaps in a religious rite, Cyrenaica, c. 200 B.C. The figure on the left is a girl with a tambourine, wearing a wreath and a sleeved jacket, Boeotia, c. 300–250 B.C. (British Museum, London)

homosexual desire—and most likely overt physical sexual expression—in a Greek woman is Sappho of Lesbos, who lived around 600 B.C.

Sappho, the "Lesbian"

> The love god with his golden curls
> puts a bright ball into my hand,
> shows a girl in her fancy shoes,
>   and suggests that I take her.
> Not that girl—she's the other kind,
> one from Lesbos. Disdainfully,
> nose turned up at my silver hair,
>   she makes eyes at the ladies.
> (Lattimore, "Anacreon" 1,
> *Greek Lyrics*)

The word *lesbian* has specific connotations of female homosexuality in today's society, but in antiquity, Lesbian referred only to someone—male or female—from the island of Lesbos, off the northern coast of Asia Minor. There is no evidence to show that the island's name had already become synonymous with female homosexuality, although the preceding translation of Anacreon's poem would certainly seem to indicate that some women from

Lesbos were already conforming to our understanding of the term. The island's females also had a reputation, real or imagined, for excessive sexual behavior in general. The latter impression may have been the result of the simple fact that the Lesbians greatly admired and praised their women's beauty—apparently even holding beauty contests. Other Greeks probably interpreted such activity as a sure sign of some kind of sexual proclivity. By the second century A.D., the tradition of "unnatural" love practices on the island had become so strong that the satirist Lucian specifically associated Lesbian women with homosexuality.

Sappho was from Lesbos, and it was probably her connection with that place more than anything else that resulted in its name eventually becoming the root for a word denoting female homosexuality. She, like her countryman and contemporary Alcaeus (see Chapter 2), was a poet and lived during the tumultuous time of political and social chaos in the island's chief city, Mytilene. Pittacus, one of the traditional "Seven Sages" of Greece, had been made "tyrant" by general agreement in an attempt to solve the problems. It was undoubtedly this situation that led to Sappho's brief exile in Sicily. Unlike that of Alcaeus, who was personally involved in the civil strife on Lesbos and speaks of it in his poetry, Sappho's verse is practically devoid of politics. In addition, unlike Alcaeus, Sappho was a woman in a male-dominated society—a fact that marks her as an extraordinary and controversial woman because of her success and lasting fame.

A biographical sketch from the second or third century A.D. relates the following details about Sappho's life:

> Sappho was a Lesbian by birth, of the city of Mytilene. Her father was Scamander or, according to some, Scamandronymus, and she had three brothers, Erigyius, Larichus and Charaxus, the eldest, who sailed to Egypt and associated with one Doricha, spending large sums on her; Sappho was more fond of the young Larichus. She had a daughter Cleis, named after her own mother. She has been accused by some of being irregular in her ways and a woman-lover. In appearance she seems to have been contemptible and quite ugly, being dark in complexion and of very small stature.
> (*Oxyrhynchus Papyrus* 1800 frag. 1)

Another, much later biography (perhaps based to some extent on the same source) corroborates some of the preceding information, confuses other, and adds more:

> Daughter of Simon or of Eumenus or of Eerigyius or of Ecrytus or of Semus or of Camon or of Etarchus or of Scamandronymus; her mother was Cleis; a Lesbian from Eresus, a lyric poetess; flourished in the 42nd Olympiad [612–608 B.C.], when Alcaeus, Stresichorus and Pittacus were also alive. She had three brothers, Larichus, Charaxus and Eurygius. She was married to a very wealthy man called Cercylas, who traded from Andros, and she had a

Figure 4.4
Representation of
Pittacus, ruler of
Sappho's home,
Mytilene, on the
island off Lesbos,
c. 600 B.C. *(Louvre,*
Paris)

daughter by him, called Cleis. She had three companions and friends, Atthis, Telesippa and Megara, and she got a bad name for her impure friendship with them. Her pupils were Anagora of Miletus, Gongyla of Colophon and Eunica of Salamis. She wrote nine books of lyric poems, and she invented the plectrum [for striking the lyre]. She also wrote epigrams, elegiacs, iambics and solo songs.

(*Suda* 107 [iv 322s. Adler])

It may appear a simple process to reconstruct the major aspects of Sappho's life from these two biographies, despite the discrepancies, but it must be remembered that they date from a period centuries after Sappho lived. Antiquity was so fascinated by her life and personality that dozens of such biographies arose. Since her poetry did not provide nearly enough detail for readers hungering for more, sensationalists simply made up information, fictionalizing large parts of her life in the process. One account, for example, has her romantically linked with Alcaeus; another has her jumping off a cliff because of unrequited love (thus one of the first to take a "lover's leap"); and her relationships with her girls were turned into sordid and shameful affairs. She was described as small, dark, and ugly, undoubtedly suggesting that men found her unattractive and that is why she turned to members of her own sex for love. She became the butt of many unflattering jokes and proverbs, and as early as the Classical period, comic playwrights exploited

Figure 4.5
Girls playing a game
of knucklebones.
Terra-cotta, 340–330
B.C. *(British Museum,*
London)

her memory frequently. Some called her "masculine" for taking up a man's profession of poet, and she also became symbolic for "unnatural" sexual acts. Not everything about Sappho was uncomplimentary, however, as indicated by the influence her poetry had on later writers and by her depiction in art and on coins from Lesbos. Nonetheless, the real Sappho fell into obscurity—thus the difficulty of trying to rediscover her today.

There can be no doubt that she came from the same aristocratic background as Alcaeus. It would be unlikely that her family remained inactive during the chaotic years in which Pittacus was raised as tyrant. As mentioned previously, it was probably the political struggles in her homeland that drove her family (or her husband's) to Sicily—apparently Syracuse, where, in later years, a statue in the town hall commemorated her brief residency. The strongest tradition makes Scamandronymus her father; as for her mother, Cleis likely is her name, since Sappho gave her own daughter that name, although the same inference would not have been lost on ancient biographers, who, if they did not have her name, may simply have assigned her the daughter's. Her daughter was understandably a major focus of Sappho's attentions:

> I have a beautiful child who looks like golden
> flowers, my darling Cleis, for whom I would not (take)
> all Lydia. . . .

Although her husband's name is given as Cercylas of Andros, it was most certainly later fabricated for its comic meaning (Prick from the Isle of Man). Whoever her husband really was, he must have had a status similar to that of Sappho's family. Since nothing is known of him, the possibility that a liaison, not a formal marriage, produced the child (however unlikely) must at least be raised. Her three brothers seem confirmed, and the escapades of the eldest, Charaxus, with a notorious courtesan in Egypt attests to the family's wealth and their apparent involvement in the Lesbian wine trade. Her brother Larichus is said to have set a better example, serving, for a while, as the official wine steward in the town hall of Mytilene, a function for young noblemen.

Sappho and Her Girls

Even in its fragmented shape, Sappho's poetry encompasses much. One scholar has remarked:

> Love and friendship were her topics . . . we can see a striking variety of mood and manner. She may be trivial, she may be profound; she enjoyed bright surfaces, but she knew something of the interior darkness. She dealt with the most slight of human experiences, and the most solemn; we encounter in her few surviving verses jokes and jealousy, religion and picnics, gossip and goddesses, children, passion, tenderness, haberdashery, orchards, lovers, enemies. She writes sometimes plainly, sometimes with amplitude; she can be subjective or objective, humorous, or melancholy, quietly wistful or violently emotional.
> (Jenkyns, *Three Classical Poets* 80–81)

However, although Sappho's poems are full of things of interest and of beauty, it is her remaining verses that detail her relationship with the circle of young girls (some hardly more than children) gathered about her on Lesbos that most concern us. These verses, incidentally, provide the fullest expression we have of aristocratic women's daily life during this period.

Sappho's exact relationship with her girls cannot be known precisely. She was not a schoolmistress, as some previously thought, nor did she run a formal institute of learning. Her poetic and musical talents made her so well known that, apparently, parents from Lesbos and other parts of Greece were willing to send their daughters to associate with her as informal members of her circle. Some have denied that this circle was something of a "finishing school" for young maidens—and to be sure, it was much more complex than such a simple characterization would imply. But it is difficult to understand how such a group could have continued to exist and why aristocratic fathers would have supported it if it had nothing to do with the need for a daughter to be as attractive as possible to a potential suitor and to marry

Figure 4.6
Greek woman in himation, Tanagra, 325–300 B.C. (Louvre, Paris)

well. In such a private group, away from the "real world," music, poetry, love, and loyalty bonded the circle together. These young women also learned elegance, grace, and the way to dress with style. It seems clear that there were other groups like Sappho's (apparently, rivalries in singing and dancing existed) and that they were an accepted part of the social fabric of Lesbos, or at least Mytilene.

It is also quite apparent that Sappho took more than a casual interest in her girls, becoming personally attached to and emotionally involved with some. Her poems reflect the seriousness of her feelings, and they clearly reveal her homosexual tendencies. In what is almost certainly the only complete poem of Sappho that we have, the frustrated poetess speaks to the love goddess, Aphrodite, much in the manner that a troubled child speaks to her mother, asking her assistance in winning the love of a girl:

> Aphrodite on your intricate throne, immortal, daughter of Zeus, weaver
> of plots, I beg you, do not tame me with pain or my heart with anguish
>
> but come here, as once before when I asked you, you heard my words
> from afar and listened, and left your father's golden house and came
>
> you yoked your chariot, and lovely swift sparrows brought you, fast
> whirling over the dark earth from heaven through the midst of the bright air
>
> and soon they arrived. And you, o blessed goddess, smiled with your
> immortal face and asked what was wrong with me, and why did I call now,
>
> and what did I most want in my maddened heart to have for myself.
> "Who now am I to persuade to your love, who, Sappho, has done you
> wrong? For if she flees, soon she'll pursue you, and if she won't take gifts,
>
> soon she'll give them, and if she won't love, soon she will love you, even if
> she doesn't want to."
>
> Come to me now again, release me from my cruel anxiety, accomplish all
> that my heart wants accomplished. You yourself join my battle.

The poem, although somewhat playful, is nonetheless serious in intent. Aphrodite is friend and protectress, but she is also the immortal goddess who makes Sappho feel the way she does for the girl. It is an earnest appeal for help and, obviously, not the first time Sappho has requested aid.

When Sappho's girls left her, it was usually because they got married. On such occasions, Sappho might participate in the festivities, and even

Figure 4.7
Representation of
Sappho (Capitoline
Museums, Rome)

write wedding songs for the ceremony, but she also had feelings of loss and hurt, which sometimes could not be suppressed. The following poem (although interpreted variously) appears to have an immediacy about it—one that resulted from Sappho seeing her former beloved with her bridegroom? It is unquestionably one of the most intense descriptions of the tortures of lost love ever composed:

> The man seems to me strong as a god, the man who sits across from
>   you
> and listens to your sweet talk nearby
> and your lovely laughter—which, when I hear it, strikes fear in the
>   heart
> in my breast. For whenever I glance at you, it seems that I can say
> nothing at all
> but my tongue is broken in silence, and that instant a light fire
>   rushes
> beneath my skin, I can no longer see anything in my eyes and my
>   ears
> are thundering,

and cold sweat pours down me, and shuddering grasps me all over,
and I
am greener than grass, and I seem to myself to be little short of
death. . . .

Other lines tend to reinforce this kind of emotional turmoil in Sappho, who writes elsewhere, "Love, looser of limbs, shakes me again, a sweet-bitter resistless creature."

In another poem, the last passage of which focuses more on a specific individual's personality than any other of Sappho's surviving verses, she details her loss of a favorite, Anactoria (which may, like the others, not be her real name), who has gone away:

Some would say an army of cavalry, others of infantry, others of
ships, is
the fairest thing on the dark earth, but I say it's whatever you're in
love with.

It's completely easy to make this clear to everyone, for Helen, who
far
surpassed other people in beauty, left behind the most aristocratic

of husbands and went to Troy. She sailed away, and did not
remember
at all her daughter or her beloved parents, but [Aphrodite] took her
aside

[three lines missing]

which makes me remember Anactoria who is no longer near,
her lovely step and the brilliant glancing of her face I would rather
see
than the Lydians' chariot or their infantry fighting in all their armor.

The comparison with Helen is significant here since the latter left all her family ties and obligations behind, driven by her sexual passion. It is clear from this parallel, from Sappho's statement of what the "fairest" thing is to her, and from the tender description of Anactoria's grace and radiance that the poet is deeply disturbed and emotionally distressed. She has lost a lover—not just an affectionate charge.

There is more such emotion in other poems, this one, unfortunately, missing some lines, but still clear in intent:

"The truth is, I wish I were dead." She left me, whispering often, and
she
said this, "Oh what a cruel fate is ours, Sappho, yes, I leave you
against
my will."

And I answered her: "Farewell, go and remember me, for you know
   how
we cared for you.
"If you do remember, I want to remind you. . . .
"and with perfume, royal, rich . . . you anointed yourself and on soft
   beds
you would drive out your passion. . . ."

Finally, Sappho expresses her feelings about Atthis, who has left, apparently preferring the company of another woman: ". . . Atthis, the thought of me has grown hateful to you, and you fly off to Andromeda." Judging from the following description, Atthis must have been a striking beauty:

. . . you, like a goddess renowned, in your song she took most joy.
   Now
she is unique among Lydian women, as the moon once the sun sets
stands out among all the stars, and her light grasps both the salt sea
   and
the flowering meadows
and fair dew flows forth, and soft roses and chervil and fragrant
   melilot
bloom.
Often as she goes out, she remembers gentle Atthis, and her tender
   heart
is eaten by grief. . . .

Other female names appear in the fragments of Sappho's poems, but none are as revealing as these. Sappho's love for her girls was innocent and lacking any sense of shame, and she would have been surprised and greatly distressed by what later tradition made of her. In her verse, she was simply describing her personal world in which feeling was so important, a world one scholar has described as follows:

The circle's present love of girl for girl . . . was a thing so different as to need another name. It was neither sanctioned nor prohibited by the community; its purpose was not generation, and its practice was consequently not deformed by fears and tabus. This love had nothing institutional to offer but (as it is portrayed in Sappho's songs) it could give its devotees delight, choice, reciprocity and a heightened sense of self. Since the question of virginity was not involved, nothing was forbidden; there was no hierarchy of gesture fixed by the nearness to a single defended goal, and so there was no shame-built need for secrecy. One caress was as sweet as another, a wreath could be as provocative as an uncovered limb, and because pleasure was luxuriously sensual but never obscene it could be thought of as a form of worship and sung

Before the Island of Dr. Moreau: Earth, Water, Beasts, and Insects—Semonides' Views on Women

"ARE WE NOT MEN?" cry out the half-animal creations in the memorable refrain from the film version of H. G. Wells's science fiction thriller, *The Island of Dr. Moreau*. The affirmation "Are we not women?" may seem just as appropriate to women today who have digested the poet Semonides' views about them—most "types" of whom, he asserts, came from animal origins.

The emphasis in this chapter is, of course, on erotic relationships, and Sappho has been presented as our most prominent example of female bisexuality in Ancient Greece. However, Sappho was a famous woman in her own right, a brilliant lyric poet, and her relationship with the young women in her charge was generally one of innocent "sisterhood" and enrichment—a rare opportunity, it seems, for them to exclusively enjoy each other's company. Nonetheless, such female associations certainly must have raised a few eyebrows in male-dominated Greece. It would be interesting to know what men were thinking. To that end, it is not inappropriate to include here Semonides' general observations on women. He was not only a near contemporary of Sappho and, like her, a lyric poet; but he was also a product of Greek island culture—in this case, Amorgos in the southern Aegean.

As one of the earliest and most extensive exposés on women in Greek literature, Semonides' piece does indeed seem written, for the most part, at the expense of women. But Greek society persisted at the expense of women. That being said, perhaps it will be more productive to cite the entire poem and then examine it in a way in which we may be able to learn more about the poet and the society in which he and Sappho lived.

On Women
In the beginning the god made various kinds of women
with various minds. He made one from the hairy sow,
that one whose house is smeared with mud, and all within
lies in dishevelment and rolls along the ground,
while the pig-woman in unlaundered clothing sits
unwashed herself among the dunghills, and grows fat.

The god made another woman from the mischievous
vixen, whose mind gets into everything. No act
of wickedness unknown to her; no act of good

in all its aspects. Finally, because this love was open and non-reproductive, an easy promiscuity was the rule, allowing love to follow always, wherever beauty was perceived.
(Burnett, *Three Archaic Poets* 226)

There is, of course, nothing in her poems that describes actual sexual contact between Sappho and the girls she loves, but it is difficult to believe that one who would so strongly vocalize and make public her erotic and

Figure 4.8   *Terra-cotta statuette of two women seated on a couch, c. 100 B.C. from Myrina in N.W. Asia Minor (British Museum, London)*

either, because the things she says are often bad
but sometimes good. Her temper changes all the time.

One from a bitch, and good-for-nothing like her mother.
She must be in on everything, and hear it all.
Out she goes ranging, poking her nose everywhere

(continued)

passionate feelings (at least, originally, within her circle) would not also have engaged in a physical relationship. There are still many who refuse to accept this as a reality, but as one scholar has correctly observed: "Few societies have been as afraid of the body as ours, and in the West none has, within history, been as solicitous as the Greek of its beauty." There is simply no compelling reason not to believe that Sappho was bisexual and, indeed, a "Lesbian" in both the ancient and modern sense of the word.

Before the Island of Dr. Moreau (continued)

Figure 4.9
Terra-cotta figure of
a woman, Corinth,
250–230 B.C.
(British Museum)

and barking, whether she sees anyone about
or not. Her husband cannot make her stop by threats,
neither when in a rage he knocks her teeth out with
a stone, nor when he reasons with her in soft words,
not even when there's company come, and she's with
    them.
Day in, day out, she keeps that senseless yapping up.

The gods of Olympus made another one of mud
and gave her lame to man. A woman such as this
knows nothing good and nothing bad. Nothing at all.
The only thing she understands is how to eat,
and even if the god makes the weather bad, she won't,
though shivering, pull her chair up closer to the fire.

One from the sea. She has two different sorts of mood.
One day she is all smiles and happiness. A man
who comes to visit sees her in the house and says:
"There is no better wife than this one anywhere
in all mankind, nor prettier." Then, another day
there'll be no living with her, you can't get within
sight, or come near her, or she flies into a rage
and holds you at a distance like a bitch with pups,
cantankerous and cross with all the world. It makes
no difference whether they are friends or enemies.
The sea is like that also. Often it lies calm
and innocent and still, the mariner's delight
in summer weather. Then again it will go wild
and turbulent with the thunder of big crashing waves.
This woman's disposition is just like the sea's,
since the sea's temper also changes all the time.

One was a donkey, dusty-gray and obstinate.
It's hard to make her work. You have to curse and tug
to make her do it, but in the end she gets it done
quite well. Then she goes to her corner-crib and eats.
She eats all day, she eats all night, and by the fire
she eats. But when there's a chance to make love, she'll
    take
the first one of her husband's friends who comes along.

One from a weasel—miserable, stinking thing.
There's nothing pretty about her. She has no kind
of charm, no kind of sweetness, and no sex appeal.
She's always crazy to make love and go to bed,
but makes her husband—if she has one—sick, when

Figure 4.10
Terra-cotta model of a woman in a bath, Rhodes, c. 450 B.C. The bath was only big enough to sit in. "She washes the dirt off her body every day twice at least, three times somedays," Semonides remarks about the "fastidious" woman. (British Museum)

he comes near her. And she steals from neighbors. She's
   all bad.
She robs the altar and eats up the sacrifice.

One was begotten from the maned, fastidious mare.
She manages to avoid all housework and the chores
of slaves. She wouldn't touch the mill, or lift a sieve,
or sweep the dung from the house and throw it out of doors,
or kneel by the fire. Afraid the soot will make her dirty.
She makes her husband boon-companion to Hard Times.
She washes the dirt off her body every day
twice at least, three times some days, and anoints herself
with perfume, and forever wears her long hair combed
and shadowed with flowers. A woman such as this
makes, to be sure, a lovely wife for someone else
to look at, but her husband finds her an expense
unless he is some baron or a sceptered king
who can indulge his taste for luxuries like her.

One was a monkey; and this is the very worst,
most exquisite disaster Zeus has wished on men.
Hers is the ugliest face of all. When such a woman
walks through the village, everybody turns to laugh.
Her neck's so short that she can scarcely turn her head.
Slab-sided, skinny-legged. Oh, unhappy man

(continued)

Before the Island of Dr. Moreau (continued)

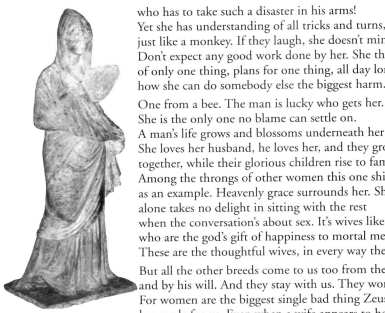

*Figure 4.11
Woman draped in her
himation, Boeotia,
300–250 B.C.
(Louvre, Paris)*

who has to take such a disaster in his arms!
Yet she has understanding of all tricks and turns,
just like a monkey. If they laugh, she doesn't mind.
Don't expect any good work done by her. She thinks
of only one thing, plans for one thing, all day long:
how she can do somebody else the biggest harm.

One from a bee. The man is lucky who gets her.
She is the only one no blame can settle on.
A man's life grows and blossoms underneath her touch.
She loves her husband, he loves her, and they grow old
together, while their glorious children rise to fame.
Among the throngs of other women this one shines
as an example. Heavenly grace surrounds her. She
alone takes no delight in sitting with the rest
when the conversation's about sex. It's wives like this
who are the god's gift of happiness to mortal men.
These are the thoughtful wives, in every way the best.

But all the other breeds come to us too from the god
and by his will. And they stay with us. They won't go.
For women are the biggest single bad thing Zeus
has made for us. Even when a wife appears to help,
her husband finds out in the end that after all
she didn't. No one day goes by from end to end
enjoyable, when you have spent it with your wife.
She will not stir herself to push the hateful god
Hard Times—that most unwelcome caller—out of doors.
At home, when a man thinks that, by the god's grace or by
men's good will, there'll be peace for him and all go well,
she finds some fault with him and starts a fight. For where
there is a woman in the house, no one can ask
a friend to come and stay with him, and still feel safe.
Even the wife who appears to be the best-behaved
turns out to be the one who lets herself go wrong.
Her husband gawps and doesn't notice; neighbors do,
and smile to see how still another man gets fooled.
Each man will pick the faults in someone else's wife
and boast of his own each time he speaks of her. And yet
the same thing happens to us all. But we don't see.
For women are the biggest single bad thing Zeus
has made for us; a ball-and-chain; we can't get loose
since that time when the fight about a wife began
the Great War, and they volunteered, and went to hell.
(Lattimore, "Semonides" 1, *Greek Lyrics*)

Semonides was a noble from Samos, a writer and man of action who actually led the colony to the island of Amorgos. He lived in an agrarian society that was becoming more urban. As a result, many women who once had labored in the field were now confined to the house. Boredom, relief from domestic chores, and the desire for betterment in economic and other ways were changing women's traditional behavior and the way in which men had traditionally viewed them. Such uneasiness is certainly inherent in Semonides. In his poem, he sticks with the customary theme that women were made from earth and water but also adds the notion that many newer "species" have arrived from beasts and insects, which is also within the tradition of "beast fables" current in his day. His world is also one that is changing dramatically for the aristocracy, who continue to view rising wealthy commoners and their more numerous lesser brethren with contempt, delighting in characterizing them as dishonest, lustful, impious, murderous, and scheming. Semonides *is* an aristocrat, and it is, therefore, no surprise to find some of his women, who are most certainly by his description of them commoners, sketched as subcreatures. (One of the most revealing aspects of the poem is the detail, usually unavailable, it supplies about village life.)

Since Semonides lived on an island, presumably his was a smaller and more observable society—and in his poem, his comments about women are directed at a familiar audience of Ionian men. In this more intimate island setting, he may have used women who were known to both him and his male listeners as the models for the "types" he describes in his poem. In other words, we may have something of an "inside joke" as partial impetus for the piece. Be that as it may, it is very much a part of human behavior (both male and female) to recognize, consciously and unconsciously, certain "types" of individuals in society.

Theophrastus would later characterize such *male* behavioral types in his *Characters* (see pages 201, 214, 226) during the Hellenistic period, and, in many respects, Semonides was doing the same thing in the seventh century—for "types" of women. Physiognomy, the identification of types of individuals from their outward appearance and behavior, had become a "science" by Theophrastus' time, but the tendency for such practices is endemic and was already well established in the universal character types presented in Greek drama, who were immediately recognizable to the audience. Ironically, what Semonides is usually criticized for—typecasting women (both negatively *and,* as we have seen in the case of the "bee-woman," positively)—establishes him as a pioneer in the development of these character types on stage (a precedent for Euripides, who, like Semonides, is often "typecast" as a misogynist).

We should also mention something about Semonides' personality that inevitably fueled the undercurrents of his poetry. It can be seen from another of his few surviving poems that, even though important and honored, Semonides had become (at least in his later days) very discouraged about life: because (as he indicates) one's goals are ultimately thwarted by old age, disease, death in battle, drowning, or even suicide. For Semonides, life was full of "bad spirits," "innumerable griefs," and "pains"—it was not just a test; it was a trial and one that we all ultimately fail. In this poem, at least, a portion of which is reproduced below, he resembles a virtuous man who has high hopes, achieves many of them, but then, despite all his successes, realizes that it is the god, not he, who controls things; in the end, all that we do is in vain:

But hope and self-persuasion keep us all alive
in our unprofitable desires. Some watch the day

(continued)

Before the Island of Dr. Moreau (continued)

for what it brings, and some the turn of years, and none
so downcast he will not believe that time to come
will make him virtuous, rich, all his heart's desire.
(Lattimore, "Semonides" 2)

It is also clear, however, from a rather revealing epigram of Semonides (perhaps produced
earlier in life) that not everything has to be dis-
appointment—even in regard to women:

No better thing befalls a man than a good wife,
no worse thing than a bad one.
(Lattimore, "Semonides" 4)

Hence, from this, he seems to be saying that the
potential for good is always there, but the experience itself can turn out badly. And it is in this
context that we should probably also consider
most of Semonides' remarks about women.

While no formal genre of satire existed in the
seventh century B.C., satire best describes the
content of Semonides' poem. Satirists by nature
are moralistic and disappointed. They soothe
their righteous indignation by exposing the
follies and wickedness of people and society
through derision, wit, and irony. Generally, their
views are honest, though exaggerated, and they
are dissatisfied with how things are when the
potential for something better is always present. If Semonides were just someone attacking
women for spite (some might say that his own
marriage went bad, prompting him to lash out,
but it could just as easily be that he found the
woman he desired and measured others' failings
against her virtue), we should properly condemn
him. But as previously noted, he is not only a
conventional man (and a literary one at that) in
a male-dominated society, he also has all the credentials of a satirist. Furthermore, as we have
seen, in his otherwise-negative appraisal of other
"types" of women, Semonides pauses to give
praise to the "bee-woman," whom every man
would like for his wife—"She loves her husband,

he loves her, and they grow old together, while
their glorious children rise to fame"—reaffirm-
ing what he states independently about a "good
wife" in the epigram above. Consequently, there
are virtuous women to be found, and those
women Semonides *does* praise. Critics may respond, yes, she is just the kind of woman a man
wants—an obedient servant who does as she is
told at the sacrifice of her own independence, as-
pirations, and self-identity. Semonides' "bee-
woman" is the ideal wife in that she is a sexless
being who would dutifully bear a limited number of children—which is exactly what a Greek
male wanted—and her "virtue" would spare him
any embarrassing gossip in the community. But
Semonides' comparison of his favorite woman to
a bee is probably more akin to Xenophon's hus-
band-wife dialogue (pp. 176–180) in which the
wife is also positively compared to a bee—in that
case, the queen bee, who presides over the hive
in matters that are not trivial and is characterized
as being "thoughtful." The only thing that can
be said with any certainty is that Semonides'
praise for one kind of woman above all others, an
example for her sex to emulate, is very typical of a
satirist's purpose—which is, ultimately, didactic.
By introducing the "bee-woman," Semonides
shows that he does not scorn all women—only
those who do not behave in a moral, proper
fashion, albeit judged by the conventional male
standards of his day.

Finally, Semonides ends his poem with general condemnation of all women as the prover-
bial "ball-and-chain" for men. However, taken in
the satiric vein we have suggested here, his comments really do not seem to be anything more
than another installment in the traditional battle
of the sexes. Whatever the case, Semonides' poem
deserves more than the superficial interpretation
it usually receives.

Harmodius and Aristogiton—Lovers Turned Assassins

One of the most famous examples of a homosexual relationship, this time in Athens under the tyrant Hippias, was that of Harmodius and Aristogiton. These men, primarily out of their affection for each other, would ultimately threaten the very existence of tyranny in the city.

By the middle of the sixth century B.C., Athens was finally beginning to emerge as a great Greek city under its first tyrant, Pisistratus, father of Hippias. Situated in Attica, a 1,000-square-mile area on a southern extension of the Greek peninsula jutting out into the sea, Athens had a long history going back to Achaean times. Its location, its control of extensive territory (the second greatest landholdings of any city-state), its proximity to harbors that could be developed—all made Athens' potential as a commercial center great. Nonetheless, it remained primarily agrarian and economically backward, lagging behind other important Greek cities such as Thebes, Sparta, Corinth, and Argos.

Athens had lost its kings by the first part of the seventh century B.C., and it had undergone most of the general political, social, and economic turmoil that had characterized the development of most Archaic Age city-states. An attempt at tyranny in the 630s B.C. failed, and the bloodbath accompanying its aftermath was certainly in large part responsible for prompting the city's first law code, attributed to Draco in 621 B.C. Traditionally, the code was harsh but was, nonetheless, an important step forward in the development of Athens, since, for the first time, the state was given some specific authority over its citizens. Order began to emerge out of chaos.

In 594 B.C., Solon, an aristocrat with commercial interests, was given extraordinary power to reform the state politically, socially, and economically. He eliminated debt-slavery and changed the Athenian political system from one based on birth to one based on wealth—in this case, those whose property produced the most would have the greatest say in government. Solon made other reforms designed to settle internal problems and also to increase the city's economic prospects, but generally, he satisfied no one, and the city remained badly factionalized. Thus, Athens was ripe for tyranny, something Solon had hoped to avoid.

In 561 B.C., Pisistratus, an ambitious nobleman, took advantage of the turmoil in Athens and seized power, becoming Athens' first successful tyrant. The initial years of his rule, however, were anything but settled, since he was thrown out twice before finally becoming permanently entrenched in 546 B.C. Pisistratus proved to be a model political boss, and it was he more than any other single individual who was responsible for bringing Athens out of the "backwoods" and making it for the first time one of the major centers in Hellas.

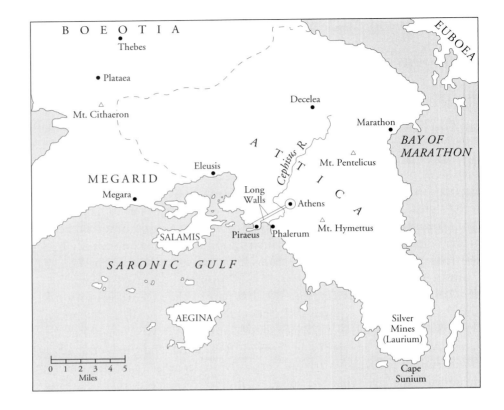

Map 9
Ancient Attica

Since Pisistratus received his support, as most tyrants did, from the masses, he took particular pains to look after their interests. He initiated a number of public works and building projects so that unemployment was low. Taxation was also light, because the tyrant himself was a millionaire with silver mines on the Thracian frontier (wealth that also paid the mercenaries who brought him to and kept him in power). Loans were made readily available to anyone who needed them, and trade was encouraged. Pisistratus also sponsored the festival of the Greater Dionysia, at which Dionysus, the god of fertility and wine and drunkenness—and special "friend" to the hardworking peasant farmers—was honored. It was at this festival, held every spring, that Greek drama was first introduced in the late 530s B.C.

At the time of Pisistratus' death in 527 B.C., few tyrants had ruled as effectively as he had—a sentiment echoed in the writings of Plato and Aristotle. He was replaced by his eldest son, Hippias. Unfortunately, Hippias had little of the charm or political savvy of his father, and although he retained enough support (and the family's silver mines) to keep himself in power, he

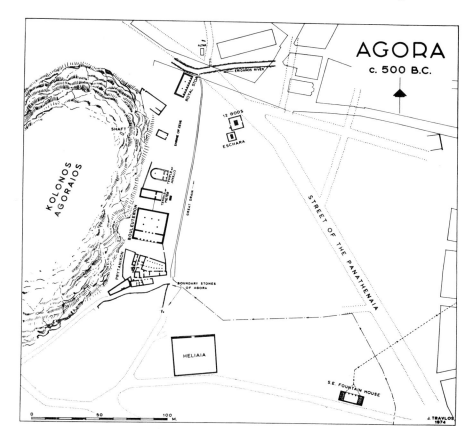

Map 10
The Athenian Agora,
c. 500 B.C. The
Athenian marketplace
and civic center, close
to the time of the
Pisistratids, was still
not very impressive
physically.

quickly alienated a good segment of the Athenian population, who found him and his tyranny repugnant. Threats of assassination were undoubtedly very real and not infrequent, but the plot that finally did materialize and resulted not in the death of Hippias, but of his brother Hipparchus, had little to do with the tyrant's ruling capabilities. In fact, the motivations appear quite ignoble. The incident involved Harmodius and Aristogiton.

Although the exact development of events leading up to the plot is somewhat confused, it seems that Hippias' brother Hipparchus (another tradition involves his brother Thettalus), who was married, became attracted to Harmodius, a beautiful youth who was the lover of a man named Aristogiton. Harmodius rejected Hipparchus' advances, but when he informed Aristogiton that he had been approached, the latter became afraid. He feared that because Hipparchus' brother was the tyrant of Athens, he could take Harmodius away from him whenever he pleased, so, it is said, the troubled lover began plotting the overthrow of the tyranny. In the meantime, Hipparchus

Figure 4.12
Traditional representations of Aristogiton (left) and Harmodius (right). (Capitoline Museums [Montemartini], Rome)

heightened Aristogiton's fears by approaching Harmodius a second time—again to no avail.

Having been rebuffed twice, Hipparchus now felt that he was the one who had been injured and began to plan his own revenge. Having no desire to use violence, he devised a subtle scheme by which he could bring shame on the family of Harmodius. He invited the latter's sister to participate as a "basket bearer" in a religious procession. This activity would have been a great honor for the family, but when the girl arrived, she was rejected and told she never would have been summoned because of her unworthiness. The insult resolved the lovers to carry out their plan.

The details of the assassination plot were worked out, and trusted associates agreed to help. The deed was to take place on the day of the great Panathenaea, the festival to the goddess Athena. Men bearing arms on that day would attract little attention, since many taking part in the procession would be carrying weapons. Harmodius and Aristogiton would attack and kill Hippias while their comrades eliminated the tyrant's bodyguards. Once these tasks had been accomplished, they could deal with Hipparchus at their pleasure. It was hoped that when others saw what was happening, they would join them in ridding the city of the tyrant and his family.

Finally, the appointed day arrived. Hipparchus supposedly had a dream the night before in which he was warned of his fate—but to no avail. The historian Thucydides describes what happened:

> At last the festival arrived; and Hippias with his bodyguard was outside the city in the Ceramicus, arranging how the different parts of the procession were to proceed. Harmodius and Aristogiton had already their daggers and were getting ready to act, when seeing one of their accomplices talking familiarly with Hippias, who was easy of access to every one, they took fright, and concluded that they were discovered and on the point of being taken; and eager if possible to be revenged first upon the man who had wronged them and for whom they had undertaken all this risk, they rushed, as they were, within the gates, and meeting with Hipparchus . . . recklessly fell upon him at once, infuriated, Aristogiton by love, and Harmodius by insult, and smote him and slew him. Aristogiton escaped the guards at the moment, through the crowd running up, but was afterwards taken and dispatched in no merciful way: Harmodius was killed on the spot.
> (6.57)

When Hippias learned what had happened, he suspected that a conspiracy was afoot, but he did not let on that he knew his brother had been killed. Instead, he instructed the armed men in the procession he had been organizing to lay down their arms and withdraw some distance away. They thought he must have something to tell them, so they did as he said. Their arms were collected by the tyrant's mercenaries, and Hippias then had those whom he suspected searched for daggers, since the usual weapons for a procession were only shield and spear. Never again was Hippias convinced that he was safe. His fears led him to be much more suspicious and oppressive in his rule, and a good number of citizens were put to death before he was finally ousted as tyrant four years later in 510 B.C.

As for Harmodius and Aristogiton, a simple twist of fate turned the fumbling lovers into heroes in later years. After Hippias' downfall, Athens emerged as a democracy in 508 B.C., and the details of what actually happened became confused. It was thought that Hipparchus—not Hippias—had been tyrant and that the pair of assassins were acting as "liberators" of their fellow citizens. The plot may actually have run deeper than it first appears, and Hippias may have had good cause to fear, for both Harmodius and Aristogiton were members of the same clan, one that had connections outside Athens and may have been growing in its hostility toward the tyrant. Hipparchus' insult to Harmodius' sister may have resulted in widespread resentment among clan members—not just the immediate family. Thus, to Hippias, and apparently to many later Athenians, Harmodius and Aristogiton not only were trying to satisfy a personal grudge but also were part of a carefully orchestrated coup attempt by the tyrant's political enemies. The two lovers may have been more substantial individuals than the preceding story suggests.

Nonetheless, they would not have spearheaded the plot if Hipparchus had not toyed with their emotions, and they were still celebrated for killing the wrong man. A statue of the "tyrannicides" was later set up in the Athenian marketplace to celebrate their mighty deed, their descendants received free meals from the state, annual sacrifices were made in their honor, and songs like the following were composed in their memory:

> I shall bear my sword in a branch of myrtle
> like Harmodius and Aristogiton
> when they killed the tyrant
> and made Athens a place of equal law.
>
> Dearest Harmodius, you are surely not dead
> but are in the Islands of the Blest, they say,
> where fleet-footed Achilles is
> and, they say, good Diomedes the son of Tydeus.
>
> I shall bear my sword in a branch of myrtle
> like Harmodius and Aristogiton
> when at the festival of Athena
> they killed the tyrant Hipparchus.
>
> Your fame shall be throughout the world forever,
> dearest Harmodius and Aristogiton,
> because you killed the tyrant
> and made Athens a place of equal law.
> (Athenaeus 659ab)

Popular belief and hatred of tyranny turned two lovers, inept bunglers more than patriots, into national heroes. Thucydides' (and also Herodotus') attempts to correct the mistaken notion that they had rid the city of tyranny went virtually unheeded, prompting him to conclude ultimately: "The Athenians are not more accurate than the rest of the world in their accounts of their own tyrants and of the facts of their own history" (6.54.1).

For the Love of Young Theodotus—Rivals Come to Blows

Although we have scattered references to homosexual behavior during the fifth century B.C. in sources such as Aristophanes' comedies, it really is not until the fourth century B.C. that we get our fullest insights into the practice. Plato, unmarried himself, gives the philosophical side of homosexual desire and love primarily in the *Symposium* and *Phaedrus,* but circumstances of actual homosexual liaisons are provided by Athenian court records. Their value rests not only in the wealth of detail they provide but also in the fact that they clearly reveal what could be said prudently in public about homosexuality at this time. It must be kept in mind, however, that the sources noted here are Athenian and may not be taken to represent homosexuality in all parts of Greece. Also, fourth-century information cannot be used to generalize about homosexuality in previous centuries.

Although Aeschines' prosecution of Timarchus (*Oration* 1) is our fullest account of homosexuality in this period, it has political overtones and was designed to bring disrepute on Timarchus for prostituting himself earlier in life. A more immediate case, not as important but still revealing, is one of a more domestic tone involving everyday people. It is a straightforward account, narrated, presumably verbatim, by one of the participants in what became a nasty love triangle. The incident's undistinguished character— unlike the more spectacular examples of Sappho and Harmodius and Aristogiton—is significant in itself, for it unequivocally demonstrates how commonplace pederasty still was at this time.

Two Athenians, one of them respected and a little too old (by his own admission) for such activity, had fallen in love with Theodotus, a boy from Plataea, a city not far from Athens. We do not know the name of the older gentleman, but his rival was named Simon—and it is clear that Simon was a jealous and impatient lover. He apparently beat the boy, inflicting serious injuries, and bullied him into doing whatever he wished. The older man, however, took the opposite approach, hoping to win the youth's affections and friendship by doing him favors. His success was such that Simon was prompted to put an end to any competition and steal the boy back.

When Simon learned that the boy was staying at his rival's house, he did not hesitate. Fortified with wine, he made his attack by night, breaking down the door of the older man's residence. Unfortunately, in his state of befuddlement, he did not meet with much success. The wronged party described what happened:

> Having discovered that the boy was with me, he came to the house at night, drunk; and bursting the door open, he broke into the women's quarters. In here were my sister and her daughters, whose lives are such models of propriety that they shrink from being seen even by the other members of the household. However, he went to such lengths of violence as to refuse to go away until those who came up, as well as those who had accompanied him, disgusted by his behavior in breaking in upon young and fatherless girls, expelled him by force.

Figure 4.13
A bisexual erotic scene between a bearded man and a beardless youth in a Hellenized setting. The Warren Silver Cup, c. 50–70 A.D. (British Museum, London)

The older man's statement is exceptional in that it clearly indicates the apparent normality of his having the young boy as his lover in a respectable household, which was also inhabited by his sister and her unmarried daughters.

Undaunted by his earlier failure, Simon continued to dog his rival. One evening when the latter was at dinner, he intruded and invited the older man outside:

> . . . he was so far from being sorry for his violent deeds that he found out where we were dining, and did a most extraordinary thing, incredible unless one realizes his insane folly: he called me outside, and as soon as I came out, he aimed a blow at me. When I stood up to him and parried his blows, he began pelting me with stones. He missed me, but struck the man who had come with him to see me—his name was Aristocritus—and the stone bruised his forehead.

Embarrassed by the whole affair and not wishing to appear foolish to his fellow citizens, the older man did not try to seek redress and hoped that the matter would pass. It did not. Realizing that Simon would not leave him alone and having no desire to give up the boy, he was at a loss as to how to proceed. He finally decided to take the lad and leave Athens on a voyage, thinking that Simon would eventually forget about him and direct his affections elsewhere.

After a sufficient amount of time had passed, the two returned, but for some reason that is never explained, the boy was placed at a friend's house while the older man stayed in Piraeus, the seaport of Athens. The separation is even more difficult to understand since the friend lived near a house that Simon had rented—and the result was predictable. As soon as Simon observed that Theodotus was back and living close by, he immediately picked up where he had left off. He gathered some friends at his house, and while they ate lunch and drank, lookouts were on the roof to watch for the boy when he ventured out. They planned to abduct him.

Coincidentally, it was at this same time that the older man came to fetch the boy. When the two emerged from the house a short time later, Simon and his drunken friends were waiting and jumped them, although several of his companions lost their nerve. Nonetheless, Simon and three friends seized the boy and began dragging him away, but he threw off the cloak by which they were holding him and ran away.

The scuffle over, the older man figured the drunken Simon and his friends would give up pursuing the lad as soon as they ran into some fellow citizens (there were no regular police in Athens), who would recognize the shamefulness of what they were about. He did not try to follow, and, thinking the boy would be safe, he took a different road to make sure he would not run into his attackers again. Things did not turn out as he expected.

Hotly pursued for a half mile, the boy took refuge in a laundry, but Simon and his friends caught him and dragged him off despite his protestations, which attracted a large crowd. The crowd decried the act and yelled out at the men, but they paid no heed, and when the laundryman and others tried to rescue the lad, they beat him even more.

As they were carrying him off down the streets, their path ironically crossed that of the older man, who, seeing that his young lover had been captured and was being badly mistreated, worked up his courage and grabbed hold of him. When he questioned Simon and his men as to why they were being so rough with the boy, they turned on him, and a fight broke out:

> The boy was hitting at them and defending his liberty. They were hitting at us, and also striking the boy in their drunken state. I was defending myself. The crowd that came up was helping us as being the injured parties. So that in all this confusion, there was not one of us who escaped without a sore head.

Though the boy was carried off anyway, the older man was apparently ultimately successful in retrieving him, for he says that when some of Simon's friends who were engaged in the fracas saw him later, they apologized, indicating that they were drunk and in the wrong for what they had done. Nothing more was heard about the matter for four years. At that time, Simon decided to bring his former rival, recently made vulnerable by a loss in a private suit, to trial on the charge of wounding him with intent to kill as a result of their rivalry over Theodotus. The punishment, if guilty, was banishment and confiscation of one's property.

Simon alleged that part of the reason the older man had enticed Theodotus away and beat him up was to get a large sum of money that Simon had given the boy to be his lover (more money, it turns out, than Simon's entire property was worth!), though he is never able to demonstrate the existence of the funds. The older man defended himself well in a speech prepared for him by Lysias (*Oration* 3), one of the great advocates of the day. He countered all the charges, revealing their absurdity:

> To mention the biggest and most glaring discrepancy of all: the fact that this man who was injured and plotted against by me, as he alleges, yet did not pluck up courage until four years later to lay his complaint before you. Other men, when they are in love and are robbed of the object of their passion and beaten besides, feel such anger that they attempt to obtain immediate vengeance; but this man has waited all this length of time.

The last sentence, in particular, is instructive, as is the following: "I have always thought it intolerable to try to hound a man out of his native land just because of our mutual rivalries for the affections of boys." That such matter-of-fact statements about pederasty are a part of testimony given in an Athenian court of law shows, once again, how common such relationships between men and boys must have been in Ancient Greece.

We do not know the fate of the boy, of Simon, or of the older man. We can probably conclude that the last was not convicted, for his defense seems a solid one, and Simon's reputation was not without blemish. However, what is clear from this example, and others discussed in the chapter, is that although the Greeks practiced bisexuality, they also accepted the additional emotional strains on individuals and society that naturally accompanied such relationships—and sometimes those strains could be very disruptive.

The Decline of Bisexuality

Interestingly, by the Hellenistic Age, which followed the death of Alexander the Great in 323 B.C., the particularism of the old city-states had broken down and been replaced by the more cosmopolitan world of the great metropolis, or mother-city. Mercenaries had replaced citizen-soldiers, and the Hellenistic monarchs' "national" armies, numbering in the tens of thousands, were drawn from a variety of sources. Institutionalized male bonding was now mostly a thing of the past, and the status of women had improved significantly. With that improvement, heterosexual romance emerged as the dominant erotic model. Homosexuality continued, but as an ethos its impact was in decline. Eventually, a changing world would take a dim view of the practice.

Suggestions for Further Reading

K. J. Dover's *Greek Homosexuality* (New York: Vintage Books, 1980) is the definitive work on the subject. A good supplement is provided by T. W. Africa, "Homosexuals in Greek History," *The Journal of Psychohistory* 9 (1982), 401–420. Additional discussion may be found in B. S. Thornton, *Eros: The Myth of Ancient Greek Sexuality* (Boulder, Colo.: Westview Press, 1998); D. Cohen, *Law, Sexuality, and Society: The Enforcement of Morals in Classical Athens* (Cambridge: Cambridge University Press, 1991); and J. J. Winkler, *The Constraints of Desire: The Anthropology of Sex and Gender in Ancient Greece* (New York: Routledge, 1990). On Eros and Greek Athletics, see T. R. Scanlon's work by that title (New York: Oxford University Press, 2002). For Sappho, see previously mentioned works by Podlecki, Burnett, Davenport, and Burn, as well as R. Jenkyns, *Three Classical Poets: Sappho, Catullus, and Juvenal* (Cambridge: Harvard University Press, 1982), and S. B. Pomeroy, *Goddesses, Whores, Wives, and Slaves: Women in Classical Antiquity* (New York: Schocken Books, 1975). For a new translation of Sappho, see M. Barnard, *Sappho: A New Translation* (Berkeley and Los Angeles: University of California Press, 1999); E. Greene's (ed.) *Reading Sappho* and *Re-reading Sappho* (University of California Press, 1998) are anthologies of scholarship on Sappho. See also D. Rayor, *Sappho's Lyre: Archaic Lyric and Women Poets of Ancient Greece* (Berkeley and Los Angeles: University of California Press, 1991); and M. Williamson, *Sappho's Immortal Daughters* (Cambridge: Harvard University Press, 1995). For Anacreon, Semonides, and Sappho, see R. Lattimore, *Greek Lyrics* (Chicago & London: The University of Chicago Press [revised and enlarged second edition], 1960). On Harmodius and Aristogiton and the political development of Athens in general, see R. Sealey, *A History of the Greek City States 700–338 B.C.,* Chapters 4–6 (Berkeley and Los Angeles: University of California Press, 1976). Thucydides and Herodotus are the major sources for the story of the "tyrannicides" and are available in numerous translations. K. Freeman's *The Murder of Herodes and Other Trials from the Athenian Law Courts* (New York: Norton, 1963) contains the text and discussion of Lysias' speech (*Oration 3*) for the defense in the Theodotus love affair.

5

The Problem with Persia

East Against West—Polygnotus, Politics, and Paintbrushes

. . . Now at this time the use of color had increased . . .
and art had become . . . highly perfected.
(Pliny, *Natural History* 35.57)

By 500 B.C., the "growing pains" of Greece were mostly over. The worst days of social, economic, and political upheaval had passed, and city-states had emerged as mature institutions. Much had been accomplished, and in many ways, the Archaic period turned out to be more of a "golden age" than Hesiod would ever have imagined. The Greeks were on the verge of the century that is usually regarded as the period of their most famous achievements, and the Archaic Age gradually gave way to the Classical. The transitional event was the Persian Wars, first in 490 B.C. and again in 480–479 B.C., wars that left a legacy of hostility between East and West that continued to erupt regularly until the middle of the fifth century. This ongoing struggle advanced the cause of a number of Greek states and politicians and, coincidentally, provided major themes for the great artists of the day. No painter blended war, art, and politics better than the most famous Greek muralist, Polygnotus of Thasos.

The Wars with Persia

By the end of the sixth century B.C., the greatest power in the East had become Persia, the latest in a long succession of empires that stretched back into the late third millennium and had included, most recently, the Neo-Babylonians and the Medes. In only half a century, Persian influence had spread from a stronghold in Iran to an area that extended from the deserts of Libya and Egypt in the West to the Indus River Valley in the East; it was by far the largest empire that had ever existed.

Such a huge empire embraced many cultures whose differences needed accommodation, and Herodotus emphasizes the point with an amusing—but still instructive—anecdote. Speaking about how "each nation would certainly think its own customs the best," Herodotus proceeds to show how the Persian king Darius made clear to some of his subjects, in this case Greeks and Indians, the diversity of the various peoples over whom he ruled:

> Darius . . . called together some of the Greeks who were in attendance on him and asked them what would they take to eat their dead fathers. They said that no price in the world would make them do so. After that Darius summoned those of the Indians who are called Callatians, who do eat their parents, and, in the presence of the Greeks (who understood the conversation through an interpreter), asked them what price would make them burn their dead fathers with fire [as most Greeks disposed of their dead]. They shouted aloud, "Don't mention such horrors!"
> (3.38)

Figure 5.1
Early gold daric issued during the reign of Darius I, symbolically representing the Persian king drawing a bow

Having already seized control of Greek city-states in Asia Minor and moving continually westward through Thrace, the aforementioned Darius I, the Great King of Persia, launched an attack on the Greek peninsula itself (see route on Map 11). The best he could do, however, was to suffer an ignominious defeat on the plains of Marathon in 490 B.C., and it was left to his son, Xerxes, to punish the recalcitrant Greeks. Darius' expedition had been primarily a punitive one, designed to repay Athens, in particular, for interfering in his affairs in Ionia. Xerxes would visit the full weight of the Persian Empire on the Greeks, and their defeat seemed a foregone conclusion.

Although it was once fashionable to regard all ancient Greeks as freedom-loving diehards, in reality, most were no different from any other people facing imminent destruction. Xerxes' call for signs of submission—earth and water—did not go unheeded in many quarters of Hellas. In Athens and Sparta, however, the mood was one of defiance, not so much because they desired a suicidal struggle with the much larger Persian force, but because they had no alternative, having executed earlier envoys from Persia.

As Greek spies continued to bring in reports confirming the incredible size of the Persian host (large, but not the "millions" Herodotus describes), those city-states who had not already surrendered sought some way to save themselves or, like Athens and Sparta, prepared to fight. Even the oracle of Apollo at Delphi on which the Greeks had learned to depend in times of

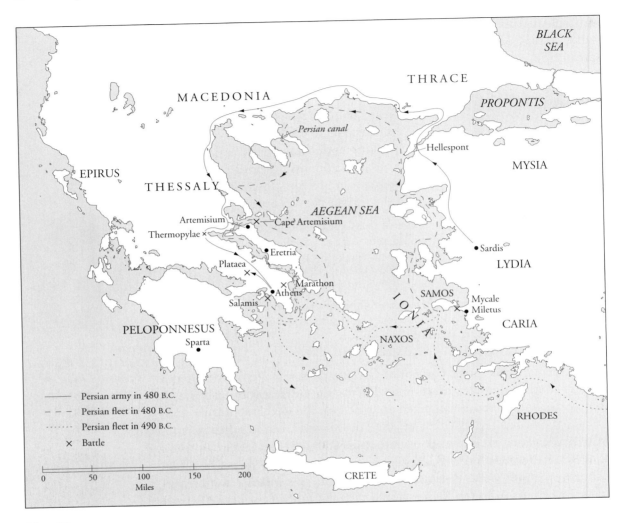

Map 11
*The invasion routes of
Darius and Xerxes*

crisis provided no assistance here, initially warning inquirers to flee to the ends of the earth to avoid the irresistible onslaught of the Persians.

Off Artemisium on the island of Euboea, the progress of the Persian fleet was impeded by Greek ships and storms, while Xerxes and his land forces encountered formidable resistance in northern Greece at the pass of Thermopylae, which provided access to the country's interior. After a valiant defense, the pass was betrayed by an opportunistic Greek, and the Persians, having broken through, now moved into the heart of Greece.

Leaving a path of destruction in his wake, Xerxes made straight for Athens, the city that had primarily been responsible for humiliating his father's forces at Marathon ten years earlier and had continued as a troublesome ob-

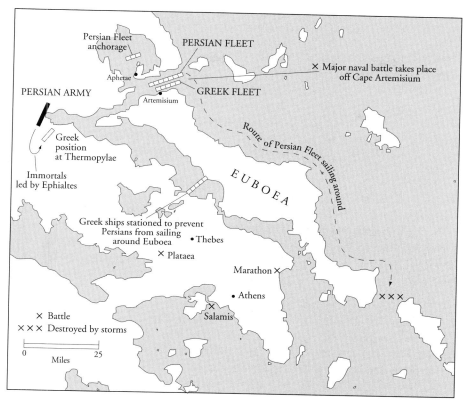

Map 12
Artemisium and Thermopylae

Persian Fleet anchorage

PERSIAN FLEET

Aphetae

× Major naval battle takes place off Cape Artemisium

GREEK FLEET

PERSIAN ARMY

Artemisium

Route of Persian Fleet sailing around

Greek position at Thermopylae

Immortals led by Ephialtes

E U B O E A

Greek ships stationed to prevent Persians from sailing around Euboea

• Thebes

× Plataea

Marathon ×

• Athens

× Battle
× × × Destroyed by storms

×
Salamis

0   25
    Miles

× × ×

struction to his desires. On arrival with his army and fleet, he found Athens practically deserted. Women, children, the aged, and the disabled had been evacuated from all of Attica to places of safety, and every able-bodied man, slave or free, foreigner or citizen, was with the fleet. A few misguided souls took up a position on the Acropolis and were put to the sword (they had incorrectly interpreted the oracle's pronouncement to defend themselves within "walls of wood" to mean a wooden fence rather than ships). Artemisium and Thermopylae had bought the time Athens had needed.

Fortunately, the Athenians had a fleet to which they could turn, but it might have been otherwise. When a rich new silver vein was discovered in the state mines at Laurium shortly after the first war with Persia, euphoric citizens wanted the proceeds divided among themselves. Those with somewhat more acumen, like the skillful Themistocles (who would eventually emerge as the most dominant political figure in Athens), knew that they had not seen the last of the Persians and urged that the funds be used to construct a fleet of 200 triremes—Athens' only salvation should the Persians return in force. For various reasons, rival politicians attempted to block

Figure 5.2
A Greek hoplite at the time of the Persian Wars, c. 480 B.C.

A "Reel" Look at Greek People III: *The 300 Spartans—* "Remember the Alamo" Greek Style

UNLIKE ROME, WHICH IS more familiar to modern audiences and offers more tantalizing fare for moviegoers, few serious films about Ancient Greece have been attempted. One of them is the 1962 historical drama, *The 300 Spartans,* based primarily on Herodotus' stirring account of the memorable last stand at the pass of Thermopylae (information pertinent to the film begins at Herodotus 7.60ff.). The Spartans and what was left of their Greek allies died valiantly while trying to obstruct King Xerxes' Persian army's march into Greece in 480 B.C. The events at Thermopylae passed into legend as a defining moment in the defense of Greek liberty.

The making of *The 300 Spartans,* however, was prompted by Cold War tensions of the early 1960s, so Herodotus and the Greeks at Thermopylae are resurrected mostly to mirror contemporary issues. Audiences of the day could not help but be reminded of the "communist scare"

when they observed an ancient Western "democratic" society making a "last stand" against despotism and the countless hoards from the "East" coming to enslave it. Unfortunately, the Spartans (and many other Greeks), who are the focus of the movie, were never democrats, maintained a slave system of their own, and their government (which the film does show correctly) never committed to the defense of Thermopylae. Nonetheless, the episode was appropriately glorified by the Ancient Greeks and a suitable mythology emerged, making the heroic stand a renewable and timely theme for modern filmmakers—dovetailing nicely with familiar outcries for freedom and liberty in our own society such as "Remember the Alamo," "Remember the *Maine,*" and "Remember Pearl Harbor."

As for the actual battle, a defensive action was planned at Thermopylae in northern Greece to delay the progress of Xerxes' great army, which

Map 13
The pass at
Thermopylae

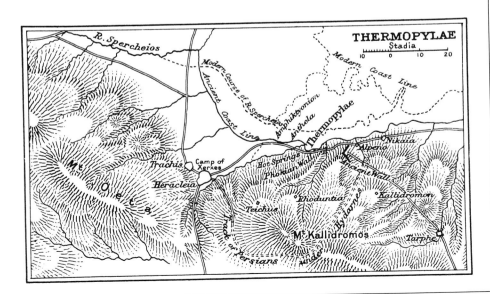

sought to break into the interior of Greece and swoop down upon Athens to the south. King Leonidas of Sparta, his bodyguard of 300, and about 7,000 Greek allies took up position in the narrow pass and awaited the enemy advance.

At first, Xerxes had nothing but contempt for the small band of defenders. For four days, he waited for them to run, but when they had not withdrawn by the fifth, he delayed no longer and sent his troops headlong into the fray, ordering them to capture those impudent and reckless people and bring them to him alive. He soon realized, however, that he had completely underestimated the fighting ability of the Greeks, particularly the Lacedaemonians, or Spartans, who decimated his ranks while suffering few losses of their own. Supposedly, Xerxes became so upset while watching the proceedings that he leaped up from his throne three times in fear for his army. Even his best warriors, inappropriately called the "Immortals," were driven back with heavy casualties.

This situation continued for two days, and Xerxes, completely frustrated by the Greeks' dogged resistance, wondered what to do next. He soon met with a bit of good luck, for a local Greek named Ephialtes, hoping to be richly rewarded, came forth and asked for an audience with the king. Ephialtes informed Xerxes of a narrow path that led over the mountain to Thermopylae, and he was paid to lead what was left of the "Immortals" and their commander, Hydarnes, around behind the Spartans and their allies.

When it became clear that the pass had been betrayed and the Persians were marching around behind them, the Greeks at Thermopylae met to discuss their course of action. Knowing that the pass was no longer defensible, most opted (or perhaps were ordered) to return to their homes. Meanwhile, Leonidas, his Lacedaemonians, and

Figure 5.3 *"Leonidas." Representation (restored) of a Spartan warrior found at Sparta which, by its archaic features, could have been fashioned soon after Thermopylae. (Sparta Museum)*

those who resolved to stay with them made ready for the final battle. They were all killed and buried where they fell. Later, inscriptions were set up to honor all those who had died at Thermopylae. For the Spartans, there was a special epitaph:

(continued)

A "Reel" Look at Greek People III: *The 300 Spartans*— "Remember the Alamo" Greek Style (continued)

Stranger, go tell the Spartans
That here we lie obedient to their commands.

As for Ephialtes' treachery, he apparently got the "reward" he deserved. Branded as a traitor by the Greeks, a price was placed on his head, and, fearing for his life, he fled to Thessaly in the north. Some time later, he returned from his self-imposed exile and was killed by a man named Athenades, although apparently for a reason unrelated to Thermopylae. Nonetheless, the Spartans greatly honored Athenades for his deed.

The movie version of these events was filmed in Greece, which itself had almost succumbed to communism directly after World War II, but *The 300 Spartans* is not set at the actual pass of Thermopylae—understandable since it is hallowed ground for modern Greeks (and probably too isolated for the cast and film crew). Unfortunately, there is no pass at the location which was chosen, and this is *the* major shortcoming of the picture. Everybody talks about the pass at Thermopylae and we see a lot of fighting for its possession, but the viewer is hard-pressed to get much of a glimpse of anything resembling the object over which everyone is making such a fuss.

Richard Egan plays Leonidas, the Spartan king who led the 300 at Thermopylae and lost his life there. Considering so little is known about the actual figure, Egan handles the role in an appropriate manner and does manage to embody much that is "Spartan" in his portrayal. He lacks, however, the characteristic beard and long hair, but in the early 1960s it was still difficult to make an unqualified hero of one so untrimmed. His city of Sparta also seems much too grandiose for its day and had no fortifications, though it probably strikes modern audiences as severe. Ralph Richardson is a cunning and manipulative

Themistocles, the Athenian counterpart of Leonidas in the film, but he seems a little too old and plays him more like a backroom politician than the great general who was certainly one of the most aggressive and effective figures from Greek or any other history. There is no evidence that the two men ever met during these proceedings, but that does not prevent Themistocles and Leonidas from becoming almost chummy in *The 300 Spartans*. The theme of Greek unity bounced around frequently by both is one also voiced in Herodotus (7.145). Themistocles' interpreting the "wall of wood" oracle and predicting the battle of Salamis in the film is justified by passages in Herodotus (7.141–143), although the latter "prediction" is incorrectly assigned to the Spartan seer Megistias.

David Farrar's Xerxes does sport a beard but a small one, and little else, including his headgear, boots, and throne, resembles existing representations of Xerxes or other Persian kings. Farrar portrays Xerxes as an appropriately pompous autocrat bent on subduing the freedom-loving Greeks and bellows suitably when required. His army, perhaps all together as large as 250,000 (not the millions indicated by Herodotus) has shrunk considerably when viewed on screen, but film dialogue about its size attempts to compensate for what we do not see. The army also appears to march in the wrong direction—up the coast rather than down it. In *The 300 Spartans*, Xerxes frees a spy who has been caught observing his march so that the latter may inform the Greeks of the size of the Persian army and discourage any resistance. In reality, spies (*not* a spy) were caught and freed by Xerxes—but this was before Xerxes had even left for Greece (7.146–147). There is also no justification for the romantic liaison between Xerxes and Artemisia, queen of Caria (see page 137), who was the Great King's close advisor and one of his fleet admirals. In the movie, she seems to pop effortlessly in and out of Xerxes' camp to flirt or give him advice between shifts with the fleet. One would think that the great naval engagement Herodotus says was taking place at the same time as Thermopylae some forty miles away at Artemisium (never referred to by name in the film and barely mentioned otherwise) would have fully occupied her time.

Historical characters on both sides such as Mardonius, Hydarnes, and the ex-Spartan king, Demaratus, among the Persians, and Megistias, Gorgo, Leonidas' wife, and his co-king, Leotychidas, are present and called by name, but others are fictional additions. The most egregious inclusion in the film is an inane romantic relationship between a young, unmarried Spartan couple. They bumble their way through the movie at the most inopportune moments and are used unnecessarily to tie up different threads of the plot. The young woman, who already appears too old not to have been married at Sparta (see pp. 162–163), though the moviemakers had to consider modern sensibilities, is apparently so attractive that she inadvertently becomes a prime reason why the pass at Thermopylae is betrayed. When she rejects the advances of Ephialtes, portrayed in the film as a mysterious, local do-nothing and sometime goat-herd, he decides to run and inform Xerxes about the secret path. He wants to get even with the Spartans for his being spurned—and pick up a few drachma (or darics) to boot. Historically, of course, Ephialtes is recorded as the betrayer of the pass, but, even so, one has to wonder why the Persians did not already know about the path since Herodotus says the Thessalians, allies of Xerxes, had used it in the past (7.215). It is unlikely the Thessalians had forgotten about it—or that other Greeks be-

sides the locals had not heard about it. Perhaps that is the real reason why the Spartan government was so reluctant to send an army to Thermopylae in the first place. Herodotus may deny it (7.175), but Spartan officials may have known beforehand that it was indefensible and could not afford the sacrifice of an army.

Greek allies at Thermopylae are included in the film, but there is no indication of their large number and they are overshadowed to prevent them distracting from the glory of the 300 Spartans. Costume on both sides should have been better considering available representations in art but are, nonetheless, convincingly "ancient" to an unknowledgeable audience. Spartan warriors look more like Graeco-Roman hybrids, although they do have the famous scarlet cloaks. The Corinthian-style helmet worn by the Spartans is seldom seen, though one of the few shown inexplicably has a hinge on the face piece! Certainly, the real Leonidas would have been more discriminating about the headgear he wore than his counterpart in the film. Xerxes' army appears motley enough to recapture a sense of the diverse groups from all over the empire which made up the army and provides the audience with a seemingly eastern appearance. Herodotus describes (7.61; 83) the Persians and Medes, the core of the army, as wearing sleeved, colorful tunics, fish-scale iron-plate breastplates, full-length trousers, and loose felt caps, which the movie recaptures in various degrees, though rather colorlessly. Wicker shields, quivers with arrows, long bows, short spears, and daggers on their right made up the soldiers' armament. Herodotus also says the Persians wore much gold. Some headgear in the movie, including turbans, is close to accurate but

(continued)

A "Reel" Look at Greek People III: *The 300 Spartans—* "Remember the Alamo" Greek Style (continued)

there is much that is hybrid or creative. Mardonius' odd-looking headdress appears something like a contemporary-style Phrygian cap but resembles more rigid helmets from that region in the next century. Particularly out of place are Xerxes' "Immortals," whose sinister black studded outfits and fin-like helmets are a far cry from the more colorful dress of the actual bodyguard (see Figure 5.4). Greek dress worn at the Isthmus conference ("assembly at Corinth" in the movie), re-created with a scriptwriter's zeal and replete with contrived dialogue, looks to be drawn from ancient-looking fabrics sold to tourists in Greek shops in the 1960s.

Military formation on both sides is mixed. There does not appear to be much on the side of the Persians except to move forward and then run away when things went badly. They also have far too much room to move about (Herodotus describes Persians actually being pushed back into the sea and drowning during the fighting [7.223]), and chariots play a major role in the battle. In his early accounting of Xerxes' army, Herodotus does mention Indian and Libyan chariots (7.86). Xerxes, too, reviews the same army while in his chariot at the beginning of the expedition. Herodotus also says that right up to the arrival at Thermopylae there was still a large contingent of Libyan chariots (7.184)—but he mentions nothing about them in his description of the actual battle. He also records that camels were among the Persian forces, but none are at Thermopylae. We are at a loss to explain the discrepancies, but one thing is clear: chariots and camels would have been useless in the narrow confines of Thermopylae. Herodotus himself says that the location was chosen to render ineffective the Persian horse (7.177)—but that does not seem to discourage the frequent cavalry maneuvers seen in the film.

Figure 5.4 *A Persian archer in ceremonial dress, probably an "Immortal" (Louvre, Paris)*

As for the Spartans, the spearhead-shaped phalanx they employ toward the end of the picture is more appropriately associated with the later Macedonians. Their spears, too, look more suitable for gardening than for battle and are far too short in length. However, the Greek capital letter "lambda" (for "Lacedaemon," the general region in which the Spartans, or "Lacedaemonians," lived) inscribed on the Spartans' shields was a known practice. They also kept step to music, a detail the filmmakers included which could have gone unnoticed, although trumpets sounded key maneuvers and a customary paean was sung as the Spartan phalanx advanced. The depiction of light-armed support troops, probably meant to be helots, fighting with the Spartans is also a positive inclusion.

In the film, Xerxes appears to have as many women in his camp as troops. There actually were women in his entourage, but it is impossible to know how many. Herodotus says they accompanied the army primarily as cooks and concubines (7.83, 7.187). There is also justification for Xerxes' pavilion in the movie. Herodotus says pavilions were provided him by locals as the expedition moved along (7.119).

According to Herodotus, Leonidas fell before the Persians, led round by Ephialtes, arrived. By that time, most spears were broken and the Spartans were fighting with their swords (7.224). The film, however, keeps the spears and places Leonidas' death only moments before a final shower of arrows disposes of the vastly outnumbered remainder of the proud Spartan troupe. Before that happens, Mardonius approaches the Spartans and tells them they will be spared if they turn over the body of Leonidas. They, of course, refuse. Herodotus mentions nothing of this, saying only that the Greeks were successful in retrieving Leonidas' body and when the Persians

with Ephialtes arrived, they pulled back behind their defensive wall to make their final stand. In the film, the opposite is shown. They march forth to encounter the Persians before finally being encircled and killed by arrows. In reality, they were charged by the Persians, the wall was demolished, and, surrounded on all sides, they were overwhelmed by missiles—not necessarily arrows, which would seem impractical at close quarters and have caused too many "friendly fire" casualties (225). Xerxes, too, lost two brothers in the battle, but neither was named "Cyrus" nor was one killed by Spartans while on patrol.

A famous quote associated with the battle of Thermopylae is attributed to a Spartan named Dieneces. When he was told that the Persians were so numerous they would blot out the sun when they fired their arrows, he contemptuously responded in typical Spartan fashion that if this were true, it would be fine with him because then they could have their battle in the shade. In the film, the comment is included but understandably assigned to Richard Egan's Leonidas at a final meeting with the Persian commander, Hydarnes. The film ends showing the modern version of the inscription set up where the Spartans fell, which is read by the film's narrator and quoted above. Leonidas' body is shown in a heap with his fellow Spartans—with no hint that Xerxes would decapitate him.

All and all, *The 300 Spartans* does try to get things right. It generally follows Herodotus' account and includes details in the script that demonstrate knowledge of the events. There are also hints of actual Spartan character and something of a feel for Ancient Greek society. However, some of that same detail is often attributed incorrectly, changed in sequence, carelessly portrayed,

(continued)

A "Reel" Look at Greek People III: *The 300 Spartans*— "Remember the Alamo" Greek Style (continued)

or altered to fit the story line, and much is created which was never there. One wonders, for example, about the origins of the detailed "plaster" relief map of Greece over which Leonidas and Themistocles discuss strategy when at the Corinth (Isthmus) meeting, or how thirty Spartans in full armor could so easily wade back and forth across a sizable inlet in chest-deep water in an attempt to kill Xerxes without being any the worse for it. Still, *The 300 Spartans* brings to life an event in Ancient Greek history with which few moderns would otherwise be familiar and remains an inspiring tale even with its shortcomings.

Figure 5.5   *View from the pass at Thermopylae. In antiquity, the sea extended to the mountains in the background. The modern version of the monument celebrating the Spartans' last stand is in the foreground.*

Themistocles' efforts, but he was a shrewd politician, and eventually his view prevailed. Fortunately, the death of Darius and the succession problems experienced by his son provided the Athenians with the additional time they needed so that the fleet was built and ready for the assault of 480 B.C.

Figure 5.6
Themistocles
(Museum of Ostia)

Themistocles and the Battle of Salamis

With Xerxes in possession of Athens, the entire Greek fleet, spearheaded by the 200 ships of Athens, rendezvoused near the island of Salamis, just off the Attic coast. As usual, opinions among the high command were divided as to how to proceed, and self-interest took precedence over sound military judgment. The Athenians, led by Themistocles, naturally wanted the entire fleet to stay and drive the Persians from their homeland. Their Peloponnesian allies, lead by Sparta, wished to withdraw south to protect their own interests before the enemy could prevent them from leaving.

The situation became critical for the Athenians, so Themistocles, after first threatening to take his ships and sail to Italy, devised a strategem that would force a battle in the narrow straits of Salamis. He secretly sent one of his own household slaves to Xerxes to inform him that the Greeks were so terrified that they were preparing to flee. If the Persians attacked immediately, the element of surprise would be theirs, and victory would be assured.

Xerxes and his commanders believed Themistocles' story. Why not? It had, after all, been a Greek who had betrayed the pass at Thermopylae. The

Map 14
The Battle of Salamis

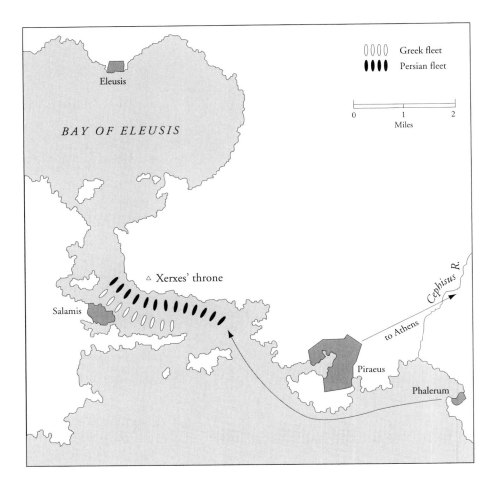

Persians began their preparations for an early-morning attack, and about midnight, their ships started to move in on the unsuspecting Greeks. Persian soldiers had already been put ashore on a nearby island for the purpose of rescuing those of their own who might fall into the water during the battle and of slaying enemy sailors in the same situation.

Unaware of Themistocles' strategem and the approaching danger, the Greeks continued to squabble among themselves. Even when they were finally informed of the Persian movement, they still refused to believe it until a Greek ship serving with the enemy (there were a number of Greeks sympathetic to or allied with the Persian cause) deserted and confirmed the story. Now convinced that the threat was real, the Greeks prepared their 380 ships for immediate action against the much larger enemy fleet; by dawn, they were assembled and ready for battle.

Figure 5.7   The straits of Salamis from the Eleusis side. On the right is the island of Salamis; on the left, Attica.

The Persians, expecting to find their adversaries sleeping and unprepared, were, instead, the ones who were caught completely off guard. Havoc ensued as the smaller, quicker Greek vessels darted in and out, ramming, breaking the oars, and smashing the rudders of their enemy's ships. In the general confusion, the Persians even crashed into one another, and their hopes of victory were quickly dashed.

The playwright Aeschylus, who participated in the battle, later described the Persian frustration in poetic terms in his play *The Persians.* An envoy returns home to relate the tragic news about Salamis to Xerxes' mother:

> . . . Warships struck their brazen beaks
> Together: a Grecian man-of-war began
> The charge, a Phoenician ornamented stern
> Was smashed; another drove against another.
> First the floods of Persians held the line,
> But when the narrows choked them, and rescue hopeless,
> Smitten by prows, their bronze jaws gaping,
> Shattered entire was our fleet of oars.
> The Grecian warships, calculating, dashed
> Round, and encircled us; ships showed their belly;

Figure 5.8
Aeschylus (Capitoline Museums, Rome)

No longer could we see the water, charged
With ships' wrecks and men's blood.
Corpses glutted beaches and the rocks.
Every warship urged its own anarchic
Rout; and all who survived that expedition,
Like mackerel or some catch of fish,
Were stunned and slaughtered, boned with broken oars
And splintered wrecks: lamentations, cries
Possessed the open sea, until the black
Eye of evening, closing, hushed them. . . .
(11.408–428)

Figure 5.9
A cup designed as the ramming prow of a Greek warship echoes Aeschylus' ". . . Warships struck their brazen beaks together. . . ." Note also the "eye" for guidance and protection.

After Salamis, the war continued to go badly for the Persians, and following major defeats in 479 B.C. at Plataea in Boeotia and near Mycale in Ionia, the second war with Persia came to an end. Athens lay in ruins, devastated by the frustrated invaders before their withdrawal, but the rebuilding process would begin immediately, and the Greeks could take pride in the fact that they had once again humbled the greatest empire on earth. This war would not be the last of the Greco-Persian altercations, but, for the time being, the recent successes paved the way for an era of increased prosperity and set the stage for the Athenian Empire.

Artemisia the Admiral—A Queen Stacks the Deck

ONE OF THE PARTICIPANTS in the battle of Salamis on the Persian side was a remarkable woman named Artemisia, queen of Caria, who, under Persian suzerainty, ruled a number of cities, including Halicarnassus. In antiquity, it was a rarity indeed to find any woman competing with men in combat on land or sea. Artemisia not only vied successfully with men, but her capabilities earned her the respect of Xerxes himself.

Artemisia commanded her own squadron of five ships in Xerxes' navy, and she was also reputed to have been one of the king's closest advisors. According to Herodotus, when she was consulted by Xerxes as to whether he should fight the Greek fleet at Salamis, Artemisia advised him against it, telling the king that the Greeks were as superior to the Persians in seamanship as men were naturally superior to women (certainly an uncharacteristic statement for a woman such as Artemisia!). Nonetheless, Xerxes ignored her advice and prepared to meet the enemy fleet.

When the Greeks sprang their trap and the battle began to go badly for the Persians, Artemisia demonstrated her resourcefulness. Herodotus writes:

> . . . Artemisia . . . gained even greater renown with the King. For when the King's fortunes had been reduced to utter confusion, at that very moment the ship of Artemisia was pursued by an Attic ship. And she, not being able to make her escape, inasmuch as there were other friendly ships in front of her and she herself happened to be nearest to the enemy, she resolved to do this, which turned greatly to her advantage when she had done it: being pursued by the Attic vessel, she charged and rammed a friendly ship, of men of Calyndus, with the king of the Calyndians himself on board, Damasithymus. Whether there had been some quarrel between her and him while they were both still at the Hellespont, I cannot say, nor whether she did what she did deliber-

ately or whether it was pure accident that the ship of the Calyndians happened to fall in her way. But when she rammed him and sank him, by her good luck she gained doubly by what she had done. For the trierarch of the Attic ship, when he saw her ramming a ship manned by barbarians, believed that Artemisia's ship was either Greek itself or must be deserting from the barbarians to the Greek side and helping them, and so he turned his line of pursuit to other vessels.

> That is the way her stroke of luck befell her, that she escaped and did not meet destruction there. But there is the additional fact that, having done evil to Xerxes, as a result of that very evil she won particular renown with him. For it is said that, as the King watched, he noticed the vessel doing the ramming, and some one of his courtiers, standing by, said, "Master, do you see Artemisia, how well she fights? And lo, she has sunk a vessel of the enemy." He asked if the action was really that of Artemisia, and they said yes, for they could clearly read the ensign on her ship. The destroyed vessel they concluded was an enemy. As I said, everything happened to her good luck in this, and most of all that the ship of the Calyndians that was destroyed had not a single man escape alive to accuse her. So Xerxes, they say, in answer to what they had told him, observed, "My men have become women, and my women men." That is what they say Xerxes said.
> (8.87–88)

Whatever the actual circumstances of Artemisia's behavior at Salamis, she did not lose her favored position with Xerxes. Later, he consulted her again on what he should do after losing most of his fleet—she urged him to retreat. He then directed her to sail a number of his children who had accompanied him on the expedition back to Asia Minor. What later services Artemisia provided for Xerxes are not known.

The Delian League and the Rise of Cimon

In 478 B.C., those Greek cities (largely Aegean or on the eastern side of the peninsula) that stood to profit most from continuing the pursuit of the Persians—and had the most to lose should they return—joined together to form the Delian League. Headquartered on the island of Delos and organized under the direction of a rejuvenated Athens, the League's members unwittingly placed themselves entirely in Athenian hands by allowing the wily Themistocles and his cohorts to draw troops and ships from trusted allies, while requiring only cash payments from the rest of the cities. This clever strategy ultimately left the latter militarily dependent. The Athenian leadership supported the idealistic purpose of the League—which was to free the Greeks of Asia Minor from Persian control—but only so long as it suited their purposes. As time went on, it became increasingly apparent that Athens' real intention was to turn the "voluntary" Delian League into its own Aegean empire.

By the late 470s B.C., Cimon had emerged as the leading politician in Athens and had assumed direction of the Delian League. Cimon was the son of the general, Miltiades, who had led Athenian troops to victory at Marathon. He used the League as a vehicle for his own success, inflicting a series of defeats on the Persians while gaining popularity at home by discovering and returning to Athens the lost "bones" of its legendary founder Theseus. It was also Cimon who fulfilled the ostensible purpose of the Delian League when, at the Eurymedon River (in southern Asia Minor) in 469 B.C., he inflicted on the Persians the most devastating defeat they ever suffered at Greek hands. In the years that followed, any remaining pretense that the Delian League was a voluntary confederation whose members were free to come and go as they pleased dissipated; as Athens continued to rebuild and prosper under Cimon's leadership, subject states were faced with two choices: submit or revolt. Most chose the path of least resistance.

East Against West—The Trojan War Renewed

Herodotus is generally regarded as the father of history and is our major source for the Persian Wars. It is clear from his writings that many fifth-century B.C. Greeks, including himself, considered the wars with Persia not as a series of random engagements but as part of an ongoing East-West struggle that began with the Trojan War. There can be no question about this view as Herodotus relates the Persians' version of how the conflict began:

> . . . the Greeks, for the sake of a woman from Lacedaemon, assembled a great army, invaded Asia, and destroyed the kingdom of Priam. Ever since that day, we have considered the Greeks our enemies.
> (1.4)

The view that *all* wars with Persia were an extension of the Trojan War was undoubtedly responsible for the following passage about the Spartan king, Agesilaus, who led an expedition against Persia in the early fourth century B.C. Cast in the role of a latter-day Agamemnon, a voice came to Agesilaus as he slept at Aulis on the eve of his departure:

> King of the Lacedaemonians, surely you know that no one has ever been made general over all Hellas save Agamemnon in former times and, now, you. Since you command the same army, war against the same enemy, and depart from the same place, it is only appropriate that you should offer the goddess the same sacrifice Agamemnon made before he sailed.
>
> (Plutarch, *Agesilaus* 6.4)

Cimon's struggle with the Persians, too, was specifically compared with the conflict at Troy, and the battle of the Eurymedon, in particular, would have been viewed as another episode in the conflict between East and West. With Cimon's victory there, another "Trojan War" had come to an end.

Comparisons with the earlier heroics at Troy were unavoidable since Cimon's Eurymedon triumph had also occurred in Asia and the magnitude of the victory was unparalleled since the days of Achilles and Agamemnon. Marathon, Salamis, Plataea, Mycale—none could compare, and as at Troy, there was a certain finality about Eurymedon. With the Greeks of Asia Minor freed, the Aegean made a "Greek lake," and the Persians in full retreat, the Greeks may have thought that the years of conflict with Asia were finally over and a new era was beginning.

Cimon, an experienced propagandist who had already exploited his popularity resulting from the recovery of Theseus' bones, styled himself the "new Theseus." He realized the benefits of fostering any parallels between his impressive victory and the one at Troy. He was one of the first politicians to recognize the advantages of surrounding himself with famous artists, poets, and writers for the purpose of utilizing their talents to promote his image and programs.

His circle probably included the poet Pindar, the tragedians Ion of Chios and Melanthius, the philosopher Archelaus, the sculptor Phidias and his brother Panaenus, the genealogist Pherecydes (always handy when a politician might need to reinforce the heroic and divine background of his family!), the artist Micon—and the greatest painter of the day, Polygnotus of Thasos.

Mixing Paint with Politics—Polygnotus the Artist

"Polygnotus of Thasos," remarks the Roman encyclopedist Pliny the Elder, "first painted women in transparent drapery, and represented their heads in multi-colored headdresses." He also:

. . . made many innovations in painting, since it was he who introduced representing the mouth as open, showing the teeth, and varying the face from the rigidity which had existed previously.
(*Natural History* 35.58)

Besides freeing the figures in his paintings from the archaic stiffness of the past, Polygnotus also broke with artistic convention by arranging individuals, or groups of individuals, on different levels, scattering them about at various points in space instead of confining them to a single ground line as had previously been done. Landscape features such as trees and rocks gave an additional feeling of depth. Also, an emotional quality appears to have characterized his work, with figures reacting to what has just happened or what is about to happen. Aristotle goes so far as to assign Polygnotus an almost didactic intent, saying that he purposefully represented men as more virtuous or better than they actually were. Polygnotus was among the first to paint with yellow ochre, but his range of color was probably more extensive than the four colors Cicero assigns to him. Nevertheless, his simplicity of color and lack of shading prompted critics in later centuries to consider him something of a "primitive." His work became so valued that it was frequently restored, and even during the early Roman Empire, the eminent rhetor Quintilian advised that any serious study of painting must begin with Polygnotus.

Innovative, brash, confident in his skills, Polygnotus spent much of his adult life in Athens and was the first known artistic advisor to an Athenian politician—Cimon, whom he recognized as his patron. Undoubtedly, it was Cimon's influence that helped the artist obtain Athenian citizenship, an honor not frequently bestowed on foreigners, but it was Polygnotus' own virtues (or lack of them) that attracted the affections of Cimon's free-spirited sister, Elpinice, who became his lover and model.

It is tempting to speculate that Polygnotus had become a member of Cimon's circle as a result of Cimon's military reduction of Thasos for bolting from the Delian League in 465 B.C. Polygnotus was a Thasian and could have been "persuaded" when the revolt was over to enter Cimon's service. However, it is likely that the association went back much earlier, for it seems certain that Polygnotus, along with fellow artist Micon, decorated the Theseum in Athens, the shrine for the bones of Theseus that Cimon had returned to the city in the mid-470s. There is also evidence to suggest that the relationship began as early as 479 B.C., when Polygnotus was painting in a shrine that was tied to the battle of Marathon, where Cimon's father had been the hero of the day.

The destruction of Athens by the Persians in 479 B.C. had left the city in ruins, but it provided an opportunity for ambitious politicians like Cimon to establish their names as builders as well as generals. Cimon's tenure in office was marked by extensive building and beautification projects, and

Figure 5.10
Vase painting (c. 460 B.C.) by the Niobid Painter in the "Polygnotean" style, perhaps copied from a mural by Polygnotus in the Theseum. (Louvre, Paris)

much of this effort could not have been realized without the spoils of the Eurymedon victory, which must have been impressive. Consequently, a large part of the reconstruction that took place during the 460s B.C. was, indirectly, a monument to Cimon's great victory.

Probably the most distinguished structure that rose out of the rubble in Athens at this time was the Stoa Poikile, or "Painted Stoa," funded by Cimon's brother-in-law, completed about 460 B.C., and, not surprisingly, partially decorated by Polygnotus, who was probably also the artistic supervisor for the building:

> Polygnotus was not just one of the common workmen, and he did not paint the Stoa for a profit, but rather he painted it for free, thus showing his patriotic zeal for the city. . . .
> (Plutarch, *Cimon* 4)

Along with other painters tied to Cimon—Micon and Panaenus, Phidias' brother—Polygnotus created a "Cimonian" picture gallery in the Stoa with paintings whose subjects and themes related, directly or indirectly, to Theseus (Cimon's political figurehead), Cimon himself, or members of Cimon's family. These paintings, which (like most large Greek murals) were not executed directly on the walls but were on wooden frames covered with boards pegged to the walls with iron pins, were still on display in the second century A.D. At that time, Pausanias described the three original works directly related to Cimon:

> . . . On the middle part of the walls Theseus and his Athenians are fighting Amazons [painted by Micon]. . . . Themiscyra fell to Heracles and the fighting force they sent against Athens was wiped out, and yet they still went to Troy and fought there against Athens and the whole of Greece. Next to the Amazons, the Greeks have just taken Troy [painted by Polygnotus] and the princes are meeting over Ajax's crime against Cassandra; the painting shows Ajax and the wives of the prisoners of war with Cassandra among them. The last part of the painting is the men who fought at Marathon [painted by Micon and/or Panaenus]; the Boeotians from Plataea and men from all over Attica are coming to grips with the barbarians: things are about equal. But in the heart of the battle the barbarians are in flight, pushing each other into the marsh, and the painting ends with the Phoenician ships, and with Greeks slaughtering barbarians as they jump into them. The hero Marathon, from whom the level ground got its name, is standing there, with Theseus rising out of the earth, and Athena and Heracles. The people of Marathon reckon to have been the first to believe Heracles was a god. In the picture of the fighting, you can most clearly make out Callimachus, who was chosen to be chief Athenian general, and General Miltiades, and the divine hero Echetlus. . . .
> (*Description of Greece* 1.15.2–4)

The first painting mentioned, Micon's *Amazonomachy* (or *War with the Amazons*), was dominated by the figure of Theseus, who, along with his fellow Athenians, is battling back the legendary women warriors. Since the Amazons came from the East, the painting symbolically represented the struggle between East and West, the West being lead by Theseus. It did not take much to realize that what was actually being commemorated here allegorically was Cimon's (the "new Theseus") recent campaigns against the Persians, the latest menace from the East to threaten Athens and the West.

Figure 5.11   *Reconstruction of the Stoa Poikile*

Figure 5.12   *The excavation site of the Stoa Poikile as it appeared in 1994. The exposed area can be compared with the drawing in Figure 5.11, where the man is standing on the steps at the left end of the structure.*

Polygnotus was responsible for the mural depicting Troy fallen, or the *Iliupersis*. It took little imagination to see how the theme would immediately evoke memories of Cimon's crushing victory over the "East" at the Eurymedon River—another Trojan War brought to a successful conclusion. As if such an allusion were not enough, Polygnotus let little doubt remain when he painted the face of Cimon's sister on one of the most prominent female figures.

Finally, there was the *Battle of Marathon*. The fact that Cimon's father, Miltiades, and his political figurehead, Theseus, were depicted so prominently in the painting left no doubt with whom it was meant to be connected.

Polygnotus was also at work in other buildings associated with Cimon. In the Theseum, the shrine Cimon had constructed for the bones of Theseus, Polygnotus and fellow artist Micon painted murals that glorified the highlights of Theseus' life and reflected indirectly on Cimon. In the Athenian sanctuary of the Dioscuri, who had their center of worship at Sparta, the same two artists painted pro-Lacedaemonian scenes—Polygnotus depicting the marriage of the daughters of Leucippus, an incident from the gods' background. Since Cimon was pro-Lacedaemonian and must have been responsi-

Women Painters—Timarete: A Brush with Fame

WE HAVE SEEN THAT Polygnotus' associate Micon, another of the great artists of the day, also painted murals for the Stoa Poikile and the Theseum; and, it appears, he had a daughter, Timarete, who established her own reputation as a painter. We do not often have an opportunity to read about women working in what most Greeks considered "male-only" occupations, but it is not uncommon to find female members of a family known for a particular craft also becoming actively involved and accepted in those professions (especially if there was no son to carry on the tradition). Timarete was still remembered in the first century A.D. when the Roman encyclopedist Pliny the Elder mentioned her as the earliest of a group of Greco-Roman women artists who were famous down to his day:

> Women, too, have been painters. Timarete, the daughter of Micon, painted a Diana on a panel of the very archaic painting in Ephesus. Irene, daughter and student of Cratinus, painted a girl at Eleusis, a Calypso, the old juggler Theodorus, and the dancer Alcisthenes. Aristarete, daughter and pupil of Nearchus, painted an Asclepius. Iaia of Cyzicus, who never married, worked in Rome during the youth of Marcus Varro [127–116 B.C.]. She used both the painter's brush and, on ivory, the graving tool. She painted women most frequently, including a panel picture of an old woman in Naples, and even a self-portrait for which she used a mirror. No one's hand was quicker to paint a picture than hers; so great was her talent that her prices far exceeded those of the most celebrated painters of her day, Sopolis and Dionysius, whose works fill the galleries. A certain Olympias, too, was a painter. About her we know only that Autobulus was her student.
> (*Natural History* 35.40)

Figure 5.13
This vase painting of Theseus and the Amazons may have been inspired by Polygnotus' work in the Theseum. It is attributed to a member of Polygnotus' group, Athens, c. 440 B.C. (British Museum)

ble for restoring the shrine after its destruction in 479 B.C., both the shrine and the paintings in it complimented Cimon's political policies.

Polygnotus' greatest works while still connected with Cimon were not in Athens but at Delphi in the Cnidian Lesche, or "Clubhouse," which was dedicated to Apollo by the people of Cnidus, a Greek city in Asia Minor. In that structure, completed shortly after the battle at the Eurymedon, Polygnotus painted what would become the most famous murals in antiquity—the *Iliupersis* (or *Troy Fallen,* a much larger version of the painting with the same name in the Stoa Poikile) and the *Nekyia* (or *Odysseus' Visit to the Underworld*).

The paintings were gigantic by contemporary standards—as may be surmised by the Lesche's 55-by-25-foot interior measurements—and their dozens of figures were arranged on at least three different levels on a surface perhaps 15 feet high. The figures approached but were somewhat less than life-size. Their themes, like the themes of most, if not all, of Polygnotus' paintings in Athens, related directly to Cimon—in this case, to the battle of the Eurymedon.

The Cnidians were members of the Delian League, and Cimon led the forces of the League at the Eurymedon. Also, it had been from the Cnidian harbors that Cimon had departed for the great battle. The Cnidians were strong devotees of Apollo, having their own important local center of worship, as well as close ties with the Delphic Apollo. Consequently, when Cimon's victory ensured their freedom from further Persian domination (they

Figure 5.14
A restoration of the precinct of Apollo at Delphi. The building with the skylight in the upper right corner of the precinct is the Cnidian Lesche (or "Clubhouse"), where Polygnotus' famous paintings of Troy Fallen (Iliupersis) *and of Odysseus' visit to the Underworld* (Nekyia) *were displayed. The large building is the Temple of Apollo, where the god's oracle was located (see Chapter 3).*

had, in the past, been subjects of the Persians), it is not difficult to understand why they would feel compelled to dedicate a great offering to Apollo at Delphi. Because Cimon had indirectly been Apollo's agent in guaranteeing Cnidian freedom, it is also easy to understand why the paintings they commissioned to be placed in their shrine would reflect favorably on him.

Besides being the "friend" and commander of the Cnidians, Cimon was also very influential at Delphi; two monuments there celebrated his family, Athens, and the Delian League. A close study of the individual mythological figures in the Cnidian Lesche's paintings reflect a solid pro-Cimonian,

Figure 5.15
Site of the Cnidian
Lesche at Delphi.
The building that
housed Polygnotus'
greatest paintings, the
Iliupersis *and* Nekyia,
was 55 feet long and
was located just in
front of the irregular
stone precinct wall
in the middle of the
photo.

pro-Thesean sentiment, which was not accidental; and Polygnotus, the artist who painted the *Iliupersis* and the *Nekyia,* was the personal friend of Cimon and had performed similar tasks for him in several buildings in Athens. Thus, the conclusion seems inescapable that, although the Lesche and its paintings may have been a thank-offering to Apollo by the Cnidians, it was also another of the many monuments that celebrated Cimon's conclusion of the wars with Persia—the final event being the great victory at the Eurymedon River.

The second-century A.D. traveler Pausanias also visited Delphi and described Polygnotus' paintings in the Lesche, although his account is much too detailed to reproduce here. A summary of his description of the *Iliupersis,* the more famous of the two works, suffices to give an impression of the character of both murals:

> As you go into the building all the right of the painting is the fall of Troy and the Greeks sailing away. Menelaus' men are getting ready for the voyage; there is a painting of the ship, with a mixture of men and boys among the sailors,

and the ship's steersman Phrontis standing amidships holding two poles. . . . Helen herself is sitting with Eurybates near her. I imagine this is Odysseus' herald, anyway he was still beardless. The servants Electra and Panthalis tie Helen's shoe and stand beside her. . . . After Helen comes Theseus' mother Aethra with close-cropped hair and Demophon, one of Theseus' children, who seems to be wondering whether he can possibly rescue Aethra. . . . In the painting the Trojan women are lamenting as prisoners. . . . Epeius is painted stripped, breaking down the foundations of the wall of Troy. Just the head of the Wooden Horse sticks out above him. Polypoetes son of Peirithous has tied a ribbon round his head, and Acamas son of Theseus stands beside him in a crested helmet. Odysseus is there, wearing a breastplate; Ajax son of Oileus is standing at the altar, holding a shield, taking his oath over the outrage on Cassandra, who is sitting there on the ground holding a statue of Athena; she must have pulled the wooden idol from its pedestal when Ajax dragged her away from the sanctuary. The sons of Atreus are painted in helmets too; Menelaus has a shield with a snake on it, alluding to the prodigy at the sacrifice in Aulis. Below them Ajax is being sworn; directly in line with the horse beside Nestor, Neoptolemus has just killed Elasus. . . . He is painted like a dying man just still breathing. Neoptolemus is striking with a sword at Astynous, who has fallen on one knee. . . . There is an altar in the painting with a frightened little boy holding onto it; a bronze breastplate is lying on the altar. . . . He has painted Laodice standing beyond the altar. . . . After Laodice comes a stone pedestal with a bronze basin on it; Medusa is sitting on the base holding onto the pedestal with both hands. . . . Among the corpses the naked man called Pelis lies flung on his back. . . . There are others higher up . . . and Coroebus. . . . Up above Coroebus are Priam and Axion and Agenor. . . . Sinon, the companion of Odysseus, and Anchialus are carrying away the corpse of Laomedon. . . . Antenor's house is here with a leopard skin hanging over the entrance, as a signal to the Greeks to leave Antenor's house alone. . . . At this point in the painting come Simonides' verses:

> Polygnotus son of Aglaophon
> of the island of Thasos has painted
> the plunder of the fortress of Troy.

(*Description of Greece* 10.25–27)

Polygnotus' great murals were an immediate success, indicated by the fact that he was voted free food and lodging for life by the "common council of Greece," which can only mean the Amphictyonic Council associated with Delphi. It becomes clear, then, why he would later paint the Stoa Poikile in Athens without charge, although he also would have had financial support from Cimon and may have been independently wealthy himself. (Polygnotus came from a family of prominent artists on Thasos and seems to have been politically active there, perhaps even connected to Archilochus, whose grandfather, Tellis, he represented in the *Nekyia*.)

Figure 5.16
Polygnotus' friend and patron, Cimon, was ostracized from Athens in 461 B.C. The Athenians voted to exile someone they considered dangerous to their democracy by writing his name on pieces of broken pottery (ostraka). If enough citizens wrote the name of the same man, he was exiled for ten years. "Cimon, son of Miltiades" is clearly inscribed on the pottery sherd on the lower left. The name of Themistocles, another of Athens' great heroes, appears on the upper right-hand piece. He, too, was exiled. Apparently, it did not pay to be too successful in Athens.

Polygnotus' later life remains unclear. It cannot be assumed that he left Athens when his patron Cimon fell from favor and was ostracized in 461 B.C., just as it cannot be assumed that Athenian politicians did not tolerate artists who were formerly associated with political enemies. The famous sculptor Phidias, for example, worked on Cimonian projects (as did his brother) before becoming closely aligned with Pericles, the man who helped engineer Cimon's exile and succeeded him politically. Ion of Chios, also one of Cimon's circle, was even hostile toward Pericles, and yet he continued to produce tragedies in Athens. Nothing indicates specifically that a change in political climate caused any decline in Polygnotus' fortunes—he was, after all, an Athenian citizen, made so as a result of his artistic achievements. In fact, there were Polygnotean paintings displayed in a building on the Acropolis that was built by Pericles. They may have been collected from other places and deposited there, but they also could have been painted by Polygnotus while Pericles ruled. If the latter is correct, then Polygnotus spent at least some of his senior years in the city, living through and contributing to the "Golden Age" of Periclean Athens.

Suggestions for Further Reading

The major ancient source for Polygnotus' paintings is Pausanias, Books 1 and 10 of *Description of Greece*. Other information about Polygnotus can be found in Plutarch's *Cimon* and Pliny's *Natural History*. A sourcebook such as J. J. Pollitt's *The Art of Greece 1400–31 B.C.* (Cambridge: Cambridge University Press, 1990) may be the best starting place. M. Robertson's *A History of Greek Art*, Vol. 1 (Cambridge:

Figure 5.17
The Propylaea, or
"front gate," to the
Acropolis in Athens
(see Figure 6.8).
The left wing of the
Propylaea (background)
displayed paintings by
Polygnotus.

Cambridge University Press, 1975) is an excellent survey on the art of Polygnotus. For the political implications of Polygnotus' paintings and his relations with Cimon, see R. B. Kebric's *The Paintings in the Cnidian Lesche at Delphi and Their Historical Context* (Leiden: E. J. Brill, 1983). Generally, see C. L. Lawton, *Attic Document Reliefs: Art and Politics in Ancient Athens* (New York: Oxford University Press, 1995); Wm. Blake Tyrrell, *Amazons: A Study in Athenian Mythology* (Baltimore: The Johns Hopkins University Press, 1989); and Tyrrell and F. S. Brown, *Athenian Myths and Institutions* (New York: Oxford University Press, 1991). J. M. Hurwit's survey *The Art and Culture of Early Greece 1100–480 B.C.* (Ithaca, N.Y.: Cornell University Press, 1985) is useful for this and previous chapters. Herodotus is the major ancient source for the Persian Wars of 490 and 480– 479 B.C. A more recent translation is by R. Waterfield, published by Oxford University Press (New York, 1998) with bibliography. Thucydides covers the period after 479 B.C.; Plutarch's lives of *Themistocles, Aristides,* and *Cimon,* and Diodorus, Book 11, are the other chief sources. Useful works on the Persian Empire and Persian relations with the Greeks are J. M. Cook's *The Persian Empire* (New York: Schocken Books, 1983); P. Green's *The Greco-*

Figure 5.18
Polygnotus could never have foreseen how far Greek painting would have progressed by the Hellenistic period, as this wildly decorative ceiling mural from a Macedonian tomb at Lefkadhia demonstrates.

Persian Wars (Berkeley and Los Angeles: University of California Press, 1998 edition); C. Hignett's *Xerxes' Invasion of Greece* (Oxford: Oxford University Press, 1963), and A. R. Burn's *Persia and the Greeks* (New York: St. Martin's Press, 1962). On the Athenian Empire, see R. Meiggs, *The Athenian Empire* (Oxford: Oxford University Press, 1972), and M. F. McGregor, *The Athenians and Their Empire* (Vancouver: University of British Columbia Press, 1987).

Other works pertinent to this chapter include H. J. Walker, *Theseus and Athens* (New York: Oxford University Press, 1995); J. Morrison and R. T. Williams, *Greek Oared Ships 900–322 B.C.* (Oxbow, 1995; reprint of the 1968 Cambridge University Press edition); Morrison and J. Coates, *Greek and Roman Oared Warships 399–30 B.C.* (Oxford: Oxbow Books, 1995); and V. Gabrielson, *Financing the Athenian Fleet* (Baltimore: The Johns Hopkins University Press, 1994).

Figure 5.19
Herodotus, the historian of the Persian Wars (left), and Thucydides, the historian of the Peloponnesian War (right). The busts of Greece's two greatest "historical minds" were joined at a later date.

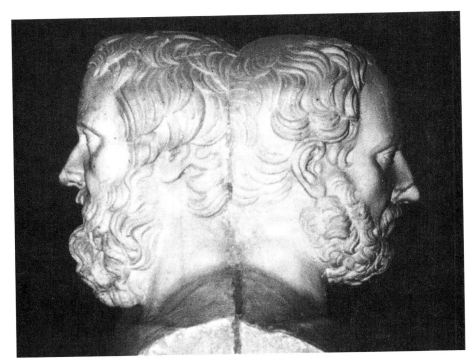

6

A Gilded Edge
for a Golden Age

Aspasia the Courtesan in Periclean Athens

*. . . our city is worthy of admiration. For we love beauty
without exaggerating its value, and we love knowledge
without becoming soft and effeminate.*
(Pericles' "Funeral Speech," Thucydides 2.40.1)

The wars with Persia had left Athens as the greatest sea power in Greece, and
Sparta continued as the dominant land power. Politically and philosophically,
the two cities were as diametrically opposed as any two entities could be. Although forced into cooperation during the Persian invasion and sometimes
sharing a mutual admiration for each other, they were frequently at odds.

By the beginning of Pericles' administration in 461 B.C., Athens' Aegean
Empire was reaching maturity, and the city's democratic system of government, not yet a half-century old, was about to enjoy the period of its fullest
expression. Fashioned in 508 B.C. by the reforms of Cleisthenes, a member
of the prominent Alcmeonid family, democracy was bred out of the civil
chaos following the expulsion of the tyrant Hippias (see Chapter 4). The last
obstacles to popular rule were removed, and the kin-based, faction-ridden
politics of the past supposedly gave way to a "one-man, one-vote" system in
which the good of society took precedence over any special interest groups.
In the "Funeral Speech" attributed to him by the historian Thucydides and
delivered in 430 B.C. (a year before his death), Pericles, a member of the same
illustrious family as Cleisthenes, would boast of democracy's merits:

Figure 6.1

The Ceramicus, or "potters' district," of Athens, where the Athenian cemetery was located (directly behind where this photo was taken) and where Pericles gave his famous "Funeral Speech." The dead could not be laid to rest within the city, and consequently, the cemetery was located outside the city walls, the foundations of which run across the center of the photo. The remains of the Sacred Gate (middle) and the Dipylon Gate, the main gate of Athens (upper middle, left), can still be seen.

Ours is a constitution which has no rival; it is a paradigm, not a copy. Our government is called a democracy because it exists for the sake of the majority and not for the few. The law guarantees that all citizens are equal with respect to their private interests, and yet claims of individual excellence are also recognized, so that when a citizen distinguishes himself in some way he is chosen for public office because of his merit, and not on the basis of his social status. Poverty is no obstacle to a man of humble origin if he can somehow benefit the city. We are free men, and we manage our public affairs as such. We are not suspicious of each other as we go about our daily business. We are not angry with our neighbor for doing what pleases him, nor do we give him looks of annoyance which, though harmless, are still irritating. While we are relaxed in private society, we are most careful not to transgress the law. We respect those who hold public office and the laws, and especially those which have been promulgated for the benefit of the injured and the unwritten laws which everyone agrees it is shameful to violate. (2.37)

Although Athens may have been in appearance and form a democracy in the ancient sense of the word, in reality, aristocrats like Pericles continued to manipulate the government. Wealth, prestige, and oratorical abilities were still the keys to political success, and few outside the traditional leading families possessed all three. A clever speech in the assembly could easily sway unknowledgeable voters, and despite glowing reports from admiring

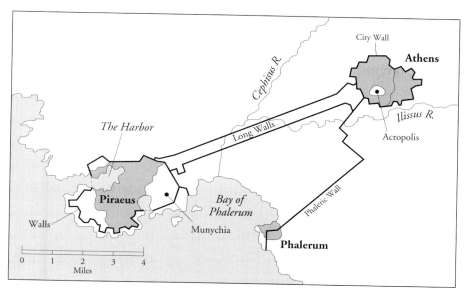

Map 15
Athens, the Piraeus, and environs

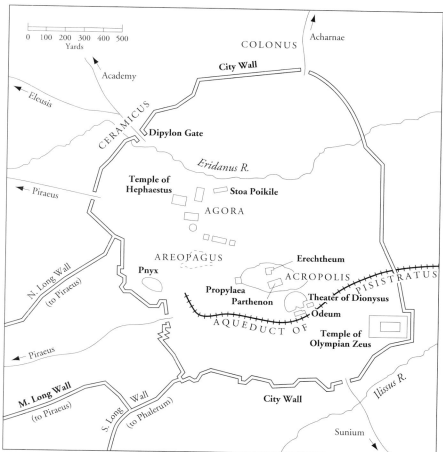

Map 16
The city of Athens

Map 17
Athenian Agora,
c. 400 B.C.: The
Athenian marketplace
and civic center close
to the time of Pericles
(see Map 10 for
comparison)

Figure 6.2
The restored west side of
the Agora, c. 400 B.C.,
the "nerve center" of the
Athenian democracy. In
these buildings, which
housed important
magistrates, the "senate,"
and archives, much of the
business of government in
Athens took place. They
are (left to right) the
Tholos, the Metroon and
old Bouleuterion, the new
Bouleuterion (behind),
the seats of "the meeting
place," the Stoa of Zeus,
and the Royal Stoa. The
Temple of Hephaestus is
above.

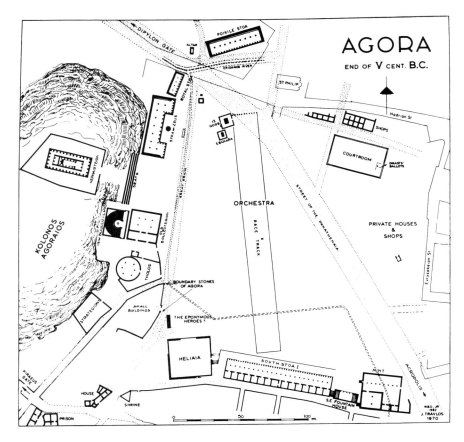

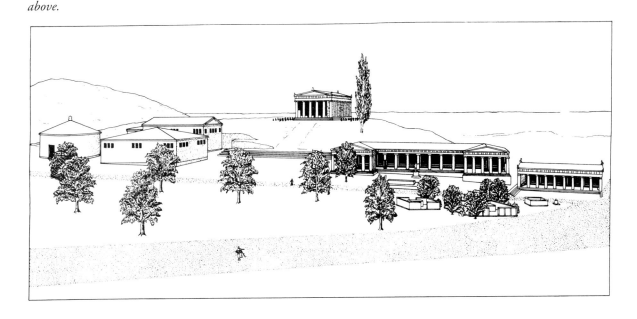

The Handicapped in Athens—A Cripple Defends His Stipend

PEOPLE WHO ARE HANDICAPPED have always had difficulty in any age, but the ancient world was particularly severe. Many would not have survived infancy, since child exposure was widely practiced and misshapen or mean-looking children were especially susceptible. Although maladies such as blindness were thought by some to be divinely inspired, most handicapped persons who lived to maturity were constantly reminded of their imperfections by the way in which society viewed them. Among the Greeks, it was not uncommon to equate ill luck with the deformed. Many, for example, would have seen the decline of Sparta in the fourth century B.C. as the direct result of its being ruled by a lame king, Agesilaus.

The gods, too, demeaned the misshapen. Hephaestus, the smith of the gods and an Olympian, was the object of ridicule and the butt of many cruel jokes because he was lame. The Greeks obviously meant for him to provide comic relief for the members of their pantheon. The humor of his defect was intensified by the fact that he, the ugliest of gods, was married to the most beautiful, Aphrodite, who was constantly cuckolding her husband. During the Hellenistic period, sculptors sought out the crippled and deformed as models in an age when realism in art was pushed to the extreme, and the grotesque became a novelty. Even people who had incurred their handicap as a result of war or an accident could suffer. A man with one eye, for instance, might be regarded as something quite evil, and the curse of the "evil eye" remains a potent force in some parts of Greece even today.

The pages of ancient history are full of the names of prominent people who had to cope with handicaps, some more successfully than others. The Roman emperor Claudius, probably the most powerful handicapped person who has ever lived, appears to have suffered neurological problems—stumbling frequently, slobbering and stammering when under stress, unable to keep his head still because of a nervous twitch. Caesar and Caligula were said to have suffered from epilepsy; Hannibal lost an eye while campaigning in Italy; Philip of Macedonia not only had an eye blinded but was also crippled in an arm and a leg. The orator Demosthenes stammered in his youth; Alcibiades had a lisp. The emperor Vitellius was lame. Philip Arrhidaeus, the half-brother of Alexander, may have been mentally retarded. There are many more examples.

Seldom, however, do we get an insight into the lot of the common handicapped person in ancient society. While we know that Pericles provided something of a welfare program for the old and the poor in Athens by paying them a small stipend for jury duty, it is clear that the state also provided a special assistance program for the handicapped. A specific example exists (Lysias, *Oration* 24) from the end of the fifth century that demonstrates some governmental support (1 obol [or $16.67 based on a modern daily wage of $100.00]) for the disabled. A cripple has been accused by someone, who has obviously taken a dislike to him, of accepting a stipend from the state when, it is charged, he is quite capable of earning a living on his own. The man, who apparently has been receiving his pension for most of his life, naturally denies that he can live without state assistance and defends his right before the Athenian Council to receive it. From his response, we can conclude that the state acted swiftly against bogus claimants, that citizens of Athens would report fakers, and that one's character was a consideration in determining whether aid was offered:

> My father left me nothing, and it is now just over two years since I ceased to maintain my mother, on her death. I have, so far, no children who will look after me. As for my work, I

(continued)

The Handicapped in Athens—A Cripple Defends His Stipend (continued)

have a skilled trade, but it is of little help, seeing that I myself can now practice it only with difficulty, and that so far I am not able to get hold of a man who will take it over for me. I have no other source of income than this pension; and if you deprive me of it, I shall in all probability be reduced to the direst straits. . . . You granted me my pension when I was younger and stronger; do not take it away now that I am older and feebler! You have always before now had a reputation for extreme compassion even towards those who are not in any distress. . . . Do not, by hardening your hearts to do me a wrong, inflict despondency on all who are in the same position as I am!

It certainly would be an anomaly, gentlemen: when my affliction was single, it is seen that I was receiving this money; but now, when old age, sickness and all the ills that come in their train are added to me, my pension is to be taken away! . . . As for my riding on horseback . . . I can deal with that quite briefly. I imagine . . . that all those who have any afflic-

tion like mine seek for some alleviation, and study how to deal with their misfortune in such a way as to make it least painful to them. I am one of these. Since it is my lot to be thus afflicted, I have discovered in riding a means of alleviating the discomforts of my longer journeys. The greatest proof . . . that it is because of my ailment and not through disrespect that I ride on horseback, is easy to convey to you: if I possessed wealth, I should ride on a saddle mule—I should not be mounting borrowed nags.

The man goes on to indicate that his handicap is so severe that he needs two crutches, whereas others only use one. He asks why, if he is so physically fit that his pension can be canceled, he would still be debarred from running for public office because he is physically disabled (obviously, then, the handicapped could not hold office in Athens). He then must refute charges that he is violent, insolent, and licentious:

I imagine, gentlemen, you are bound to distinguish between persons for whom it is possible to behave with arrogance, and those for whom it is impossible. Arrogant behavior is certainly not *probable* in those who are poor and in greatly straitened circumstances, but rather in those whose possessions far exceed their needs. Nor is it possible in those who are physically disabled, but in those who have complete confidence in their strength; nor in those who are already advanced in years, but in those who are still young and who have equally youthful minds. The rich can use their wealth to buy off any danger that threatens them; the poor are compelled by their ever-present necessity to exercise moderation. The young expect to be excused by their elders; but the latter when they commit an offense meet with reprobation alike from young and

Figure 6.3   A miniature representation of women at work in a bakery, Thebes, 525–475 B.C. (Louvre, Paris). Sights such as this would have been common in the daily working life of Athens and other Greek cities.

old. The strong have it in their power, even when they themselves are in no way ill-treated, to browbeat whomever they wish; the delicate are unable to defend themselves against the aggressor when they are ill-treated, or, if they wish to inflict injury, to get the better of their victim.

The crippled man must also deal with accusations about his bad character. It is said that his shop is frequented by undesirables:

> Every one of you is in the habit of visiting, say, the perfumier, or the barber, or the cobbler, and so on. The greatest number go to those who have set up shop nearest the market-place, and the least to those who are farthest away from it. So that if any of you means to condemn the character of those who visit me, obviously he will equally be condemning those who spend time in other establishments. If he does this, then he is condemning the whole of Athens—for all of you are accustomed to call on tradespeople and pass your time somewhere or other.
>
> However, I see no reason why I should trouble you at any greater length by a too-detailed defense. . . . I implore you, gentlemen, retain towards me the same attitude as of old: do not deprive me of the only share in my country which fate has granted me. . . . It was because, gentlemen, Providence had denied us a share in the great public offices that the State decreed us this money, thinking that all fortune, good or bad, is to be shared in common by the community as a whole. Surely, then, my lot would be wretched indeed if, while disbarred by my affliction from any share in the greatest and most splendid activities, I were further to be stripped . . . of that which the State granted expressly with a view to compensating those who are in this position. . . .

After presenting himself as a defender of democracy and one who risked his life in the chaotic civil strife that followed the conclusion of the Peloponnesian War, the man concludes:

> Do not, therefore . . . when I have done no wrong, mete out to me the same treatment that you do to those who are loaded with crimes! Pass on me the same verdict as you did at all your other sessions, bearing in mind that I am not here as an administrator of public funds, to render account of my office; nor as the holder of any magistracy, to submit to an examination of my tenure. No, I am here to defend my pittance merely. Thus, gentlemen, you will all show your recognition of justice. I, in return for your bounty, shall be filled with gratitude. . . .

Figure 6.4
A Greek barber and his client (Indiana University Museum of Art)

scholars of past centuries, Athenian peasant farmers were in no rush to exercise their new-found franchise. Apathy is an unavoidable by-product of a free political system, and it existed in ancient Athens as it does today.

Pericles ensured that citizens would complete the governmental tasks assigned or voted to them by offering pay for most positions, a practice for which he was criticized. But Pericles was a practical man. Attendance at the assembly was considered a citizen's responsibility—and it was unpaid. The assembly was often dismissed for lack of a quorum. Slaves even had to be assigned to strike the backs of unconcerned citizens heading away from the assembly with a chalk-covered or painted rope, an embarrassing indication that they were shirking their responsibilities.

Despite its shortcomings, Athenian society was as open as any has ever been—perhaps more open if the outrageous remarks made by comic playwrights about contemporary figures are any indication. In addition, the fact that about two-thirds of the male population had some function in the city's government, paid or not, is truly remarkable and probably unparalleled. The same situation could not be said to exist at rival Sparta.

Sparta had developed along completely different lines from Athens and, with a minor exception or two, from all other Greek states. Located in the southern part of the Peloponnesus in the district known as Laconia, Sparta became a militaristic state with totalitarian tendencies primarily out of the need to keep a large, restive slave population in check. These slaves, or serfs, were called *helots*. They were largely the former citizenry of Messenia, an area to the west of Laconia that Sparta had earlier conquered and added to its territory.

The Spartans were reminded almost constantly of the explosive situation they had created by enslaving a native population on its own land, especially when that population greatly outnumbered them. Helot revolts, which were actually lengthy wars in some cases, pressed the Spartans sorely, and by the end of the seventh century B.C., their unorthodox military system was probably in place. Its totalitarian character also conveniently imposed "equality" on its citizenry and solved the particular social and economic problems that had been disturbing Sparta. This system was an easy one (as are all totalitarian states) for the great Spartan families, not always in conformity with the "robotic character" of the community, to manipulate.

Pericles, in the same funeral speech quoted previously, compared the Spartan system unfavorably with what he found so praiseworthy in the Athenian:

> Ours is a city open to all people. We never resort to the expulsion of foreigners or keep anyone from learning or seeing anything which might help our enemies if not kept secret. For we place our trust primarily in courageous

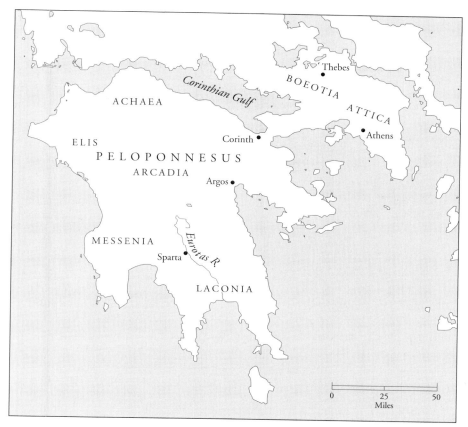

Map 18
*The Peloponnesus.
Sparta is located in the
southern part, along
the Eurotas River.*

Figure 6.5
*Ancient Sparta. The
remains of the later
large theater (c. first
century B.C.) lie below
the tree-covered heights
that were once the
Spartan acropolis.*

Spartan Wives—Sex and the State

ACCORDING TO TRADITION, IT was the legendary lawgiver, Lycurgus, who reformed Sparta and turned it into a totalitarian, militaristic state. We really do not know who this Lycurgus was, and it is doubtful that such a person was actually responsible for the unusual system that evolved at Sparta. Nevertheless, a Spartan citizen of classical times would never have questioned the belief that Lycurgus *had* given Sparta its *Eunomia,* or well-ordered laws.

Among the many practices Lycurgus supposedly instituted at Sparta, one of the more interesting related to the preparations of young girls for marriage and what might be expected of them after they became wives. Because they would produce the future Spartans, women at Sparta were much better treated than they were elsewhere in Greece, but they also experienced much that females in other Greek cities probably would have considered intolerable. If Plutarch is to be believed, the following account in his life of *Lycurgus* (14–16) was the typical situation. It should be explained beforehand that the Spartans apparently engaged in eugenic breeding as a means, in the state's view, to ensure a "quality" population. They also attempted to make the bride appear "boylike" on her wedding night, presumably to help the husband make the sexual transition from a male (see Chapter 4 on bisexuality) to a female partner more easily. Plutarch's statement that Spartan women were in "full bloom and ripeness" when they married might be misconstrued using today's standards. It is unlikely they were much older than the fourteen-year-old Athenian wife whom Xenophon, an admirer of Sparta, mentioned was still learning her household responsibilities (see p. 168). Finally, wives (and children) apparently did not live with their husbands until the latter received their allotment of land from the government when they were thirty years old.

Like everything else in a totalitarian society, marriage for women at Sparta seems to have been regarded mostly as another way of serving the state:

> [Lycurgus] ordered the maidens to exercise themselves with wrestling, running, throwing the quoit, and casting the dart, to the end that the fruit they conceived might, in strong and healthy bodies, take firmer root and find better growth, and withal that they, with this greater vigor, might be the more able to undergo the pains of childbearing. And to the end he might take away their overgreat tenderness and fear of exposure to the air, and all acquired womanishness, he ordered that the young women should go naked in the processions, as well as the young men, and dance, too, in that condition, at certain solemn feasts, singing certain songs, whilst the young men stood around, seeing and hearing them. . . . Nor was there anything shameful in this nakedness of the young women; modesty attended them, and all wantonness was excluded. It taught them simplicity and care for good health, and gave them some taste of higher feelings, admitted as they thus were to the field of noble action and glory. Hence it was natural for them to think and speak as Gorgo, for example, the wife of Leonidas, is said to have done, when some foreign lady, as it would seem, told her that the women of Lacedaemon were the only women in the world who could rule men. "With good reason," she said, "for we are the only women who bring forth men." [See also p. 129.]

These public processions of the maidens, and their appearing naked in their exercises and dancings, were incitements to marriage, operating upon the young with the rigor and certainty, as Plato says, of love, if not of mathematics. . . .

In their marriages, the husband carried off his bride by a sort of force; nor were their brides ever small and of tender years, but in their full bloom and ripeness. After this, she who superintended the wedding comes and clips the hair of the bride close around her head, dresses her up in man's clothes, and leaves her upon a mattress in the dark; afterwards comes the bridegroom, in his everyday clothes, sober and composed, as having supped at the common table, and, entering privately into the room where the bride lies, unties her virgin zone, and takes her to himself; and, after staying some time together, he returns composedly to his own apartment, to sleep as usual with the other young men. And so he continues to do, spending his days, and, indeed, his nights, with them, visiting his bride in fear and shame, and with circumspection, when he thought he should not be observed; she, also, on her part, using her wit to help and find favorable opportunities for their meeting, when company was out of the way. In this manner they lived a long time, insomuch that they sometimes had children by their wives before ever they saw their faces by daylight. Their interviews, being thus difficult and rare, served not only for continual exercise of their self-control, but brought them together with their bodies healthy and vigorous, and their affections fresh and lively, unsated and undulled by easy access and long continuance with each other; while their partings were always early enough to leave behind unextinguished in each of them some remaining fire of longing and mutual delight. After guarding marriage with this modesty and reserve, [Lycurgus] was equally careful to banish empty and womanish jealousy. For this object, excluding all licentious disorders, he made it, nevertheless, honorable for men to give the use of their wives to those whom they should think fit, that so they might have children by them. . . . Lycurgus allowed a man who was advanced in years and had a young wife to recommend some virtuous and approved young man, that she might have a child by him, who might inherit the good qualities of the father, and be a son to himself. On the other side, an honest man who had love for a married woman upon account of her modesty and the well-favoredness of her children, might, without formality, beg her company of her husband, that he might raise, as it were, from this plot of good ground, worthy and well-allied children for himself. And indeed, Lycurgus was of a persuasion that children were not so much the property of their parents as of the whole commonwealth, and, therefore, would not have his citizens begot by the first-comers, but by the best men that could be found; the laws of other nations seemed to him very absurd and inconsistent, where people would be so solicitous for their dogs and horses as to exert interest and to pay money to procure fine breeding, and yet kept their wives shut up, to be made mothers only by themselves, who might be foolish, infirm, or diseased; as if it were not apparent that children of a bad breed would prove their bad qualities first upon those who kept and were rearing them, and well-born children, in like manner, their good qualities. These regulations, founded on natural and social grounds, were certainly so far from that scandalous liberty which was afterwards charged upon their women, that they knew not what adultery meant. . . .

Figure 6.6
A Spartan warrior

action, not in secret plans and deceptions. As far as education is concerned, our enemies seek to make themselves brave by vigorous training begun in early youth; but, even though our lifestyle is an easygoing one, we are just as prepared as they are to meet dangers. This proved by the fact that the Lacedaemonians do not invade our territory by themselves, for they bring all their allies with them. We, on the other hand, attack a neighbor's country without help, and we usually prevail without much difficulty even though we are fighting on foreign soil and against men who are defending their homes. They have not yet experienced the fullness of our strength because we must give our attention to the navy and, at the same time, send out our own citizens on land expeditions. And yet, if they attack some small part of our army and win, they boast that they have routed us all; but when they are defeated they say that it was our entire army that worsted them. Indeed, we are better off because we have chosen to meet danger in a relaxed fashion and without severe training, and with a bravery which is inspired by our way of life and not by laws; for we are not distressed beforehand at the prospect of pain, and yet when the time comes we prove that we are just as courageous as those who are always undergoing strenuous training.
(Thucydides 2.39)

When Pericles made his comparison between Athens and Sparta, the inevitable had already taken place. Always quarreling with each other, always suspicious and looking after their own interests, Athens and Sparta had finally gone to war, and the control of Hellas was at stake. While professing the role of defender of liberty and democracy, Pericles had, in reality, been unerringly guiding Athens' imperialistic fortunes, stepping on the toes of Sparta, its allies, Persia, and whoever else got in the way. He increased the influence and power of the Empire wherever he could. His luck finally ran out, however, when the conservative Spartans, goaded by their worried allies and fearful of eventually being cut off and overwhelmed, answered Pericles' designs with a war cry.

The Peloponnesian War, as it is called, lasted from 431 to 404 B.C. It was the most destructive war in Greek history, and the Greeks would never recover from its effects, suffering a politically disastrous fourth century and eventual conquest by Philip of Macedonia in 338 B.C. Before that happened, however, Greek society enjoyed its greatest period of prosperity, and Athens, more than any other city, was the center of the cultural and intellectual activity that distinguished the mid–fifth century B.C. For this reason, the rule of Pericles is usually referred to as the "Golden Age."

The Golden Age of Athens

Whereas the Peloponnesian War was still a number of years in the future, the military situation in Greece stabilized after a half-century of almost constant warfare. First, the Persians, scarred by decades of unsuccessful war with the Greeks, made peace in 449 B.C. Then, Athens and Sparta ended their on-again, off-again hostilities in 445 B.C. Funds that had previously been earmarked for the Athenian war chest could now be used to complete the rebuilding and beautification of the city. Tribute from the Athenian Empire was funneled, not without objections (Pericles' moving of the Delian League treasury from Delos to Athens in the late 450s to protect it, ostensibly, from Persian threats had already produced howls of protest), into Pericles' building and artistic programs. In his life of *Pericles,* Plutarch gives a glowing report on the scale of the ambitious general's plans for Athens:

> . . . he brought forth and proposed to the people great building projects and far-reaching artistic programs requiring an extended application of labor, so that, no less than those who were in the fleet or guarded the borders, or took part in military expeditions, the population at home would have a claim to derive benefit from and have a share in the public funds. For this undertaking the materials used were stone, bronze, ivory, ebony, and cypress-wood, and the artists who labored on them and wrought works of art were builders, modellers, bronze-workers, stone-cutters, dyers, workers in gold and ivory, painters, embroiderers, and engravers; and those concerned with the organization and transport of the materials were, on the sea, the merchants, sailors, and ships' pilots, and, on land, the wagon-makers, those who bred draught animals, wagon

drivers, rope makers, linen-weavers, road workers, and miners. Thus each art, just as each general has his own army under him, had its own private throng of laborers organized like an army, acting as an instrument and body of public service; so, to sum the whole thing up, briefly, the opportunities for service reached every age and type, and they distributed the wealth accordingly. (12.5–7)

Assisting Pericles as his artistic supervisor was his friend and confidant, Phidias, the greatest of all Greek monumental sculptors and probably the most celebrated artist active in Athens during the Golden Age. Foremost among Pericles' architects were Ictinus and Callicrates, whose most famous creation, the Parthenon, became the crowning jewel of their patron's building program. High atop the Acropolis (the rock plateau, now sacred ground, on which Athens had begun), the Parthenon was designed to be the largest temple of its style on the Greek peninsula. Begun in 447 B.C., it was basically complete when dedicated in 438 B.C.; Phidias and his artisans had only to complete the decoration.

The Parthenon was a temple for Athena, the city's patron deity, and a symbol of Athens' democracy, wealth, and, of course, piety. It was also a war

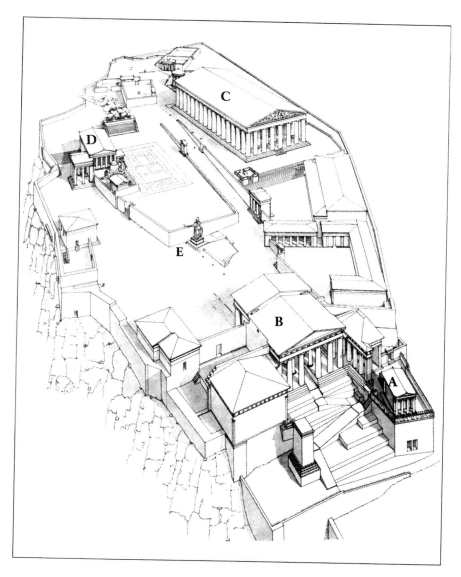

Figure 6.8
Reconstruction of the Acropolis in Athens. Important buildings were as follows: (A) the Temple of Nike, (B) the Propylaea, (C) the Parthenon, and (D) the Erechtheum. Phidias' statue of Athena Promachos (E) is also represented.

memorial, built with funds from the old Delian League, and, like a phoenix rising from the ashes, it signaled the final rebirth of Athens out of the flames of 479 B.C. Its artwork recalled mythical themes relating to Athena and Athens and, like Polygnotus' paintings (see Chapter 5), had meanings that could be related to both past and present events.

Phidias fashioned the impressive gold and ivory cult statue that towered almost 40 feet inside the Parthenon's shadowy interior. With the exception of the great gold and ivory seated statue of Zeus at Olympia that was later included among the Seven Wonders of the Ancient World, the Athena

Figure 6.9
The Parthenon, jewel of Pericles' building program in Athens. Callicrates and Ictinus were the architects. Phidias, Pericles' friend, lent his artistic expertise, and he had a hand in fashioning the sculptures that adorned the Parthenon. Phidias also constructed the impressive cult statue of Athena that stood inside the building.

Parthenos was his most impressive work. One ancient account describes it as follows:

> In the temple which they call the *Parthenon* . . . the cult image itself is made of ivory and gold. In the middle of her helmet there is placed an image of a sphinx, and on each side of the helmet griffins are represented . . . griffins are beasts which look like lions but have the wings and beak of an eagle. . . . The statue of Athena stands upright and wears a tunic which reaches to the feet and on her breast the head of Medusa, made of ivory, is represented. In one hand she holds a figure of Victory about [8 feet] high and in the other she holds a spear; at her feet is placed a shield, and near the shield is a serpent. . . . On the base the birth of Pandora is represented in relief.
> (Pausanias 1.24.5–7)

Previously, Phidias had raised on the Acropolis a bronze statue of Athena Promachos that was 30 feet tall. Her helmet, shield, and spear evoked memories of the battle of Marathon, spoils from which had financed her creation. The story goes that the sun's reflection off the top of the statue could be seen by sailors at sea some miles away.

As a friend of Pericles, Phidias was vulnerable to attack from his patron's political enemies. A frontal assault on the great man himself could be dangerous, and a much safer tactic was to try to discredit him by accusing his

Figure 6.10
Marble statuette of Athena. This is a Roman copy from the second century A.D. that, while about one-twelfth the size of the original, closely resembles Pausanias' description of the Athena Parthenos. The spear could have rested in the bend of her left arm. (National Museum, Athens)

associates of wrongdoing. Phidias, it was said (Plutarch, *Pericles* 13.9), assisted Pericles in satisfying his lust by providing free-born women for him to seduce. He was actually charged with embezzling some of the gold (or ivory) that he had been given for the statue:

> Being a friend of Pericles and having considerable influence with him, he on that account had a number of jealous enemies; these enemies decided to test

Figure 6.11
Female figures from the east pediment of the Parthenon. Fashioned by Phidias and his team of sculptors, they are probably (left to right) the goddess Hestia, and Dione, whose daughter Aphrodite reclines in her lap. These and other sculptures from the Parthenon are part of the collection known as the "Elgin Marbles" and are now displayed in the British Museum in London.

the populace by bringing a charge against Phidias, in order to find out what the popular judgment would be against Pericles. Having bribed a certain Menon, one of Phidias' co-workers, they had him sit down in the agora as a suppliant and beg for immunity in return for giving information and making a charge against Phidias. The man was received as a witness by the people, and an inquiry was held in the assembly, but acts of theft were not proven. For right from the very beginning and on the advice of Pericles Phidias had so worked and put in place the gold for the image that it was quite possible to remove it and test its weight. And this is what Pericles challenged his accusers to do.

(Plutarch, *Pericles* 31.2–3)

Plutarch states that, ultimately, the enemies of Pericles and Phidias were successful in having the artist hauled off to prison, where he died from disease or poison. We know that, in fact, he was banished—if not for the charge of embezzlement, then something else politically inspired—and went to Olympia, where he completed his Zeus. His departure apparently did little to quell the rumors of his guilt, for a story was later circulated (as Aristophanes indicates in his *Peace* [605–611]) that Pericles had precipitated the Peloponnesian War as a way to cover his own complicity in the theft!

Aspasia, the Courtesan

The exact same charges lodged against Phidias (obviously stock insults—procuring free-born women for Pericles and prompting him to begin the Peloponnesian War—without any real meaning) were also hurled at another of the general's close associates, Aspasia. She was Pericles' most intimate of companions and probably had more influence on him than any other person:

> Aspasia, some say, was courted by Pericles since she was a very wise and statesmanlike woman. For even Socrates would visit her on occasion with his well-known friends, and her own intimates brought their wives to listen to her even though she managed a business that was neither seemly nor respectable: she raised young girls as courtesans.
> (Plutarch, *Pericles* 24.5)

Aspasia is the most famous woman of whom we know in fifth-century Athens. (With the possible exception of Sappho, she is probably the most

Figure 6.12
Aspasia (Vatican Museums, Rome)

famous woman in all of Greek history.) She added a sparkle all her own to the city's "Golden Age." Born in the Ionian city of Miletus, she was the daughter of a citizen named Axiochus. Whether she was orphaned at an early age and sold into slavery by unconcerned relatives or her father simply could not afford or did not want to keep her, we do not really know. (Perhaps her father dedicated her to a temple of Aphrodite, an honorable way of disposing of unwanted female children, who then would be trained as priestesses and serve the goddess with their bodies.) In any case, she lost her freedom and eventually became a professional prostitute, or, more accurately, a courtesan.

Courtesans (*hetairai*) were much more than common prostitutes and were highly desired and much-prized companions. Beautiful and charming, women who became courtesans were usually purchased at a young age by keen-eyed "older" courtesans, who, aware they would not always attract the attentions they once commanded, trained these girls in the arts of love and lived off their skills. Courtesans were among the most educated people of the day, for their clients were the elite of society, and sexual gratification was not always enough to please a high-ranking and intelligent patron. Philosophy, history, politics, science, art, and literature were all necessary tools if a courtesan expected to be successful.

Since most probably received a percentage of their earnings, a much-sought-after courtesan like Aspasia (*Aspasia* means "the desired one," so it is unlikely that this was her given name) would have been in a position to buy her freedom early in life. Alternatively, an adoring client (or clients), like Sappho's brother, who supposedly bought the freedom of the woman with whom he was involved in Egypt (see Chapter 4), might purchase her release for her. Freedom, too, might be granted outright by a madam, although the latter certainly would have had to have the reputed "heart of gold" to have done so. (If a courtesan had begun as a temple prostitute, she would have been released once she had fulfilled her obligation to the goddess.)

Once freed, a courtesan, unless she married, usually continued to ply her trade, and some became quite wealthy and influential. Aspasia, the tradition states, "emulated a certain Thargelia, an Ionian woman of earlier times and went after men of the greatest power" (Plutarch, *Pericles* 24.2). More handsome than beautiful, her grace, intelligence, and style were enough to win the biggest prize of the day in Athens—Pericles.

When Aspasia came to Athens is not known. The city was attracting much attention all over the Greek world because of Pericles' building program and the flourishing artistic and intellectual atmosphere that existed there. Tribute from the Athenian Empire ensured a steady source of wealth, and there were unlimited opportunities for the enterprising to "make a fast

Figure 6.13
A small terra-cotta representation of a courtesan entertaining her client. Aspasia was a courtesan and trained young girls to serve in the profession. (Louvre, Paris)

buck." Aspasia may have been one of the many who were lured to Athens at this time to profit from such a lucrative situation—as well as to enjoy the excitement and the company of talented men.

For some time, Athens had run state-owned brothels; in addition, there were private ones, and such businesses never died for lack of a customer (although some of the latter must certainly have died from venereal disease, which would have been a very real problem!). The typical male attitude toward sex in Athens seems to be summed up by one citizen's statement that wives were for legitimate children and looking after the house, but "we have call girls for our pleasures and mistresses to daily refresh our bodies" (Ps. Demosthenes 59.122). There was always room for a new whoring establishment, as long as it was registered and paid the required special tax.

Though only in her mid-twenties, Aspasia was probably already raising young girls as courtesans and running a "house" (the later gossipmonger Athenaeus says she imported large numbers of beautiful women and filled all of Greece with her prostitutes). The opportunities in Athens would have made it profitable to do so. Her clientele would have been, of course, of very high calibre, and she would not have had to put out a welcome mat to ensure a "healthy" traffic. The fame of well-known courtesans was not restricted to local gossip. Her reputation undoubtedly had preceded her arrival in town.

Aspasia's house must have quickly become the fashionable place for gentlemen of quality to rendezvous. Beauty, erotic satisfaction, stimulating conversation, the finest food and drink—all could undoubtedly be had there. At one time or another, most of the city's important figures—politicians, playwrights, philosophers, artists, and literary celebrities—passed through her door. It seems ironic that men who otherwise excluded women from politics and gave so little attention to their capabilities would earnestly solicit Aspasia's advice on weighty matters and place such high value on her opinions. Although she held no official position and certainly was not considered "respectable" by Greek standards, it was precisely her freedom from conventional restraints that allowed Aspasia to become as influential as she was in Athens.

Aspasia's influence must have grown considerably after she became the mistress of the most powerful man in Athens, Pericles, probably in the mid-440s B.C. Some like to believe that the great general, at least twice her age, was so smitten with Aspasia that he immediately divorced his wife and came to live with her. It is more likely that Pericles had previously become dissatisfied with his marriage (although knowing Aspasia certainly might have enhanced that dissatisfaction) and had already divorced his wife—perhaps as many as five years earlier.

A Contemptuous Son—Xanthippus Dishonors Pericles

CHILDREN OF PROMINENT PEOPLE often have trouble escaping the long shadows cast by their famous fathers or mothers, and, unfairly perhaps, their shortcomings are overemphasized by an expectant society. In ancient Athens, Pericles' eldest son, Xanthippus, shared few of his father's abilities, but, despite his inadequacies, he seemed to feel he was "owed" everything that went along with his parent's celebrity. We seldom have an opportunity to look into the domestic squabbles of the major figures in antiquity, but Plutarch, at least, relates some of the tradition about the son's selfish attacks on his father. We have no way of knowing what effect Pericles' divorce had on Xanthippus (who must have been close to twenty when it happened) or his cohabitation with Aspasia. However, if what Plutarch says about Xanthippus as a mature adult is true, it would appear that he had always been spoiled and disagreeable:

> Xanthippus, the eldest of [Pericles'] legitimate sons, was a spendthrift by nature, who had married a young and extravagant wife. . . . Xanthippus resented his father's passion for economy and the meager allowance he was given, and still

more the fact that he only received it in small amounts. He therefore approached one of Pericles' friends and borrowed money from him, pretending that this was on Pericles' instruction. When the friend later asked for repayment, Pericles, so far from settling the debt, brought an action against him. Young Xanthippus was furious and began openly to abuse his father, telling stories to raise a laugh against him about his management of affairs at home and his conversations with sophists. For example, there was an athlete who had accidentally hit Epitimus the Pharsalian with a javelin and killed him, and Pericles wasted an entire day, according to Xanthippus, arguing with Protagoras as to whether, "in the strictest sense," it was the javelin, or the man who threw it, or the judges of the games, who should be held responsible for the accident. According to Stesimbrotus it was also Xanthippus who put about the scandalous story concerning his own wife's association with Pericles, and he says that to the very end of Xanthippus' life the quarrel between him and his father was never made up. . . .
> (*Pericles* 36.1–3)

Whatever the case, the two lived together as "man and wife" to the end of Pericles' life, even though the state would not have recognized their marriage (only citizens could marry and produce children who would be citizens). They had at least one child. The depth of Pericles' love for Aspasia—later writers (Plutarch, *Pericles* 24.6; Athenaeus 589de) also liked to point out that Pericles kissed Aspasia every morning when he left and again when he returned home, which must not have been a typical practice or they would not have made so much of it—is demonstrated by his compulsion to live with his mistress. Although cohabiting might not "raise many eyebrows" in today's society, such a relationship for an Athenian citizen—let alone someone of Pericles' stature—was totally unacceptable.

Ironically, Pericles himself had been responsible for authoring some of the very citizenship laws he was disregarding, and ultimately, there was a

Figure 6.14
A rare example of a couple showing public affection in Greek society. Such practices apparently fueled controversy over the already sensational relationship between Pericles and Aspasia, who supposedly were known to have kissed whenever Pericles left and returned home. (Chicago Art Institute)

price to pay. Late in his life, when plague claimed his legitimate sons and he had no legal heir, he pleaded before the assembly to confer citizenship on his son by Aspasia. The Athenians were not compelled to do so, but always swayed by an emotional appeal and recognizing the debt they owed the great man for all his past years of service, they agreed. This son, Pericles, would later serve the state at the highest levels.

Unconventional relationships always attract public attention, but when they involve such high-profile personalities as Aspasia and Pericles, who also had political enemies with whom to contend, we should expect a large body of negative comment. The comic poets were particularly unkind, identifying Aspasia with women in mythology who had made heroes like Heracles look ridiculous or caused their death. She was styled as a "dog-eyed whore," Pericles' Hera, and the end-product of pederasty. Her son was previously held up as an object of ridicule, his illegitimate status in society affirmed in the theater before the citizenry of Athens.

Bad feeling ran so high at times that actual charges, including impiety, were lodged against Aspasia in court—by a comic playwright, no less—and Pericles, who was being attacked indirectly, is said to have handled her defense (Plutarch, *Pericles* 32.1–3; Athenaeus 589de). She was viewed as being too political and having too much influence over Pericles and his policies. Some were convinced that she had prodded him into a nasty war with Samos

Newlyweds—Ischomachus' Conversation with His Bride

WHILE THE RELATIONSHIP OF Aspasia and Pericles was certainly an unconventional one in Greek terms, an insight into what was more typical, in respect to a properly married couple, is provided by Xenophon (c. 430–356 B.C.) in a literary treatise called the *Oeconomicus*—on the proper management of a household. This narrative, unique in Greek literature, represents a discussion between a husband named Ischomachus and his much younger wife (she is 14 and he is about 30, typical ages for both sexes at the time of a first marriage) and is set in Athens in the latter part of the fifth century B.C. It is part of a longer dialogue that is taking place between the philosopher Socrates and his friend Critobulus. At one point in the narrative, Socrates tells Critobulus about a conversation he once had with Ischomachus—after a chance meeting with him at the Stoa of Zeus (see Map 17) in the Athenian Agora—about his relationship with his wife when they were first married, years before. Xenophon, who was a disciple of Socrates, relates the narrative as if it were one he had overheard, but, while the story of Ischomachus and his wife (as well as the rest of the dialogue) may be based on an actual recollection, it is, for the most part, a literary embellishment.

Just *how* typical this marital relationship in ancient Greece was and how much of it is Xenophon's own idea of how a marriage should be "managed" is impossible to know. (The notion that Xenophon is actually detailing his own relationship with his wife, Philesia, has not received much recent support.) Xenophon was himself a wealthy, conservative Athenian with pro-Spartan tendencies, which caused him problems (he was a close friend of the Spartan king Agesilaus), and militarily, he had served in the Athenian cavalry and, later, as a mercenary for the Persian prince, Cyrus. As an author, apart from his philosophical and other writings, he was the best-known historian of the early fourth century B.C., producing, most importantly, a history of his time called the *Hellenica*.

Modern readers may find parts of the *Oeconomicus* narrative cited here humorous, but this was never the intent of Xenophon. Also, with respect to Socrates, while the topic of Ischomachus' marital relationship would definitely have piqued his ethical interests, if he truly found Ischomachus' reflections more interesting "than . . . an account of the most splendid athletic competition or horse-race" (see page 177), then from everything else we know about this earthy philosopher, it must have been a "slow day."

Here, the conversation between Socrates and Ischomachus has already begun, and the latter is responding to Socrates' question about how he spends his time (*Oeconomicus* 7.3– 43):

". . . I certainly do not spend time indoors, for my wife is more than capable of managing everything inside the house, even by herself."

I [Socrates] said, "I should very much like you to tell me, Ischomachus, whether you yourself trained your wife to become the sort of woman that she ought to be, or whether she already knew how to carry out her duties when you took her as your wife from her father and mother."

"What could she have known when I took her as my wife, Socrates? She was not yet fifteen when she came to me, and had spent her previous years under careful supervision so that she might see and hear and speak as little as possible. Don't you think it was adequate if she came to me knowing only how to take wool and produce a cloak, and had seen how spinning tasks are allocated to the slaves? And besides, she had been very well trained to control her appetites, Socrates," he said, "and I think that sort of training is most important for man and woman alike."

"Ischomachus," I asked, "did you train your wife yourself in other respects so that she would be competent to deal with matters that concern her?"

"No, by Zeus," said Ischomachus, "at least, not until I had sacrificed to the gods and prayed that I might be successful in teaching and she in learning what was best for both of us."

"Did your wife sacrifice along with you and offer the same prayers?" I asked.

"Oh, yes, very much so, and she vowed and prayed fervently to the gods that she might become the sort of woman that she ought to be, and she made it clear that she would not neglect what she had been taught."

"By the gods, Ischomachus," I said, "tell me what you began by teaching her, since I would rather hear you describing that than giving an account of the most splendid athletic competition or horse-race."

Ischomachus replied, "Well, Socrates, as soon as she was sufficiently tamed and domesticated so as to be able to carry on a conversation, I questioned her more or less as follows: 'Tell, me, wife, have you ever thought about why I married you and why your parents gave you to me? It must be quite obvious to you, I am sure, that there was no shortage of partners with whom we might sleep. I, on my part, and your parents, on your behalf, considered who was the best partner we could choose for managing an estate and for children. And I chose you, and your parents, apparently, chose me, out of those who were eligible. Now if some day the god grants us children, then we shall consider how to train them in the best way possible. For this will be a blessing to us both, to obtain the best allies and support in old age. But at present we two share this estate. I go on paying everything I have into the common

Figure 6.15   *Red-figure vase showing Athenian bride and groom, 440–420 B.C. (British Museum, London)*

fund; and you deposited into it everything you brought with you. There is no need to calculate precisely which of us had contributed more, but to be well aware of this: that the better partner is the one who makes the more valuable contribution.'

"In reply to this, Socrates, my wife answered, 'What should I be able to do to help you? What ability have I got? Everything depends on you. My mother told me that my duty is to practice self-control.'

(continued)

Newlyweds—Ischomachus' Conversation with His Bride (continued)

"'By Zeus, wife,' I said, 'my father said the same to me. But self-control for both man and woman means behaving so that their property will be in the very best condition and that the greatest possible increase will be made to it by just and honorable means.'

"'And what do you envisage that I might do to help improve our estate?' asked my wife.

"'By Zeus, wife,' I said, 'try to do as well as possible what the gods have given you the natural ability to do, and which the law encourages, as well.'

"'And what is that?' she asked.

"'I suppose,' I said, 'that they are not trivial matters, unless of course, the activities that the queen bee presides over in the hive are trivial. Wife, the gods seem to have shown much discernment in yoking together female and male, as we call them, so that the couple might constitute a partnership that is most beneficial to each of them. First of all, so that the various species of living creatures may not become extinct, this pair sleeps together for the purpose of procreation. Then this pairing provides offspring to support the partners in their old age, at least in the case of human beings. And finally, human beings do not live outdoors like cattle, but obviously have need of shelter.'

"'Those who intend to obtain produce to bring into the shelter need someone to work at the outdoor jobs. For ploughing, sowing, planting, and herding is all work performed outdoors, and it is from these that our essential provisions are obtained. As soon as these are brought into the shelter, then someone else is needed to look after them and to perform the work that requires shelters. The nursing of newborn children requires shelters, and so does the preparation of bread from grain, and likewise, making clothing out of wool. Because both the indoor and the outdoor tasks require work and concern, I think the god, from the very beginning, designed the nature of woman for the in-

Figure 6.16 *Terra-cotta figure of a woman grinding wheat at a basin, Rhodes, 450 B.C. Ischomachus' wife would have been expected to perform such "indoor" domestic tasks—or assign them to slaves. (British Museum, London)*

door work and concerns and the nature of man for the outdoor work. For he prepared man's body and mind to be more capable of enduring cold and heat and travelling and military campaigns, and so he assigned the outdoor work to him. Because the woman was physically less capable of endurance, I think the god has evidently assigned the indoor work to her. And because the god was aware that he had both implanted in the woman and assigned to her the nurture of newborn children, he had measured out to her a greater share of affection for newborn babies than he gave to the man. And because the god had also assigned to the woman the duty of guarding what had been brought into the house, realizing that a tendency to be

Figure 6.17   Xenophon emphasizes the importance of a marriage producing children. Pictured here are two "baby bottles" in the form of mice. (British Museum, London)

afraid is not at all disadvantageous for guarding things, he measured out a greater portion of fear to the woman than to the man. And knowing that the person responsible for the outdoor work would have to serve as defender against any wrong doer, he measured out to him a greater share of courage.'

"'Because it is necessary for both of them to give and to take, he gave both of them equal powers of memory and concern. . . . And he gave them both equally the ability to practice self-control too, when it is needed. And the god granted the privilege to whichever one is superior in this to gain a larger share of the benefit accruing from it, whether man or woman. So, because they are not equally well endowed with all the same natural aptitudes, they are consequently more in need of each other, and the bond is more beneficial to the couple, since one is capable where the other is deficient.'

"'. . . The law . . . yokes together husband and wife, and just as the god made them part-

ners in children, so the law has appointed them partners in estate. And the law declares honorable those duties for which the god has made each of them more naturally capable. For the woman it is more honorable to remain indoors than to be outside; for the man it is more disgraceful to remain indoors than to attend business outside. If someone behaves in a way contrary to the nature the god has given him, perhaps his disobedience will not escape the notice of the gods, and he will pay a penalty for neglecting his proper business or for performing his wife's work. It seems to me,' I added, 'that the queen bee toils constantly at such work appointed by the god.'

". . . My wife asked, 'Shall I have to do this too?'

"'Certainly,' I replied, 'you will have to stay indoors and send forth the group of slaves whose work is outdoors, and personally supervise those whose work is outdoors. Moreover, you must receive what is brought inside and dispense as much as should be spent. And you must plan ahead and guard whatever must remain in reserve, so that the provisions stored up for a year are not spent in a month. And when wool is brought in to you, you must see that clothes are produced for those who need them. And you must also be concerned that the dry grain is in good condition for eating. However,' I said, 'one of your proper concerns, perhaps, may seem to you rather thankless: you will certainly have to be concerned about nursing any of the slaves who becomes ill.'

"'Oh, no,' exclaimed my wife, 'it will be most gratifying if those who are well cared for will prove to be thankful and more loyal than before.'"

Ischomachus went on: "I was delighted with her response and said, 'Wife, because of such thoughtful actions on the part of the

(continued)

Newlyweds—Ischomachus' Conversation with His Bride (continued)

Figure 6.18   *Women conversing at a fountain. One of the few regular opportunities women such as Xenophon's wife had to go outside and chat at length with their neighbors was fetching water for the household from the local fountain. Hydria, Athens, 520–500 B.C. (British Museum, London)*

queen bee, isn't the relationship of the bees to her, too, of such a kind that when she deserts the hive, not one of the bees considers staying behind, but all follow her?'

"My wife replied, 'It would surprise me if the leader's activities did not apply more to you than to me. For if you were not concerned that supplies were brought in from outside, surely my guarding the things indoors and my budgeting would seem pretty ridiculous.'

"And I replied: 'Yes, but my bringing in supplies would appear just as ridiculous if there were not someone to look after what has been brought in. Don't you see how people pity those who draw water in a leaky jar, as the saying goes, because they seem to labor in vain?'

"'Yes, by Zeus,' said my wife, 'they are truly miserable if they do that.'

"'But, wife, your other special concerns turn out to be pleasant: whenever you take a slave who has no knowledge of spinning, and teach her that skill so that you double her value to you; and whenever you take one who does not know how to manage a house or serve, and turn her into one who is a skilled and faithful servant and make her invaluable; and when-

ever it is in your power to reward the helpful and reasonable members of your household and to punish any of them who appears to be vicious. But the sweetest experience of all will be this: if you prove to be better than I am and make me your servant. Then you will have no need to fear that as your years increase you will be less honored in the household; but you may be confident that when you become older, the better partner you have been to me, and the better guardian of the estate for the children, the greater the respect you will enjoy in this household. For it is not because of youthful grace that beautiful and good things increase for human beings, but rather because of their virtues,' I said. As far as I can recall, those are the kind of subjects, Socrates, that I believe I discussed with her first."

Xenophon's remarks have, unfortunately, been misconstrued by some feminists, who see the tract as a negative piece about women. However, Sarah B. Pomeroy has correctly stated in her translation and interpretation of the dialogue: "A careful reading of the *Oeconomicus* will show that Xenophon by no means considered the domestic realm as inferior. . . . Xenophon asserts that women and men are complementary in their biological nature and therefore in their contributions to the domestic economy, but this difference does not imply inequality. Like Plato in the *Republic*, Xenophon makes it clear that the soul has no sex; men and women are endowed with a potential for moral equality." (Xenophon, *Oeconomicus*, 88) in 441 B.C. because her native city, Miletus, was involved in a territorial dispute with the island. Other stories, as mentioned earlier, made her responsible for the outbreak of the Peloponnesian War. Pericles was dead and the war had been raging for six years when Aristophanes wrote in his *Acharnians* (525–531):

> when some drunken youths went for the whore Simaetha
> and stole her away,
> then the Megarians, garlicked with the pain,
> stole in return two whores of Aspasia.
> Then the start of the war burst out
> for all Hellenes because of three strumpets.
> Then Pericles the Olympian in his wrath
> thundered, lightened, threw Hellas into confusion. . . .

Clearly, the Athenians exacted their toll from those who turned the public's eye.

Her relationship with Pericles would have placed Aspasia in contact, if she were not already, with some of the greatest freethinkers and intellectuals of the day in Athens. Pericles, who was rather aloof and distant from the people he ruled (an interesting disposition for a man who styled himself a democrat), liked to associate with such types. He was clearly on the "cutting edge" of intellectual curiosity in Athens, certainly a rare quality in a politician—and one that had little appeal to the typical voter, who was usually suspicious of anyone who questioned the traditional values of society. Aspasia's apparent receptiveness to new ideas and intellectual inquiry was something the two had in common. It is doubtful, however, that Aspasia would have ever met the man who apparently first whetted Pericles' appetite for knowledge, Anaxagoras of Clazomenae. He was Pericles' close friend and teacher, though intellectual soul mate might be a more proper description since the two men did not differ much in age.

Anaxagoras was the first philosopher to take up residence in Athens, and he brought the Greek Enlightenment, the rational inquiry into knowledge that had begun with Thales (see Chapter 2) in Ionia in the sixth century B.C., to the city's doorstep. Primarily an astronomer, his radical views about the gods and the universe (considered atheistic by contemporary standards) and his association with Pericles (which, as we have already seen, always invited attacks from political enemies) forced him to flee Athens around 450 B.C. This was probably before Aspasia had arrived, so her knowledge about him and his teachings must have been secondhand.

Since Aspasia is credited with having rather formidable rhetorical skills, she would have acquired some of her training from one or more of the sophists ("wise men") present in Athens at this time. She is even jokingly referred to as a "female sophist." Sophists were a logical outgrowth of the

Greek Enlightenment. They were mostly itinerant teachers, who traveled from city to city teaching, for a fee, a variety of subjects—but mostly oratory and those skills that enhanced one's chances for material success. The prosperity and charged atmosphere of Periclean Athens made it the place to be. The city attracted sophists (probably made welcome by Pericles himself) like a magnet, creating an intellectual revolution and bringing new ideas that both confused and confounded the typical Athenian.

The sophists were the first to offer some form of higher education to Athens' elite, and they professed the radical view that education could be used to prepare someone for a vocation. That was bad enough for many Athenians, always leery of new ideas, but they also viewed these teachers of their youth as corrupt, immoral (or at least amoral), and exorbitant in their fees. Not all sophists were, of course, but it did not really matter. Their rejection of conventional religion was sufficient reason in the eyes of most to condemn them as subversives and as dangers to society. Aristophanes parlayed these fears, real or imagined, into a delightful comedy about the sophists entitled *The Clouds,* in which he charges them with impiety and corrupting the youth of Athens.

The one sophist whom Aspasia was certain to have known (and by whom she was most likely influenced) was Pericles' friend Protagoras of Abdera:

> Protagoras was the first to maintain that there are two sides to every question, opposed to each other, and he even argued in this fashion, being the first to do so. Furthermore he began a work thus: "Man is the measure of all things, of things that are that they are, and of things that are not that they are not." He used to say that soul was nothing apart from the senses . . . and that everything is true. In another work he began thus: "As to the gods, I have no means of knowing either that they exist or that they do not exist. For many are the obstacles that impede knowledge, both the obscurity of the question and the shortness of human life." For this introduction to his book the Athenians expelled him; and they burnt his works in the market-place, after sending round a herald to collect them from all who had copies in their possession.
>
> He was the first to exact a fee of a hundred minae and the first to distinguish the tenses of verbs, to emphasize the importance of seizing the right moment, to institute contests in debating, and to teach rival pleaders the tricks of their trade. . . .
> (Diogenes Laertius 9.51–52)

Although all of the preceding claims for Protagoras cannot be substantiated (or even understood), he is generally regarded as the greatest of the sophists. His maxim "Man is the measure of all things" is, more or less, the single saying with which the group has most often been identified. Convinced of the fallibility of the senses and, therefore, the unreliability of religion and science, Protogoras believed that knowledge, morality, and justice were implanted in all men. Although nothing could be known with absolute certainty, one could still lead a life of reason without it. What he seems to be implying is that one is in a position to control his or her own destiny and that understanding comes from within—not from any traditionally or artificially conceived system that has been applied from outside. Certainly, such ideas, although blasphemous to most, would have been attractive to both Pericles and Aspasia, two people who had undeniably taken charge of their own destinies.

We definitely know that Aspasia had a long and lasting friendship with Socrates, who must have been about her age. The diminutive man with the homely face is generally regarded as the father of Western ethical philosophy. He was apparently fascinated with the intellectual capabilities of Aspasia (not to mention her physical attributes, for unlike his pupil Plato, there was not much of the puritan in Socrates).

Figure 6.19
Socrates (Louvre, Paris)

If they met soon after Aspasia arrived in Athens, when both would have been in their twenties, their intellectual development may have had some parallels. Aspasia was influenced by the sophists, and although Socrates was not a sophist and rejected much of what they embraced as truths, he, too, had attended their lectures and considered their teachings. He was also reputed to have been the student of Archelaus, who was a disciple of Pericles' close friend Anaxagoras. There was certainly some common intellectual ground between the two—even detractors called her a "Socratic" and Plato playfully portrayed her as the philosopher's instructor—and we must suppose that Aspasia had some role in helping Socrates refine his own ideas—including those about women.

Socrates' appreciation of Aspasia and her abilities is also indicated by the fact that she is mentioned in the works of several of his students. Plato's *Menexenus,* for example, though not to be taken seriously, has Socrates refer to a funeral oration he heard Aspasia composing, leaving him to conclude that she was responsible for Pericles' funeral oration—obviously playing on the tradition that Aspasia's rhetorical skills (from which Pericles must have benefited) were impressive. In his *Oeconomicus,* Xenophon has Socrates defer to the absent Aspasia, who, he says, knows more than he about whether a wife becomes a good one as the result of training she receives from her husband—implying that Aspasia certainly would not think so.

Another less-known writer of Socratic dialogues, Aeschines of Sphettus, produced an *Aspasia* that features the remarkable woman in a fictitious conversation with Xenophon and his young wife and that is intent on displaying Aspasia's "womanly ability" and asserting her belief in the equality of male and female in marriage. A portion of the dialogue, repeated by Cicero (*De Inventione Rhetorica* 1.31), runs as follows:

> "If your neighbor had gold that was purer than yours," Aspasia asked Xenophon's wife, "would you rather have her gold or yours?" "Hers," was the reply. "And if she had richer jewels and finer clothes?" "I would rather have hers." "And if she had a better husband than yours?" At the woman's embarrassed silence, Aspasia began to question the husband, asking him the same things but substituting horses for gold and land for clothes and asking him finally if he would prefer his neighbor's wife if she were better than his own. At his embarrassed silence, reading their thoughts, she said, "Each of you would like the best husband or wife: and since neither of the two of you has achieved perfection, each of you will always regret this ideal."

Although the Socratics apparently found Aspasia a useful tool through which to express a point of view, they never would have included her if she had not come to represent these views in the mind of Socrates himself and of most educated Greeks.

Among other intellectuals, artists, and literary figures active in Athens during the Golden Age, Aspasia probably would have been acquainted with Herodotus. His complimentary remarks about Pericles' family, the Alcmeonids, in his *Persian Wars* (e.g., 6.115, 121–124) strongly suggest Pericles' patronage while he was writing his landmark history in Athens. However, in 443 B.C., Herodotus would join those Pericles sent to help settle the new colony at Thurii in Italy (interestingly, it was the general's sophist friend Protagoras who drew up a law code for the new city), so if he knew Aspasia, it could have been only for a few years. Of course, Herodotus may have returned to Athens periodically, and if he did, we might expect that he would be entertained by Pericles and Aspasia. Some believe that Herodotus was disturbed by Pericles' war with Samos, where the historian had earlier in his life taken refuge from tyranny (see Chapter 2). If so—and the popular tradition was that Aspasia had goaded Pericles into that war—then the friendship may have been strained after Samos was brutally reduced in 439 B.C.

We would also expect that Aspasia knew the great playwrights, though judging from their unflattering comments, we can probably safely eliminate writers of comedies from her circle of friends! Aristophanes may even have had her in mind as a model for his main character when he wrote his *Lysistrata* in 411 B.C., although Aspasia would have been long past her prime (or been dead). Like Aspasia, Lysistrata was outspoken, held her own with men, and was dissatisfied with women's subservient role in Athens. Although some moderns mistakenly interpret these qualities as indications of feminist inclinations on the part of Aristophanes, nothing could be further from the truth. It is those very qualities that Aristophanes is deriding for the benefit of the males in his audience. If Aspasia did provide any inspiration for the character of *Lysistrata*, Aristophanes was paying her a backhanded compliment at best.

Of the three great tragedians of fifth-century Athens, Aeschylus, the most religious and conservative, was too old for Aspasia to have known. He died in Sicily in 456 B.C., although he had been in Athens for the early part of Pericles' rule. Sophocles and Euripides, however, were close in age to Pericles, and Aspasia undoubtedly was familiar with both.

Sophocles was probably not much more than an acquaintance. Like his fellow tragedians, he was as much a philosopher as those who were so labeled, since he considered such questions as why human beings, particularly the innocent, suffer and what man's relationship is to the gods. More moderate in his religious beliefs than Aeschylus, he was still a conservative. For Sophocles, the gods directed people's fate, predicting—as in the case of Oedipus, who was destined to kill his father and marry his mother—through oracles what was to happen. What the gods foretold, however, did

Figure 6.20
Sophocles (Capitoline
Museums, Rome)

not necessarily have to end in tragedy. One could behave with moderation, holding in check the character faults that, if allowed to interact negatively with those of others, would only end in disaster. It is doubtful that Aspasia and Pericles, who associated with freethinkers and sophists, would have felt comfortable with Sophocles—nor he with them. However, it would not be fair to assert that they would have found Sophocles disagreeable simply because of differing views on religion. There are indications of other possible frictions.

In his play *Antigone,* Sophocles considers the question of whether a citizen should obey the laws of the state even when they go against divine or natural law, which is one's instinctive feeling of what is morally correct. Antigone defies Creon's order that her brother, who had attacked Thebes and perished fighting her other brother for possession of the city (both brothers died in a duel), should go unburied as a punishment. The denial of a proper burial is not right in the eyes of the gods, and the conflict between Creon and Antigone ultimately ends in tragedy for them both.

It would be difficult to disassociate this theme from Pericles' running of the Athenian Empire, which oftentimes overlooked morality in favor of political expedience. (It would be equally difficult not to regard Oedipus, who in *Oedipus Rex* [c. 430 B.C.] has eyes but cannot see his own tragedy building before him, as representative of Pericles, or at least Athens, blindly blundering into the destructive Peloponnesian War.) Certainly, there were citizens in Athens who disapproved of many of Pericles' policies, although they may have been in the minority and were not always able to express their dissent effectively. It may be that Sophocles was using his drama to represent an actual "crisis of conscience" that was disrupting Athenian society.

This assertion is not a new idea. Even ancient tradition indicates that the Athenians elected Sophocles a general as a result of his *Antigone* after it was produced, probably in 441 B.C. Sophocles had been an imperial treasurer the year before when Pericles was reorganizing the Empire for more efficient collection of tribute, largely for his building program. Plutarch, at least, says (e.g., *Pericles* 23.1, 28.4–6) that critics complained that the funds, meant for protection against Persia, were being used improperly. Sophocles, in his position, would have known about any problems or improprieties firsthand, and he may have sided with the critics and begun to form the idea for his *Antigone*. The same year the play was apparently written and produced, Pericles had instigated a bitter, and to some, unnecessary war with Samos (the one Aspasia had supposedly urged him to start). The next year Sophocles was elected general with Pericles. The conclusion that the play is interwoven with current politics seems unavoidable. Sophocles had little or no military experience, a point with which Pericles had confronted the playwright, and his election seems just the kind of thing disgruntled citizens might do to protest policies with which they disagreed.

In the same play, Sophocles uses Antigone to express what must come close to his own views about the family. Antigone's initial motivation for her act of defiance comes from her loyalty to and love for her brother. If this play is any indication, Sophocles firmly embraces the traditional, conservative concept of the family. It is unlikely he would have approved of the cohabitation and production of children out of sanctioned wedlock by Aspasia and Pericles. A close association with the couple would have indicated to others that he condoned such relationships.

Finally, Pericles did not approve of the playwright's apparent penchant for pursuing boys. He obviously had made mention of it on more than one occasion, a fact about which Sophocles himself joked (Athenaeus 603c–604d = Ion of Chios frag. 8). Everything considered, there does not seem to be enough common ground to postulate a close relationship between Aspasia and Sophocles.

The last major figure in Periclean Athens whom we might be able to relate to Aspasia is Euripides. Nothing indicates that he served in any official capacity in Athens, and there is no information about his participation in

Figure 6.21
Euripides (Capitoline Museums, Rome)

military campaigns or personal contact between him and Aspasia or Pericles. Nonetheless, he must have known Pericles more than casually. Ancient biographical information lists, credibly, among his associates Pericles' intellectual companions Anaxagoras, Protagoras—and Socrates, Aspasia's close friend. Certainly, his views, particularly about the gods, were quite different from those of his traditional contemporary playwright, Sophocles, and were closer to what we have indicated for the sophists. Like Aspasia and Pericles, Euripides might be characterized as a freethinker, an experimenter who was willing to inquire into things even though the process might produce unsettling results.

In his plays, the gods are mostly symbolic, and tragedy results from the inability of his characters to keep their own emotions under control. Human beings are ultimately responsible for their actions, and moderation is best if one wishes to avoid disaster. Euripides' search for human causation places him in the forefront of the development of psychology, for some of his character studies, particularly of women, are brilliant analyses of the range of emotion. He was revolutionary in the writing of tragicomedies, which traditionalists would have seen as demeaning the genre. Aspasia probably would have smiled. Euripides had such an unnerving effect on Athenian audiences, and his radical ideas (charges of impiety were alleged) were so disturbing, that he often found himself and his plays the objects of contempt and derision. Such criticism probably contributed to his ultimate departure for Macedonia, where he died.

We might suppose, however, that from what we know about Aspasia, she would have been sympathetic with Euripides' more realistic portrayal of people on stage. Even his most famous women, Medea and Phaedra—who are classic psychological characterizations that helped establish the unfounded tradition that Euripides must have been a woman hater—may have been modeled to some extent on the strong, assertive Aspasia. Certainly, she was one of the few female sources to whom Euripides could turn and intellectually discuss the nature of women. After all, it was the male audiences of Athens who regarded these characters with horror. Most females probably could have sympathized at least with the motivations that caused them to do what they did.

Unconventional—and unpopular—people usually seek out others sympathetic to their ideas and views, especially if they are also the object of frequent ridicule and jokes. That reason alone is enough to suggest a friendship between Euripides and Aspasia, even though the tradition states he was somewhat of a loner.

Although it is difficult to postulate any political position for Euripides while Pericles was alive, his characterization of Athens as the "holy and unconquered land" in the *Medea*, produced at the beginning of the Peloponnesian War in 431 B.C., might indicate approval with how Pericles was running things. This seems likely, for by 415 B.C., the playwright was apparently quite upset with the direction in which Athens was being led by Pericles' successors. His *Trojan Women*, produced the year after Athens had brutally reduced Melos and was now contemplating the invasion of Sicily, may warn of the dangers of such actions and the fate all empires, including the Athenian, must face. Hecuba, the mother of the great slain Trojan warrior Hector, states at the fall of Troy:

. . . O Troy, once
so huge over all Asia in the drawn wind of pride,
your very name of glory shall be stripped away.
They are burning you, and us they drag forth from our land
enslaved. O gods! Do I call upon those gods for help?
I cried to them before now, and they would not hear.
Come then, hurl ourselves into the pyre. Best now
to die in the flaming ruins of our fathers' house!
(1276–1283)

Thucydides Survives the Plague

SHORTLY AFTER THE PELOPONNESIAN War began, Athens was hit by a devastating plague (brought in by the fleet) that lingered for several years and killed thousands. Pericles witnessed the deaths of his two legitimate sons, Xanthippus and Paralus, and his sister before he, too, apparently succumbed in his sixties in 429 B.C. Because of her closeness to Pericles, it is remarkable that Aspasia (and her son by him) did not also die. Perhaps she, like the young Thucydides, who later became a historian and described the plague in his chronicle of the Peloponnesian War, did have the disease but was able to survive it.

In his *History,* Thucydides, contemptuous of divine explanations, took his inspiration from the sophists, usually emphasizing rational inquiry and scientific investigation. A keen observer of the human condition, Thucydides painstakingly detailed the course of the plague, which, despite innumerable modern attempts, still eludes a precise identification. Also a moralist, perhaps Thucydides clouded the issue for us by purposely confusing the symptoms for dramatic effect. His description of the disease's progress from the head to the extremities might be, in reality, a moral metaphor for Athenian imperialism, which he may have believed was a ruinous policy. Beginning at the head (Athenian leadership), the disease of "immorality" had spread to the body (Athens) and then the extremities (the Empire). It could only, like the actual plague, ultimately destroy the "patient" through a kind of natural retribution.

Whatever the case, Thucydides' personal experience with the catastrophic illness provides a remarkable and poignant insight into how the people of Athens had to cope with death all around them within the city while the Peloponnesian War raged outside:

> It first began, it is said, in the parts of Ethiopia above Egypt, and thence descended into Egypt and Libya. . . . Suddenly falling upon Athens,

it first attacked the population in Piraeus—which was the occasion of their saying that the Peloponnesians had poisoned the cisterns, there being as yet no fountains there—and afterwards appeared in the upper city, when the deaths became much more frequent. All speculation as to its origin and its causes, if causes can be found adequate to produce so great a disturbance, I leave to other writers, whether lay or professional; for myself, I shall simply set down its nature, and explain the symptoms by which perhaps it may be recognized by the student, if it should ever break out again. This I can the better do as I had the disease myself, and watched its operation in the case of others.

That year then is admitted to have been otherwise unprecedently free from sickness; and such few cases as occurred all ended in this. As a rule, however, there was no visible cause; but people in good health were all of a sudden attacked by violent heats in the head, and redness and inflammation in the eyes, the inward parts, such as the throat or tongue, becoming bloody and emitting an unnatural and fetid breath. These symptoms were followed by sneezing and hoarseness, after which the pain soon reached the chest, and produced a hard cough. When it settled in the heart, it upset it; and discharges of bile of every kind named by physicians ensued, accompanied by very great distress. In most cases also an ineffectual retching followed, producing violent spasms, which in some cases ceased soon after, in others much later. Externally the body was not very hot to the touch, nor pale in its appearance, but reddish, livid, and breaking out into small pustules and ulcers. But internally it burned so that the patient could not bear to have on him clothing or linen even of the very lightest description; or indeed to be otherwise than stark naked. What they would have liked best would have been to throw themselves into cold water; as indeed was done by some of the neglected sick, who plunged into the rain-tanks in their agonies of unquenchable thirst; though it made no difference whether they drank little or much. Besides this, the miserable feeling of not being able to rest or sleep never ceased to torment them. The body meanwhile did not waste away so long as the distemper was at its height, but held out to a marvel against its ravages; so that when they succumbed, as in most cases, on the seventh or eighth day to the internal inflammation, they had still some strength in them. But if they passed this stage, and the disease descended farther into the bowels, inducing a violent ulceration there accompanied by severe diarrhoea, this brought on a weakness which was generally fatal. For the disorder first settled in the head, ran its course from thence through the whole of the body, and even where it did not prove mortal it still left its mark on the extremities; for it settled in the privy parts, the fingers, and the toes, and many escaped with the loss of these, some too with that of their eyes. Others again were seized with an entire loss of memory on their first recovery, and did not know either themselves or their friends. . . . Some died in neglect, others in the midst of every attention. No remedy was found that could be used as a specific. . . . Strong and weak constitutions proved equally incapable of resistance. . . . By far the most terrible feature in the malady was the dejection which ensued when anyone felt himself sickening, for the despair into which they instantly fell took away their power of resistance, and left them a much easier prey to the disorder; besides which there was the awful spectacle of men dying like sheep, through having caught the infection in nursing each other. This caused the greatest mortality. On the one hand, if they were afraid to visit each other, they perished from neglect; indeed many houses were emptied of their inmates for want of a nurse; on the other, if they

ventured to do so, death was the consequence. This was especially the case with such as made any pretensions to virtue: honor made them unsparing of themselves in their attendance in their friends' houses, where even the members of the family were at last worn out by the moans of the dying, and succumbed to the force of the disaster. Yet it was with those who had recovered from the disease that the sick and the dying found most compassion. These knew what it was from experience, and had now no fear for themselves; for the same man was never attacked twice—never at least fatally. And such persons not only received the congratulations of others, but themselves also, in the elation of the moment, half entertained the vain hope that they were for the future safe from any disease whatsoever.

An aggravation of the existing calamity was the influx from the country into the city, and this was especially felt by the new arrivals. As there were no houses to receive them, they had to be lodged at the hot season of the year in stifling cabins, where the mortality raged without restraint. The bodies of dying men lay one upon another, and half-dead creatures reeled about the streets and gathered round all the fountains in their longing for water. The sacred places also in which they had quartered themselves were full of corpses . . . for as the disaster passed all bounds, men not knowing what was to become of them, became utterly careless of everything, whether sacred or profane. All the burial rites before in use were entirely upset, and they buried the bodies as best they could. Many, from want of the proper appliances, through so many of their friends having died already, had recourse to the most shameless sepultures: sometimes getting the start of those who had raised a pile, they threw their own dead body upon the stranger's pyre and ignited

(continued)

Thucydides Survives the Plague (continued)

it; sometimes they tossed the corpse which they were carrying on the top of another that was burning, and so went off.

Nor was this the only form of lawless extravagance which owed its origin to the plague. Men now coolly ventured on what they had formerly done in a corner and not just where they pleased, seeing the rapid transitions produced by persons in prosperity suddenly dying and those who before had nothing succeeding to their property. So they resolved to spend quickly and enjoy themselves, regarding their lives and riches as alike things of a day. Perseverance in what men called honor was popular with none, it was so uncertain whether they would be spared to attain the object; but it was settled that present enjoyment, and all that contributed to it, was both honorable and useful. Fear of gods or law of man there was none to restrain them. As for the first, they judged it to be just the same whether they worshipped them or not, as they saw all alike perishing; and for the last, no one expected to live to be brought to trial for his offenses, but each felt that a far severer sentence had been already passed upon them all and hung over their heads, and before this fell it was only reasonable to enjoy life a little.

Such was the nature of the calamity, and heavily did it weigh on the Athenians, death raging within the city and devastation without. (2.48–54)

When Pericles died in 429 B.C., Aspasia apparently sensed that the political tide was finally turning against aristocratic rule in democratic Athens. Nonaristocrats, once contemptible and considered unfit for high office, were now gaining support and becoming popular among the common voters, who were tired of being pushed around by their noble overlords. She took up with a rich commoner named Lysicles, who was a wool merchant, and groomed him for success. Undoubtedly, the tradition that she immediately helped him obtain high office is a true one, for her experience and capabilities were a valuable resource to anyone she chose to favor. She would not have wasted her time on Lysicles had he not shown potential, for she was not the kind of woman to associate with unambitious and untalented men.

How long Aspasia lived into the Peloponnesian War is unknown. Our information, meager as it is, runs out only a year after Pericles' death, when Lysicles was killed fighting in Asia Minor as general. Aspasia would probably have been in her early forties, so despite two tragedies in quick succession, she could have survived at least another twenty years or more. She may have retired into seclusion or even moved from Athens, since there was bound to be continued hostility toward her as the war took its toll and her former defenders were felled by the sword or old age. However, her relationship with Socrates may indicate that she stayed.

Some Greek Views on Old Age—From Solon to Euripides

MANY TODAY ARE PROBABLY surprised to learn that Pericles, for example, died in 429 B.C. when he was in his mid-sixties—from plague, no less. It is a common belief that people in Ancient Greece did not live so long. Yet, clearly, many did. The historian Polybius, for example, succumbed in his eighties after falling from his horse; and the orator Demosthenes poisoned himself when he was 62. Aristotle died at 63; Plato, when he was at least 80. The playwright Aeschylus was 69; Sophocles was about 90. The sophist Gorgias of Leontini outdid just about everyone by living approximately 107 years.

This is only a small list of famous Greeks who lived past age 60. A review of literary and inscriptional remains will produce many more, and one need only point to other indicators that confirm a sizable number of sexagenarians and beyond in Greek society. At Sparta, one could not even sit on the Gerousia, or Spartan "Sen-

ate," until reaching the age of 60; and in most cities in Greece, active military service ended at age 60. It is also reasonable to suggest that if so many prominent people in Greece lived past 60—and a good many of them did not die from old age—then there must have been countless other men and women about whom we know nothing who also reached advanced age. That number would obviously have been much smaller, proportionally, than it is today. The practice of child exposure, slavery, as well as continual warfare, plagues, and general poor living conditions, contributed to a lower median age for ancient Greeks than might be inferred from the examples given here. Nonetheless, a poem attributed to the great Athenian lawgiver Solon suggests that 70 was not an unusual age to attain—in fact, it seems expected. In the poem, ten different ages of man, each seven years long, are delineated, from infancy to death:

> A child in his infancy grows his first set of teeth and loses them
>   within seven years. For so long he counts as only a child.
> When the god has brought to accomplishment the next seven-year period,
>   one shows upon his body the signs of maturing youth.
> In the third period he is still getting his growth, while on his chin
>   the beard comes, to show he is turning from youth to a man.
> The fourth seven years are the time when every man reaches his
>   highest point of physical strength where men look for prowess achieved.
> In the fifth period the time is ripe for a young man
>   to think of marriage and children, a family to be raised.
> The mind of a man comes to full maturity in the sixth period,
>   but he cannot now do as much, nor does he wish that he could.
> In the seventh period of seven years and in the eighth also
>   for fourteen years in all, his speech is best in his life.
> He can still do much in his ninth period, but there is a weakening
>   seen in his ability both to think and to speak.
> But if he completes ten ages of seven years each, full measure,
>   death, when it comes, can no longer be said to come too soon.

(Lattimore, "Solon" 5, *Greek Lyrics*)

(continued)

Some Greek Views on Old Age—From Solon to Euripides (continued)

To be sure, most ancient societies have had "passages of life" poems, and this one is reminiscent of earlier ones—probably even modeled somewhat on them. Nonetheless, references contained in it (for example, the late marriage age for men and the emphasis on good speech) are particularly Greek, and it would therefore appear that the poem generally embraces what Hellenic society expected from life. Solon obviously considered it not uncommon for a man to live to about 70. Elsewhere, he indicates that even 80 (which he apparently reached himself) was possible and desirable—as long as one remained mentally active.

Although the Greeks had a good chance of reaching old age, they do not seem to have viewed life during the later years as very pleas-ant—death was just around the corner. One need only remember the Underworld scene in Book 11 of the *Odyssey* where Achilles' ghost issues its chilling admonition to the visiting Odysseus that it would rather be the slave of the poorest ploughman than king over all the dead. Probably the most common reason stated in Greek literature for having children was so that they could care for their parents in old age, a time that, as seen from the following early poems, seemed to offer nothing but difficulties, disappointments, and fear. In the seventh century B.C., Mimnermus of Colophon would have thought that Pericles and the others we have mentioned had already lived too long; he recommended 60 as the ideal age to die. What followed, in his opinion, was not worth experiencing:

> What, then, is life if love the golden is gone? What is pleasure?
> 　　Better to die when the thought of these is lost from my heart:
> the flattery of surrender, the secret embrace in the darkness.
> 　　These alone are such charming flowers of youth as befall
> women and men. But once old age with its sorrows advances
> 　　upon us, it makes a man feeble and ugly alike,
> heart worn thin with the hovering expectation of evil,
> 　　lost all joy that comes out of the sight of the sun.
> Hateful to boys a man goes then, unfavored of women.
> 　　Such is the thing of sorrow the god has made of old age.
> (Lattimore, "Mimnermus" 1)

Some believe that Solon's more positive picture of aging is a direct response to the gloom of Mimnermus, whose sentiments were not isolated. Anacreon of Teos (sixth century B.C.) adds his "two cents" when he complains:

> I have gone gray at the temples,
> yes, my head is white, there's nothing
> of the grace of youth that's left me,
> and my teeth are like an old man's.
> Life is lovely. But the lifetime
> that remains for me is little.
> For this cause I mourn. The terrors
> of the Dark Pit never leave me.
> For the house of Death is deep down
> underneath; the downward journey
> to be feared, for once I go there
> I know well there's no returning.
> (Lattimore, "Anacreon" 5)

Most other existing examples from Greek literature do nothing to dispel the notion that old

Figure 6.22   *"Grandmother" figures, holding infants (British Museum, London)*

age was not a joyous time of life. Fictional characterizations of the elderly, particularly in Greek comedies, also do little positive for them.

In his final years, Plato may have hoped to realize the sentiment he expressed in the *Laws* that the aged were due the utmost respect; but Aphrodite was probably more realistic when she said old age was hated even by the gods. Perhaps the realities of old age and its alternative were best summed up by the tragic playwright Euripi-

des, who himself lived to be about 80. In his play the *Alcestis* (ll.669–672), he wrote:

> It is meaningless, the way the old men pray for
>   death
> and complain of age and the long time they
>   have to live.
> Let death only come close, not one of them
>   still wants
> to die. Their age is not a burden any more.

Socrates' students who mention Aspasia in their dialogues were active mostly in the fourth century B.C. They were just being born when Pericles died, when Socrates himself had only recently turned 40 and his reputation was emerging most forcefully. If these students had some personal acquaintance with Aspasia, it is more likely that they would have written about her and have had Socrates refer to her if they had firsthand knowledge of the relationship. Plato, for instance, may be representing himself when he has Menexenus tell Socrates that he has met Aspasia many times and knows what she is like. Their work may be an indication that Aspasia remained active in Athens for another decade or two.

Whenever Aspasia died, her memory continued strong. Admired or hated, one thing is clear: If only because of her decided influence on so many of its "architects," Aspasia deserves to be called the gilded edge to the Golden Age of Athens. But she was also a force herself. Few females in Greece were as politically powerful, albeit indirectly, and influential. The copious insults and character smears are testimony to the stature she achieved in a male-dominated society.

Suggestions for Further Reading

Thucydides and Plutarch's life of *Pericles* are the best ancient sources for the period. *Pericles* 24 has the fullest account of Aspasia. Sourcebooks such as C. W. Fornara's *Archaic Times to the End of the Peloponnesian War* (Cambridge: Cambridge University Press, 1983) and Pollitt's work cited in Chapter 5 are useful collections for Aspasia, Phidias, and Periclean Athens. A major treatment of Aspasia is M. M. Henry's *Prisoner of History: Aspasia of Miletus and Her Biographical Tradition* (New York: Oxford University Press, 1995). Of related interest is D. Hamel, *Trying Neaira: The True Story of a Courtesan's Scandalous Life in Ancient Greece* (New Haven: Yale University Press, 2003). On women in general, E. Fantham et al.'s study *Women in the Classical World* (New York: Oxford University Press, 1994) is the best starting place. Also of interest are M. Lefkowitz and M. B. Fant, *Women's Life in Greece & Rome* (Baltimore: The Johns Hopkins University Press, 1983); R. Hawley and B. Levick, *Women in Antiquity: New Assessments* (New York: Routledge, 1995); I. McAusland and P. Walcot (eds.), *Women in Antiquity* (New York: Oxford University Press, 1996); S. Murnaghan and S. R. Joshel (eds.), *Women and Slaves in Greco-Roman Culture* (New York: Routledge, 1998); and J. Rowlandson (ed.), *Women and Society in Greek and Roman Egypt* (Cambridge: Cambridge University Press, 1998). For Greek women, specifically, see S. Lewis, *The Athenian Woman* (New York: Routledge, 2002); S. Pomeroy (see also Chapter 4), *Spartan Women* (New York: Oxford University Press, 2002); M. Dillon, *Girls and Women in Classical Greek Religion* (New York: Routledge, 2002); S. Blundell, *Women in Ancient Greece* (Cambridge, Mass.: Harvard University Press, 1995), and Blundell and M. Williamson, *The Sacred and the Feminine in Ancient Greece* (New York: Routledge, 1998); H. King, *Hippocrates' Women: Reading the Female Body in Ancient Greece* (New York: Routledge, 1999); L. K. Taaffe, *Aristophanes and Women* (New York: Routledge, 1994); B. Cohen, *The Distaff Side: Representing the Female in Homer's* Odyssey (New York: Oxford University Press, 1995); and M. Lefkowitz, *Women in Greek Myth* (Baltimore: The Johns Hopkins University Press, 1990). On this and related topics in Chapter 6, see also J. Davidson, *Courtesans and Fishcakes: The Consuming Passions of Classical Athens* (New York: St. Martin's Press, 1998). For Semonides, see

H. Lloyd-Jones, *Females of the Species: Semonides on Women* (London: Gerald Duckworth & Co. Ltd., 1975). On the *Oeconomicus,* see S. Pomeroy's *Xenophon: Oeconomicus. A Social and Historical Commentary* (Oxford: Clarendon Press, 1994). Also of interest is L. Cohn-Haft, "Divorce in Classical Athens," *JHS* 115 (1995): 1–14. For Pericles and Athens, see D. Kagan's *Pericles of Athens and the Birth of Democracy* (New York: Free Press, 1991) and A. J. Podlecki's *Pericles and His Circle* (New York: Routledge, 1998).

On fifth-century Athens, see the studies by Meiggs and McGregor in Chapter 5. For Thucydides, pertinent works are G. Cawkwell, *Thucydides and the Peloponnesian War* (New York: Routledge, 1997); R. Luginbill, *Thucydides on War and National Character* (Boulder, Colo.: Westview Press, 1999); G. Crane, *Thucydides and the Ancient Simplicity: The Limits of Political Realism* (Berkeley and Los Angeles: University of California Press, 1998); and S. Hornblower, *Thucydides* (Baltimore: The Johns Hopkins University Press, 1987). V. Ehrenberg's *The People of Aristophanes* (New York: Schocken Books, 1962) is a sociological study of the people of Athens, including personalities discussed in this chapter, as seen through the eyes of Aristophanes in his plays (also pertinent for Chapter 7). A Lesky's *Greek Tragic Poetry* (New Haven, Conn.: Yale University Press, 1983) and H. D. F. Kitto's *Greek Tragedy: A Literary Study* (London: Methuen, 1966) are excellent studies of the works of Aeschylus, Sophocles, and Euripides. See, also, P. Wilson, *The Athenian Institution of the Khoregia: The Chorus, the City, and the Stage* (Cambridge: Cambridge University Press, 2000). P. Cartledge's *Sparta and Lakonia: A Regional History 1300–363 B.C.,* 2nd ed. (London: Henley & Boston, 2001) provides a recent overview of Sparta.

For other topics touched on in this chapter, consult R. Garland, *The Eye of the Beholder: Deformity and Disability in the Graeco-Roman World* (Ithaca, N.Y.: Cornell University Press, 1995); J. De Romilly, *The Great Sophists in Periclean Athens* (New York: Oxford University Press, 1992; B. S. Strauss, *Fathers and Sons in Athens: Ideology and Society in the Era of the Peloponnesian War* (Princeton, N.J.: Princeton University Press, 1997); and S. Lewis, *News and Society in the Greek Polis* (Chapel Hill: University of North Carolina Press, 1997). On old age, see T. M. Falkner, *The Poetics of Old Age in Greek Epic, Lyric, and Tragedy* (Norman: University of Oklahoma Press, 1995); Falkner and J. de Luce, *Old Age in Greek and Latin Literature* (Albany, N.Y.: SUNY Press, 1989); and R. B. Kebric, "Old Age, the Ancient Military, and Alexander's Army: Positive Examples for a Graying America," *Gerontologist* 28 (1988): 298–302. For medicine, see J. Longrigg, *Greek Rational Medicine* (New York: Routledge, 1993), and Longrigg (ed.), *Greek Medicine: From the Heroic to the Hellenistic Age—A Source Book* (Routledge, 1998). On the Acropolis, see J. M. Hurwit's *The Athenian Acropolis: History, Mythology, and Archaeology from the Neolithic Era to the Present* (Cambridge: Cambridge University Press, 2000).

General Reading

On general topics, see C. B. Patterson, *The Family in Greek History,* Rev. ed. (Cambridge, Mass.: Harvard University Press, 2001); S. B. Pomeroy, *Families in Classical and Hellenistic Greece* (New York: Oxford University Press, 1997); L. C. Nevett,

House and Society in the Ancient Greek World (Cambridge: Cambridge University Press, 1999); J. K. Davies, *Democracy and Classical Greece,* 2nd ed. (Cambridge, Mass.: Harvard University Press, 1993); and R. Osborne, *Classical Landscapes with Figures: The Ancient Greek City and Its Countryside* (London: G. Philip, 1987). On Athens and its democracy, see C. W. Fornara and L. J. Samons, *Athens from Cleisthenes to Pericles* (Berkeley and Los Angeles: University of California Press, 1991); C. Starr, *The Birth of Athenian Democracy* (New York: Oxford University Press, 1990); R. J. Littman, *Kinship in Athens 600–400 B.C.* (New York: Lang, 1990); D. Stockton, *The Classical Athenian Democracy* (New York: Oxford University Press, 1990); A. H. M. Jones, *Athenian Democracy* (Baltimore: The Johns Hopkins University Press, 1986); N. F. Jones, *The Associations of Classical Athens: The Response to Democracy* (New York: Oxford University Press, 1999); D. Boedecker and K. Raaflaub (eds.), *Democracy, Empire, and the Arts in Fifth-Century Athens* (Cambridge, Mass.: Harvard University Press, 1998); J. W. Roberts, *City of Socrates* (New York: Routledge, 1987); and A. Powell, *Athens and Sparta: Constructing Greek Political and Social History from 478 B.C.* (New York: Routledge, 1991). On Sparta, see Cartledge's other works, *The Spartans: The World of the Warrior-Heroes of Ancient Greece* (Woodstock and New York: The Overlook Press, 2003), *Spartan Reflections* (Berkeley and Los Angeles: University of California Press, 2001), and, with A. Spawforth, *Hellenistic and Roman Sparta,* 2nd ed. (New York: Routledge, 2001). Additional useful studies include S. Hodkinson, *Property and Wealth in Classical Sparta* (Duckworth and the Classical Press of Wales, 2000). N. M. Kennell, *The Gymnasium of Virtue: Education and Culture in Ancient Sparta* (Chapel Hill: University of North Carolina Press, 1996); Powell and S. Hodkinson, *The Shadow of Sparta* (New York: Routledge, 1994); L. F. Fitzhardinge, *The Spartans* (New York: Thames & Hudson, 1980); and the venerable W. G. Forrest, *A History of Sparta 950–192 B.C.* (New York: Norton, 1968). For the Peloponnesian War, Kagan's four-volume *History of the Peloponnesian War* (Ithaca, N.Y.: Cornell University Press, 1969–1987) is the most thorough treatment. On dining, see A. Dalby, *Siren Feasts: A History of Food and Gastronomy in Greece* (New York: Routledge, 1997); P. Garnsey, *Food and Society in Classical Antiquity* (Cambridge: Cambridge University Press, 1999); and Dalby and S. Grainger, *The Classical Cookbook* (New York: Oxford University Press, 1996).

7

Rowdies, Rogues, and Robbers

The Other Side of the Law in Fifth- and Fourth-Century Athens—Eratosthenes the Adulterer, Conon the Thug, "Clytemnestra" the Poisoner, Diogeiton the Embezzler, and Phormio the Con-Artist

Cleon: "I admit that I am a thief. You are not."
Sausageseller: "By Hermes . . . I am; and I perjure myself
even when there are eye-witnesses."
(Aristophanes, *Knights* 296–298)

When weighed from a distance, the passage of time inevitably causes "Golden Ages" to take on a luster they never had, making it difficult for us to distinguish the pyrite, or "fool's gold," from the nuggets. Conceivably, we live in a Golden Age today, although, bombarded daily with society's seemingly endless problems, few would think so. Like Hesiod, we fondly look back to what we think were happier, more prosperous times.

In Athens, there is no question that brilliant achievements took place during its "Golden Age," some having lasting impact. Pericles realized something special was happening when he referred to Athens as "the school of Hellas" in his Funeral Speech. Nonetheless, the city had always been full of those who cared nothing for art, beauty, philosophy, or anything else that did not fill their bellies, provide a jingle in their purses, or satisfy their desires below the belt.

As in any society, a certain—and in Athens, apparently considerable—segment of the population engaged in unlawful or disruptive behavior. It is ironic that in the city that many regard as the birthplace of the Western legal tradition, the "Thieves Market," where people knowingly bought stolen goods, was located right next door to the city's chief law court! One would certainly have to conclude that the Athenians were a tolerant people.

With the state having such an apparently relaxed attitude about lawbreakers and no meaningful police force, respectable Athenians must have constantly been on guard to protect themselves and their families from every sort of crime. Individuals were primarily responsible for bringing wrongdoers to court, and it was in the courts that the state assumed a major role in trying to see that justice was done. Predictably, the many courts of Athens were constantly in session, filled with what one comic playwright characterized as "the cheap, courtroom cant of this flabby, subpoena-serving, shyster-jargoned degeneration." Athenians were so litigious that the same playwright had one of his characters, jaded by it all, observe: "*That,* Athens? Don't be ridiculous. Why, I can't see even a single lawcourt in session" (Aristophanes, *Clouds,* ll. 206–208).

Figure 7.1

The excavated ancient Agora, or "marketplace," of Athens (foreground). Here or near here, much of the action described in this chapter took place.

Some Negative Characters from Theophrastus

ONE OF PEOPLE'S FAVORITE pastimes is watching and observing other people. From an individual's particular appearance or behavior, we have a tendency, consciously or unconsciously, to "categorize" or "typecast" that person. In Ancient Greece, this predilection was perhaps even more pronounced. One of the reasons was the widespread influence of drama, particularly tragedy, in which universal types—rather than real individuals—were portrayed on stage. Consequently, associating people one encountered in daily life with types seen on stage was almost unavoidable (the influence is still apparent in our movies today). By the Hellenistic period, this process had contributed to the development of an entire pseudoscience known as "physiognomy," the judgment of character from appearance.

The Peripatetic School, founded by Aristotle, was particularly keen in pursuing this line of inquiry, and Aristotle's successor, Theophrastus (c. 370–285 B.C.), was a major practitioner. Theophrastus produced a sketchbook of thirty different *Characters,* which revealed the broad array of "types" one might encounter in society.

Although his character sketches are not descriptions of named individuals whom we can precisely identify, they are nonetheless composites and representative of a number of real people whom Theophrastus had personally observed. "Negative" characters are not lacking, as can be seen in the following example. (Two other examples appear later in the chapter, on pp. 214 and 226.)

The Man Without Moral Feeling

Lack of moral feeling is willingness to do or say what is disgraceful. The man without moral feeling is the kind who will take an oath with no sense of responsibility, since he does not mind letting himself in for hard words or even downright abuse. By nature he is a base kind of person, lacking the most elementary sense of decency and capable of absolutely anything. Dead sober, he will do a belly dance when he is supposed to be part of a comic chorus; and at a puppet show he goes around collecting the penny admission from everybody and arguing with pass-holders who think they have a right to watch free. Very likely he runs a shady hotel or a whore-house, too, or collects taxes. Town crier, gambler, cook—no trade is too disgraceful for this fellow. He leaves his mother without support in her old age; he gets hauled into court for petty theft and knows the inside of the town jail better than his own house.

[This man also seems to be the sort who gets a crowd around him and lectures his listeners in a loud, cracked voice, trading arguments and abuse. And some of them arrive in the middle of his tirade, while others leave without bothering to hear it all; but he obliges with a summary of whatever is left out, convinced that there's no occasion so proper for a display of his lack of moral feeling as when he has an audience.]

In court, moreover, he is capable of playing any role: defendant, plaintiff, or witness. Sometimes he gets out of testifying by swearing ignorance; or he may appear in court as a witness, with stacks of evidence inside his coat and whole handfuls of documents. He knows a good many rascals, and he will not disqualify even the worst of them from high office. More than that, he lends money to these fellows the moment they ask for the loan—collecting interest, to be sure, at a rate of three obols in twelve, not yearly or monthly but daily. He gets the interest from their businesses, too, and makes the rounds of baker's and fishmonger's with the money stuffed into his cheek.

[They are a troublesome lot, always ready with an insult and talking so loudly that the market-place and the shops echo.]
(*Characters* 6)

Ultimately, most lawbreakers were dealt with and received their punishment, but the fact that there were so many "services" to help defendants get out of a pinch indicates that taking someone to court guaranteed nothing. Another comic poet joked during the fourth century B.C. that legal ploys were so common one could pick them up with the groceries while shopping at the market:

> . . . You will find everything sold together in the same place at Athens—figs, *summoners,* bunches of grapes, turnips, pears, apples, *witnesses,* roses, medlars, haggis, honeycombs, chickpeas, *lawsuits,* beestings, beestings-pudding, myrtle, *allotment machines,* iris, lambs, *waterclocks* [with which to time speakers in court], *laws, indictments.*
> (Eubulus as quoted by Athenaeus 14.640b–c)

The history of law and order at Athens is a muddled affair at best. As mentioned in Chapter 4, the first law code was traditionally attributed to Draco in 621 B.C. If the actual tenor of the code was anything like its memory, then clearly, the tolerance for lawbreakers—of any kind—or slackers had worn rather thin:

> One penalty was specified for nearly all offenders, death; so that those convicted of idleness were put to death, and those who stole vegetables or fruit were punished in the same way as temple-robbers or killers. Consequently, Demades in later times was a hit when he said that Draco wrote his laws in blood, not in ink. Draco himself, they say, when asked why he fixed death as the penalty for most offenses, answered that he thought small offenses deserved it, and he knew no greater penalty for great ones.
> (Plutarch, *Solon* 17.2–4)

By 594 B.C., however, we are told that Solon's reforms had swept away Draco's laws except for those regarding homicide and that he had instituted a new and more comprehensive code, displaying it on wooden blocks for all to see. Eventually, this code, with additional laws and amendments, was inscribed on stone and formed the legal foundation for the Classical period in Athens—the so-called law of Solon.

Subsequently, any citizen was able to propose a new law, and if it was approved by the majority of the assembly, it became law. The new law was then inscribed in a public place so that all could refer to it, but this procedure caused problems because, over a period of time, the laws of Athens literally became spread all over town. Until the end of the fifth century B.C., there does not appear to have been any central place where one could go to find a specific law. Consequently, wronged people looking to prosecute had first to wander through various buildings, reading as they went, to discover the official version of the law that applied to them! Fortunately, some effort was made to place related laws in the same general vicinity, but we can still imagine some poor soul in search of an obscure statute haunting the porticoes of temples, stoas, and monuments, wondering whether he was ever going to get his lawsuit moving.

As already indicated, the law and the courts of Athens were a favorite topic of the comic poets, and taking a potentially confusing situation such as the one previously described to the extreme was one of their specialties. In his fullest exposé on the subject, the *Wasps*, Aristophanes, in the form of an old man named Philocleon, unerringly pokes fun at the sizable number of people in Athens who seem to thrive on jury duty: "What *I* like's a little lawsuit, chopped up fine and stewed in its own juice" (ll. 510–511).

A large percentage of elderly sat on Athenian juries as the aged were more available for service. Sitting on a jury was also a change from what was an otherwise boring routine for many. It gave a feeling of importance, usefulness—and excitement. Jury duty also supplied a livable (but meager) wage, comprising a form of welfare for older citizens who had little or no income—not to mention opportunities for bribery:

> "No sooner do I go inside than a tender hand steals into mine, still warm from tapping the Treasury. And then they beg, and bow, and wheedle, and whine. 'Father,' they say (they call me Father), 'pity me, Father' . . . Do you think that a Very Important Person like that would know that I was alive, if I hadn't acquitted him once before?"
> (*Wasps* 553–558)

If we were to believe Aristophanes (and one always has to be aware that caricatures were oftentimes more important to the comic playwright than reality), old people were falling over one another to serve. In this case, Philocleon's son has had to lock him in his house and station guards at the door to prevent him from hurrying down to the courts. Aristophanes humorously characterizes Philocleon's "disease" thus:

> He's a JURY-addict! Most violent case on record.
> He's wild to render verdicts, and bawls like a baby
> if ever he misses a seat on the very first bench.
> He doesn't get any sleep at night, not a wink.
> Or, if he closes his eyes a speck, he's in Court—
> all night his mind goes flapping around the water-clock.
> You know those pebbles that the Jurors drop into the urns
> marked *Guilty* and *Not Guilty,* to record their votes on the verdict?
> Well, he's squeezed *his* pebble so often and so hard
> that when he wakes up, he has three fingers stuck together,
> like someone putting incense on the festival altar.
> And worse. Let him see the name of a fathead faggot

scrawled on a wall—"*I letch for Demos; he's a doll*"—
and he scratches beside it, "*I itch for the Jury; it's a jewel.*"
Once his rooster didn't crow till sundown. Know
what he said? "That cock's corrupt! The officials under investigation
bribed him to wake me up too late for Court!"
Now he shouts for his shoes right after supper;
he's over there *way* before dawn, and goes to sleep
clutching a courtroom column just like a barnacle.
And nasty—watch him in action! When he takes his wax tablet
to fix the penalty, he always draws the Long Line:
everyone gets the maximum sentence from him!
Then off for home like a bee—or a *bumble*-bee—
wax just plastered underneath his fingernails.
He's petrified that he might run out of those pebbles
he uses for voting; so he keeps a *beach* in the house.
In sum, he's insane; the more we reason with him,
the more he judges everybody else. Absolutely
hopeless. Incurable.
(*Wasps* 87–113)

Although the courts of Athens provided a never-ending stream of material for contemporary comics, they also provide us with some of the most

Figure 7.2
Small representations of the types of comic actors in masks who appeared in the plays of Aristophanes (British Museum, London)

realistic and invaluable insights into the lives and characters of typical Athenian citizens that we possess. A number of prosecution and defense speeches survive from the late fifth and fourth centuries B.C., mostly prepared by orators such as Lysias, Isocrates, Demosthenes, Antiphon, and Isaeus, for their clients' use in court. They expose a human side of Athens that we would not otherwise have. Through them, we become acquainted with the Athenians and their city on their own terms. We do not have to guess, for everything is laid out for us in rare and welcome detail. Here is illustrated life on the local level. We see people involved in the same kinds of situations and problems that affect all societies and families when human beings of every social strata, age, and moral outlook live and work together.

An accused adulterer, ruffian, poisoner, embezzler, and con-artist have unknowingly added a significant chapter to our knowledge of classical Athens.

Eratosthenes—An Adulterer's Luck Runs Out (c. 400 B.C.)

Euphiletus' wife was not the first to be seduced by Eratosthenes. His conquests were reputed to be numerous, and he apparently had little difficulty in winning over the affections of the women he pursued. He was a professional adulterer, and one day his roving eye fell on another victim—his last, although he could not have known it at the time.

Eratosthenes first saw Euphiletus' wife (her name is not known), ironically, at the funeral of her mother-in-law. Conceiving a desire for her, he bided his time, learning more about Euphiletus' household, particularly which of the maids went to the market. Eventually, he approached that maid and asked that she convey his secret longings to her mistress. For whatever reason, the wife was receptive to Eratosthenes' advances, and a liaison began.

Up to this point, by Euphiletus' own admission, his wife had been a model to her sex: "She was a clever housewife, economical and exact in her management of everything." He wished her to be content and happy, but at the same time, he thought it proper to keep a watchful eye on her. However, when she bore him a son, his trust for her became complete. That, he would later complain, was the beginning of his undoing.

Euphiletus' house was a small one (his description of its interior is the most complete that we have). The men's and women's quarters were separated, the former being downstairs, the latter, upstairs. The two were connected only by a ladder. Euphiletus, however, decided to reverse this arrangement:

> After the birth of my child, his mother nursed him; but I did not want her to run the risk of going downstairs every time she had to give him a bath, so I

Figure 7.3
Central section of a funeral procession for a Greek doctor named Patron (late first century B.C.), showing—and naming—his wife and two daughters (left). It was at a similar solemn affair that Eratosthenes first spotted Euphiletus' wife. (Louvre, Paris)

myself took over the upper story, and let the women have the ground floor. And so it came about that by this time it was quite customary for my wife often to go downstairs and sleep with the child, so that she could give him the breast and stop him from crying.

This arrangement was more than satisfactory for the wife—and for Eratosthenes—since in his concern over spouse and child, Euphiletus had provided his own house as a convenient rendezvous for the two lovers. While he slept upstairs, they made love below.

The affair went on for some time, and the husband, continuing to praise his wife and thinking her the most chaste woman in Athens, suspected nothing; but one day he arrived home earlier than expected from the country. Unaware that he had an uninvited guest in his house, Euphiletus dined, and later, when the baby started crying, he directed his wife to go downstairs to feed him. She hesitated at first, perhaps realizing that the maid, hoping to draw attention to Eratosthenes' presence, was purposely pinching the child to make him cry. She told Euphiletus that his long absence made her want to remain with him. However, Euphiletus became so annoyed that he finally insisted that she leave and attend the baby. "Oh, yes!" she recovered beautifully. "To leave *you* alone with the maid up here! You mauled her about before, when you were drunk!" Euphiletus laughed, and his wife got

Figure 7.4
Terra-cotta model of a woman asleep in a bed, Eretria (?), third century B.C. The bed has a wooden frame and flexible sleeping surface held by thongs. Euphiletus' wife would go downstairs to sleep in the women's quarters and attend her child—and her lover. (British Museum, London)

up and went out the door, locking it as if it, too, were part of the joke. Tired from his journey, the trusting husband soon drifted off to sleep, awakened only briefly by the sound of creaking doors.

His wife returned just before morning and unlocked the door. When her husband asked about the creaking sounds he had heard, she offered that she had to go next door to rekindle the baby's lamp, which had gone out during the night. Euphiletus was satisfied with the explanation, although he thought he noticed that his wife was wearing makeup. This would have been entirely inappropriate—especially since her brother had died recently. Still, he suspected nothing. The lovers had escaped detection and had turned what had been a "close call" into an entire night of unconcerned pleasure.

More time passed, and the affair continued to go on right under Euphiletus' nose, but one day, as he was coming home, an old hag stopped him. She had been sent by Eratosthenes' former mistress, who had recently discovered why her lover had not been by to see her and was now bent on revenge:

> "Euphiletus," she said, "please don't think that my approaching you is in any way due to a wish to interfere. The fact is, the man who is wronging you and your wife is an enemy of ours. Now if you catch the woman who does your shopping and works for you, and put her through an examination, you will discover all. The culprit," she added, "is Eratosthenes from Oea. Your wife is not the only one he has seduced—there are plenty of others. It's his profession."

So saying, she left. Euphiletus, shocked, began remembering the night of the creaking doors, when his wife had locked him in his room—and her rouged face! Now realizing the truth, he immediately sought out the servant the old hag had identified. Removing her to the house of a friend, he threatened her with punishment if she did not tell the truth, but he offered his pardon if she did. The maid pretended to know nothing at first, but when Euphiletus mentioned Eratosthenes by name, she broke down and, reminding her master of his promise to do her no harm, told him all she knew. She

Figure 7.5
Reconstructions of
actual Athenian
houses. Some of the
action described in this
chapter took place in
dwellings similar to
these.

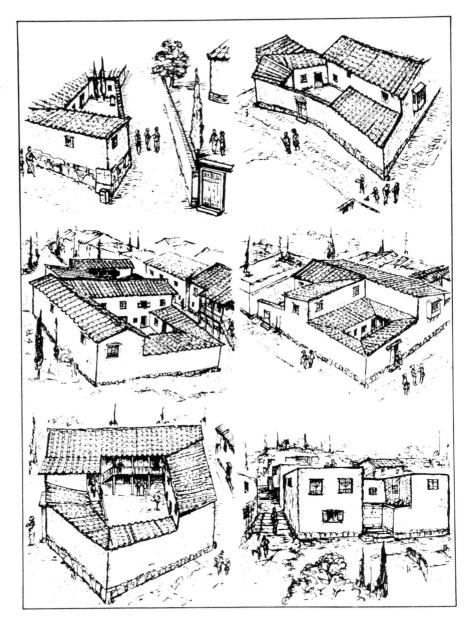

told how Eratosthenes had approached her with a message for her mistress after the funeral, how his persuasions eventually won her over, how he gained access to the house, and how while Euphiletus had been out of town, his wife had attended a religious service with Eratosthenes' mother to make everything seem proper. Euphiletus swore the woman to secrecy, and then he detailed how he wanted her to help him catch the lovers together in his house. Helpless to do otherwise, she agreed.

A few days later, Euphiletus dined at home with a relative who had just returned from the country, then went off to bed after his guest had left. Not much later, the maid, as directed, awakened him with the news that Eratosthenes was in the house. Euphiletus told her to watch the door while he slipped out and rounded up as many of his neighbors as he could find. When he had collected them, they obtained torches and entered his house. Euphiletus describes what happened next:

> We forced the bedroom door. The first of us to enter saw him still lying beside my wife. Those who followed saw him standing naked on the bed.
>
> I knocked him down . . . with one blow. I then twisted his hands behind his back and tied them. And then I asked him why he was committing this crime against me, of breaking into my house.
>
> He answered that he admitted his guilt; but he begged and besought me not to kill him—to accept a money-payment instead.
>
> But I replied:
>
> "It is not I who shall be killing you, but the law of the State, which you, in transgressing, have valued less highly than your own pleasures. You have preferred to commit this great crime against my wife and my children, rather than to obey the law and be of decent behavior."

Euphiletus executed Eratosthenes on the spot—which, according to Athenian law, was a justifiable act in these circumstances.

Even though the wronged husband was entitled to dispose of the adulterer in this fashion—although usually the guilty party would pay a sum of money, as Eratosthenes himself was quick to point out—the dead man's relatives brought charges of murder against Euphiletus. They contended that Eratosthenes had not been caught "in the act" and killed, as the law allowed, but that the murder was premeditated. They said that Euphiletus had seized Eratosthenes in the street, dragged him off from an altar where he had taken refuge, and murdered him. Consequently, Euphiletus was charged with homicide and brought before the court. The penalty, if one was found guilty, was death, although after the first day of trial, the accused could voluntarily go into exile and his property would be confiscated.

Certainly, some parts of Euphiletus' story are shaky: His naivete over such a long period of time seems suspect, and it was most convenient that Euphiletus just happened to bring his relative home for dinner the exact night Eratosthenes was killed. He could claim that he had been entertaining his guest—not planning a murder as the prosecution charged. His success in rounding up a number of neighbors at night at a moment's notice was also more than fortunate, although he emphasizes how difficult it had been

Figure 7.6
A woman cowers timidly inside, fearing the approach of a drunken reveler (presumably her husband), who brandishes a torch and threatens to break down the door. Wine, as evidenced in this chapter (see also Chapter 4 on Theodotus), was often the cause for domestic and other violence in ancient Athens. (The Metropolitan Museum of Art)

to collect them. We might also wonder if he would want to expose himself to the kind of embarrassment and ridicule that revealing his wife's adultery firsthand would cause. There is good reason to believe that he knew what was going on under his roof, but why he waited to act at this time and what his ulterior motives (if any) were, are difficult to determine. Nevertheless, no one came forward to dispute his testimony, and there were many to support it. Although we do not know the findings of the court, it is probably safe to assume that he was found innocent.

Adultery was a serious business, since for purposes of inheritance and ancestral worship, blood line could not be a matter of question. The violation of his wife, who would have been automatically divorced by her actions, and household—as well as Eratosthenes' reputation as a philanderer—would have been enough for most jury members to set Euphiletus free and feel his savage behavior justified. The fact that Lysias (*Oration* 1), one of the great advocates of the day, prepared the defendant's speech may demonstrate that the case was not open and shut for Euphiletus. As part of his strategy, he took the position that the law itself instructed that he must kill the malefactor. This, of course, was not true, but it helped establish the sense that he had not been taking the law into his own hands. Euphiletus appears to have represented himself cleverly—as a man protecting not only his own household but also the community.

A Casual Act of Violence—Conon the Thug and His Sons (c. 340 B.C.)

Ariston's problems first began while he was on garrison duty on the Attic frontier, when the sons of Conon pitched their tent close to him and his companions. Their unrefined habits, coarse language, and drunkenness, quite alien to the lifestyle of Ariston and his friends, inevitably spilled over into their preserve, despite their attempts to keep to themselves. There could be no peace as long as Conon's sons were around. To be sure, they were an undesirable lot:

> They used to begin drinking immediately after lunch, and continue all day long. This they did every day during all the time we were on garrison duty. Our way of life was the same out there as at home. Thus, when the time came for others to have dinner, these men would be playing drunken tricks, for the most part on our servants, but in the end upon us too. They used to pretend that the servants annoyed them with the smoke of their cooking, or that they were impertinent—any kind of excuse; and for this they used to thrash them and empty the chamber-pots over them and urinate at them. There was no sort of disgusting outrage they left undone.

Ariston and his companions told their neighbors to stop pestering them, but their efforts were met with insults, so they went to the garrison commander and protested. He apparently had already been informed of their rowdiness, and making a personal visit to their tent, he censured them for their unruly behavior. Conon's sons were unimpressed, giving him a dose of the same medicine for which they had become famous around camp. The commander's harsh words did little more than resolve the brothers to take revenge and attack Ariston's tent that evening. If a number of officers and men had not come to their rescue when they heard the commotion raised by Conon's drunken progeny, Ariston and his compatriots might have been badly injured. As it was, they escaped with minor damage, but the bad feelings would continue even after the men finished their tour of duty and returned home. (They were not professional soldiers, but members of Athens' citizen militia.) However, Ariston took a cautious approach, deciding that the best course was to try to avoid contact with his antagonists—and, in the future, others like them.

One day while Ariston was taking an evening stroll with a friend in the Athenian marketplace, Ctesias, one of Conon's sons, saw him and, drunk as usual, yelled out at him. Muttering something inaudible to Ariston, he then rushed off to a suburb of Athens where his father and some friends were engaged in a drinking party at the house of a comrade who owned a laundry. He apparently had little trouble coaxing the revelers to follow him, for they soon caught up with Ariston and his friend, who were still walking in the market, and attacked them:

> We happened to have turned back, and were again walking in about the same place, near the Monument, when we encountered them. As we came close, one of them, I don't know which, fell upon my friend Phanostratus and held him, while Conon and his son and Theogenes attacked me. First they tore off my clothes, then they tripped me up, threw me into the mud, jumped on me and kicked me with such violence that my lip was cut through and my eyes were closed up. In this state they left me, unable to get up or utter a word.

The assailants then peppered him with filthy words, and Conon, who was over 50 at the time, imitated a victorious cock in a cockfight, a popular sport in Athens. Jokingly, he crowed like a rooster and flapped his arms against his sides like wings. When he and his friends had left (taking their victim's cloak with them), some bystanders carried Ariston, naked, to his home, where his mother and servants, greatly distressed, began screaming and crying to the extent that the neighbors inquired about what was happening. After they had calmed down, they decided to take him to a public bath and clean him up before summoning a physician. On the way, they met Meidias, one of Ariston's relatives, who, with a friend, was coming home from dinner. They accompanied Ariston to the baths and remained while the doctor examined him. Since he was so weak, he spent the night at Meidias' house, which was nearby:

> Such, then, was the immediate condition to which I was reduced by the blows and injuries I had received. Later, the doctor said that the swellings on my face and the cuts and bruises gave no great cause for alarm. But a high temperature followed, and continued without intermission, together with sharp and violent pains throughout my whole system, and especially my sides and abdomen. I was unable to take any food; and as the doctor said, if a sudden discharge of blood had not relieved me at the most painful and critical moment, I should have died of suppuration. As it was, the loss of blood saved my life.

Figure 7.7
Building foundation in the Athenian Agora that has tentatively been identified as the Athenian prison. If so, this is where troublemakers of the sort mentioned in this chapter were imprisoned. It would also be where Socrates was confined and executed.

Ariston recovered and eventually took the matter to court. As might be expected, when Conon realized that he was involved in serious litigation and that there was no escaping the suit, he utilized every dodge imaginable—bluffing, stalling, and irrelevantly claiming that his son was illegitimate and a "victim of society." He produced the sworn statements of false witnesses, who, by their names, were recognizable as his cronies and partners in mischief and crime, men who were at the drinking party the night of the incident. He had other ploys, just as contemptible, that he planned to use during the trial, but Ariston exposed them all. Among other things, he revealed that in his boyhood, Conon had belonged to a gang that called itself the Huns and included in its membership a man the state had already executed. These hooligans had gone so far as to feed themselves from the offerings others made to the dead.

Demosthenes (*Oration* 54), the greatest orator of the fourth century B.C., prepared Ariston's case, making it clear that the medical evidence undermined whatever bogus evidence the defense could produce. The known good character of Ariston, the reputable witnesses who supported his claims, and Conon's general reputation as a troublemaker also worked against him. As every responsible citizen's nightmare, he undoubtedly received the punishment he deserved.

The Offensive Man

OFFENSIVENESS CAN BE DEFINED with no difficulty: it is amusing yourself in an obtrusive, objectionable way. The offensive man is the kind who exposes himself when he passes respectable married women on the street. At the theater he goes on clapping after everyone else has stopped and hisses the actors who are public favorites; should there be general silence for a moment, he cocks his head and lets out a belch to make the audience turn round in their seats.

What's more, during the busiest part of the day downtown he strolls over where nuts and berries are on sale, and stands there munching them without paying while he talks to the poor merchant. He shouts a greeting to someone he hardly knows, too, and uses the man's name in a familiar way; or he calls, "Stop a minute!" to people who are obviously in a hurry; or if you have just lost an important case, he stops you outside the courtroom and jokes about what happened. He also goes shopping personally for fancy items—and lays out money for a party-girl. Then he shows off his purchase to everybody he meets, with an invitation to stop by and sample this specialty. And he lounges around outside the barber shop explaining in full detail his intention to get drunk.

He damns fortune-tellers up and down, too, with his mother just back from seeing one, and during the service of prayer and libation he lets the cup drop and laughs as if he had done something clever. Or while the others are all quietly listening to the playing of a girl entertainer, he makes himself conspicuous by clapping time and whistling along with the music and then criticizing her for stopping so soon. At a formal dinner he goes to spit across the table and hits the waiter. (Theophrastus, *Characters* 11)

In-Law Problems—A Poisonous Stepmother? (c. 420 B.C.)

Philoneos took a long draught and keeled over dead. His companion became deathly ill and died three weeks later. Philoneos' concubine, a slave trying to win back her master's love, unknowingly served the two men their fatal doses—for which she was tortured and executed—thinking it was a love potion. Philoneos' friend's wife, his second, escaped punishment even though she had devised the entire scheme. Years later, her stepson, now of legal age, charged her with murder. The young man explained:

There was in our house an upper room, which Philoneos used to occupy whenever he had business in town. This Philoneos was an honest, respectable man, a friend of my father's. He had a concubine, whom he was intending to dispose of to a brothel. My step-mother, having heard of this, made a friend of the woman; and when she got to know of the injury Philoneos was proposing to do her, she sent for her. When the woman came, my step-mother told her that she herself also was being wrongly treated, by my father; and that if the woman would do as she said, she was clever enough to restore the love of Philoneos for his concubine, and my father's love for herself. As she expressed it, hers was the creative part, the other woman's part was that of obeying orders.

The woman innocently and eagerly offered her cooperation, and some time later, it happened that both Philoneos and the young man's father had business at the seaport of Athens, the Piraeus. The father was leaving on a trip to the island of Naxos, and his friend was going to attend a religious ceremony in honor of Zeus. The two decided to accompany one another to the harbor, and Philoneos thought it would be agreeable to treat his departing friend to a feast after he performed his religious duties. His concubine went along to assist with the sacrifice, and with the banquet. She carried a drug, which she had received from her co-conspirator and thought was a love potion.

After completing the religious ceremonies, the two men sat down to dinner, and the concubine began serving them. She had not yet decided when to administer the drug, but after considering her options, she thought it best to wait until after they had eaten:

> When they had finished dinner, they naturally—as one of them was sacrificing to Zeus and entertaining a guest, and the other was about to set off on a voyage and was dining with his friend—they naturally were proceeding to pour libations, and accompany them with an offering of incense. Philoneos's concubine, as she was serving them with the wine for the libation—a libation that was to accompany prayers destined, alas . . . not to be fulfilled—poured in the poison. And in the belief that she was doing something clever, she gave the bigger dose to Philoneos, thinking that perhaps the more she gave him, the more he would love her. She still did not know that she had been deceived by my step-mother, and did not find out until she was already involved in disaster. She poured a smaller dose for my father.
>
> The two men poured out their libation; and then, taking in hand that which was their own destroyer, they drained their last draught.

Before he died, the boy's father indicated that he thought he had been poisoned by his wife. This attempt was not the first one she had made on his life, since he had previously caught her concocting "love potions" meant for him, and even the household slaves knew about it. He enjoined his son to avenge his murder.

Presumably, the son had to grow up with his half brothers in the same household as the woman he suspected of killing his father—a difficult situation at best. How much time passed before he reached his majority is not clear. When he was finally old enough to charge his stepmother with murder, the concubine was long dead, and there was not much corroborating evidence to support his claim. To make matters worse, his own half brothers created an almost Cinderellan dilemma for him by challenging his allegations and denying that their mother conspired to kill their father. They did not question the facts he presented—only the motive—arguing that their mother's only guilt was trying to recover their father's affections by having the concubine administer a love potion to him. The terrible result surprised her as much as anyone.

Although this explanation may seem a little feeble to us today, the traffic in love and other potions was very intense in antiquity, and sometimes a mistake in a pinch or measure of an ingredient was the difference between life and death. Obviously, "overdoses" were not uncommon occurrences, and attributing the husband's death to such a mistake was believable in the eyes of many.

Nonetheless, the young man could not understand why his half brothers were so adamantly protecting their mother when she had killed the man who was also their father. They should be helping him, he argued, but they had no desire to learn the truth. If they did, they could simply question knowledgeable household slaves under torture (necessary in legal matters) to obtain the facts, but they would not. Still, they "know for certain" that their mother committed no crime.

The case certainly would not have been an easy one to decide—especially since it was between in-laws and half brothers (the eldest of the latter handled his mother's defense, since a woman could not defend herself in court). The young man's determination to pursue the matter after so many years would seem to be to his credit, but his arguments, prepared by a prominent advocate, Antiphon (*Oration* 1), could not be conclusive. The most crucial evidence in his favor—testimony by slaves familiar with his stepmother's questionable activities—was apparently not available to him, and this fact gives the case another interesting aspect.

If slaves who had been his father's were no longer his to command, then it follows that they were not now his property and lived in a household separate from his own. Consequently, the matter of inheritance comes up. If the son had been disinherited in favor of his half brothers, there was an additional motivation for his striking out at his stepmother at the earliest opportunity. Despite the cordiality expressed during the trial, the family could not have been on very good terms with one another. The half brothers may have known nothing about their mother's innocence or guilt—their father was dead and had been dead for some time. Nothing could change that. Their main interest in opposing their half brother, therefore, may have been to protect their inheritance, for if their mother were found guilty, most certainly they would have lost it all.

Did the woman purposely kill her husband? It seems likely, but we will never know for sure. If she did, it would not be the first time a disgruntled spouse acted to dispose of an unwanted mate—or to put the interests of natural children above those of a stepchild.

Diogeiton—A Grandfather Turns Embezzler (c. 400 B.C.)

Diogeiton's brother Diodotus was a wealthy businessman. Diogeiton, apparently hoping to benefit in some way from Diodotus' success, convinced his brother to marry within the family—ostensibly to preserve the fortune from outsiders—and offered his daughter as the best possible candidate. (Uncles marrying nieces was allowable under Athenian law.) Diodotus took his brother's advice and married his niece, and the union produced two sons and a daughter.

Some years later, Diodotus was called up for active military service, and realizing that he could be killed, he wished to put his affairs in order. Since Diogeiton was his brother (and father-in-law) and his children's grandfather (and uncle), Diodotus believed him best suited to be the children's guardian in case something happened. He gave Diogeiton his will and a sizable amount of money. He outlined his various finances in detail, and he left specific instructions about what his wife and daughter were to receive (essentially, as dowries for future marriages). He then deposited a sealed copy of this information at his house and went off on campaign. Unfortunately, he was killed at Ephesus in Asia Minor.

Apparently, Diogeiton was the only one notified of Diodotus' death, for he was able to conceal the fact from the rest of the family and moved to secure his brother's fortune before anyone else found out. He knew he would have to remove the copy of the sealed documents Diodotus had left at home if he were going to be successful, so using as his excuse his need to refer to them for business matters, he was able to obtain them. Consequently, after embezzling almost everything for himself, he finally revealed his brother's death.

Diodotus' wife and children performed the customary funeral rites and then lived for a year at the Piraeus, where all their provisions had been left. When these ran out, Diogeiton took charge as the executor of his brother's estate and guardian of his children. He sent the children back to Athens and married off his daughter again, using for her dowry the money Diodotus had designated (of course, keeping some of it for himself).

Eight years passed, and when the elder of Diodotus' two sons reached legal age, the greedy grandfather summoned both boys and informed them

Pasion—Former Slave Turned Wealthy Citizen Banker at Athens

SOME OF THE MOST interesting cases preserved for us from the law courts of ancient Athens concern a man named Pasion (especially Isocrates, *Oration* 17; and Demosthenes, *Orations* 36, 45) and his family. A former slave, Pasion had become a banker and a citizen—and died perhaps the wealthiest man in Athens. It is not surprising that a man of such circumstance would occasionally find himself involved in legal troubles, and records, including statements by his son Apollodorus (who was frequently involved in court after his father's death), reveal the details of Pasion's life. His "rags to riches" story provides an unusual insight into how a former slave was able to throw off his shackles, raise himself and family to the heights of the same society that had enslaved him—and have slaves of his own.

Slavery in Ancient Greece was not practiced uniformly, and Athens and Sparta are the best examples. Sparta had a built-in system of slavery, having suppressed the native population of neighboring Messenia in the eighth century B.C. The Spartan servile population was referred to as helots, and because they outnumbered their masters by a significant margin, they always provided a potential threat to Spartan security. At Athens, when Solon abolished debt-slavery in the sixth century B.C., the Athenians were obliged to obtain their slaves through the traditional methods—prisoners of war, piracy, and unwanted children. Once a slave population had been established, slaves bred new slaves. Athens, or more properly the 1,000-square-mile area of Attica, had a slave population at its height of up to 100,000. Since most Greek slaves were ethnically indistinguishable from their masters, it was difficult to know strictly from appearance who was a slave and who was not. They wore similar clothes, worked the same jobs, and earned the same wages as free men. Indeed, outside of Athens, wherever debt-slavery continued, former citizens were still enslaved. An imperfect accent was certain betrayal of nonlocal roots, but even so, everyone knew who was slave and who was not. The law also reinforced a slave's status.

Practically everyone, from whatever economic strata, owned at least one slave. The wealthier one was, the more slaves one had. The households of prominent individuals were run by slaves, usually under the supervision of the wife (see, for example, Ischomachus' instruction to his wife, p. 179) or a senior slave. There were, of course, escapes, but it was difficult for a runaway slave to find refuge. Marriage was encouraged because it was thought unlikely that a slave would abandon a wife and children. There was also an unwritten law that fugitive slaves were to be returned, but many who had been born into slavery had no idea where to go, anyway. An example from the Peloponnesian War also illustrates the frustration. The Spartans offered refuge to all runaway slaves from Athens, and then simply re-enslaved those who took them up on the offer. Except at Sparta, where the helots were under continual supervision, the Greeks do not appear to have feared their slaves as the Roman did. The scale and diversity of the institution in Greece never approached that in Italy and Sicily.

It appears there was little or no moral issue over slavery in Ancient Greece because no particular group of individuals was enslaved by another. Human servitude was a fact of life, and, while it was an unpleasant situation to contemplate, theoretically, anyone might become a slave at any time. An ocean voyage could end a person's independence if captured by pirates since he would be sold into slavery unless a ransom could be arranged. A neighbor of Pasion's son, for example, was seized by privateers at sea, ironically while pursuing some runaway slaves of his own, and was himself shackled and enslaved at Aegina before being ransomed.

Figure 7.8 *A well-attired and disinterested maid shades her mistress from the sun. (British Museum, London)*

Slaves, of course, were property. At the lowest level, a slave who had accepted his status might be treated like a member of the household. An unskilled slave could, however, get stuck in the Athenian state mines and, depending on the work, might not live long. Female slaves could end up in brothels, some state run, or as courtesans, which was preferable to a common prostitute, as seen in the case of Aspasia (see pp. 171–196). She owned and trained ladies of her own and profited from their charms. Slaves who were highly skilled could usually look forward to better treatment. There was no good reason to mistreat a slave who brought in profits, although there were always some sadistic masters. Skilled slaves enjoyed a greater amount of freedom while

plying their trades, shared earnings with their masters, could purchase slaves to assist them, and typically had opportunity to buy their own freedom and that of their family. They would then continue to ply their trade and be counted among the large population of freedmen in the city. Pasion was one such person, who also became a citizen.

Public slaves performed the duties of clerks and other functionaries for the city, while "Scythian archers" served as Athens' police force. From the way in which Aristophanes makes light of the latter in his comic play, *Lysistrata,* one wonders if they did much more than escort drunk citizens

(continued)

Pasion—Former Slave Turned Wealthy Citizen Banker at Athens (continued)

home at night. The city could also offer to purchase the freedom of a particularly civic-minded slave. In the case of slaves giving testimony in law courts, it was accepted only under torture. Interestingly, Pasion, a former slave, went to great lengths to prevent such from happening to an individual identified as a slave in one of his own court proceedings (Isocrates 17.13ff.), which his accuser only regarded as an additional sign that Pasion was guilty.

As for Pasion, he was born about 430 B.C. and while his name is Greek, his background was probably Phoenician. He was purchased by two Athenian bankers, Archestratus and Antisthenes, and near the end of the fifth century, he began working for them. Because of his good character and honesty (Demosthenes 36.43–44; 52.29), Pasion earned his owners' respect and, eventually, was freed and assumed responsibility for the business. By 394/393 B.C., he apparently owned the bank, probably first leasing then purchasing it from his former masters. Pasion had also married because it was about this same time that his first son, Apollodorus, was born. Nothing is known about his wife, Archippe, except that she, like Pasion, would not have been a citizen. She must have been considerably younger than her husband because a second son was not born until 380 B.C., at which time Pasion would have been about fifty.

394/393 B.C. appears to have been a particularly notable year for another reason—Pasion landed in court for the first time. A young nobleman from the kingdom of Bosporos in the Crimea accused Pasion of refusing to return a substantial sum of money he had deposited (Isocrates, *Oration* 17). It is difficult to know if the charge was valid because we do not know the result of the trial. All we do know is that Pasion's reputation for honesty did not suffer, and in the years that followed, his bank prospered—unlikely

if he had been found guilty. Many merchants in the Piraeus, where Pasion's bank was located, were his customers, as well as the general, Timotheus (Demosthenes, *Oration* 49), businessmen, and the father of the orator Demosthenes. Demosthenes, himself, was involved in legal disputes concerning Pasion's family long after the latter had died.

In the years that followed, Pasion gave the city a thousand shields, produced in his own shield factory—ostensibly a wartime gift to curry favor with the Athenians. Such generosity did not go unnoticed, and for his efforts, which included other benefactions, he was awarded Athenian citizenship (Demosthenes 59.2). It was rare for someone not born an Athenian, and in this case a former slave, to be voted such an honor. After becoming a citizen, Pasion continued to contribute mightily by outfitting and providing crews for five naval vessels, or triremes (Demosthenes 45.85), at a time when it was common for two wealthy citizens to share such duties for a single ship. Citizenship also allowed Pasion to own property. By the time of his death, he had real estate, including his house in the Piraeus and blocks of apartments he rented, worth about 20 talents.

In 380 B.C., Pasion's second son, Pasicles, was born. Some fourteen years had passed since the birth of his eldest son, which seems a long time. After Pasion's death, the circumstances would fuel suspicion, though it could not be proved, that the child was the result of an adulterous affair involving Pasion's young wife (Demosthenes 45.83–84). Late in the 370s, Pasion had more legal troubles. By that time, his health was failing, he was having trouble seeing, and it was difficult for him to come and go from his home to Athens (Demosthenes 52.13). He had previously turned daily banking operations over to a freedman named Phormio, who was almost a mirror reflection of his own early experience. (Note: This is not the Phormio discussed on pp. 223–228.) Phormio was not Greek and had been purchased in the slave market, taught to write, trained to manage Pasion's business affairs, and was eventually freed. He, too, would be made a citizen in 361 B.C. Pasion trusted Phormio completely and, in case something happened to him, he leased Phormio the bank and shield factory so that they would remain intact until both sons reached maturity and could legally divide their inheritance. When Pasion died in 370/69 B.C., he willed his widow, Archippe, to Phormio. This apparently was not an uncommon business practice (Demosthenes 36.28–29), particularly among bankers, and was done to further ensure Pasion's holdings, discourage fortune hunters looking for rich widows, and prevent Archippe from remarrying and risk having new children and in-laws fight over his legacy. Pasion's older son, Apollodorus, was now about 24. Judging from subsequent legal actions, he was a quarrelsome sort. Pasion's arrangements may also have been designed to protect his younger son's interests from his older brother until Pasicles came of age. At the time of his death, Pasion had amassed a fortune of at least 70 talents, or the modern equivalent of about $22,000,000, assuming gold was the standard (talents are weight mea-

surements, and an Attic talent is about 910 ounces: $70 \times 910 \times \$350$ an ounce). By way of comparison, John Jacob Astor, the richest man in America in 1848, was worth $20,000,000.

Pasion's legal problems did not die with him. Apollodorus moved from the family house in Piraeus to the country and was prosecuted not long after by one of his father's former claimants, who renewed his attempt to secure money he said was owed him. We do not know the outcome of that trial, but from this point on, Apollodorus was a frequent face in Athenian courts. Furthermore, after Phormio married Archippe in accordance with Pasion's will (and produced children by her, further proof of her young age), Apollodorus resented it and forced legal disputes with Phormio for years to come. When his mother, Archippe, died, Apollodorus' personal attacks increased. He not only charged Phormio with fraud and ingratitude but also attempted to prove the marriage to his mother was illegal and that his younger brother, who continually sided with Phormio, was actually Phormio's adulterous son by Archippe (Demosthenes 45.83-84). It is interesting that in these same legal actions, Apollodorus' unkind words about Phormio's former status as a slave indicate that he had forgotten (or purposely avoided) his roots were chained to the same institution.

of their inheritance, indicating an amount that was only a small fraction of what it was actually worth. Not only that, but he also complained:

> I have spent a good deal of my own money on your upbringing. While I had it, I didn't mind; but now, I'm badly off myself. So therefore, as you have come of age and reached manhood, you must begin now and see about earning your own living.

The boys had some idea of the real worth of their inheritance, and the prospect of being cheated out of it and reduced to beggary—by their own grandfather-uncle, no less!—brought them to tears. They ran to their mother, who was equally upset, and together they implored her second husband, Phaedrus (the children's stepfather), to intercede. The mother begged him to call a meeting of her father and other family members. She stated emphatically that even though she was not used to speaking before men (a revealing indication of just how much women were throttled in discussing even family affairs), the enormity of the wrong being done compelled her to act. Phaedrus agreed to pursue the matter.

Phaedrus familiarized the other family members with the situation, and a meeting was arranged at which Diogeiton would be questioned. The latter was initially reluctant to attend, but he finally acquiesced. At the assembly, the angry mother was not shy about expressing her contempt for Diogeiton's treatment of her children:

> You who are their father's brother . . . and also my father, and so both uncle and grandfather to them! If you felt no shame before any human being, you ought to have dreaded the anger of Heaven. . . .

Diogeiton had been greedy but not clever. In his haste to get rid of the copy of Diodotus' instructions, he was careless and had not destroyed the evidence. He had simply tossed it away. Ironically, the children found the document while their mother was moving out of the old house to go live with her new husband, and they brought it to her. Consequently, she had known for years the exact terms of her dead first husband's will, and she was fully armed with the details when she dressed down her father's disgraceful behavior—producing the documents in question and revealing their contents.

Why she had not come forth earlier cannot be known. Perhaps she had been willing to let her father's "minor" indiscretions go up to this point, but once she realized that he was also planning to cheat her children out of everything that was theirs, she could not remain quiet. Not only had Diogeiton misrepresented the terms of the will and deprived the rightful heirs of their inheritance, but also money from his dead brother's investments had continued to accrue and make him even richer. He was the worst possible kind of person, she thought:

> And you did not hesitate to turn out these children, your own grandsons, from their own home, dressed in rags, barefoot, without an attendant, without a coverlet, without a cloak, deprived of the household goods which their father had bequeathed them, and of the money which he had deposited with you. And now you have children by my step-mother, and these you are rearing in the enjoyment of all the blessings of wealth. That is all as it should be; but at the same time you wrong my sons, turning them ignominiously out of their home with the determination to reduce them from wealth to beggary. In these actions, you show no fear of Heaven, no shame before me, your

daughter, who share with you the knowledge of the facts, and no respect to your brother's memory. No: we are all, in your eyes, subordinated to money!

The family was dumbfounded by the facts and empathized with the children, remembering their dead father and deploring the way in which a covetous brother had betrayed his trust. Nevertheless, they apparently brought no pressure on Diogeiton, for the case ended up in court, and the stepfather argued it well in a model speech prepared by Lysias (*Oration* 32). A long list of additional examples demonstrated how Diogeiton had juggled his books to defraud his grandchildren, claiming to have spent more on them than he actually had and manipulating business deals so that they would suffer from any losses incurred, while he alone would reap the profits of a successful venture.

Diogeiton may still have been acquitted, but the evidence for his avarice was so overwhelming that the children probably received what was rightfully theirs. The concern over finding a trusted agent to dispose of one's property according to one's will was a real one for many Athenians. The jurors, thinking about the future dispersal of whatever property they might own, no doubt felt that the same thing could happen to them. A verdict to convict may have convinced the jurors that they were taking a step in the right direction to discourage such practices.

Phormio—The Con-Artist (c. 360 B.C.)

Chrysippus could never have foreseen all the problems in store for him when he entered into what he thought was a typical business deal with Phormio, a merchant-trader. Phormio apparently had a knack for bilking unsuspecting investors into underwriting his trading ventures. An alien residing in Athens, Chrysippus had in good faith lent money to the swindler on what was known as a "bottomry contract," an early form of shipping insurance whereby he advanced Phormio a large sum on the security of goods equal to twice the value of the loan. In this case, the goods were to be sold on arrival at Bosporus in the Crimea. Phormio was then to return with a different cargo to dispose of in Athens. From the profits of the two cargoes, Chrysippus' original investment was to be repaid with 30 percent interest. If no return cargo were shipped, Phormio was to pay a fine of over twice the amount of Chrysippus' loan. He also had the option, it seems, simply to pay back the original loan with interest. This type of loan was common, although risky (vessels were often lost at sea, leaving the lender with nothing). But the prospect of an easy and substantial profit prompted even those of a conservative nature sometimes to take the gamble.

Phormio's conniving started immediately. Without the knowledge of Chrysippus, he secured additional loans from two other men; one of them, Lampis, was the owner of the ship that was to transport Phormio's cargo. Phormio apparently used none of Chrysippus' money—if he did, he placed none of the goods purchased with it on the ship. He seems to have spent only as much as the other men had advanced him to purchase his cargo. Consequently, it looks as though Phormio put nothing of his own into the venture, as his contracts demanded, and that he was hoping to profit illegally from the use of other people's money while incurring no risk to himself. One would think that his investors would have been more watchful, but they obviously were not.

What Phormio's exact plan was is not clear, but the cargo he was to sell in Bosporus could not even begin to cover his debt to all three investors. Since the latter two had contracted only for the outward voyage (and both accompanied him on the trip), perhaps he hoped to sell the cargo he had bought with their money at such a profit that he could repay them and still have some left for himself. If not, he may have thought he could fall back on Chrysippus' contribution to make up the difference and still realize a sizable gain. It may be, however, that he had planned to defraud all three from the start and keep all the proceeds for himself. Whatever the case, it seems that Chrysippus, in particular, had the best chance of coming up empty in the deal.

Unaware of his associate's deception and not knowing that his part of the cargo had never even been loaded, Chrysippus naively gave Phormio letters that outlined the details of his business arrangement with the latter. These letters gave instructions about the unloading, inspection, and protection of the goods and were to be delivered to his slave, who was wintering in Bosporus, and to a business partner who was also there. The letters, of course, were never delivered.

Once at Bosporus, Phormio's initial attempts to sell the cargo he had brought were unsuccessful, for a war had badly disrupted the local economy. This situation caused problems, since Lampis and the other creditor who had loaned him money for the voyage now wanted their share of the profits. Phormio was apparently able to make excuses and convinced them to return to Athens without him. However, they told him to load whatever he was supposed to have purchased for the return trip with Chrysippus' money. (Clearly, they knew that Chrysippus was a fellow investor, but they could not have known at this time the precise details of his involvement.) Phormio said he was unable to comply, because he had not yet sold what he had brought. He would stay until he had completed his dealings in Bosporus, then sail to Athens, presumably promising to pay them when he arrived.

Figure 7.9
Scenes of merchant ships, perhaps similar to the one whose cargo Chrysippus underwrote, being attacked by pirates or warships of an unfriendly state. Such business ventures were risky for much could happen to a ship at sea. (British Museum, London)

The departure of Lampis' ship conveniently left Phormio out of his investors' reach and in possession of *all* their capital—certainly a dream situation for a con-artist. He could have capitalized on the situation had it not been for Lampis' greed. Not wishing to return to Athens without a cargo, he so overloaded his ship that it sank not far from port. Lampis survived the ordeal (nothing is said of the other creditor who presumably was also on board), but a large number of his crew were lost, causing a great deal of mourning in Bosporus. People were quick to comment about how lucky Phormio had been not to have sailed on the ship or put any of his merchandise on it, and he, too, commented likewise.

Although there is certainly no conclusive evidence to support the idea, Phormio's devious personality and the circumstances surrounding the wreck make it almost irresistible for us not to at least suspect his hand at work. Such a convenient disaster, so close to port, right after he and his creditors had cordially parted company, their differences apparently resolved, with plenty of witnesses, would have solved all Phormio's problems. If his two creditors had drowned with the others, it would have relieved him completely of all his obligations to them. He could have said he had settled his accounts with them before they sailed, and as for Chrysippus, any story he wanted to tell him about why he was no longer obliged to him would do— such as that the cargo he had purchased with the latter's money was now lying

The Lover of Bad Company

LOVE OF BAD COMPANY and rascally behavior is a passion for the vicious. It marks the kind of man who imagines that he will find out what life is really about and become a terror if he associates with people convicted of crimes against the state. Or when you describe somebody as respectable this fellow will reply, "So it would appear . . ." and then go on to argue that really nobody can claim respectability—people are all alike. A remark like "What a respectable man so-and-so is" he turns into a joke.

Moreover it's the rascal, he argues, who turns out to be the real gentleman if you put him to the test. Some of what you hear about such men is true, he admits, but other things aren't. "They're clever and good-natured, the kind who won't let a friend down," he maintains; and he champions anyone like this with all his might as the most capable person he ever met. In addition, he listens sympathetically whenever a rascal is be-ing prosecuted in a court of law or called on to make a public defense of his record. "Remember, you're trying the case, not the man," he will say to the jury every time; and he calls the defendant a watchdog of the people's interests, on the lookout against lawbreakers. "We won't have anybody left to worry about good government," he adds, "if we can't stand by fellows like this."

You also find him playing the protector of worthless men, or trying to get a jury packed for dirty work in the courtroom. And if he is called in to give an individual opinion, he puts the arguments of the opposing sides in an unfavorable light.

[It could be said generally that sympathy with rascally behavior represents the next thing to rascality itself; and there is some truth in the old saying about birds of a feather.]
(Theophrastus, *Characters* 29)

---

on the ocean floor. Consequently, if no one were there to dispute him, Phormio could have maintained that he had honored his contracts all around—and kept everything for himself.

Whether Phormio actually did have something to do with the ship's sinking, we do not know. (Lampis apparently was not suspicious.) When Lampis returned to Athens, he informed Chrysippus, upon the latter's inquiry, that he had received from Phormio neither a return cargo nor cash to settle their contract. Chrysippus then began to believe that he had been cheated.

Phormio finally turned up in Athens some time later, and when he did, Chrysippus confronted him and demanded payment. To put Chrysippus off, Phormio promised that he would comply, but he soon reneged, forcing Chrysippus, in conjunction with another of his partners who apparently had shared in the initial investment, to pursue the matter legally. At first, he had the support of Lampis, who continued to deny that Phormio had ever put the required goods on his ship or given him money. It was even Lampis who led Chrysippus to Phormio when the former wanted to serve him with

a summons but did not know where to find him. But Phormio was eventually able to "buy off" Lampis, ironically, with money owed to Chrysippus. Lampis then changed his story to support Phormio's claim that he had not violated his contract and that the loss of the ship relieved him of any responsibility. When Lampis was reminded of his earlier charges against Phormio—and there were witnesses to substantiate what he had said—he replied that he must have been out of his mind when he made them.

Phormio employed as much legal trickery as he could to avoid being prosecuted. The matter first went through arbitration, but the arbitrator, a friend of Phormio's, wished neither to rule against him nor to get into trouble for siding with him. The case finally came before an Athenian court. There, Chrysippus and his partner, in an argument prepared for them and attributed to Demosthenes (*Oration* 34), summarized some of the major points undermining Phormio's defense and made it appear an impossible one:

> Now, in the light of the facts themselves, consider in your own minds, men of the jury, what means the man was likely to have for discharging the debt. He sailed from this port without having put the goods on board the ship, and having no adequate security; on the contrary, he had made additional

loans on the credit of the money lent by me. In Bosporus he found no market for his wares, and had difficulty in getting rid of those who had lent money for the outward voyage. . . .

The two men were aided in their case by the fact that in all their long experience of doing business in Athens, they had never appeared in any lawsuit. They continued to pile up detailed evidence that defied the logic and challenged the accuracy of Phormio's defense, substantiating clearly his chicanery. We would hope, then, that the jury ruled in their favor, for in this case, at least, it seems clear that the accused deserved punishment.

In his play *The Clouds* (ll. 445–451), Aristophanes has his major character, the debt-ridden, hard-pressed Strepsiades, respond to the chorus when they ask him to make known his wishes, that his desire is to perfect and profit from an expertise in the art of deceiving and misleading people. He wants to be, to use his words:

A CHEATER, a BASTARD, a PHONEY, a BUM
SHYSTER, MOUTHPIECE, TINHORN, SCUM,
STOOLIE, CON-MAN, WINDBAG, PUNK,
OILY, GREASY, HYPOCRITE, SKUNK,
DUNGHILL, SQUEALER, SLIPPERY SAM,
FAKER, DIDDLER, SWINDLER, SHAM . . .

Judging from the examples described in this chapter, it appears that Strepsiades' desires (and worse), although expressed by a fictional literary character, could be encountered all too frequently in the streets of Classical Athens. Aristophanes understood well the character of more than a few of his fellow citizens.

Suggestions for Further Reading

Most of the more interesting cases from the law courts of Classical Athens, the source for much of the detail in this chapter, can be found with commentary in Freeman's previously cited collection (Chapter 4), *The Murder of Herodes and Other Trials from the Athenian Law Courts.* See also C. Carey, *Trials from Classical Athens* (New York: Routledge, 1997), J. Trevett, *Apollonius the Son of Pasion* (New York: Oxford University Press, 1992), and I. Worthington (ed.), *Demosthenes: Statesman and Orator* (New York: Routledge, 2000). Several of Aristophanes' plays provide much contemporary chatter about the working of the law and court system in Athens—most notably, *Wasps,* which is humorous but still revealing. Along this line, see D. M. MacDowell, *Aristophanes and Athens: An Introduction to the Plays* (New York: Oxford University Press, 1995). On law in Athens, see MacDowell's *The Law in Classical Athens* (Ithaca, N.Y.: Cornell University Press, 1978); S. C. Todd, *The Shape of Athenian Law* (New York: Oxford University Press, 1993);

M. Ostwald, *From Popular Sovereignty to the Sovereignty of Law: Law, Society and Politics in Fifth-Century Athens* (Berkeley and Los Angeles: University of California Press, 1990); M. R. Christ, *The Litigious Athenian* (Baltimore: The Johns Hopkins University Press, 1998); V. J. Hunter, *Policing Athens: Social Control in the Attic Lawsuits 420–320 B.C.* (Princeton, N.J.: Princeton University Press, 1994); and, on women specifically, R. Just's *Women in Athenian Law and Life* (New York: Routledge, 1991) and R. Sealey's *Women and Law in Classical Greece* (Durham: University of North Carolina Press, 1990). See, also, I. Arnaoutoglou, *Ancient Greek Laws: A Sourcebook* (New York: Routledge, 1998). Related works are D. M. Schaps, *Economic Rights of Women in Ancient Greece* (Edinburgh: Edinburgh University Press, 1981); N. Demand, *Birth, Death, and Motherhood in Classical Greece* (Baltimore: The Johns Hopkins University Press, 1994); M. Golden, *Children and Childhood in Classical Athens* (Baltimore: The Johns Hopkins University Press, 1993); and L. G. Mitchell, *Greeks Bearing Gifts: The Public Use of Private Relationships in the Greek World, 435–323 B.C.* (Cambridge: Cambridge University Press, 1998).

Also of interest are N. R. E. Fisher, *Slavery in Classical Greece* (London: Classical World Series, 1993); Y. Garlan, *Slavery in Ancient Greece* (Ithaca, N.Y.: Cornell University Press, 1988); J. M. Hall, *Ethnic Identity in Greek Antiquity* (Cambridge: Cambridge University Press, 2000); L. Casson, *Travel in the Ancient World* (Baltimore: The Johns Hopkins University Press, 1994); P. de Souza, *Piracy in the Graeco-Roman World* (Cambridge: Cambridge University Press, 1999); F. Meijer and O. van Nijf's sourcebook, *Trade, Transport and Society in the Ancient World* (New York: Routledge, 1992); and C. A. Faraone, *Ancient Greek Love Magic* (Cambridge, Mass.: Harvard University Press, 2001 edition). Generally, for this period, see B. S. Strauss, *Athens after the Peloponnesian War: A Study of Class Factions and Policy 403–386 B.C.* (Ithaca, N.Y.: Cornell University Press, 1987); and P. George, *Barbarian Asia and the Greek Experience: From the Archaic Period to the Age of Xenophon* (Baltimore: The Johns Hopkins University Press, 1994).

8

Hellenistic Science, Technology, and Fantasy

Alexander and His Submarine Adventure

*It is true indeed that these and many other things have
been invented several times over in the course of ages. . . .*
(Aristotle, *Politics* 1329^{b}25)

In the first half-century following the Peloponnesian War, the Greeks became increasingly susceptible to external manipulation. Torn by years of in-
ternecine strife and bankrupt in manpower and funds, no city-state could
firmly assert itself. Persian gold, more often than not, was the key to success
or failure. What the great Persian kings of the early fifth century B.C. could
not do with their armies, their mediocre successors in the fourth century accomplished with cash, making the Greeks dependent on it, manipulating
them by closely controlling the flow.

The predictable result was that Philip of Macedon and his son Alexander eventually subdued the discordant Greeks and placed the stamp of hege-
mony on Hellas. Viewed only as a temporary evil at first, the conquerors
soon demonstrated their permanence as the rule of the Successors sup-
planted that of Philip and Alexander. Helpless to do otherwise, the Greeks
stood idly by and watched as their world became Macedonian.

Much had occurred before that process was completed. Philip's life was
cut short when he was assassinated in 336 B.C. (see pages 232–235), and
Alexander took his place as king of Macedonia and leader of the Greeks. In
that role, he launched a great expedition against the Persian Empire, a cam-

Figure 8.1
Alexander the Great.
Inheriting the throne
of Macedonia from
his father, Philip,
Alexander established
an empire that
stretched from Libya
to India. His death
in 323 B.C. at age
32 ushered in the
Hellenistic Age.
(Louvre, Paris)

paign his father had originally planned, but one that Alexander now took upon himself and carried out beyond Philip's wildest dreams.

Leaving his capital of Pella in Macedonia in 334 B.C., Alexander crossed the Hellespont and arrived in Asia Minor (see Figure 8.6, page 236) with an army that numbered 40,000 infantry and 5,000 calvary. In a ten-year campaign unrivaled in the annals of military history, he destroyed the old Persian Empire and created a new one that stretched from Libya to India. Alexander defeated the armies of Persia at the Granicus River (334 B.C.), at Issus (333 B.C.), and at Gaugamela (331 B.C.), prompting the Great King Darius III to flee before the latter two battles had even been decided. In the meantime, he had freed Egypt from Persia (332 B.C.), become its pharaoh, and established the city of Alexandria, which would emerge as the greatest city in the world in the period following his death.

By 330 B.C., Babylon and Susa were Alexander's, and he had captured and burned Persepolis, the throne-capital of Persia. By the time he crossed the Indus River in 326 B.C. (the first confirmed date in Indian history), Darius had been killed by his own nobles, Alexander had traversed the Hindu

The Death of Philip—Pausanias, the Assassin

IF ALEXANDER HAD NOT become the imposing figure he did, we probably would have heard much more about his father, Philip. It was Philip who originally cast the long shadow of fame, and Alexander himself initially must have wondered whether he could ever escape from under it. The fourth-century B.C. historian Theopompus proclaimed in his *Philippica* (now lost) that Europe had never produced such a man as Philip, who was recognized by the Macedonians as their greatest king. Before his assassination in 336 B.C. at age 46, he had literally transformed Macedonia from an assortment of tribes and races into a unified kingdom and people, changed its character from rural to urban, and built the most modern, efficient, and formidable army of his day. The legacy of his 23-year rule was the first "national state" in Europe, the first national capital at Pella, and the first national army.

What follows is an account, by the first-century B.C. chronicler Diodorus of Sicily, of Philip's assassination. While some of its detail might be questioned, modern scholars have generally been willing to accept the main narration of events. The assassin was named Pausanias, who was one of Philip's own bodyguards. The event took place in the theater at Aegae (modern Vergina), the ancient capital and cult center of the royal house—and the burial place of the Macedonian kings. The occasion was the celebration of a marriage between Philip's daughter by Olympias of Epirus (also the mother of Alexander) and Olympias' brother, the king of Epirus (an uncle-niece marriage). This marriage was designed to strengthen the ties between the royal families of Macedonia and Epirus and also to reaffirm Olympias' status (and, coincidentally, Alexander's place in the succession), since Philip had recently remarried—for the seventh time! Multiple marriages were not unusual because they established political ties between royal houses

Figure 8.2 *Portrait of Philip represented as Zeus on a tetradrachm.*

or powerful allies and helped to guarantee a surviving heir to the throne. They could also cause emotional strain on the parties involved.

Diodorus describes the day of the murder:

Finally the drinking was over and the start of the games set for the following day. While it was still dark, the multitude of spectators hastened into the theater and at sunrise the parade formed. Along with lavish display of every sort, Philip included in the procession statues of the twelve gods wrought with great artistry and adorned with a dazzling show of wealth to strike awe in the beholder, and along with these was conducted a thirteenth statue, suitable for a god, that of Philip himself, so that the king exhibited himself enthroned among the twelve gods.

Every seat in the theater was taken when Philip appeared wearing a white cloak, and by his express orders his bodyguard held away from him and followed only at a distance, since he wanted to show publicly that he was protected by the goodwill of all the Greeks, and had no need of a guard of spearmen. Such was the pinnacle of success that he had attained, but as the praises and congratulations of all rang in his ears, suddenly without warning the plot against the king was revealed as death struck. We shall set forth the reasons for this in order that our story may be clear.

There was a Macedonian Pausanias who came of a family from the district Orestis. He was a bodyguard of the king and was beloved by him because of his beauty. When he saw that the king was becoming enamored of another Pausanias (a man of the same name as himself), he addressed him with abusive language, accusing him of being a hermaphrodite and prompt to accept the amorous advances of any who wished. Unable to endure such an insult, the other kept silent for the time, but, after confiding to Attalus, one of his friends, what he proposed to do, he brought about his own death voluntarily and in a spectacular fashion. For a few days after this, as Philip was engaged in battle . . . Pausanias stepped in front of him and, receiving on his body all the blows directed at the king, so met his death.

The incident was widely discussed and Attalus, who was a member of the court circle and influential with the king, invited the first Pausanias to dinner and when he had plied him till drunk with unmixed wine, handed his unconscious body over to the muleteers to abuse in drunken licentiousness. So he presently recovered from his drunken stupor and, deeply resenting the outrage to his person, charged Attalus before the king with the outrage. Philip shared his anger at the barbarity of the act but did not wish to punish Attalus at that time because of their relationship, and because Attalus's services were needed urgently. He was the [uncle] of the Cleopatra whom the king had just married as a new wife and he had been selected as a general of the advanced force being sent into Asia, for he was a man valiant in battle. For these reasons, the king tried to mollify the righteous anger of Pausanias at his treatment, giving him substantial presents and advancing him in honor among the bodyguards.

(continued)

Figure 8.3   *The theater at Aegae (modern Vergina) in which Philip was assassinated by Pausanias in June 336 B.C. (partially excavated)*

The Death of Philip—Pausanias, the Assassin (continued)

Pausanias, nevertheless, nursed his wrath implacably, and yearned to avenge himself, not only on the one who had done him wrong, but also on the one who failed to avenge him. In this design he was encouraged especially by the sophist Hermocrates. He was his pupil, and when he asked in the course of his instruction how one might become most famous, the sophist replied that it would be by killing the one who had accomplished most, for just as long as he was remembered, so long his slayer would be remembered also. Pausanias connected this saying with his private resentment, and admitting no delay in his plans because of his grievance he determined to act under cover of the festival in the following manner. He posted horses at the gates of the city and came to the entrance of the theater carrying a Celtic [sword] under his cloak. When Philip directed his attending friends to precede him into the theater, while the guards kept their distance, he saw that the king was left alone, rushed at him, pierced him through his ribs, and stretched him out dead; then ran for the gates and the horses which he had prepared for his flight. Immediately one group of the bodyguards hurried to the body of the king while the rest poured out in pursuit of the assassin; among these last were Leonnatus and Perdiccas and Attalus. Having a good start, Pausanias would have mounted his horse before they could catch him had he not caught his boot in a vine and fallen. As he was scrambling to his feet, Perdiccas and the rest came up with him and killed him with their javelins.

Such was the end of Philip, who had made himself the greatest of the kings in Europe in his time, and because of the extent of his kingdom had made himself a throned companion of the twelve gods. He had ruled [almost] twenty-four years.
(16.92.5–95.1)

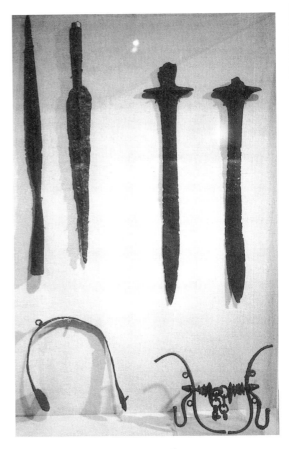

Figure 8.4   *The location and circumstances surrounding the discovery of these weapons and horse bit and bridle piece during the excavation of King Philip's tomb make it reasonable to suggest they were directly involved in events related to his assassination. (Thessalonike Museum)*

Aristotle (*Politics* 1311[b]), who was at the court of Philip and in a position to know, affirms that Pausanias acted because Philip had permitted the insult by Attalus and his friends; and, indeed, this could have been the *only* reason: Pausanias was seized by the emotion and opportunity of the moment, killed Philip on impulse, ran to where he knew horses would be (including his own?), tripped, and was killed by pursuing bodyguards, who, having failed once in their duty, were now more intent on dispatching the assassin before he escaped than on preserving him to provide possible information about a conspiracy! The true circumstances may be no more complex than this, but hindsight has provided a multiplicity of ancient and modern conspiracy theories that im-

plicate Alexander, Olympias (or both), Alexander's friends, Attalus, other claimants to the throne, and Persian agents or Greek "freedom fighters." As in any assassination of so significant an individual, the truth may never be known, but most of those who were under suspicion were prosecuted, and, if judged guilty, were executed. Eventually all (with the exception, of course, of Alexander's mother, Olympias) who were thought to have some connection with the deed met untimely ends.

Figure 8.5 The reconstructed cremated remains of Philip of Macedonia, father of Alexander the Great (Thessalonike Museum)

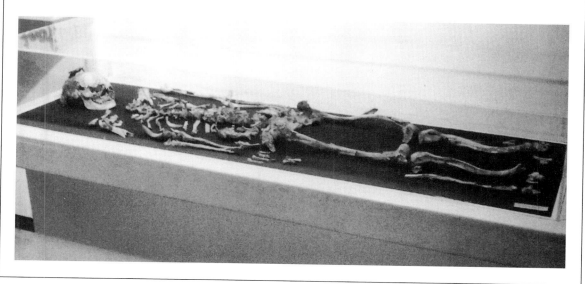

Kush into the primitive regions of Bactria and Sogdiana, and he had successfully weathered every military contingency and hostile people imaginable. He also had to deal with illness, wounds, and, worst of all, plots against his life involving even members of his high command. His attempts to adapt his rule to so diverse a population and area had caused disgruntlement among his racist Macedonian troops. Through it all, Alexander survived, forging well into India before his Macedonians, thinking themselves halfway round the world, refused to go farther. After fighting his way down the Indus River, surviving the deserts of Pakistan and Iran, and overcoming other obstacles, Alexander successfully concluded his campaign early in 324 B.C. at Susa, just north of the Persian Gulf.

The last year of Alexander's life was a hectic one. Plans to circumnavigate the Arabian peninsula never reached fruition. Grumblings among the ranks, trouble with trusted administrators, personal tragedy, revolts in the far reaches of the Empire, problems in Greece, and difficulty in tying together the various threads—ethnic, racial, religious, political, and other— that would ultimately form the fabric of a new empire all took their toll. On June 10, 323 B.C., Alexander the Great succumbed after a brief illness (precipitated by a heavy drinking bout) while residing in the palace of Nebuchadrezzar in Babylon. He was thirty-two years old.

Alexander's death in 323 B.C. ushered in the Hellenistic Age, and seldom, if ever, has any period in history so successfully combined chaos with creativity. Forged in the wars of the Successors, Alexander's generals, and steeled by economic and social upheaval, the Hellenistic world produced a remarkable record of scientific and technological achievement before it was overwhelmed by the onslaught of the Romans—a disturbing reminder that periods of continual warfare can be as much stimuli to progress as detriments.

Figure 8.6
Alexander's army crossed the Hellespont from Europe into Asia at this point, proceeding from the ancient site of Sestos on the right to Abydos (modern Canakkale) on the left. A century and a half earlier, Xerxes' army had crossed in the opposite direction at the same place—on a pontoon bridge—to begin the Second Persian War with the Greeks (see Chapter 5).

Figure 8.7
The new creativity of the Hellenistic period was also reflected in the realism and emotionalism of its art, as expressed in this representation of the Trojan priest Laocoön and his sons entwined in a huge serpent's coils. (Vatican Museums, Rome)

Already before the third century B.C., the fertile imagination of Greek thinkers had proposed an atomic theory, suggested rational explanations for the workings of the universe, advanced a rudimentary theory of evolution, and offered other equally amazing proposals on a variety of subjects. It would be the Hellenistic period, however, that witnessed the maturation of Greek science and technology. Hellenistic thinkers projected a heliocentric solar system, measured the circumference of the earth to within about 100 miles of modern estimates, and advanced medical studies (see box, pages 239–241). Inventors like Ctesibius of Alexandria created pneumatic devices that opened and closed doors by themselves and moved statues, and numerous other engineering and mechanical feats that seem to us staggering for that day were brought to fruition. The theories, proposals, and accomplishments of these few centuries would have lasting influence well into the Roman Empire, providing impetus, inspiration, and guidance for all forms of creative activity. The steam engine of Hero of Alexandria (first century A.D.)

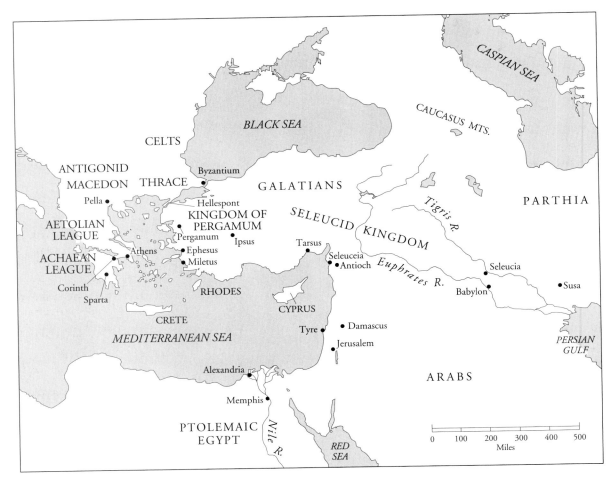

Map 19
The Hellenistic world

and other remarkable achievements that were to come lay within the same Hellenistic tradition. What was not yet possible had at least been thought about—evidenced by a fictitious submarine adventure attributed to Alexander the Great.

The Beginnings of Science Fiction

If they could have, the same ancient scientists, technologists, and engineers who made the aforementioned discoveries would undoubtedly also have devised ways to explore the three realms that have always fascinated humans most: the depths of the sea, the sky, and, of course, space. Unfortunately, they had neither the knowledge nor the tools to make these realms accessible.

Erasistratus, the Physician—and Psychologist

IN THE FIFTH CENTURY B.C., Hippocrates and his school at Cos revolutionized the science of medicine by looking for human rather than divine causes for illness. Although such an approach was a momentous leap forward, the first rational physicians were still a long way from fully understanding the workings of the human body. Unfortunately, a number of their authoritative but erroneous pronouncements about good health became so firmly entrenched that they lasted for centuries—even though empirical evidence existed to dispute them. One of the theories attributed to them concerned the four humors: blood, phlegm, black bile, and yellow bile. The theory offered that as long as these fluids remained in balance, a person was "in good humor" (an expression still in common use today, although few comprehend its original meaning), or in good health. Bleeding a sick patient, it was thought, was one way to adjust the balance, and this practice remained a vital part of medical treatment well into the modern era!

There are countless examples in human history of the perpetuation and rigid defense of erroneous notions—rational solutions shoved aside in favor of ridiculous alternatives are not hard to find. Our knowledge of medicine, for instance, might have been enhanced significantly if some of the work and ideas of the third-century B.C. Hellenistic physician Erasistratus had been widely adopted. Erasistratus rejected the doctrine of humors (which, unhappily, Galen would reassert in

(continued)

Figure 8.8 Clamps, saws, blades, drills, and other tools and devices used by ancient Greek physicians, from the sanctuary of Asclepius, the god of healing, at Epidaurus (Epidaurus Museum)

Erasistratus, the Physician—and Psychologist (continued)

the second century A.D. and, because of his stature, would help perpetuate into modern times). Along with his older contemporary Herophilus, Erasistratus carried out groundbreaking medical research in Alexandria, Egypt. Erasistratus was interested primarily in physiology; Herophilus was more concerned with anatomy. Both might properly be called the "founders" of their respective fields.

Herophilus' research resulted in very modern conclusions about the nature and function of the brain, heart, nerves, and other organs—although, unlike his younger colleague, he continued to adhere to the humoral theory. Erasistratus subsequently elaborated on Herophilus' theories. Their work would not be surpassed until Harvey's investigations in the seventeenth century. Both men arrived at many of their doctrines through the vivisection of condemned criminals, a practice that horrified some and would later earn the condemnation of the Christian fathers.

Although Erasistratus was wise enough to abandon the four humors, he still did not fully comprehend many things about the body. He believed, for example, that blood was carried by veins but erroneously asserted that the arteries were filled with air. Nevertheless, many sick people during the Hellenistic period must have benefited from his work and also from the correct application of treatments such as opiates for pain and exercise, diet, massage, and baths for other maladies.

Before coming to Alexandria, Erasistratus, originally from Ceos, resided at the court of Seleucus, founder of the Seleucid Kingdom in Asia. There, he was physician and friend to the royal family. Plutarch involves him in a rather dramatic and Euripidean episode that, if accurate, attests to the physician's talents in the area of psychology as well as medicine. The incident concerns the young wife of Seleucus, Stratonice, and the king's son, Antiochus, who has fallen hopelessly in love with her:

It appeared that Antiochus had fallen in love with Stratonice, who was still a young girl, although she had already borne a child to Seleucus. Antiochus was distressed and for a time he struggled to conceal his passion. But at last he decided that his malady was incurable, his desires sinful and his reason too weak to resist them: he therefore determined to make his escape from life and to destroy himself gradually by neglecting his body and refusing all nourishment, under the pretext that he was suffering from some disease. Erasistratus, his physician, found no difficulty in diagnosing his condition, namely that he was in love, but it was less easy to discover with whom. He made a habit of spending day after day in the young prince's room, and when any particularly good-looking girl or young man entered, he would study his patient's face minutely and watch those parts and movements of the body which nature has formed so as to reflect and share the emotions of the soul. Sure enough, when anybody else came in, Antiochus remained unmoved, but whenever Stratonice visited him, as she often did either alone or with Seleucus, all the symptoms which Sappho describes immediately showed themselves: his voice faltered, his face began to flush, his eye became languid, a sudden sweat broke out on his skin, his heart began to beat violently and irregularly, and finally as if his soul were overpowered by his passions, he would sink into a state of helplessness, prostration and pallor.

Besides all this, Erasistratus reflected, it was most unlikely that the king's son, if he had fallen in love with any other woman, would have persisted to the point of death in saying nothing about it. He saw the difficulty of revealing a secret of this nature to Seleucus, but still, trusting in the king's affection for his son, he ventured to tell him one day that love was the disorder from which Antiochus was suffering, a love that could neither be satisfied nor cured. "How is it incurable?", the king asked him in astonishment. "Because," Erasistratus replied, "he is in love with my wife." "Well then, Erasistratus," said the king, "since you are my son's friend, could you not give up your wife and let him marry her, especially when you see that he is my only son, the only anchor of our troubled dynasty, and this is the only means of saving him?" "You are his father," the physician answered, "would you do such a thing if Antiochus were in love with Stratonice?" "My friend," replied Seleucus, "I only wish that someone, whether a god or a man, could turn this passion of his towards her. I should be happy to give up my kingdom if only I could save Antiochus."

Seleucus uttered these words with deep emotion, and wept as he spoke, and thereupon the physician clasped him by the hand and said, "Then you have no need of Erasistratus: you, sire, are a father, a husband and a king, and you are also the best physician for your own household." After this Seleucus summoned the people to meet in full assembly and announced that it was his will and pleasure that Antiochus should marry Stratonice, and that they should be proclaimed King and Queen of all Upper Asia. He believed, he said, that his son, who had always been accustomed to obey his father, would not oppose his desire, and that if his wife should be unwilling to take this extraordinary step, he

Figure 8.9 *Bust identified as Seleucus, founder of the Hellenistic Seleucid kingdom (Louvre, Paris)*

would appeal to his friends to persuade her to accept as just and honorable whatever seemed right to the king and advantageous to the kingdom. This is how Antiochus came to be married to Stratonice, so we are told.
(*Demetrius* 38)

Indeed, it has been only in the twentieth century that science and technology have made such ventures commonplace—although we have only begun to explore the depths of the ocean and space. For the ancients, the possibilities of conquering these realms seemed so remote that speculation about such adventures was to be found more in literature than in scientific treatises.

Not surprisingly, most of this literary speculation had about it a definite air of the fantastic—it was not meant to be taken seriously.

The human imagination, however, does provide stimulus for future generations, and there has seldom been anything proposed in the past that has not become, or at least had potential to become, a reality in later ages. Within the past hundred or so years, for example, classic science fiction writers like Jules Verne and H. G. Wells fascinated their readers with technological wonders. At the time, their visions went beyond the capabilities of contemporary scientists and technocrats, but their science fiction has become our science fact. Many of their ideas, which some might consider fairly recent, have a history that goes back many centuries. For instance, those who look to Jules Verne for the first extensive account of a trip to the moon will undoubtedly be amazed to learn of a much earlier voyage that took place during the Roman Empire in the second century A.D.—a totally facetious visit to the lunar surface concocted by the Greek satirist Lucian:

> [We] sailed off at dawn before a moderate wind. Around noon . . . a typhoon suddenly hit us. It spun the ship around and lifted it about thirty miles high in the air. But, before it could let us drop back into the water, as we hung suspended in the sky, a wind filled our sails and carried us along. For seven days and nights we sailed the air. On the eighth we sighted a large land mass like an island in the sky. It was round and, illuminated by some immense light, shone brightly. We put in there, anchored, and disembarked, and, upon reconnoitering the countryside, found it was inhabited and under cultivation. During the day we could see no other land about but, when night came on, we saw a good many other islands the color of fire, some bigger than ours and some smaller. Below was another land mass with cities, rivers, seas, forests, and mountains; we guessed it was our own earth . . . the land we were in was what appeared to people on earth as the moon.
> (*A True Story* 1.9–11)

Lucian's adventures do not stop at the moon, for he visits other heavenly bodies and even becomes involved in a war between moon- and sun-people. Not surprisingly, he has warned his audience in advance that they will find his "True Story" the most outrageous yarn they have ever heard. He does not disappoint. Nevertheless, his piece is of interest if only because he has the boldness to conceive of a trip to another body in space. Also, the method by which he has chosen to transport himself to the moon is revealing: He does not attempt to invent some fantastic kind of machine but is content to work within what he knows. The ship he is traveling on gets caught in a typhoon, and a wind fills its sails and carries it to the moon. Although impossible, of course, there is still a certain logic to this reasoning. Since Lucian chose a familiar

Aristarchus, the Astronomer

AS LONG AS THERE have been human beings, the heavens have attracted perhaps more interest (and misunderstanding) and provided more fascination than any other aspect of our environment. Our earliest records indicate a preoccupation with the planets and stars, largely for religious reasons. That interest has remained unabated to our own day, although our primary motivations for studying the heavens, aside from curiosity, do not always parallel those of antiquity. Early astronomers, however, were uncannily adept at their craft, and some of their achievements were quite remarkable.

In Greece, by the Hellenistic period, an astronomer from Samos named Aristarchus (third century B.C.) had hypothesized some of the basic concepts on which the modern understanding of our solar system rests. Aristarchus' investigations caused him to break away from much of the conventional—and erroneous—wisdom about the universe. His rational observations of the heavens led him to spectacular conclusions: It was he who first proposed a heliocentric hypothesis. He also believed that the earth rotated diurnally and recognized that the sun (and other stars) was incredibly far away and of immense size—over 300 times larger than earth. His treatise *On the Sizes and Distances of the Sun and Moon* is still extant.

Aristarchus' views, however, were too far ahead of his time, and his ideas about the size of the cosmos boggled the minds of contemporary scientists. Like many other Hellenistic revelations, his discoveries had only superficial impact on a world that preferred to look to less demanding, long-standing explanations. It would be another 1,800 years before Copernicus "discovered" what Aristarchus had already known. Our major source for Aristarchus' heliocentric hypothesis is

Archimedes, who reviews the theory with a large dose of skepticism:

> You are aware that universe (cosmos) is the name given by most astronomers to the sphere whose center is the center of the Earth, and whose radius is equal to the distance between the center of the Sun and the center of the Earth. This is the common account as you have heard from astronomers. But Aristarchus of Samos brought out a book consisting of some hypotheses, wherein it appears, as a consequence of assumptions made, that the [real] universe is many times greater than the one just mentioned. His hypotheses are that the fixed stars and the Sun remain unmoved, that the Earth revolves about the Sun in the circumference of a circle, the Sun lying in the middle of the orbit, and that the sphere of the fixed stars, situated about the same center as the Sun, is so great that the circle in which he supposes the Earth to revolve bears such a proportion to the distance of the fixed stars as the center of the sphere bears to its surface. Now it is easy to see that this is impossible; for, since the center of the sphere has no magnitude, we cannot conceive it to bear any ratio whatever to the surface of the sphere. We must however take Aristarchus to mean this: since we conceive the earth to be, as it were, the center of the universe, the ratio which the earth bears to what we describe as the "universe" is the same as the ratio which the sphere containing the circle in which he supposes the earth to revolve bears to the sphere of the fixed stars. For he adapts the proofs of his results to a hypothesis of this kind, and in particular he appears to suppose the magnitude of the sphere in which he represents the earth as moving to be equal to what we call the "universe."

(*The Sand-Reckoner,* Introduction)

mode of transport and made the circumstances—not his vessel—responsible for what happened, he was simply extending the limits of what the technology of his day would allow through natural causation. Consequently, he has kept the notion of such a voyage within the realm of possibility.

Lucian's fascination with the possibility of "space travel," despite his exaggerated and ridiculous development of the story, is clear. He would not have chosen to exploit the topic if he did not have some interest in it—and in this respect, he is a continuation of the Hellenistic obsession with science, technology, and fantasy. This is further demonstrated by the fact that he not only took his audience to the moon but also convinced them that Archimedes, the greatest of the Hellenistic technocrats and inventor of numerous marvelous machines, had devised a heat ray that destroyed anything it touched. Although theoretically possible, there is absolutely no evidence for the existence of such a weapon or its use in antiquity. On this occasion also, Lucian has employed his imaginative powers to turn Hellenistic creativity into science fiction.

Alexander's Submarine

With writers such as Lucian spreading tales about outer space and Hellenistic technological fantasies, it is not surprising to find the same tradition continuing into the third century A.D. in the form of the *Alexander Romance.* Better known as Pseudo-Callisthenes, the *Romance* is completely unhistorical and exaggerated. It had its origins in the Hellenistic period and was falsely attributed to Callisthenes, a relative of Aristotle, who had, in fact, been the official historian of Alexander the Great's expedition until his death in 327 B.C. It is actually a collection of anonymous romantic and marvelous stories about the great conqueror. These stories started forming before Alexander died, and they predictably grew and became more exaggerated as the centuries wore on. They appear to have reached orthodox form as a continuous narrative—perceived as the work of a single author—in the third century A.D.

Few works have rivaled the *Romance's* popularity through the ages, and with the exception of the Bible, no other book has been translated into more languages. The original version no longer exists, so we cannot know exactly what it contained, but among the stories included in the tradition are Alexander's experience in a remarkable flying machine and the first detailed account of a submarine adventure. These two ideas would certainly have appealed to the Hellenistic mentality.

It is no surprise to find Alexander portrayed as the conqueror of the sky and the sea: Feats that are not possible for mere mortals are reserved for those who have been made "bigger than life"—elevated to the status of superhumans or demigods. The plethora of novels, pseudohistories, romances, and folktales of peoples from Europe to Central Asia about Alexander made him the equal of any task. Thus, he *could* be transported through the air in a flying machine powered by griffins (mythological creatures with an eagle's head, wings, and the body of a lion); and he *could* view the wonders of the ocean's depths in a glass submersible.

Of the two adventures, the air voyage became the better known— probably because it seemed more of a feat to stay aloft in the air than it did to sink beneath the sea—but in terms of Hellenistic science and technology, the submarine adventure is unquestionably the more interesting. Alexander's flying machine is totally absurd; however, the submarine, although impractical, is in design and concept about as close as possible to what the technology of the day would allow. Like Lucian's trip to the moon, the story has a bit of the rational about it, although it also appears in a totally ridiculous context. The narrative, unfortunately, has been altered, interpolated, and corrupted without mercy. The design of the vessel; its contents; the people, land, and objects involved; the situation and motivation; the undersea world—these and many other details differ in each of the numerous versions that now exist. However, the earliest and simplest rendition of the submarine adventure we possess—although a late one (sixth century A.D.)—may be close to the original. It has been succinctly summarized as follows:

> Alexander and his army, marching by the shore of Ocean, found a giant crab which with difficulty they killed. In it were found six magnificent pearls and this gave the king the idea of exploring the submarine world in search of more. He had a large glass vessel constructed protected by an iron cage and provided with a small hatch in the bottom, through which he might thrust his hand and pick up pearls from the sand. In this contraption Alexander has himself lowered into the sea at the end of a long chain, after arranging with his men to draw him up again when he twitched the chain. Twice when he has descended to about half the length of the chain a fish brushes against it and causes Alexander's men to haul him up again. He persists, however, and at the third attempt is lowered to the full length of the chain, 308 cubits. At this moment a giant fish appears, seizes the vessel in its mouth and swims off with it, dragging the four ships and 350 men responsible for lowering the glass vessel behind it. It swims for more than a mile and finally deposits Alexander on the shore half dead with terror and blessing Providence for his lucky escape.

(Ross, "Alexander and the Faithless Lady: A Submarine Adventure," 5)

We would like to believe that there is generally some noble purpose that motivates technological progress—like improving the human condition. This is, of course, not always true, and it is certainly not true in the case of the

Alexander submarine episode. Not even curiosity seems to play a role (although it would become a major motivation in some later versions of the story). What motivates the originator of this account is nothing more than the prospect of gain. Alexander believes he can find more of the pearls that he and his army discovered in the crab they killed. Technology is thus linked here solely to gain—and if such a submersible were possible, the writer can think of no better way to employ it than to gather treasure from the sea. Such a prospect would certainly have excited Hellenistic rulers—and Roman emperors.

Before accusing the author of being too narrow and self-serving in his conception of how such a revolutionary device might be utilized, it should be pointed out that our knowledge of the undersea world allows us a perspective that was not available to the ancients. In antiquity, there were only a few reasons that would compel someone to dive beneath the sea. Most, if not all, were associated with profit; for example, diving for sponges and shells, gathering rare fish, recovering objects from shipwrecks—and collecting pearls. The risks and fears that went along with entering an unknown world would not have been worth taking if there had not been a healthy profit motive. The proposal of a manned submersible was simply making more sophisticated a practice that had been going on for centuries: Pearl diving would become more efficient, and the deeper waters, unreachable by conventional means, could be made accessible. The desire to devise a way to harvest the treasure fields in the depths of the sea found expression in the world of the fanciful with Alexander's descent.

Although putting such an underwater vessel to use in the manner described in the *Alexander Romance* may be nothing more than an older version of "If I had Aladdin's lamp, I would . . . ," it could also be a reflection of a changing attitude toward the practical application of technology. To be sure, military technology grew quite sophisticated during and after Hellenistic times. Its sole purpose was the destruction of one's enemies—a type of gain—but the general application of nonmilitary technology for economic gain does not seem to have become widespread. Perhaps, then, this version of the story is an early indication of a changing attitude that would come to characterize a more technologically oriented, profit-minded world that would reach full expression during the Middle Ages.

The way in which the author goes about constructing Alexander's fictitious underwater device is, like his proposed use of it, quite rational and within the context of the times. He had obviously thought much about it. Any successful submersible must include at least (1) a watertight and waterproof casing; (2) a way to see outside for purposes of observation, avoiding obstacles, and determining direction; (3) an air supply; and (4) a method of submerging and resurfacing.

Figure 8.10
Alexander's submarine adventure as portrayed in a fourteenth-century illuminated French manuscript of the Alexander Romance *(The Bodleian Library, Oxford)*

Remarkably, Alexander's submersible met all these requirements—at least theoretically. His vessel was made of glass. By itself, glass satisfied three of the four requirements: it was waterproof and watertight; it was transparent (also eliminating the need for interior lighting at shallow depths); and it could hold air. Glass floats for fishing nets have been in use for as long as there has been civilization, and Alexander's submersible was really nothing more than a large version of a glass float. Thus, he was protected from the sea, could see outside, and had a supply of air, albeit a limited one, to breathe.

Some way also had to be devised to force the glass bubble beneath the water, and the "inventor" of Alexander's vessel handled that in simple fashion by enclosing it in an iron cage, the weight of which would make it sink. To retrieve it, just as simple a method was employed—the cage and bubble were attached to a heavy chain that was worked by men in ships on the surface. The chain also served as a means of communication, for when Alexander twitched it, his men knew that he wished to be brought up. How he twitched the chain is not made clear, but presumably it could be accomplished by Alexander's simply shifting his weight back and forth while standing in the vessel. This entire concept was merely an elaboration of a procedure already used by ancient divers, who had ropes attached to their waists that connected them with the surface. When their lungs were empty, they yanked the rope as a signal to pull them up.

The "designer" of Alexander's craft also realized that there had to be some way of gathering the pearls once they had been sighted, so he provided the submersible with a small hatch (by which the occupant also entered and left) in the bottom, which could be opened whenever Alexander spied some treasure. Placing the hatch at the bottom of the vessel could have been accidental, but it is more likely that it was put there as a result of the kind of experiments mentioned in a work called the *Problems*, erroneously attributed to Aristotle. The *Problems* contains a discussion on diving in which the fact is mentioned that an overturned bucket will retain air underwater—a reality that Aristotle must have known and probably stated, for any peasant who owned a bucket was capable of the same observation. The man who concocted Alexander's submersible, too, had to have been aware that as long as there was air in the vessel he envisioned, a hatch on the bottom could be safely opened without fear of water flooding the compartment.

Theoretically, Alexander's submersible was about as sophisticated as it could be. In practical terms, however, the results would not have been positive. Making a glass vessel big enough to hold a man while remaining watertight and waterproof would have presented quite a challenge. The other complications are obvious—apparently, the author was not aware of what the pressures of the sea would do to his fragile vessel 308 cubits (about 460 feet) down, the stated depth to which Alexander supposedly descended. When compared even with the earliest successful submersibles of a few centuries ago, Alexander's craft seems a rather clumsy device, but the concept should not be ridiculed. A little over 130 years ago, Jules Verne got his astronauts to the moon by shooting them out of a great cannon embedded in the ground, a notion that may seem absurd to most of us today but was based on the best technological thinking of his day (although interest in some variation of the concept has been renewed by modern space theorists).

Myth Becomes History

Alexander's submarine adventure demonstrates how ancient science, technology, and fantasy are not as strange bedfellows as they might first appear, but like Archimedes' heat ray, Alexander's fictional feat has taken on a historicity it never had. Myth has become reality, and legend has become fact. By the thirteenth century, for example, Roger Bacon, depending on the earlier account of the astronomer Aethicus Ister, had accepted the tradition of Alexander's submersible as absolute fact. His stature contributed to the story's acceptance down to the present day.

Incredibly, almost every modern publication, serious and popular, on the subject of submersibles and their history begins with the tradition of Alexander's "diving bell." Some even go so far as to give the year and location of its use—most frequently, the siege of Tyre in 332 B.C. One work tells us, for example, that Alexander was perhaps the first monarch in recorded history to become a diver when, in 300 B.C., he was lowered into shallow waters in a glass barrel to observe marine life. At least by this account, supplying air to Alexander would not have been a problem, since by 300 B.C., he had already been dead for twenty-three years! A quagmire of inaccuracies, misunderstandings, and misplaced credulity has resulted concerning the real nature of Alexander's adventure—all the more incomprehensible, since the absurdity of the account is obvious to anyone familiar with the comparatively large and accessible body of ancient historical material about Alexander. A brief review of that evidence will restore Alexander's adventure, once and for all, to the realm of romance where it properly belongs.

The main historical tradition of Alexander is preserved in five ancient writers: Arrian, Plutarch, Quintus Curtius, Diodorus, and Justin. Together, they provide a fairly full account of the exploits of the Macedonian monarch. Had Alexander really done something as spectacular as descend beneath the waves in any kind of submersible, it could not have gone unnoticed—there would have been some prominent mention of it. But there is none; there is nothing remotely related. Furthermore, the same tradition includes much anecdotal and questionable material, some of which borders on or is of a fantastic nature. Yet, even the most outrageous of these passages contains no hint of a submarine adventure. Neither can any reference be found in the scores of fragments from the numerous histories about Alexander that no longer exist. If ancient writers troubled themselves to record, for example, a story about Alexander traveling to Iasus on the coast of Asia Minor to view a boy riding on a dolphin, they certainly would not have overlooked the first deep-sea adventure. The obvious conclusion is that the episode never occurred—until it appeared in the fictitious pages of Pseudo-Callisthenes.

As for the siege of Tyre, the historical event to which Alexander's alleged descent is most often attached, there are detailed accounts of it in Arrian, Diodorus, and Curtius. This was a likely setting for underwater exploits, since Tyre was an island city, completely surrounded by water, and much of the action during Alexander's seven-month siege took place offshore. However, the

Map 20
Alexandria. The cultural and intellectual center of the Hellenistic world, Alexandria was founded by Alexander the Great soon after his conquest of Egypt in 332 B.C. Capital of the Ptolemies, it boasted the Great Library and Museum (described as "part of the royal palaces"), the Lighthouse of Pharos, one of the Seven Wonders of the Ancient World, and was home to many of the great thinkers and inventors of the day.

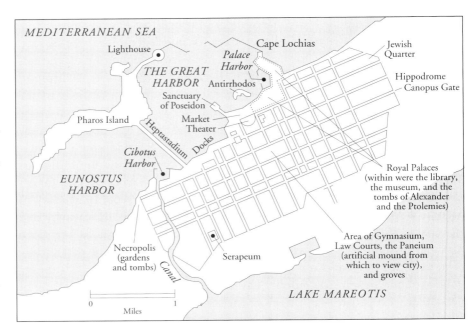

only underwater operations mentioned by these sources were carried out by the Tyrians *against* Alexander. Arrian (2.21.6) says that divers were sent out to cut the rope anchor cables on Alexander's ships, prompting the Macedonians to replace them with chain cables (perhaps inspiring Pseudo-Callisthenes to have Alexander's submersible attached to a chain rather than a rope). Curtius (4.3.10) also mentions Tyrian divers, but in a different capacity: They undermined the foundations of the causeway that Alexander was building out to the city and so caused its collapse. It is possible that there were other, similar kinds of underwater activities—perhaps even some from Alexander's side—but all were of the type that we generally equate with the duties of "frogmen." There was no submersible at Tyre.

Although there is no historical basis for Alexander's submarine experience at Tyre, it is understandable how such an impression could have arisen. A tradition, brewing since the Hellenistic period and reaching maturity in late antiquity, had Alexander descending beneath the waves in a submersible. It was a part of a body of countless stories about him, historical and otherwise, that had been circulating orally and in written form for centuries. The exact circumstances of the undersea adventure were vague (it was inserted in Pseudo-Callisthenes as a letter Alexander had supposedly written to his mother, Olympias, about his wanderings), and no specific location was mentioned. The process of mingling the historical with the non-historical then began.

Figure 8.11
Aristotle. Aristotle's presence at the court of Philip and the tradition that the great scholar tutored Alexander gave credence to the belief in later ages that he had fashioned an underwater vessel for Alexander.

It was well known that Aristotle (384–322 B.C.) had been at the court of King Philip, Alexander's father, and many ancient sources state that one of Aristotle's duties there was to educate Alexander. To what extent Aristotle actually did influence Alexander is a matter of debate, but no one can argue that the two were not associated in some fashion. It has already been noted that although it was popularly believed that Aristotle was the author of a work called the *Problems,* he probably was not. Nevertheless, the mistaken impression that he did write the work was obviously current in late antiquity—and undoubtedly much earlier. (Thus far, then, we have Aristotle and Alexander together, and the belief that Aristotle was responsible for the ideas contained in the *Problems.*)

In the *Problems,* as we have seen, there is a discussion about diving, which states that overturned buckets will retain air when they are forced into the water. A diver can, thereby, utilize the air collected in this manner to remain underwater an extended period of time. The logical extension of this concept was a primitive diving bell of some sort. The popular impression of later ages was that Aristotle was a wonder-worker—few would have questioned his ability to design such an underwater vessel. Through hindsight, it was presumed that he produced one for his favorite student, Alexander, to use in his wars.

Once this idea had been established, an appropriate location was needed in which to set the episode, and Tyre was the logical choice. Why Tyre? Because,

A "Reel" Look at Greek People IV: *Alexander the Great—* A Less Than "Great" Rendition

CONSIDERING THAT ALEXANDER THE Great's 10-year expedition from Macedonia into India and back to Babylon, a distance of over 11,000 miles, has been described as the greatest military campaign of all time and the man himself as the most brilliant field commander in history, Hollywood has paid scant attention to him. Critics not fully familiar with his credentials routinely place Napoleon above him, and, to this date, so have the movies (although a new major film is forthcoming). Previously, the only attempts in the last half-century to deal with the staggering saga of Alexander have been the epic 1955 treatment *Alexander the Great* starring Richard Burton, an ill-fated attempt at a T.V. series in the 1960s featuring William Shatner of *Star Trek* fame, and a PBS miniseries in the early 1980s that has been almost forgotten.

Alexander's story, understandably, is difficult to retell—one too remote to automatically attract the interest of a modern film audience that is unfamiliar with Macedonia, and one which involves a complicated personality over which scholars have spilled much ink trying to get right. Many today have heard Alexander's name and that he did something "great," but it is easier to relate to Napoleon. He at least is a more recent and seemingly more romantic figure from France who warred successfully against countries of which most audiences have heard, until stopped by the Russian winter at Moscow. Truth be told, Alexander was stopped by nothing, be it weather, topography, climate, or opponents. He never suffered defeat and, unlike Napoleon, who commanded a Franco-European army fighting opponents organized in a recognized style of European warfare, Alexander successfully expanded his core of Macedonians and Greeks into a multinational, multireligious force that ultimately numbered over 100,000. That army, held together only by

his force of personality, fought every kind of foe in every type of circumstance imaginable over a 10-year period. When he died unexpectedly at age 32 in 323 B.C., Alexander had conquered a quarter of the world. Whatever one ultimately thinks of him, few personalities in history have had such an impact. The film version of *Alexander the Great* does manage to recapture some of the well-known vulgate tradition about Alexander, but, generally, it falls short in impressing the viewer of the full magnitude of his story. It is also rife with historical errors.

While *Alexander the Great* lacks much, many omissions are no fault of its own. Since the film was made in 1955, the scholarship on Alexander has advanced considerably, major excavations at the Macedonian capital of Pella have taken place, and most impressive of all, the Macedonian Royal Tombs, including that of Alexander's father Philip, were discovered at Aegae (modern Vergina) in 1977. These tombs, in particular, have advanced considerably our knowledge of how Macedonian royalty lived and died during the era of Alexander, and even the cremated remains of Philip have been recovered (Figure 8.5). Artifacts include remarkable examples of royal paraphernalia, arms and armor, and silver and bronze wine vessels, presumably used at court. One of the few things in *Alexander the Great* to which more than passing attention is paid was the reproduction of classical pottery. Judging from Royal Tomb contents, however, it is more likely that finely crafted silver or bronze vessels would have been used in the film's drinking scenes at court. Also, paintings of the type found on Royal Tomb walls would have made nice substitutes for the neo-concrete murals and other wall decoration shown in *Alexander*. Inspiration from these same tombs as well as excavations at Pella would also, presumably, have helped the

Figure 8.12   *Some excavated remains of Pella, once the capital of Philip and Alexander*

filmmakers understand that simply reproducing details from earlier Greek society to re-create Macedonian settings for the picture will not do. Examples of sculpture, for instance, range from Greek archaic to classical, and Myron's famous discus-thrower ("Discobolus") somehow ends up at Philip's palace—as do curious-looking reproductions of the "Lions of Naxos." Architecturally, the film depends on examples of earlier Greek temples, simply turning them inside out to make interiors for Macedonian buildings. A Spanish village inadequately substitutes for Pella (although the countryside could pass for that surrounding Aegae). The Persians fare even worse in respect to their surroundings with representations from earlier Assyrian art and religion decorating their hangouts.

Even without the new discoveries, however, *Alexander the Great* has enough historical problems to cause the informed viewer to wince. Much that is crucial to Alexander is missing. There is no defining sack of Thebes, which reinforced Alexander's kingship and power after Philip's death for any Greeks still in doubt about his control over them. The key battle of Issus in 333 B.C. is not depicted at all, and the name appears only on a backdrop "map" that frequently covers the screen while a narrator tells us what Alexander has been up to in newscast fashion. At the actual battle of Issus, the Persian king Darius III fled, leaving his family behind to fall into Alexander's hands. In *Alexander,* Darius' mother,

(continued)

A "Reel" Look at Greek People IV: *Alexander the Great—* A Less Than "Great" Rendition (continued)

wife, and children have to wait another two years before they are gathered after Alexander's final battle with Darius on "the plains of Babylon" (actually, Gaugamela in 331 B.C.). Also present among the family is Roxane, the Sogdian princess whom Alexander would not encounter and marry until some years later, and who is erroneously portrayed as Darius's daughter. Alexander's closest friend, Hephaestion, who should have had a dominant role in the film, is barely noticed. Egypt, where Alexander was first declared a "god," a theme closely followed in the film, and where the future city of Alexandria was established, is referred to only in passing. India, too, receives a narrator's scant mention, while Alexander's pivotal battle with the Indian prince Porus at the Hydaspes River (326 B.C.) and subsequent Indus River campaign on which Alexander received his almost fatal wound are entirely overlooked. Memnon of Rhodes, the Greek who participated in the Persian resistance to Alexander, has inexplicably been made an Athenian and shows up now and again as a defender of Greek liberty before being killed at the Granicus River (334 B.C.). The real Memnon was never so altruistic and lived past Granicus another year, posing a most serious threat to Alexander's progress. Memnon's wife, Barsine, played by Claire Bloom, is somehow elevated to a major role in the film. She is with her husband at Athens, where she first meets and "falls" for Alexander. After Memnon's death, the real Alexander would father a son by Barsine, apparently hinted at in the film when she is captured (erroneously) at Miletus and the romance is "consummated" in 1950s asexual style. The child is never seen, but Barsine now accompanies Alexander as something of a "conscience" for the remainder of the film. It is also she who will rally other women to burn Darius' palace and is with Alexander at Susa when he marries Roxane and at his

death soon after. All this is fiction, and such egregious errors make the film an almost worthless guide to the real Alexander's life.

Richard Burton was probably a good cast for the role of Alexander. He was of average height for his day, as was Alexander, close to the right age when Alexander dies, was fond of drink (little of which is exhibited in the movie until the end, although the real Alexander was a heavy drinker), and thrived on playing complicated, moody characters. No one will ever agree exactly on the nature of Alexander's true personality, but there is much beneath the skin of the real man that most actors could not duplicate on screen. Burton exudes Alexander's confidence because he is supposed to, always seems troubled, agitated, or impatient (perhaps partly because of the ridiculous blond hairpiece he wears), and dominates everything and everybody around him. As a restive youth (Burton is not a convincing teenager), he competes with his friends in stilted athletic contests that look to be drawn right out of Leni Riefenstahl's *Olympia* (1938), and listens with them eagerly as a predictable Aristotle chirps on endlessly about Greek superiority to everybody else. When his father is killed, Alexander grabs hold of the expedition and is off to Persia within a blink of an eye. Actually, it was not until two years after Philip's death, in 334 B.C., that the expedition departed.

Philip, portrayed by Fredric March, drinks heavily, limps from a wound (though is still able to dance a mocking "Hitlerian" jig on a rock high above the Greek dead at Chaeronea), and points to a scar below his eye, which was actually put out by a spear or an arrow. Apparently the filmmakers thought that a man with only one eye was not a very appealing idea. March does have a beard and is vaguely reminiscent of the features of a possible forensic reconstruction of the real Philip's face of-

Figure 8.13 *Presumed armaments of Philip of Macedonia discovered in the larger of the Royal Tombs at Vergina, ancient Aegae. (Thessalonike Museum)*

fered back in 1983, but he never ages and the real Philip, judging from his actual remains and armor (prop-room issue in the picture), was a man of small stature. That, however, probably would not have been noticeable since Alexander was also said to be shorter than his friend Hephaestion, and it would appear that Macedonians, in general, were not a tall people. March's Philip seems somewhat remote from the birth of his own son (perhaps purposeful to reinforce the idea in the film that Alexander's actual father was a god), does not appear to know what his son's name means in Greek ("Little Lion"?), and fears Alexander from the day of his birth. The tensions underpin much of the early going of the film. In contrast, the real Philip was a man in charge.

The role of Alexander's mother, Olympias, seems mostly to verify her son as a "god" and to get back at Philip for his infidelities and mistreatment. Ultimately, Olympias goads one of Alexander's "friends," Pausanias, who has been insulted at court by Philip, into killing her husband by getting Pausanias drunk and filling his ear with poison about her husband. That, of course, bears no resemblance to the actual circumstances of the assassination (see p. 232). In the film, Philip is stabbed on the steps of the palace in Pella (not in the theater at Aegae) and Pausanias is immediately apprehended and then killed by Alexander himself—purposely leaving the viewer to wonder

(continued)

A "Reel" Look at Greek People IV: *Alexander the Great—* A Less Than "Great" Rendition (continued)

Figure 8.14   The gold box, or larnaca, *from Philip's tomb which contained the king's cremated remains (see Figure 8.5). Note the royal starburst emblem on its lid. (Thessalonike Museum)*

if Alexander had not been somehow involved with his mother in the plot. While the possibility has excited many, it cannot be verified.

Such tensions between father, mother, and son may have some justification in the ancient sources, but the movie seems intent on developing what amounts to a dysfunctional Shakespearean family performing in a stage play rather than a film. Here and elsewhere, Burton seems to forget he is playing Alexander and slips off into the role of Hamlet or some other of the English bard's troubled youths. Perhaps Burton was still in character from his role in *The Robe,* where

he often looks aimlessly out in the distance after being mysteriously seized by the power of Jesus' robe and babbles to confused bystanders around him, "Were you out there . . . ?"

The use of thousands of extras from the Spanish army to re-enact the "mighty" battles may have been much ballyhooed at the time, but there is little to be seen of the famed Macedonian phalanx or any sort of tactics on either side in battles. One does note spears at times resembling the famed Macedonian long pikes, but they seem to shorten noticeably (probably too hard to manipulate) when on the march or in combat. In all the battle scenes, the fighting inevitably ends up with unlikely swordplay, and whoever has a spear seems to wave it around aimlessly not really knowing what to do with it. The variety of armor and military dress in the film has little to do with actual examples, and one does not know what to make of the fur "booties" (and furs) sometimes worn by the actors. One of the few things that actually does have some relevance is the well-known "starburst" symbol of Macedonian royalty, which is crudely painted mostly on the shields of the cavalry. Unfortunately, the Macedonian cavalry did not carry shields. Alexander's own inadequate armor is usually worn without tunic or any type of undergarment, which must have chafed Burton no end, and decorations on it have been curiously lifted from the breastplate of the Prima Porta statue of the Roman emperor Augustus, who lived three centuries later. One would think that the art directors could have at least copied the armor Alexander is shown wearing while engaging Darius in the famous mosaic from Pompeii. The greatest shortcoming of Burton's accoutrements, however, is the various prop helmets he wears. One has a face mask that opens and closes like cupboard doors whenever he feels the need and could not appear more ridiculous.

At the end, Alexander just seems to run out of gas. By that time, we have also. The film has disintegrated into a mishmash of error, misplaced scenarios, and confused impressions about the man, and we do not know exactly what to make of the movie's finale. From everything negative that has happened and the deaths of his father and those who had been his friends, Alexander apparently has a revelation. The "King of kings" discards his selfish ambition and reaches a new understanding: it is the hearts of men that must be conquered—not their lands. He subsequently embraces a new theme of the "Unity" or "Brotherhood of Man," a notion still current in the scholarly community when the film was made—but *never* in the manner implied in the film. At Susa, Alexander does go on to marry Darius' daughter (actually Stateira, who is mentioned in the credits, but is replaced in the film by Roxane), while his officers, too, take noble Persian wives. Diversity is accomplished, and a new order is created. All will live as one in "heart and mind." All are "alike under the eyes of god." "*He* is the father." The unions have barely finished, however, when Alexander becomes unsteady, loses his grip on a ridiculous-looking tall vessel of wine, and collapses. He is not a god after all, though he is still destined to fulfill the prophecy of a short life like Achilles (did not a familiar carpenter's son also live a short life?). His own slated apotheosis has apparently been interrupted by his realization that there is really only "one god."

If anyone watching the film for two hours fifteen minutes still did not understand where it was going, everything suddenly becomes clear. Hollywood has managed, as it almost always does in films with ancient themes, to tie Alexander with Christianity. Even Alexander's submarine adventure would have had a more relevant place in this film than such a notion! Nonetheless, Alexander's men still parade by him in a final display of respect, and Alexander still gives up the ghost with the famous last words, "To the strongest," attributed to him when he is asked to whom he left his kingdom ("empire" in the film). One would think a man who has found the true religion would be more of a pacifist. At the last, however, Burton's confused Alexander apparently found the true god easier than he did the right place and time to expire since the historical Alexander did not die until the following year, perfectly content with Zeus—and in Babylon, *not* Susa. It does not really matter, however. The film had died long before.

Figure 8.15
Statuette of Alexander
discovered at
Alexandria, the city he
founded, first century
B.C.

as noted previously, there were operations on the water and, most importantly, evidence of *underwater* activities that would have begged the use of a submersible. But this was not the only reason that Tyre became the location for the adventure. Diodorus, for example, speaks of some rather fantastic technological devices that were employed in the battle for the city:

> They had a wealth of catapults and other engines employed for sieges and they had no difficulty in constructing more because of the engineers and artisans of all sorts who were in the city. All kinds of novel devices were fashioned by them, so that the entire circuit of the walls was covered with machines. . . . The Tyrians had bronze workers and machinists, and contrived ingenious countermeasures. Against the projectiles from the catapults they made wheels with many spokes, and, setting these to rotate by a certain device, they destroyed some of the missiles and deflected others, and broke the force of all. They caught the balls from the stone throwers in soft and yielding materials and so weakened their force. . . . They forged great tridents armed with barbs and struck with these at close range the assailants standing on the towers. . . . They thought of another ingenious device also to offset the Macedonian fighting qualities. . . . They fashioned shields of bronze and iron and, filling them with sand, roasted them continuously over a strong fire and made the sand red hot. By means of a certain apparatus they then scattered this over those Macedonians who were fighting. . . . With their firethrowers they discharged huge red-hot masses of metal into the press of the enemy . . . the Tyrians rigged marble wheels in front of the walls and causing these to rotate by some mechanism they shattered the flying missiles of the

The Bigger and Better Weapon: Demetrius' Siege of Rhodes— A "Colossal" Undertaking

FEW RULERS IN THE Hellenistic period—let alone antiquity—were as obsessed with developing the ultimate weapon as Demetrius Poliorcetes was. The son of Alexander's general Antigonus the One-Eyed, Demetrius survived the squabbles of the Successors long enough to establish himself on the throne of Macedonia in 294 B.C. However, his high-handed manner, rash temperament, and poor judgment caused him to lose the throne and ultimately to be captured in battle and die a prisoner of his adversary Seleucus in 283. His son was able to reestablish the family in power in the 270s, and the Antigonid house would rule Macedonia until it was overthrown by Rome in 168 B.C.

In his earlier days, Demetrius was frequently in the shadow of his more illustrious father. When the latter was killed at Ipsus, the greatest battle among the Successors, in 301 B.C., Demetrius emerged as an independent contender for the remains of Alexander's empire. He had already established himself as a major military force during his famous siege of Rhodes (305–304 B.C.), and although unsuccessful, Demetrius had earned there the nickname Poliorcetes, "Besieger of Cities," because his war engines were among the most incredible ever fashioned up to that time. The most impressive was called the Helepolis, the "City-Taker," and the historian Diodorus provides the fullest account of it and other aspects of the siege:

> Demetrius, who was besieging Rhodes, failing in his assaults by sea, decided to make his attacks by land. Having provided therefore a large quantity of material of all kinds, he built an engine called the helepolis, which far surpassed in size those which had been constructed before it. Each side of the square platform he made almost 75 feet in length, framed together from squared timber and fastened with iron; the space within he divided by bars set about 18 inches from each other so that there might be standing space for those who were to push the machine forward. The whole structure was movable, mounted on eight great solid wheels; the width of their rims was three feet and these were overlaid with heavy iron plates. To permit motion to the side, pivots had been constructed, by means of which the whole device was easily moved in any direction. From each corner there extended upward beams equal in length and little short of 150 feet long, inclining toward each other in such a way that, the whole structure being nine stories high, the first story had an area of forty-three hundred square feet and the topmost story of nine hundred. The three exposed sides of the machine he covered externally with iron plates nailed on so that it should receive no injury from fire carriers. On each story there were ports on the front, in size and shape fitted to the individual characteristics of the missiles that were to be shot forth. These ports had shutters, which were lifted by a mechanical device and which secured

Figure 8.16   *Portrait of Demetrius Poliorcetes on a tetradrachm*

(continued)

The Bigger and Better Weapon: Demetrius' Siege of Rhodes (continued)

the safety of the men on the platforms who were busy serving the artillery; for the shutters were of hides stitched together and were filled with wool so that they would yield to the blows of the stones from the ballistae. Each of the storys had two wide stairways, one of which they used for bringing up what was needed and the other for descending, in order that all might be taken care of without confusion. Those who were to move the machine were selected from the whole army, three thousand four hundred men excelling in strength; some of them were enclosed within the machine while others were stationed in its rear, and they pushed it forward, the skillful design aiding greatly in its motion. He also constructed penthouses—some to protect the men who were filling the moat, others to carry rams—and covered passages through which those who were going to their labors might go and return safely. Using the crews of the ships, he cleared a space 800 yards wide through which he planned to advance the siege engines he had prepared, wide enough so that it covered a front of six curtains and seven towers. The number of craftsmen and laborers collected was not much less than thirty thousand.

As everything, therefore, because of the many hands was finished sooner than was expected, Demetrius was regarded with alarm by the Rhodians; for not only did the size of the siege engines and the number of the army which had been gathered stun them, but also the king's energy and ingenuity in conducting sieges. For, being exceedingly ready in invention and devising many things beyond the art of the master builders, he was called Poliorcetes; and he displayed such superiority and force in his attacks that it seemed that no wall was strong enough to furnish safety from him for the besieged. Both in stature and in beauty he displayed the dignity of a hero, so that even

those strangers who had come from a distance, when they beheld his comeliness arrayed in royal splendor, marveled at him and followed him as he went abroad in order to gaze at him. Furthermore, he was haughty in spirit and proud and looked down not only upon common men but also upon those of royal estate; and what was most peculiar to him, in time of peace he devoted his time to winebibbing and to drinking bouts accompanied by dancing and revels, and in general he emulated the conduct . . . of Dionysus among men; but in his wars he was active and sober, so that beyond all others who practiced this profession he devoted both body and mind to the task. For it was in his time that the greatest weapons were perfected and engines of all kinds far surpassing those that had existed among others. . . . (20.91–92)

The Colossus of Rhodes

The Rhodians stopped Demetrius' giant engines by flooding the ground in front of them, making it impossible for them to move. Demetrius eventually tired of the lengthy and unprofitable siege and sailed away, leaving his remarkable war machines behind for the Rhodians, who sold them and used the proceeds to construct the Colossus of Rhodes. The Colossus was a huge bronze statue of the sun god Helios, patron deity of the island, and one of the Seven Wonders of the Ancient World.

Fashioned by the sculptor Chares of Lindus, a native of Rhodes and pupil of the great Lysippus, the giant statue was another example of Hellenistic technological skills and the emphasis on "bigness." It was about 120 feet high (150 with its base) and took twelve years (292–280 B.C.) to complete at a cost of 300 (presumably gold) tal-

Figure 8.17   The head of the Colossus of Rhodes may have closely resembled this almost contemporary representation of Helios on fourth-century B.C. didrachm from Rhodes.

ents, a sum impossible to calculate precisely today but certainly in the many millions of dollars. Philon of Byzantium (second century B.C.) gave the following account of the Colossus:

> . . . At Rhodes was set up a Colossus 120 feet high, representing the Sun. . . . The artist expended as much bronze on it as seemed likely to create a dearth at the foundries; for the casting of this statue was the world's (triumph) in metal-working. . . . The artist fortified the bronze from within by means of iron scaffolding and squared blocks of stone, whose connecting rods bear witness to hammering of Cyclopean force, and indeed the hidden part of the labor is greater than the visible. . . . He constructed beneath it a base of white marble, and on this, working out the proportion, he first fixed the feet of the Colossus up as far as the ankle-bones, on which the god, 120 feet high, was to be erected. As the top of the base was already so high as to over-top other statues, it was not possible to lift the rest of the statue and place it in position above; so the ankles had to be filled in and the whole to rise on the top (by stages) like a building; for the same reason, in the case of other statues, artists make

a model first, then divide it up and cast the parts separately, and lastly join them all together again in erecting it; so here, when the first bit had been cast, the second was modeled on the top of it, and when that had been cast the third was built on to it, and so on, using always the same device of construction. The sculptor then continually piled up round the as yet uncompleted parts of the Colossus a vast mound of earth, which hid the completed parts and allowed the casting of the next stages at ground level. So, going up bit by bit towards the goal of his endeavor, at the expense of 500 talents of bronze and 300 of iron, he made his god equal to the God, raising a work mighty in its boldness; for he gave the world a second Sun to match the first.

(*The Seven Wonders of the World,* Chapter 4)

The popular fiction that the Colossus bestrode the harbor at Rhodes belongs to the imagination of a fifteenth-century writer, and the small evidence we do have suggests instead a statue like that illustrated in Figure 8.18, shading his eyes, most likely facing east, looking at the rising sun, and located *behind* the harbor in a spot where everyone could see it.

Philon mentions that 500 talents (weight) of bronze were used in the construction of the statue. If his figure is accurate, this is the equivalent of 12½ tons of bronze. For a statue so large, such a small amount of bronze would require the outer skin of the Colossus to be almost coin thin—probably not cast as Philon suggested but beaten into thin plates. Consequently, the main support would have come from the "iron scaffolding and squared blocks of stone" inside. Chares appears to have designed his work to withstand almost every environmental condition,

(continued)

The Bigger and Better Weapon: Demetrius' Siege of Rhodes (continued)

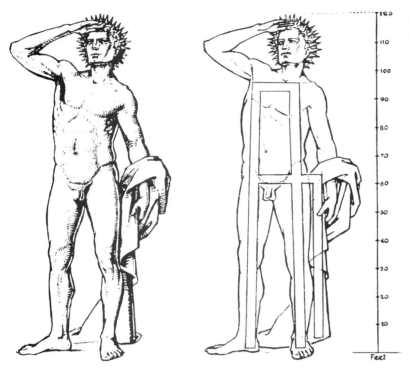

Figure 8.18
Probable pose of the Colossus of Rhodes and positioning of supports inside

but he apparently failed to consider the one that ended the Colossus' brief existence. Fifty-four years after its erection, it became the victim of an earthquake, which caused the statue to bend at the knees and fall to the ground, where it lay in ruins for almost 900 years.

The story of the Colossus ends in the seventh century A.D. when the Saracens devastated Rhodes and supposedly broke up the statue's re-mains and sold them to a Jewish merchant. The tradition is a strong one (albeit containing some absurdities), but one has to wonder, considering the value of bronze, how it could have survived all those centuries. An oracle supposedly forbade any attempts to raise the Colossus, and similar religious taboos may have surrounded the great wreck. Yet, it seems almost logical to assume that the "mining" of the site had begun earlier.

catapults and, deflecting them from their course, rendered their fire ineffective. . . . In sum, the Tyrians defended themselves strongly in all regards and showed themselves well provided with the means of defense.
(*History* 17.41.3–45.5)

With such a "high-tech" atmosphere associated with the siege of Tyre, it would not have been difficult for writers even less critical than Diodorus to insert Alexander's submarine into their more romantic accounts of the episode.

Furthermore, all existing versions of Alexander's underwater experience include some type of frightening undersea creature, ranging from a giant fish to other monsters. Interestingly, both Diodorus and Curtius (whose critical acumen can also be questioned) include in their accounts of the siege of Tyre the appearance of a huge sea monster that threatens Alexander's progress in humbling the city.

Finally, Diodorus and Curtius make the suggestion that Alexander's siege of Tyre actually evolved as a clash between the king and Poseidon, god of the sea—because Alexander's success ultimately depended on his "conquest" of the waters surrounding Tyre. Consequently, the impression took hold that this contest was not between armies but between a god and a man (who was viewed by some as a god, or at least superhuman). Later ages would have found it reasonable that Alexander employed fantastic devices, such as a submersible, to win his battle with Poseidon, and he ultimately did conquer the sea and Tyre.

All these diverse elements came together to form a specific tradition, albeit a *false* one, that Alexander had employed his submarine at the siege of Tyre.

A Submersible in Antiquity?

Although a deep-sea submersible as "sophisticated" as the one Alexander is described as having was beyond the technological capabilities of the day, is there any evidence to show that the principle outlined in the *Problems,* which was commonly known, was ever applied in antiquity to a larger bucket? Was there ever a simple diving bell that could hold a person? The answer is no. There is no evidence for the practical application of the concept on a large scale until long after antiquity. It took that long, apparently, to master all the problems of construction, material, air supply, lighting, and manipulation. Difficulties with the last may be reflected in the fact that Pseudo-Callisthenes provided Alexander's imaginary vessel with four ships and 350 men to handle it. Or perhaps the ancients were just not interested in developing a diving bell. This would not be the first time that something

Hero of Alexandria's "Steam Engine"

ALTHOUGH HERO LIVED IN the first century A.D., he was a continuation of the Hellenistic tradition of technology and invention that had been centered at Alexandria in Egypt. Among his creations was a ball rotated by steam—a steam engine—which he described in his *Pneumatica* (2.11) and which has been reconstructed by Landels (*Engineering in the Ancient World* 28).

Such a machine could have revolutionized ancient society, and the question of why Hero never developed his "steam engine" on a larger scale is a much-debated one. Some find the answer in sociological and economic explanations, but it may be, as one recent authority has stated, that "the construction of the steam engine had to wait until it was possible to make iron pipes and put them together with screws" (Drachman, *The Mechanical Technology* 206).

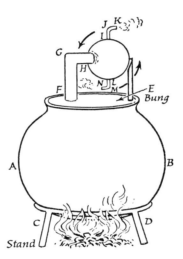

Figure 8.19   A reconstruction of Hero's "steam engine." Pressure builds up in the cauldron, and steam passes through the pipe FGH into the sphere, from which it escapes at various points, but mainly through the bent tubes IJK and LMN. As the steam is forced out in one direction through the outlets, it causes a reaction thrust in the opposite direction, which makes the sphere revolve.

theoretically possible was not pursued in antiquity. We would have difficulty today understanding a conscious decision not to pursue to its logical conclusion any idea that could have a revolutionary impact on society—or make a profit. Hero, for example, after toying with his steam engine model, apparently did not try to develop a large-scale version—nor did anyone else.

Perhaps it could not be done, but a primitive heat ray such as the one erroneously ascribed to Archimedes was also within the realm of the technology of the day—and yet it, too, was never developed.

As for the diving bell, perhaps no one could see what advantage it would really have over conventional methods of moving about underwater. Free divers could dive just as deep—for a primitive diving bell could only have been used in shallow water—their movements were not as restricted, they could accomplish more in less time, and perhaps best of all, their cost was minimal. But other considerations may have also played a part, and they should at least be mentioned.

For many ancient believers, the sea was sacred, and plunging a large object like a diving bell into it was blasphemous and might earn the retribution of the gods. Also, the risk of drowning may have scared some away. References in ancient literature to deaths at sea are not at all positive, for if the body were not recovered, it could not be given a proper burial, and the soul was doomed to roam forever with no hope of finding peace. The prospects of a death *below* the sea trapped in a diving bell had no appeal. In addition, there was the fear of what the depths of the sea might contain. The types of scary creatures Alexander meets in the various accounts of his undersea adventure are probably an expression of this fear. In the rendition with which we have been dealing, a giant fish takes Alexander's submersible in its mouth, drags it and the men and ships handling the vessel for more than a mile, and then deposits the great Alexander half dead on the shore "counting his lucky stars" that he is still alive. This certainly could not have been an encouraging prospect. This same fish story may be a variation of the Jonah and whale theme in the Bible—the idea expressed here that the sea will not tolerate anything sinful. Lucian had already parodied the whale theme in his writings, and its influence might also be seen in the Alexander adventure—a reflection, perhaps, of the view of some Judeo-Christians in the Roman Empire that the purity of the ocean's depths should not be sullied by the sins of man. Hence, Alexander was "spit out."

Why even the simplest type of shallow-water diving bell was never developed in antiquity remains a mystery. We can understand, however, the mythologizing process of assigning unattainable feats to famous individuals, for it is a process that continues today. It is not uncommon for things that are quasi-historical, or completely fictional, to take on the air of undisputed fact. We continue to enjoy reading or hearing about superhuman exploits that make an impressive figure even more impressive—and that includes Alexander. At the same time, however, we cannot allow the myth to obscure (or become) fact. In the case of Alexander's submarine adventure, we must return it to the realm of fantasy, where it properly belongs.

The Ordinary Becomes the Extraordinary: Ptolemy V, the Rosetta Stone, and the Decipherment of Egyptian Hieroglyphs

Figure 8.20   Ptolemy I, the former general of Alexander the Great and founder of the Ptolemaic dynasty in Egypt

WE MAY END THIS final chapter with a "beginning" that Ptolemy V, the much-overtaxed monarch of Hellenistic Egypt from 205 to 180 B.C., unknowingly provided for us—the means to decipher Egyptian writing, a skill that had been lost since the fifth century A.D.

One of the three major kingdoms that were ultimately carved out of Alexander's old empire, Egypt was ruled by the family of Ptolemy I, the former general of the Macedonian warlord who seized Alexander's body and brought it to Egypt. Able to fend off all challenges from other Successors, who tried to dislodge him, Ptolemy eventually declared himself king (305 B.C.)—or, more traditionally, pharaoh—and proceeded with the building of Alexandria (where Alexander's body

was ultimately laid to rest). His son and successor, Ptolemy II (Ptolemy became the dynastic title for Egypt's rulers), expanded the Ptolemaic overseas empire and developed Alexandria (see Map 20) as a cultural, artistic, and learning center—completing such memorable additions as the Great Library, Museum, and Zoo, and the Pharos lighthouse, which eventually became one of the Seven Wonders. Subsequent Ptolemies are generally regarded as less capable and had to weather constant external and internal problems. Fortunately, they had Egypt's tremendous wealth to help counterbalance whatever they lacked in talent or opportunity. Ptolemy V was particularly harassed. While still a child, he succeeded his father after the latter's murder, and in the following years, he was faced with internal revolts and the loss of most overseas possessions. In 197 B.C. at Memphis, a commemoration ceremony of the accession of Ptolemy V Epiphanes ("Made manifest"), as he would be called, took place. On March 27 of the following year, a general council of priests from all over Egypt assembled at Memphis to celebrate this event in a way described in the "Rosetta Stone," destined to become one of the most famous inscriptions from the ancient world. However, it is not the content of the inscription that concerns us. The text is of interest but not remarkable: Ptolemy is honored as benefactor (especially) to the temples and priests of Egypt—and to all his subjects. What *is* of importance is that the decree on the stone was written in two languages, Greek (the language of the Ptolemies) and Egyptian, and three scripts—Greek (all capital letters), hieroglyphs (the formal pictorial script of Egypt), and demotic (a more common, extremely cursive Egyptian script derived from hieroglyphs). The knowledge of ancient Greek had never been forgotten—and having for the first time all three scripts together on

Figure 8.21
The Rosetta Stone (with restorations). It measures 3 feet 9 inches in height, 2 feet 4½ inches in width, and is 11 inches thick. It weighs almost three-quarters of a ton. In its original state, the monument was probably 5–6 feet tall. (British Museum, London)

the same stone saying the same thing was the crucial element that ultimately led to the unraveling of the "mysterious" writings of the ancient Egyptians.

After centuries of neglect, the aforementioned Rosetta Stone (portions of it missing) was discov-ered by Napoleon's soldiers when they demolished an old wall in 1799 at Rosetta (Rashid)—hence the name—a small village in the western Nile Delta. Following the French capitulation to the

(continued)

The Ordinary Becomes the Extraordinary (continued)

Figure 8.22   *A close-up of the face of the Rosetta Stone, showing the three distinct scripts. At the top is the hieroglyphic script; in the middle is the demotic, or cursive Egyptian script; and at the bottom is Greek. Note the elongated oval cartouches in the hieroglyphic script, which contain the names of royalty like Ptolemy V.*

British in 1801, the Stone, weighing almost three-quarters of a ton, came into British hands and was transported to England, arriving the following year. Subsequently, copies of the text were made and distributed to scholars while the Stone, itself, was put on permanent display at the British Museum in London, where it is still exhibited today. However, it would ultimately be a young

French scholar named Jean-François Champollion (1790–1832) who began to discover the key to the problem of decipherment in 1822 and is generally acknowledged as the "Father of the Decipherment of Hieroglyphs." A major breakthrough in solving the mystery involved the assumption that the six elongated ovals, or cartouches, in the hieroglyphic text on the Rosetta Stone always contained a royal

Figure 8.23   Champollion, the French scholar who deciphered the Egyptian hieroglyphs with the aid of the Rosetta Stone

name—in this case that of Ptolemy (that is, Ptolemy V), who was mentioned in the Stone's Greek text. Once the hieroglyphic equivalent of Ptolemy's name in Greek was established, the first step toward formulating a general system of decipherment had been taken, and today, the once-closed archives of Egyptian history are fully known to us. What follows are some excerpts from the more-complete Greek text on the Rosetta Stone. (Most missing lines from the hieroglyphic text can be restored from a later copy of the decree found in 1898; the rest can only be reconstructed from the demotic portion of the Stone.)

The inscription begins, typically, with the standard salutations (with Ptolemy hailed by his names and titles throughout):

In the reign of the young one who has succeeded his father in the kingship, lord of diadems, most glorious, who has established Egypt and is pious towards the gods, triumphant over his enemies, who has restored the civilized life of men . . . . . . the living image of Zeus, son of the Sun, PTOLEMY, LIVING FOR EVER, BELOVED OF PTAH, in the ninth year . . .

Then comes the decree, itself, preceded by additional preliminary detail:

DECREE. There being assembled the Chief Priests and Prophets and those who enter the inner shrine for the robing of the gods, and the Fan-bearers and the Sacred Scribes and all the other priests from the temples throughout the land who have come to meet the king at Memphis, for the feast of the assumption by PTOLEMY, THE EVER-LIVING, THE BELOVED OF PTAH, THE GOD EPIPHANES EUCHARISTOS, the kingship in which he succeeded his father, they being assembled in the temple in Memphis on this day declared . . .

Eventually, we get to the reasons why Ptolemy is being honored:

Whereas king PTOLEMY, THE EVER-LIVING, THE BELOVED OF PTAH, THE GOD EPIPHANES EUCHARISTOS, the son of King Ptolemy and Queen Arsinoe, the Gods Philopatores, has been a benefactor both to the temples and to those who dwell in them, as well as all those who are his subjects, being a god sprung from a god and goddess (like Horus the son of Isis

(continued)

The Ordinary Becomes the Extraordinary (continued)

and Osiris, who avenged his father Osiris)
(and) being benevolently disposed towards
the gods, has dedicated to the temples revenues
in money and grain and has undertaken
much outlay to bring Egypt into prosperity,
and to establish the temples,
and has been generous with all his own
means; and of the revenues and taxes levied
in Egypt some he has wholly remitted and
others has lightened, in order that the people
and all the others might be
in prosperity during his reign. . . .

The decree continues at some length in a similar vein, then finally the priests indicate what they are going to do to honor their benefactor:

. . . WITH PROPITIOUS FORTUNE:
It was resolved by the priests of all the temples
in the land to increase greatly the existing
honors of
King PTOLEMY, THE EVER-LIVING, THE BE-
LOVED OF PTAH, THE GOD EPIPHANES EU-
CHARISTOS, likewise of those of his parents the
Gods Philopators, and of his ancestors . . . and
to set up in the most prominent place of every
temple an image of the EVER-LIVING King
PTOLEMY, THE BELOVED OF PTAH, THE
  GOD
EPIPHANES EUCHARISTOS,

an image which shall be called that of 'Ptolemy,
the defender of Egypt', beside which
shall stand the principal god of the temple,
. . . and that the priests shall pay homage
to the images three times a day, and put
upon them the sacred garments, and perform
the other usual honors such as are
given to the other gods in the Egyptian
festivals; and to establish for King PTOLEMY,
THE GOD EPIPHANES EUCHARISTOS,
    sprung of
King Ptolemy and Queen Arsinoe, the Gods
Philopators, a statue and golden shrine in
each of the
temples, and to set it up in the inner chamber
with the other shrines. . . . And a festival shall be
kept for King PTOLEMY . . . yearly in the temples
throughout the
land. . . .

In the end, we are told what anyone who had the endurance to read the entire decree already knew:

. . . This decree shall be inscribed
on a stela of
hard stone in sacred [that is, hieroglyphic] and
native [that is, demotic] and Greek characters
and set up in each of the first, second and
third [rank] temples beside the image of the
ever-living king.

Suggestions for Further Reading

The Greek Alexander Romance is available in the Penguin edition (1991) by R. Stoneman. On Hellenistic science and technology, see G. Sarton, *A History of Science: Hellenistic Science and Culture in the Last Three Centuries B.C.,* Vol. 2 (New York: Norton Library, 1970); G. L. Irby-Massie and P. T. Keyser, *Greek Science of the Hellenistic Era* (New York: Routledge, 2002); and J. W. Humphrey et al., *Greek and Roman Technology* (New York: Routledge, 1997). J. G. Landels, *Engineering in the Ancient World* (Berkeley and Los Angeles: University of California Press, 1981), and J. Evans, *The History and Practice of Ancient Astronomy* (New York: Oxford

University Press, 1998), are also useful. For the Rosetta Stone, see R. Parkinson, *Cracking Codes: The Rosetta Stone and Decipherment* (Berkeley and Los Angeles: University of California Press, 1999), and C. Andrews, *The British Museum Book of the Rosetta Stone* (New York: Dorset Press, 1981).

General Reading

Pertinent studies include S. Hornblower, *The Greek World, 479–323 B.C.* (New York: Routledge, 1984); L. A. Tritle, *The Greek World in the Fourth Century: From the Fall of the Athenian Empire to the Successors of Alexander* (New York: Routledge, 1996); G. Shipley, *The Greek World After Alexander, 323–30 B.C.* (New York: Routledge, 2000); F. W. Walbank, *The Hellenistic World* (Cambridge, Mass.: Harvard University Press, 1993 [revised edition]); P. Green's massive *Alexander to Actium: The Historical Evolution of the Hellenistic Age* (Berkeley and Los Angeles: University of California Press, 1990); and Chr. Habicht, *Athens from Alexander to Antony* (Cambridge, Mass.: Harvard University Press, 1997). On Macedonia, see R. M. Errington, *A History of Macedonia* (Berkeley and Los Angeles: University of California Press, 1990); E. Borza, *In the Shadow of Olympus: The Emergence of Macedon* (Princeton, N.J.: Princeton University Press, 1992 [second revised edition]), and *Makedonika* (Claremont, Calif.: Regina Books, 1995). The most extensive treatment is *A History of Macedonia, Vol. 2: 550–336 B.C.* (Oxford: Oxford University Press, 1979) by N. G. L. Hammond and G. T. Griffith, and *Vol. 3: 336–167 B.C.* (1988), by Hammond and Walbank. On Philip and Alexander, see also Hammond, *Philip of Macedonia* (Baltimore: The Johns Hopkins University Press, 1994); *Alexander the Great: King, Commander and Statesman* (Park Ridge, N.J.: Noyes Press, 1980), and *The Genius of Alexander the Great* (Chapel Hill: University of North Carolina Press, 1997). Also on Alexander, J. M. O'Brien's *Alexander the Great: The Invisible Enemy* (New York: Routledge, 1992) examines the king's personality as affected by Dionysus, the god of wine, and includes an extensive bibliography. See, too, A. B. Bosworth, *The Legacy of Alexander: Politics, Warfare and Propaganda under the Successors* (New York: Oxford University Press, 2002); *Alexander the Great in Fact and Fiction* (2000), edited with E. J. Baynham; *Alexander and the East: The Tragedy of Triumph* (1997); and *Conquest and Empire: The Reign of Alexander the Great* (Cambridge: Cambridge University Press, 1988). Notable treatments of Alexander are also by Green (1991 reprint); Hamilton (1973); and Lane Fox (1973). On women, see E. Carney, *Women and Monarchy in Macedonia* (Norman: University of Oklahoma Press, 2000); and S. Pomeroy, *Women in Hellenistic Egypt: From Alexandria to Cleopatra* (New York: Shocken Books, 1984). On Alexandria and the Great Library, J-Y. Empereur's *Alexandria Rediscovered* (New York: Braziller, 1998); R. MacLeod (ed.), *The Library at Alexandria* (New York: Palgrave/Macmillan, 2002), and L. Canfora's *The Vanished Library: A Wonder of the Ancient World* (Berkeley and Los Angeles: University of California Press, 1990) are available. For the "Seven Wonders," see J. and E. Romer's *The Seven Wonders of the World: A History of Modern Imagination* (New York: Holt, 1995); and P. Clayton and M. Price (eds.), *The Seven Wonders of the Ancient World* (New York: Barnes & Noble Books reprint, 1993).

Epilogue

The Hellenistic world would survive its founder only a little over a century and a half before it succumbed to Rome—the new ruler of the Mediterranean. Nevertheless, the influence of the Greek people we have studied here and countless others continued to have an incalculable effect on the society of their conquerors. Much of Roman culture was founded on the Greek, although the Romans were generally unwilling to acknowledge any contributions made by a people they had subjugated.

Even before 146 B.C., the date by which Greek autonomy was at an end and the great Hellenistic monarchies humbled, Romans had already absorbed many of the traditions of their Eastern neighbors. Their alphabet, for example, was based on a version of the Greek. It was a Greek, a former Roman slave who took the name Livius Andronicus, who founded Roman literature in 240 B.C. The earliest Roman history was written by a Roman—in Greek. Roman comedy, already popular in the third century B.C., was modeled directly on Greek examples. The major Roman gods and goddesses were essentially borrowed from the Greeks and given different names. Much in Roman art and architecture was Greek-inspired. Even the famous gladiatorial contests that so many automatically associate with Rome had Greek inspiration.

After being conquered, Greeks filled many of the skilled positions in Roman society. A large percentage of the teachers, artists, sculptors, craftsmen, scientists, scholars, mathematicians, inventors, philosophers, musicians, and physicians was Greek. Many had begun their experience with the Romans as slaves. Some became freedmen and citizens. Those who remained slaves and were unskilled were a mainstay of Roman agriculture—and a cause for concern in the form of rebellions and uprisings. Certainly, the superstructure of Roman society rested firmly on many Greek supports. This fact held true over the centuries as the Roman Republic evolved into the Roman Empire.

Ironically, in the fifth century A.D. it was the Eastern, or Greek, half of the Roman Empire that outlasted the Latin West, which fell mostly into barbarian hands. Civilization was older and more deeply rooted in the East than it was in the West, a stabilizing factor when the Empire came under stress. The East had also been the population and economic center. Taking its language, culture, and philosophical inspiration (tempered by oriental influences and Christian beliefs) largely from Greeks, the East continued as the Byzantine Empire. Constantinople, the capital of the Later Roman Empire, now became the Byzantine capital.

Figure E.1
The walls of
Constantinople

For centuries, the Byzantines continued to maintain a remarkably high level of culture, while the West floundered in the hands of semibarbaric kings and nobles. When Constantinople finally did fall to the Turks in 1453 A.D., many of the scholars, teachers, and artists who had been instrumental in preserving and perpetuating the language and culture of the ancient Greeks took their knowledge westward. There, they helped sow the seeds for the Italian Renaissance and the final recovery of Medieval Europe.

The shadow cast by the people of Ancient Greece still looms large in today's society. We continue to call ourselves by names like Jason, Helen, and Philip. Many words in our vocabulary (including "history," "philosophy," "geometry," "mathematics," "physics," "economics," and "geography") have Greek origins, particularly in technical and scientific fields. The names of many trees, flowers, animals, insects, and even "dinosaurs" would be very different if there had been no Greek language. We have called the cars we drive "Apollo," "Phoenix," and "Omega." We have assigned names from Greek mythology to our space program and rockets. Many businesses bear names like "Atlas," the Greek titan who held up the world, as do our streets. One also can usually find an "Athens," a "Sparta," a "Syracuse," a "Troy," a "Homer," or an "Alexandria" on the maps of most states.

Figure E.2
A view of the Bosphorus, the winding strait that separates Europe (left) and Asia (right) and leads to the Black Sea, from the ancient location of Constantinople (formerly the Greek city of Byzantium). In the background is the Bosphorus bridge and the sprawl of today's Istanbul.

The spirit, at least, of our democratic system had its beginnings in ancient Athens. We frequently see buildings and houses in our cities modeled on Greek architecture. If someone asks if you are "in good humor," you might as well be in fifth-century B.C. Greece, for that is when the expression arose. The Olympic Games are our only world festival, and it is doubtful they (or organized competitive sport, for that matter) would exist without the Greek model. Christianity has been affected by earlier Greek religious and philosophical beliefs. Greek drama remains a viable part of our theatrical tradition.

So much around us has been inspired by the ancient Greeks—affecting our lives, our daily routines, and our traditions—sometimes it is hard not to imagine that the people we have discussed are still out there somewhere, silently smiling over our shoulders.

Appendix

People of Atlantis: Plato's Imagination—or Recycled Minoans?

Few stories have been as enduring and fascinating as that of the lost continent of Atlantis and its people. In the past few decades alone, the lure of Atlantis has evoked a number of books (added to the estimated thousands already produced), expeditions, and television specials, and, it would seem, interest has not waned since the myth was first introduced by the Greek philosopher Plato almost 2,400 years ago. The Atlantis story is better known to a far greater body of neophyte historians than more traditional topics, but the entire foundation of the story is dubious at best. It rests solely on material from two of Plato's dialogues, the *Timaeus* and *Critias*. If they had been lost, we would never have heard of Atlantis. Apparently, certain details from Plato's works became part of the public domain and were interpreted out of context—for the story had taken on a life of its own well before the modern era. Read all at once, the story of Atlantis is a mishmash of myth, philosophy, speculation, anachronism, melodrama, and fiction. Trying to cut through all the layers of the tale in search of some historical truth is almost impossible. However, if there ever was a historical germ for the story of Atlantis, the best candidate remains the Minoan island of Thera, about seventy miles to the north of Crete.

As seen in Chapter 1 (pages 4–5), the Minoans were an extremely sophisticated and advanced pre-Greek civilization centered on the island of Crete in the Eastern Mediterranean Sea. But the Minoans also had an extensive trading empire that took them all over the Mediterranean (and probably along the Atlantic seaboard, though such travel would have been restricted), and they established communities as on Thera, where an important

Figure A.1
Plato (Capitoline Museums [Montemartini], Rome)

Minoan site, Akroteri, is now being excavated. Beginning around 1650 B.C., a series of volcanic eruptions disturbed Thera, later culminating (c. 1628 B.C.) in a tremendous explosion that ripped it apart. The original configuration of the island remains a matter of debate, but what is left today are high, semicircular portions of what apparently had once been the island's outer rim—and a still-active volcano in the middle of the water below (previously the island's center?). There are a number of parallels between Plato's story of the lost continent of Atlantis and what happened at Thera, prompting various suggestions that the two may be one and the same. Before proceeding with this discussion, however, it is useful to introduce some material Plato relates about Atlantis.

Plato first tantalizes us about Atlantis in his *Timaeus* (24e ff.), where he introduces it as part of a broader philosophical discussion (supposedly taking place in Athens around 425 B.C.) between Socrates, Plato's own mentor, and a trio of guests. It is Critias (actually, a cousin of Plato's mother) who raises the subject, stating that his grandfather (almost ninety at the time) had told him the story of Atlantis when he was a boy. He had originally heard it from the sixth-century B.C. Athenian lawgiver and poet Solon, who was also one of the traditional "seven sages" of Greece. Solon supposedly had been told the tale while in Egypt on his fabled (and chronologically flawed) travels by a mysterious "very old priest" of a people who claimed an ancient relationship with Athens. The priest informed Solon that he and his fellow Greeks were like children in their grasp of actual antiquity compared with the Egyptians, revealing in the process (implausibly) that there had been *multiple* destructions and resurrections of humankind—written records of which had been preserved "from earliest times" in their temples. Such records revealed that 9,000 years previous, before the greatest of all destructions by water (apparently, prior even to the traditional Gilgamesh and biblical flood stories), Solon's own Athens had had a prior existence and was preeminent among all the cities of the world in government, achievements, and warfare. The astonished Solon (perhaps he was only an apprentice sage at this juncture) begged the old priest to go on—and in the course of his tale, the priest explains how Athens once protected the entire free world against the aggressions of the people of Atlantis:

> . . . Our records tell how your city checked a great power [Atlantis] which arrogantly advanced from its base in the Atlantic ocean to attack the cities of Europe and Asia. For in those days the Atlantic was navigable. There was an island opposite the strait which you call (so you say) the Pillars of Heracles, an island larger than Libya and Asia combined; from it travelers could in those days reach the other islands, and from them the whole opposite continent which surrounds what can truly be called the ocean. For the sea within the strait we were talking about is like a lake with a narrow entrance; the outer ocean is the real ocean and the land which entirely surrounds it is properly termed continent. On this island of Atlantis had arisen a powerful and remarkable dynasty of kings, who ruled the whole island, and many other islands as well and parts of the continent; in addition it controlled, within the strait, Libya up to the borders of Egypt and Europe as far as Tyrrhenia [Tuscany]. This dynasty, gathering its whole power together, attempted to enslave, at a single stroke, your country and ours and all the territory within the strait. It was then, Solon, that . . . your city [Athens] . . . overcame the invaders and celebrated a victory; she rescued those not yet enslaved from the slavery threatening them, and she generously freed all the others living within the Pillars of Heracles. At a later time there were earthquakes and floods of extraordinary violence, and in a single dreadful day and night all your fighting men were swallowed up by the earth, and the island of Atlantis was similarly swallowed up by the sea and vanished; this is why the sea in that area is to this day impassable to navigation, which is hindered by mud just below the surface, the remains of a sunken island.

Thus far, the story has all the trappings of a script for the next Indiana Jones movie: a lost island-continent about which no one, except for a few

Figure A.2
The steep, rugged remains of the interior rim of the volcanic island of Thera (modern Santorini), overlooking the caldera. Is it the origin of the Atlantis myth?

people (mostly from the same family), had ever heard existed in an antediluvian world 9,000 years before with an heretofore unknown alter-Athens. Its "history" was recorded only in a mysterious "written record" preserved in Egyptian temples and passed on to Solon by "a very old priest." Plato goes on to develop the Atlantis story further in the *Critias,* detailing the origins, resources, geography, degeneration, and other aspects of the island civilization before his narrative breaks off abruptly. Debate has raged as to why he never finished the dialogue—but the simplest explanation may be that offered by Plato himself in the *Timaeus* (21c), where he says that Solon, too, never finished his poem about Atlantis. Interestingly, Plato's "unfinished" narrative in the *Critias* ends with the degeneration of Atlantis, which is just where his earlier story about Atlantis' destruction begins in the *Timaeus*. Hence, the convenient dovetailing of the two parts of the story would seem to indicate that Plato purposefully stopped where he did for dramatic effect—a case of *in medias res*. Whatever the reason, Plato does manage to include a physical description of the capital city of Atlantis before ending:

> . . . the inhabitants proceeded to build temples, palaces, harbors and docks, and to organize the country as a whole in the following manner. Their first work was to bridge the rings of water round their mother's original home [their mother, as the story goes, was Cleito, who with the god Poseidon, produced the subsequent occupants of Atlantis, named after the eldest of their children, Atlas, first king of Atlantis. Poseidon had received the island initially as part of his share when the gods distributed the earth among themselves. Cleito was the daughter of one of the original "earthborn" inhabitants of the island, and once Poseidon had intercourse with her, he fortified the hill where she lived and enclosed it with two concentric rings of land and three of sea], so forming a road to and from their palace. This palace they proceeded to build at once in the place where the god and their ancestors had lived, and each successive king added to its beauties, doing his best to surpass his predecessors, until they had made a residence whose size and beauty were astonishing to see. They began by digging a canal three hundred feet wide, a hundred feet deep and fifty stades [a stade = 607 feet] long from the sea to the outermost ring, thus making it accessible from the sea like a harbor; and they made the entrance to it large enough to admit the largest ships. At the bridges they made channels through the rings of land which separated those of water, large enough to admit the passage of a single trireme, and roofed over to make an underground tunnel; for the rims of the rings were of some height above sea-level. The largest of the rings, to which there was access from the sea, was three stades in breadth and the ring of land within it the same. Of the second pair the ring of water was two stades in breadth, and the ring of land again equal to it, while the ring of water running immediately round the central island was a stade across. The diameter of the island on which the palace was situated was five stades. It and the rings and the bridges (which were a hundred feet broad) were enclosed by a stone wall all round, with towers and gates guarding the bridges on either side where they crossed the water. The stone for them, which was white, black and yellow, they cut out of the central island and the outer and inner rings of land, and in the process excavated pairs of hollow docks with roofs of rock. Some of their buildings were of a single color, in others they mixed different colored stone to divert the eye and afford them appropriate pleasure. And they covered the whole circuit of the outermost wall with a veneer of bronze,

they fused tin over the inner wall and orichaic gleaming like fire over the wall of the acropolis itself. [No one, including Plato, seems to know exactly what "orichaic" is. He says it was known only by name in his time but that it was plentiful at Atlantis and only gold was a more valuable metal. The name comes from a Greek word literally meaning "mountain copper," but whether it was a yellow ore, an alloy of copper, or brass, as suggestions have offered, it was treated by the ancients as a fabulous metal. In the Middle Ages, it was mentioned as very precious but known only by report. Apparently, nobody ever really knew what it was, and it became that elusive metal that everyone desired but that was to be found only in unspecified locations or lost worlds like Atlantis.]

The construction of the palace within the acropolis was as follows. In the center was a shrine sacred to Poseidon and Cleito, surrounded by a golden wall through which entry was forbidden, as it was the place where the family of the ten kings was conceived and begotten; and there year by year seasonal offerings were made from the ten provinces to each one of them [Poseidon, it is said, had originally divided the island up equally among his ten sons (five sets of twins) by Cleito; hence, the ten provinces]. There was a temple of Poseidon himself, a stade in length, three hundred feet wide and proportionate in height, though somewhat outlandish in appearance. The outside of it was covered all over with silver, except for the figures on the pediment which were covered with gold. Inside, the roof was ivory picked out with gold, silver and orichaic, and all the walls, pillars and floor were covered with orichaic. It contained gold statues of the god standing in a chariot drawn by

Figure A.3
Ruins of the Minoan settlement of Akroteri on Thera—a part of Plato's city of Atlantis?

six winged horses, so tall that his head touched the roof, and round him, riding on dolphins, a hundred Nereids (that being the accepted number of them at the time), as well as many other statues dedicated by private persons. Round the temple were statues of the original ten kings and their wives, and many others dedicated by kings and private persons belonging to the city and its dominions. There was an altar of a size and workmanship to match that of the building and a palace equally worthy of the greatness of the empire and the magnificence of its temples. The two springs, cold and hot, provided an unlimited supply of water for appropriate purposes, remarkable for its agreeable quality and excellence; and this they made available by surrounding it with suitable buildings and plantations, leading some of it into basins in the open air and some of it into covered hot baths for winter use. Here separate accommodation was provided for royalty and for commoners, and, again, for women, for horses and other beasts of burden, appropriately equipped in each case. The outflow they led into the grove of Poseidon, which (because of the goodness of the soil) was full of trees of marvelous beauty and height, and also channeled it to the outer ring-islands by aqueducts at the bridges. On each of these ring-islands they had built many temples for different gods, and many gardens and areas of exercise, some for men and some for horses. On the middle of the larger island in particular there was a special course for horse-racing; its width was a stade and its length that of a complete circuit of the island, which was reserved for it. Round it on both sides were barracks for the main body of the king's bodyguard. A more select body of the more trustworthy were stationed on the smaller island ring nearer the citadel, and the most trustworthy of all had quarters assigned to them in the citadel and were attached to the king's person.

Finally, there were dockyards full of triremes and their equipment, all in good shape.

So much then for the arrangement of the royal residence and its environs. Beyond the three outer harbors there was a wall, beginning at the sea and running right round in a circle, at a uniform distance of fifty stades from the largest ring and harbor and returning on itself at the mouth of the canal to the sea. This wall was densely built up all round with houses and the canal and large harbor were crowded with vast numbers of merchant ships from all quarters, from which rose a constant din of shouting and noise day and night. (*Criti.* 115c ff.)

The simplest explanation for Plato's entire narrative about Atlantis is that it is another fanciful creation of the philosopher's mind that, ultimately, squares very nicely with the "ordered" societies he presents in the *Republic* and *Laws*. Plato offers an imaginary "perfect" society that existed somewhere in the Atlantic, sometime in the remote, distant past. It degenerated from its divine nature to baseness and was punished by the gods with destruction in Sodom and Gomorrah fashion. Interestingly, it was a heroic Athens that checked the power of Atlantis-run-amuck—but, alas, it, too, was helplessly swept under by the same deluge that overcame the wretched citizens of Atlantis. This was not a result of any moral offense Athens had committed—just the opposite. Athens appears to have inherited all the perfection that Atlantis had lost before it perished—and it would be noble Athens, not Atlantis, that would in future be born again in a Platonic fashion of reincarnation. Plato, it seems, juxtaposed the two cities precisely to make a moral point. Also, Plato could not very well explain how a deluge that wiped Atlantis, an entire continent, off the face of the earth spared its fiercest opponent, Athens. And how could Solon (not to mention everyone else) be surprised to learn of the existence of a previous Athens if it had never perished in the first place?

There is also a problem of nomenclature in the Atlantis dialogues. Plato has Critias state (*Criti.* 113ab) that his listeners might be surprised to hear foreigners in his stories about Atlantis referred to by Greek names. The reason for this, he explains, is that when Solon learned the Egyptians had translated the original names into their own language, he simply reversed the process and retranslated them back into Greek. (Critias even states, presumably, that he still possessed Solon's original manuscript of these names!) Anyone who has actually tried to do what Critias suggests—to retranslate names, especially unfamiliar ones—would have to conclude that Solon's complete success in doing so was a neat trick in itself. Likewise, Solon would have had to have utilized the same process to identify location names. Atlantis, for example, was named after Poseidon's son, Atlas. Poseidon and Atlas were both names the Greeks used. What, then, was the lost continent called before Solon retranslated its name back to Atlantis? Athens, too, would have to have gone by an Egyptian name until resurrected by Solon's pen. Of course, Solon did mention (*Tim.* 21e) that, among the Egyptians, Athena was called Neïth. Perhaps, then, Athens had been known as "Neïtherland" (or some such name) for most of the previous 9,000 years. While all this may be a nice rhetorical exercise on Plato's part, its implausibility certainly places additional strain on the credibility of the entire Atlantis story.

The example of an Atlantis obliterated may have been an apt one for Plato's contemporary audience. Plato viewed the Greek city-state as an ideal institution. The people who populated the institution, however, could lead it astray. Ideally, in Plato's mind, classical Athens had been like Atlantis—an example of good government, cultural achievement, and, in its case, a "school of Hellas." Also, like Atlantis, Athens ruled over a large Mediterranean empire and had many triremes (Atlantis' "triremes" are, unfortunately, anachronistic); ultimately, it was the expansion of that empire and quarrels with Sparta that led to the destructive Peloponnesian War. Most of Plato's life was postwar, and the difficult problems that dogged the Athenians well into the fourth century were Plato's problems as well. The story of Atlantis could well have been an allegory in which Plato warns that noble Athens, which had once stood against Atlantis, had now *become* Atlantis— an ideal society fallen from grace. It was, perhaps, time to return to the ideals that had once made "both" the cities of Athens great.

If Plato did not intend his discussion of Atlantis to relate to the "degeneration" of Athens during his own time, then one question must be answered: Why was Athens included in the Atlantis story at all? If it were just an account of a lost continent, there was no need to mention Plato's hometown; the story would have read just as well without it. Instead, it is clear that Plato's main intent is to celebrate *Athens*—Atlantis is secondary. Critias states in the *Timaeus* (25e ff.) that he had only been reminded of the story of Atlantis by Socrates' own discussions on the ideal society the previous day. Proceeding, he offers up the Athens of the Atlantis myth as the ideal society for which Socrates is searching. It is this early, idealistic phase of Athens that is really the core around which the entire myth is built. At first, Critias does little to inspire our confidence, struggling to remember a story he had heard as a boy, admitting he had "rehearsed" details overnight before repeating them to his friends. But any doubts about his memory are quickly dispelled. Not only does he recount the tale with the expertise of a rhetorician as accomplished as Plato, but he also provides "off the top of his head" the precise lengths and dimensions of buildings, canals, rings, horse tracks, and just about everything else that can be measured (aping Plato's own obsession with precise measurements and circles). At one point in his comments, Critias muses about how difficult it is to find a suitable story on which to base what one wants to say. In the story of Atlantis, Plato apparently found his.

Whether ideas such as these were in Plato's mind when, late in life, he wrote about Atlantis, there could still be, as we mentioned earlier, a historical germ to the Atlantis story—the volcanic destruction of the Minoan island Thera. The Greeks were notoriously lacking when it came to time-reckoning, geography, and their early history (see Thucydides' comment, page 116). Consequently, locations, circumstances, and chronology often became confused, and details changed or became embellished (even fabricated). Stories could become so muddled over the centuries that it was impossible to ascertain the true circumstances of an event.

As an example of how something like the Atlantis myth could get started, let us use some details about the great city of Carthage in Africa. Similar to Atlantis, Carthage, traditionally founded in 814 B.C., ruled a western Mediterranean empire that stretched to the Atlantic, had a large war and merchant fleet—and used elephants, which Plato says were plentiful at Atlantis. In Roman times, at least, Carthage had a system of interconnecting harbors (with a channel to the sea, as at Atlantis), walls, and a circular military harbor with an islet in the center containing the fleet commander's pavilion (like the citadel on the innermost circle of land mentioned at Atlantis). Certainly, this "maze" of channels, connecting walls, and harbors—one of which was circular—is akin to the circles of water and land described as surrounding the capital at Atlantis. In the days of Greek colonization, it had been Carthage that had largely prevented Greeks in any number from populating the Western Mediterranean, and certainly, subsequent Greek tradition would not have been oblivious—or complimentary—to the once-threatening power. This is not to say that it is only memories of past association with Carthage that are responsible for Plato's Atlantis—there is no evidence, for example, that the harbor system just described at Carthage even existed in Plato's day, and Carthage was not destroyed until the second century B.C., long after the philosopher's death. It is simply an illustration about how, if Carthage had existed during a period without historical records, the various fragments from its actual history could have become distorted over the centuries and emerged in a later time as a story not unlike that of Atlantis—a great empire with many ships that had circular waterways around its principal city, ruled a large portion of the earth, used elephants, and was ultimately destroyed. A similar kind of distorted tradition about Thera may have produced the main ingredients for the Atlantis story.

We have already seen how Thera (today, the Greek island of Santorini, a popular tourist destination) was largely destroyed in a volcanic catastrophe. There are certainly some interesting parallels between what we know about Thera and the Atlantis saga. The latter highlights a conflict between Athens and Atlantis. The well-known Greek myth of Theseus and the Minotaur has as one of its motivating themes a previous war between Athens and Crete. Thera is not Crete—but the story is set in the same general locale, and both Crete and Thera were Minoan properties at one time. It may also be worth noting that the Theseus-and-Minotaur confrontation on Crete is set in a labyrinth, while the circles of land and water at Atlantis' capital form a maze (or labyrinth?) of sorts. Furthermore, Atlantis is described as mostly mountainous, and it would seem, much of old Thera (as today) rose straight up from the sea in precipitous cliffs.

The story goes on to say that Atlantis was submerged under a great deluge. Obviously, when Thera exploded, a deluge of sea water poured into and filled what had been blown away. Atlantis was said to have disappeared in a single day and night. The major destruction at Thera must have taken place in a similar time frame (as with Mt. Vesuvius' destruction—though a much lesser eruption—of Pompeii and Herculaneum in 79 A.D.). Violent

Figure A.4
Scenes of Minoan urban, country, and seafaring activities from a fresco at Akroteri on Thera. Did memories of such help to spawn the Atlantis saga?

earth tremors from the eruption certainly must have spawned tidal waves. (Residents of Hawaii, for example, like to point out to visitors today that waves generated by underwater tremors are constantly striking the islands, most of them, fortunately, unnoticeable since they have lost their impact after traveling hundreds of miles. Some tsunami, however, have not been so gentle—one wiping out a major portion of downtown Hilo in 1960.) Considering the many small islands in the vicinity of Thera, as well as the close-by shoreline of Greece, and (more so) Crete, and Asia Minor, it is likely that some areas were washed over, with large loss of life—an episode that folk memory would certainly not forget. Also, the debris—and land shifting that likely took place as a result of the volcanic activities—could have choked formerly usable harbors, created "sandbars" in previously navigable sea, and generated the stories about an entire former continent resting just beneath the sea. Certainly, building material and other trappings of daily life would also have been found embedded in the mud for years to come, further generating ideas about a lost world under the waves. Superstitious sailors who had witnessed such may have subsequently hit sandbars while sailing elsewhere in the Mediterranean (even great distances away) and concluded this was all part of the same huge submerged lost continent—"Atlantis." Today, the remains of Thera form a circle of sorts, still difficult for modern cruise ships to navigate. The channels are carefully marked to keep ships from running aground. The outline in Figure A.5, based on a map that appears from its details to be late sixteenth century, shows that the configuration of Thera

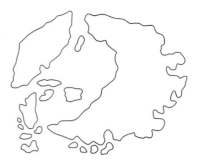

Figure A.5
An outline of Thera (modern Santorini) from an old map reprinted in C. G. Doumas, Santorini, *Editions "Hannibal," Athens (no date). If accurate, Thera's configuration has changed considerably over the centuries.*

differed from what it is today—and was even more hazardous for ships to navigate. What was left of Thera after the eruption 3,600 years ago may very well have appeared to sailors trying to navigate between the pieces as a series of circles, which could have begun the story of the Atlantis circles.

Atlantis is described as controlling a vast empire from somewhere in the Atlantic, outside the Pillars of Heracles. As mentioned earlier, the Minoans had an extensive Mediterranean trading empire (Thera was part of that empire) that may even have reached to the Atlantic seaboard. Location has been a major stumbling block for those who wish to identify Thera with Atlantis—the two are at the opposite ends of the Mediterranean—and even guides on Thera today reluctantly concede that its Atlantic locale makes it unlikely Thera is the actual Atlantis. However, this really is not the stumbling block it may first appear to be. Anyone who has studied folktale, myth, and saga knows that locations in stories such as the one about Atlantis can easily become confused over time. Even ancient sailors tossed about by storms in waters with which they were familiar sometimes could not tell precisely where they were until they saw something familiar—and that could take days or even weeks. They might even be washed up on shores they knew nothing about—a situation demonstrated in literature, at least, in the *Odyssey* and the *Aeneid.* When they returned to their homes, they must have carried with them stories about their experiences beyond the "edge of the known world"—even, perhaps, stories about the great ocean itself, to the west. We can offer speculation on how the story of Atlantis might have arisen, been spread, and become vulgate.

Let us suggest that a story began circulating in the prehistoric Mediterranean world about the destruction of Thera, which was subsequently expanded to include the collapse of the entire Minoan society—which had been a very advanced society—in the following centuries. As the generations passed, the actual location (Egyptian tradition may have already established a "western" setting for the story since Thera was, indeed, west of the

Figure A.6
A Minoan woman in a fresco from Akroteri. A citizen of Thera— or a "lost" resident of Atlantis?

Nile) and circumstances of the eruption and the Minoans, who were assimilated into Bronze Age Greek society, were forgotten—"because" as we are reminded in the *Timaeus* (21d) "of the lapse of time and the death of those who took part in it the story has not lasted till our day." However, a story about a mysterious land that had been populated by a remarkable people and had sunk beneath the sea persisted—and continued to grow on its own. Add to this mix stories resulting from the Greek tin trade in the Western Mediterranean—Spain, for example, and Britain, too, through indirect or perhaps even direct intercourse. Stories about the latter, in particular, a distant, little-known island nation in the Atlantic, rich in tin (interestingly, Atlantis' inner walls were covered with tin) could very well have been the beginning of the setting for Atlantis in the Atlantic, which, of course, was "to the west." Then came the collapse of Bronze Age Greece c. 1100 B.C., and passing through the illiterate jumble of the Dark Age that followed, the resultant tale about Atlantis could have emerged into the rejuvenated Greek world (c. 750 B.C.) as a combination of all the elements described above—a lost civilization (such as the Minoans) that had ruled a large empire from an island continent (such as Britain) in the Atlantic that produced a special wondrous metal, orichaic (a confused memory of tin), and was destroyed (as was Thera) and sank beneath the sea. Memories of the end of the Mycenaean world probably would have made the emphasis on destruction and utter ruin all the more intense.

In the subsequent period of colonization, many Greeks migrated westward, mingling with the powerful Carthaginians, memories of whom may also have contributed to the Atlantis story. So, too, the new westward emphasis made the Atlantic Ocean more relevant—but it was still largely imposing and unknown. Plato's own comment that the seas in the area of Atlantis, once navigable, were no longer so may indicate that he, at least, knew of no Greek who had successfully entered the Atlantic; however, his observation may be meaningless. He had little or no geographical knowledge about the area and was vulnerable to any unsubstantiated rumor that came his way, and if Greeks were restricted from sailing into the Atlantic, it would have been more a matter of Carthaginian obstruction than navigable waterways. Even then nothing stopped Pytheas of Massalia (modern Marseilles in France) from sailing into the Atlantic and apparently circumnavigating Britain only a few decades after Plato's death. Conversely, the Mediterranean was now mostly a known entity—Atlantis, it may have been concluded, could never have existed in the Mediterranean because somebody would have known at least something about it. Therefore, Atlantis, like all fantasy lands and utopias (nowhere lands), had to have existed in an appropriate far-off, little-known setting (not unlike the wild stories about lost civilizations, dinosaurs, and Tarzan that used to come out of Africa before it was fully explored). That setting, in the west, one with enough water to overflow an entire continent, must have been somewhere in the Atlantic. Residual parts of the old Atlantis tale that placed it in the Mediterranean were now, perhaps, transformed into portions of the island continent's African and European empire. The addition of Athens to the story had to have been a late one, and probably Plato's own creation. Athens was not a major player in the Greek world until relatively late. An Athenocentric core to the Atlantis story certainly would have enhanced Athens' status in the Greek world (giving it, literally, unheard-of longevity and prestige) and suited Plato's own moral purposes very nicely.

This example, then, is a way—founded on constructs not atypical of myths—in which various elements may have arisen and come together to form the Atlantis story. How important the story was before Plato detailed it cannot be gauged. It may not even have existed—or it may have been a minor tradition. But Plato attempts to raise it to the status of Homer's and Hesiod's epics, saying that it would have been even more celebrated had Solon completed the full story. The whole matter is probably best summed up for us in an implied observation by Aristotle (Strabo 2.102; 13.598), Plato's own pupil, that the man (Plato) who *made up* Atlantis also made it *disappear.* We shall have to keep Atlantis and its people in the realm of our imaginations for now—at least until underwater archaeologists stumble over a sign reading "Atlantis City Limits."

Glossary and Pronunciation Guide

Included here are brief descriptions of major historical figures, sites, and other terms mentioned in the text. The pronunciation is indicated for most entries, though it should be noted that consistency is not always possible and pronunciation will inevitably vary among instructors.

Achaeans (a-kē´ans), name applied by Homer to the Bronze Age inhabitants of Greece (i.e., Achaean civilization); frequently synonymous with Mycenaeans

Achilles (a-kil´-ēz), hero of Homer's *Iliad* and greatest of the Greek warriors at Troy

Acropolis (a-krop´-ō-lis), the "high place" in a Greek city; a fortified plateau, as in Athens, on which the Parthenon and other buildings, mostly religious in nature, were set

Aegean (ē-jē´-an), body of water east of the Greek peninsula that was a center of Greek life and activity and whose islands were home to many Hellenes

Aeschylus (es´-ki-lus), 525–456 B.C., first of Athens' great tragedians, who wrote the *Agamemnon* and *Persians* among other plays; along with Sophocles and Euripides, one of the three greatest Greek tragedians

Agamemnon (ag-a-mem´-non), king of Mycenae who, in the *Iliad,* was commander-in-chief of the Greeks at Troy

agora (ag´-ō-ra), the bustling central area of a Greek polis; typically included the marketplace and civic buildings and was the site where important public and private business transpired

Alcaeus (al-sē´-us), c. 600 B.C., early lyric poet from Mytilene on Lesbos who supported the ideals of the aristocracy

Alexander, 356–323 B.C., Macedonian king who conquered the Persian Empire and set the stage for the Hellenistic world

Alexandria, city in Egypt founded by Alexander in 332 B.C.; became the capital of the Ptolemies and the cultural and intellectual center of the Hellenistic world

Anaxagoras (an-ak-sag´-ō-ras), c. 500–428 B.C., first philosopher-scientist to come to Athens, and a friend of Pericles

Antigonus (an-tig´-ō-nus), 382–301 B.C., general and successor of Alexander; father of Demetrius Poliorcetes; patriarch of the Antigonid house that would establish itself in Macedonia

Antiphon (an´-ti-fon), c. 480–411 B.C., Athenian orator whose speeches for defendants and prosecutors provide interesting insights into Athens' legal system

Apollo (a-pol´-ō), god of prophecy, rationality, and music; had major centers of worship at Delphi and on Delos

Archaic period, 750–500 B.C., the "formative" period of the historical Greeks following the Dark Age; characterized by social upheaval, political experimentation, colonization, and lyric poetry

Archilochus (ar-kil´-ō-kus), active 680–640 B.C., individualistic warrior-poet from Paros whose poems were among the earliest reflections of the changing world of the Greek aristocracy

Arion, active 628–625 B.C., greatest singer and musician of his day; patronized by Periander, tyrant of Corinth

Aristarchus (ar-is-tar′-kus), c. 310–230 B.C., Hellenistic astronomer from Samos who proposed a heliocentric solar system

aristocracy, a small, dominant ruling group whose position in society is determined solely by birth

Aristogiton (ar-is-tō-jī′-ton), he and his lover Harmodius assassinated Hipparchus in Athens in 514 B.C. and were later mistakenly celebrated as "tyrannicides"

Aristophanes (ar-is-tof′-a-nēz), c. 450–385 B.C., greatest of the Greek comic playwrights, who reveals much about Athens and Athenians in plays such as *Clouds, Lysistrata,* and *Wasps*

Aristotle (ar′-is-tot-l), 384–322 B.C., one of the greatest Greek thinkers and scientists; reputedly tutor to Alexander

Artemisia (ar-tē-miz′-i-a), queen of Caria and admiral of Xerxes; fought at Salamis in 480 B.C.

Artemisium (ar-tē-mizh′-i-um), cape off the northeastern tip of Euboea where the Greek navy engaged the Persians in 480 B.C.

Aspasia (as-pā′-shi-a), courtesan, intellectual, and mistress or "wife" of Pericles, on whom she exerted great influence

Athena (a-thē′-na), patron goddess of Athens

Atlantis, name of the lost island continent mentioned by Plato in the *Critias* and *Timaeus;* the original tradition of the story may have begun with the eruption of the Minoan island of Thera, modern Santorini, c. 1628 B.C.

Attica (at′-i-ka), district of east-central Greece in which Athens is located

Boeotia (bē-ō′-sha), primarily agricultural district of central Greece north of Attica; home of Hesiod and Pindar; location of Thebes

Callicrates (ka-lik′-ra-tēz), with Ictinus, architect of the Parthenon in Periclean Athens

Cimon (sī′-mon), c. 512–450 B.C., son of Miltiades and leading conservative politician in Athens in the 460s B.C. who crushed the Persians at the Eurymedon River and was patron to Polygnotus

Cleisthenes (klīs′-the-nēz), established democracy in Athens in 508 B.C.

Cleon (klē′-on), d. 422 B.C., first nonaristocratic political leader in Athens; frequently parodied in Aristophanes' plays

Cnidus (nī′-dus), Greek city on the southern coast of Asia Minor that was a member of the Delian League and dedicated the Cnidian Lesche at Delphi

colony, an independent extension of a mother-city founded abroad, usually to relieve social pressures at home

Corinth (kor′-inth), major Greek commercial center and rival of Athens; located at the isthmus of Corinth

Crete (krēt), a large Mediterranean island southeast of the Greek peninsula that was home to the Minoans

Croesus (krē′-sus), d. 546 B.C., last king of Lydia in Asia Minor, who was defeated and killed by Cyrus the Persian

Croton (krō′-t′n), Greek city in southern Italy that produced many famous athletes including Phayllus and Milo

Darius (da-rī′-us), Great King of Persia, 521–486 B.C.; **Darius III,** 336–330 B.C.

Dark Age, period of difficulty c. 1100–750 B.C. in Greece that followed the collapse of Achaean society

Delian League, confederacy of Greek states formed in 478 B.C. to fight the Persians; became the foundation of Athens' Aegean Empire

Delos (dē′-los), island in the Cyclades that was sacred to Apollo and was headquarters of the Delian League

Delphi (del´-fī), sacred shrine and site of the oracle of Apollo located on Mt. Parnassus above the Gulf of Corinth

Demetrius, 336–283 B.C., son of Antigonus, besieger of Rhodes in 305 B.C., and king of Macedonia, 294–288 B.C.

Demosthenes (dē-mos´-the-nēz), 384–322 B.C., greatest Athenian orator, whose speeches reveal much about Athens and its legal system and who led the opposition to Philip of Macedonia's intervention in Greece

Draco (drā´-kō), magistrate (archon) who traditionally gave Athens its first law code in 621 B.C.

Elis (ē´-lis), district in Greece on the western side of the Peloponnesus where Olympia is located

Ephialtes (ef-i-al´-tēz), Greek who betrayed the pass at Thermopylae in 480 B.C.

Erasistratus (er-a-sis´-tra-tus), Hellenistic physician whose studies in human physiology were revolutionary

Erechtheum (er-ek-thē´-um), temple on the Acropolis in Athens begun in 421 B.C.

Eupalinus (ū-pal´-i-nus), engineer who built the tunnel of Eupalinus on Samos during the tyranny of Polycrates

Euripides (ū-rip´-i-dēz), 485–406 B.C., Athenian tragic playwright who, along with Aeschylus and Sophocles, was one of the three greatest Greek tragedians

Eurymedon (ū-rim´-e-don), river in south-central Asia Minor where Cimon crushed the Persians in 469 B.C.

Halicarnassus (hal-i-kar-nas´-us), important Greek city on the southern coast of Asia Minor where Herodotus was born; capital of Queen Artemisia; member of the Delian League; and home to King Mausolus, builder of the "Mausoleum," one of the Seven Wonders of the Ancient World

Harmodius (har-mō´-di-us), Athenian "tyrannicide" who, along with his lover Aristogiton, assassinated Hipparchus in 514 B.C.

helot (hel´-ot), one of the servile population of Sparta whose labors supported the warrior class

Hera (hē´-ra), wife of Zeus; goddess of childbirth and marriage

Hero, active c. 62 A.D., mathematician and inventor who lived in Alexandria and devised a working model of a steam engine

Herodotus (hē-rod´-ō-tus), born c. 484 B.C., "Father of History" and the major historian of the Persian Wars

Herophilus (her-ō´-fi-lus), Hellenistic physician whose studies in human anatomy were revolutionary

Hesiod (hē´-si-od), epic poet who lived in Boeotia c. 700 B.C. and wrote the *Theogony* and *Works and Days*

Hipparchus (hi-par´-kus), brother of the Athenian tyrant Hippias; assassinated by Harmodius and Aristogiton in 514 B.C.

Hippias (hip´-i-as), Pisistratid tyrant of Athens, 527–514 B.C.; brother of Hipparchus

Hippocrates (hi-pok´-ra-tēz), 469–399 B.C., Greek physician whose school sought human rather than divine explanations for illness and supported the theory of the "four humors"

Homer, thought to have imposed artistic unity on the *Iliad* and *Odyssey,* probably in the eighth century B.C.

hoplite (hop´-līt), heavily armed Greek infantryman who fought in a formation called the phalanx

Ictinus (ik-tī´-nus), with Callicrates, the architect of the Parthenon in Periclean Athens

Iliad (il´-i-ad), Homer's epic poem about the "Wrath of Achilles" during the Trojan War

Ionia (ī-ō´-ni-a), area along the central coastline of Asia Minor inhabited by Greeks who spoke the Ionic dialect and where the cultural rejuvenation of Hellas began after the Dark Age; traditional birthplace of Homer, history, and philosophy

Isthmian Games, one of the four "circuit" games of Greece; held at Isthmia near Corinth every two years and sacred to Poseidon

Lacedaemonians (las-ē-dē-mō´-ni-an), generally, Spartans

Laconia (la-kō´-ni-a), district in the southern Peloponnesus where Sparta is located

Leonidas (lē-on´-i-das), Spartan king who died defending the pass at Thermopylae in 480 B.C.

Lesbos (lez´-bos), Greek island off the northern coast of Asia Minor; home of the poets Sappho and Alcaeus

Lesche (les-kā´), "clubhouse" at Delphi built by the Cnidians; housed Polygnotus' greatest paintings

Leuctra (lūk´-tra), site in Boeotia where Spartan military power was eclipsed when defeated by Thebes in 371 B.C.

Lucian (loo´-shen), born c. 120 A.D., Greek satirist living during the Roman Empire who described an early trip to the moon

Lycurgus (li-kur´-gus), traditional lawgiver of the Spartans

Lysias (lis´-i-as), c. 459–380 B.C., major Greek orator whose speeches give many insights into the Athenian legal system

Macedonia (mas-e-dō´-nī-a), kingdom to the north of Greece that first became a major political power under Philip and then Alexander

Marathon, site in Attica 26 miles northeast of Athens where the Athenians defeated the Persians in 490 B.C.; Phidippides (fī-dip´-pi-dēz) traditionally began his run to Athens from here

Miletus (mī-lē´-tus), important Greek city in southern Ionia on the coast of Asia Minor; home of Thales, father of Greek philosophy

Miltiades (mil-tī´-a-dēz), c. 550–489 B.C., father of Cimon and general most responsible for Athenian victory at Marathon in 490 B.C.

Minoans, non-Greek inhabitants of Crete whose civilization had reached an advanced state by about 2000 B.C.

Mycale (mik´-a-lē), site in southern Asia Minor where the Greeks defeated the Persians in 479 B.C. to end the Second Persian War

Mycenae (mī-sē´ne), foremost of the Achaean citadels and traditional home of Agamemnon; located in the northeastern Peloponnesus

Mytilene (mit´l-ē´-nē), chief city on Lesbos

Nemean (nē-mē´-an) **Games**, one of the four "circuit" games of Greece held every two years at Nemea in the northeastern Peloponnesus and sacred to Zeus

Odyssey (od´-i-si), Homer's epic poem about the "Return of Odysseus" following the Trojan War

Olympia (ō-lim´-pi-a), chief center of worship for Zeus; located in Elis in the western Peloponnesus and where the Olympic Games were held

Olympic Games, most important of the four "circuit" games in Greece; held at Olympia every four years and sacred to Zeus

ostracism, constitutional process in Athens instituted c. 487 B.C. by which politicians considered dangerous to the state could be exiled for ten years

Panathenaean Games, most prestigious of local Greek games held in Athens in conjunction with the Panathenaea, a yearly celebration of Athena's birthday

pankration (pan-krā´-shi-un), grueling athletic event that was a combination of boxing, wrestling, judo, and brawling

Paros (par´-os), Greek Aegean island in the Cyclades group; home of Archilochus; and member of the Delian League

Parthenon (par´-the-non), Athena's temple on the Acropolis in Athens built between 447 and 438 B.C. during Pericles' administration

Pasion Former slave who rose to wealth and citizenship in fourth-century B.C. Athens

Pausanias (po-sā´-ni-as), (1) Greek traveler and geographer who recorded his observations in his *Description of Greece* in the second century A.D.; (2) assassin of Philip of Macedonia

Peloponnesian War, great destructive war between Athens and Sparta that lasted from 431 to 404 B.C. and ended with Athens' defeat

Peloponnesus (pel-ō-po-nē´-sus), the "island of Pelops"; southernmost part of the Greek peninsula where Mycenae, Corinth, Argos, and Sparta are located

pentathlon (pen-tath´-lon), the "five events," which included the 200 meters, long jumping, throwing the javelin and discus, and wrestling

Pericles (per´-i-klēz), c. 495–429 B.C., architect of Athens' "Golden Age" during the mid–fifth century B.C.

phalanx (fā´-langks), the formation in which hoplites fought

Phayllus (fī-lus), legendary athlete from Croton who tradition says jumped 55 feet in the long jump sometime in the early fifth century B.C.

Phidias (fid´-i-as), greatest of the monumental classical sculptors, who supervised the decoration of the Parthenon; constructed the cult statue of Athena inside; and fashioned the golden statue of Zeus, one of the Seven Wonders of the Ancient World, at Olympia

Philip, king of Macedonia, 359–336 B.C.; conqueror of Greece; father of Alexander the Great

Pindar (pin´-dar), c. 518–438 B.C., prominent Greek poet known especially for his poems celebrating victorious athletes

Piraeus (pī-rē´-us), the seaport of Athens

Pisistratus (pi-sis´-tra-tus), Athens' first tyrant, 561–527 B.C., father of Hippias and Hipparchus

Plataea (pla-tē´-a), Boeotian city near the northern border of Attica where the Greeks defeated the Persians in 479 B.C.

Plato (plā´-tō), c. 429–347 B.C., one of the greatest Greek philosophers and political theorists; founder of the Academy; author of the *Republic,* the *Laws,* the *Apology,* and other influential works, including the *Critias* and *Timaeus,* which preserve the tradition about Atlantis

Plutarch (plōō´-tark) Greek biographer who lived in the Roman Empire during the first–second century A.D. and wrote parallel *Lives* of famous Greeks and Romans

polis (pō´-lis), a Greek city-state

Polycrates (pō-lik´-ra-tēz), tyrant of Samos during the second half of the sixth century B.C.

Polygnotus (pol-ig-nō´-tus), greatest of the Greek muralists; painted the *Iliupersis* and *Nekyia* at Delphi and was artistic advisor to Cimon

Propylaea (prop-i-lē´-a), the gateway to the Acropolis in Athens

Protagoras (prō-tag´-ō-ras), best known of the sophists who came to Athens and taught during the mid–fifth century B.C.

Ptolemy (tol´-e-mi), general of Alexander, Successor, and founder of the Ptolemaic dynasty in Egypt

Ptolemy V (210–180 B.C.), minor king of Egypt, whose reign produced the Rosetta Stone

Pythian (pith´i-an) **Games,** one of the four "circuit" games in Greece held every four years at Delphi in honor of Apollo

Rosetta Stone, priestly decree (196 B.C.) from the reign of Ptolemy V that was found at Rosetta in Egypt in 1799 and whose text provided Champollion with the key to deciphering Egyptian hieroglyphs

Salamis (sal´a-mis), island off the Attic coast where the Greek fleet destroyed the Persian navy in 480 B.C.

Samos (sā´-mos), Ionian island off the coast of Asia Minor that became a naval power and cultural center under Polycrates in the sixth century B.C. and remained an important player in Greek affairs throughout the Classical period

Sappho (saf´-ō), famous poetess who lived on Lesbos c. 600 B.C.

Seleucus (sē-lū´-kus), general of Alexander, successor, and founder of the Seleucid dynasty in Syria, Mesopotamia, and Iran

Semonides (se-mon´-i-dēz), mid–seventh century B.C., lyric poet of Amorgos, whose poems on women and other topics reflect a satiric, moralizing tone

Socrates (sok´-ra-tēz), 469–399 B.C., father of Western ethical philosophy

Solon (sō-lon), archon and poet who reformed Athens politically, socially, and economically in 594 B.C.

sophists (sof'-ists), teachers who provided the first opportunity for higher education in Athens, emphasizing rhetorical skills and the fallibility of the senses

Sophocles (sof'-ō-klēz), 496–406 B.C., Athenian tragic playwright who, with Aeschylus and Euripides, was one of the three greatest Greek tragedians

Sparta, the foremost military power in Greece, located in the southern Peloponnesus

stoa (stō'-a), a long, colonnaded Greek building with shops and offices usually fronting the agora

Thales (thā'-lēz), active c. 585 B.C., father of Western philosophy; from Miletus

Thasos, island in the northern Aegean just south of Thrace

Themistocles (thē-mis'-tō-klēz), c. 528–462 B.C., prominent Athenian politician who helped save the Greeks during the Second Persian War

Theophrastus (thē-ō-fras'-tus), succeeded Aristotle as head of the Peripatetic School and was author of the *Characters*

Thermopylae (ther-mop'-i-lē), pass in northern Greece that was dramatically defended against the Persian invasion in 480 B.C.

Thucydides (thū-sid'-i-dēz), c. 460–400 B.C., the historian of the Peloponnesian War

Thurii (thoo'-ri-i), colony founded in Italy in 443 B.C.

trireme (trī'-rēm), major form of Greek warship during the Classical period

Troy, site in the northwest corner of modern Turkey where the Trojan War occurred

Tyre (tīr), Phoenician city attacked and taken by Alexander in 332 B.C. after a lengthy siege

Xenophon (zen'-ō-fon), historian, essayist, disciple of Socrates (dialogues), and soldier

Xerxes (zurk'-sēz), great king of Persia, 485–465 B.C.

Zeus (zūs), Greek sky god who presided over the other gods on Olympus

Acknowledgments

Chapter 1

Translations in this chapter are by R. Lattimore: Archilochus and Tyrtaeus, in *Greek Lyrics,* University of Chicago Press (Chicago, 2nd ed., 1960), © 1960 by Richmond Lattimore. Reprinted by permission. H. D. Rankin: Archilochus, in *Archilochus of Paros,* Noyes Press (Park Ridge, N.J., 1977). A. P. Burnett: *Mnesiepes Inscription* E[1] II 22–54, in *The Archaic Poets: Archilochus, Alcaeus, and Sappho,* Harvard University Press. Copyright © 1983 by Anne Pippin Burnett. Reprinted with permission by Gerald Duckworth & Company, Ltd. G. Davenport: Archilochus, in *Archilochus, Sappho, Alkman: Three Lyric Poets of the Late Greek Bronze Age,* University of California Press (Berkeley and Los Angeles, 1980), © 1980 The Regents of the University of California. Richmond Lattimore: Lines 433–436 from Aeschylus, *Agamemnon,* in *Complete Greek Tragedies,* ed. Grene & Lattimore. Copyright 1953, 1951 by the University of Chicago Press. Reprinted by permission. D. Parker: Aristophanes, *The Wasps,* 1117–1119, from *Three Comedies: The Birds, The Clouds, The Wasps* (Ann Arbor: The University of Michigan Press, 1969). Reprinted by permission. Homer: *The Iliad,* 21.110–113, by Richmond Lattimore. Copyright 1951 by the University of Chicago Press. Reprinted by permission. Reprinted by permission of the publishers and the Loeb Classical Library from Hesiod, *Homeric Hymns, Epic Cycle, Homerica* (*Battle of Frogs and Mice* 11, 5–6, 8, 124–131, 161–167, 199–250, 259–270, 302–303), by Hugh G. Evelyn-White, Cambridge, Mass.: Harvard University Press, 1914. The Loeb Classical Library® is a registered trademark of the President and Fellows of Harvard College. Reprinted by permission of the publishers and the Loeb Classical Library from Plutarch, *Moralia,* Vol. 3 (*Moralia,* 208c, 210e, 212f, 240e, 241f,

242c), by Frank C. Babbitt, Cambridge, Mass.: Harvard University Press, 1928. The Loeb Classical Library® is a registered trademark of the President and Fellows of Harvard College. Reprinted by permission of the publishers and the Loeb Classical Library from Diogenes Laertius, *Lives of Eminent Philosophers,* Vol. 2, 6.38–40, by R. D. Hicks, Cambridge, Mass.: Harvard University Press, 1925. The Loeb Classical Library® is a registered trademark of the President and Fellows of Harvard College. J. S. Watson: Quintilian, *Institutes of Oratory,* Vol. 2, Bell and Daldy (London, 1871). J. M. Edmonds: Archilochus, in *Elegy and Iambus,* Vo. 2, Loeb Classical Library and William Heinemann, Ltd. (London, 1931).

Chapter 2

Translations in this chapter are from A. N. Athanassakis: Hesiod, *Theogony,* 26–34, 81–96, *Works and Days,* 174–176, and *Shield,* The Johns Hopkins University Press (Baltimore, 1983). Theognis of Megara in *Greek Lyrics,* by Richmond Lattimore. Copyright © 1960 by the University of Chicago Press. Reprinted by permission. R. Lattimore: Theognis and Alcaeus, in *Greek Lyrics,* University of Chicago Press (Chicago, 1960), © 1960 by Richmond Lattimore. All rights reserved. Mary R. Lefkowitz and Maureen B. Fant, eds.: Thucydides 6.59, No. 22, in *Women's Life in Greece and Rome: A Source Book in Translation,* © 1982 Johns Hopkins University Press. Reprinted by permission of Johns Hopkins University Press and Gerald Duckworth & Co., Ltd. B. Jowett: Aristotle, *Politics,* 1.1259a, The Modern Library (New York, 1943). Reprinted by permission of the publishers and the Loeb Classical Library from Diogenes Laertius, *Lives of Eminent Philosophers,* Vol. 1, 1.22–27, by R. D. Hicks, Cambridge, Mass.: Harvard University Press, 1925. The Loeb Classical Library® is a registered trademark of the President and Fellows of Harvard College. C. W. Fornara: Athenaeus, in *Archaic Times to the End of the Peloponnesian War,* 540d–f, No. 32, Cambridge University Press (New York, 2nd ed.: 1983). Copyright © 1983. Reprinted with the permission of Cambridge University Press. Herodotus, *The History,* 1.24, 3.60, by D. Grene. Copyright © 1987 University of Chicago Press. Reprinted by permission.

Chapter 3

Translations in this chapter are from Herodotus: *The History,* 1.53–56, by D. Grene. Copyright © 1987 University of Chicago Press. Reprinted by permission. F. J. Nisetich: Pindar, *Victory Songs,* Olympian Ode 13.24–31, The Johns Hopkins University Press (Baltimore, 1980). Copyright © 1980. D. C. Young: Pindar, "Pythian Ode," 8.83–87, in *The Olympic Myth of Greek Amateur Athletics.* Copyright © 1985 Ares Publishers, Inc. Used courtesy of Ares Publishers. S. G. Miller: Euripides, *Autolycus,* Frag. 282 (95–96); *Palatine Anthology,* 11.82 (65); Pausanias 5.6.7–8 (56), 5.16.2–8 (57), 6.14.5–8, 6.11.2–9 (60–61); and Suetonius, *Nero,* 2.3 (82), in *Arete,* Ares Publishers, Inc. (Chicago, 1979). Used courtesy of Ares Publishers. J. Swaddling: Epictetus, *Dissertations,* 1.6.23–29, from *Ancient Olympic Games,* Copyright © 1980. By permission of the University of Texas Press. W. E. Sweet: *IAG* 63 and Syll³ 802 in *Sport and Recreation in Ancient Greece: A Sourcebook with Translations,* Oxford University Press (New York, 1987), © 1987 by Oxford University Press. All rights reserved.

Chapter 4

Translations in this chapter are from Lysias, *Oration* 3, from *The Murder of Herodes and Other Trials from the Athenian Law Courts,* by Kathleen Freeman, reprinted by permission of Hackett Publishing Co., Inc. Copyright © 1963 by W. W. Norton & Company, Inc., copyright renewed © 1991 by Liliane Clopet, reprinted 1994 by Hackett Publishing Co., Inc. All rights reserved. R. Lattimore: Anacreon and Semonides, in *Greek Lyrics,* by Richmond Lattimore. Copyright © 1960 by the University of Chicago Press. Reprinted by permission. Reprinted by permission of the publishers and the Loeb Classical Library from *Greek Lyrics,* Vol. 1, Sappho, by David A. Campbell, Cambridge, Mass.: Harvard University Press, 1988. The Loeb Classical Library® is a registered trademark of the President and

Fellows of Harvard College. R. Jenkyns: Sappho, in *Three Classical Poets: Sappho, Catullus, and Juvenal.* Copyright © 1982 by The President and Fellows of Harvard College. Reprinted by permission of Harvard University Press. Mary R. Lefkowitz and Maureen B. Fant, eds.: Sappho, in *Women's Life in Greece & Rome,* Nos. 1–5, The Johns Hopkins University Press. Copyright © 1992. Reprinted by permission of Johns Hopkins University and Gerald Duckworth & Co., Ltd. J. H. Finley (Crawley translation): Thucydides, 6.57, *The Peloponnesia War,* The Modern Library (New York, 1951). C. W. Fornara, Athenaeus, in *Archaic Times to the End of the Peloponnesian War,* No. 659ab, No. 39A, Cambridge University Press (New York, 2nd ed., 1983). Copyright © 1983. Reprinted with the permission of Cambridge University Press.

Chapter 5

Translations in this chapter are from Herodotus: *The History,* 3.38, 8.87–88, by D. Grene. Copyright © 1987 University of Chicago Press. Reprinted by permission. S. G. Benardete, trans.: Aeschylus, *The Persians,* in *The Complete Greek Tragedies, Aeschylus II,* lines 408–428, Grene & Lattimore, eds. Copyright © 1956 by the University of Chicago Press. Reprinted by permission. J. J. Pollitt: Pliny, *Natural History,* 35.57–58; and Plutarch, *Cimon* 4.6, in *The Art of Ancient Greece: Sources and Documents* (Prentice-Hall, Inc., Englewood Cliffs, N. J. 1965). Reprinted by permission of Jerome J. Pollitt and the publisher. P. Levi: Pausanias, Description of Greece, 1.15.2–4, 10.25–27, in *Guide to Greece,* Vol. 1, by Peter Levi (Penguin Classics, 1971). Copyright © Peter Levi, 1971. Pliny the Elder: *Natural History,* 35.40, in M. R. Lefkowitz's and M. B. Fant's *Women's Life in Greece & Rome,* No. 181, The Johns Hopkins University Press, copyright © 1982. Reprinted by permission of Johns Hopkins University and Gerald Duckworth & Co., Ltd.

Chapter 6

Translations in this chapter are by Stylianos V. Spyridakis and Bradley P. Nystrom: Thucydides, Pericles "Funeral Speech" 2.40.1, 2.37, 2.39, in *Ancient Greece: Documentary Perspectives,* pp. 10–15. Copyright © 1985 by Kendall-Hunt Publishing Company. Used with permission. Lysias: *Oration* 24 from *The Murder of Herodes and Other Trials from the Athenian Law Courts,* translated by Kathleen Freeman, reprinted by permission of Hackett Publishing Co., Inc. Copyright © 1963 by W. W. Norton & Company, Inc. C. W. Fornara, Plutarch, *Pericles* 24.5, No. 96, and Aristophanes, *Acharnians,* lines 525–531, No. 123, in *Archaic Times to the End of the Peloponnesian War,* Cambridge University Press (New York, 1983). Copyright © 1983. Reprinted with the permission of Cambridge University Press. J. Dryden: Plutarch, *Lycurgus,* 14–16, in M. R. Lefkowitz's and M. B. Fant's *Women's Life in Greece & Rome,* No. 89, The Johns Hopkins University Press, copyright © 1982. Reprinted by permission of Johns Hopkins University and Gerald Duckworth & Co., Ltd. J. J. Pollitt: Plutarch, *Pericles,* 12.5–7 (115–116), and 31.2–3 (66), and Pausanias, 1.24.5–7 (69), in *The Art of Ancient Greece: Sources and Documents.* Reprinted by permission of Jerome J. Pollitt and the publisher. S. B. Pomeroy: Xenophon, *Oeconomicus* 7.3–43, in *Xenophon: Oeconomicus: A Social and Historical Commentary,* 7.3–43, The Clarendon Press (Oxford, 1994). Used by permission of the author. Reprinted by permission of the publishers and the Loeb Classical Library from Diogenes Laertius, *Lives of Eminent Philosophers,* Vol. 2, 9.51–52, translated by R. D. Hicks, Cambridge, Mass.: Harvard University Press, 1965. The Loeb Classical Library® is a registered trademark of the President and Fellows of Harvard College. M. B. Fant: Aeschines of Sphettus in Cicero, *De Inventione Rhetorica,* 1.31, in E. Cantarella, *Pandora's Daughters,* The Johns Hopkins University Press (Baltimore, 1987). R. Lattimore: Euripides, *The Trojan Women,* lines 1276–1283, in *Complete Greek Tragedies,* Vol. II. Copyright © 1958 by the University of Chicago Press. Reprinted by permission. R. Lattimore: *Alcestis,* lines 669–672, in *Complete Greek Tragedies,* Vol. III. Copyright © 1955 by the University of Chicago Press. Reprinted by permission. R. Lattimore: "Solon 5," "Mimnermus 1," and "Anacreon 5," in *Greek Lyrics,* Copyright © 1960 by the University of Chicago Press. Reprinted by permission. I. Scott-Kilvert: Plutarch, *Pericles* 2.48–54, in *The Rise and Fall of Athens,* Penguin Classics (Baltimore, 1960), © 1960 Ian Scott-Kilvert. R. Crawley (with modifications by M. I. Finley): Thucydides 2, 48–54, in *The Portable Greek Historians,* The Viking Press, Inc. (New York, 1959).

Chapter 7

Translations in this chapter are by R. E. Wycherley: Aristophanes, *Knights,* 296–298, and Eubulus quoted by Athenaeus, 14.46b–c, in *The Athenian Agora,* Vol. 3: *Literary and Epigraphical Testimonia.* © The American School of Classical Studies at Athens (Princeton, 1957). Used with permission. W. Anderson: Theophrastus, *The Character Sketches,* 6, 11, and 29, The Kent State University Press (Kent, 1970). D. M. MacDowell: Plutarch, *Solon* 17.2–4, in *The Law in Classical Athens,* Cornell University Press (Ithaca, 1978). D. Parker: Aristophanes, *The Wasps,* 553–558, 87–113, from *Three Comedies: The Birds, The Clouds, the Wasps* by Aristophanes (Ann Arbor: The University of Michigan Press, 1969). Used with permission. Lysias: *Orations* 1 and 32, Demosthenes: *Oration* 54, and Antiphon: *Oration* 1, from *The Murder of Herodes and Other Trials from the Athenian Law Courts,* translated by Kathleen Freeman, reprinted by permission of Hackett Publishing Co., Inc. Copyright © 1963 by W. W. Norton & Company, Inc. All rights reserved. Reprinted by permission of the publishers and the Loeb Classical Library from *Demosthenes,* Vol. IV, *Oration* 34, translated by A. T. Murray, Cambridge, Mass.: Harvard University Press, 1936. The Loeb Classical Library® is a registered trademark of the President and Fellows of Harvard College. W. Arrowsmith: Aristophanes, *The Clouds,* New American Library (New York, 1962). Copyright © 1962 by William Arrowsmith. Used by permission of Dutton Signet, a division of Penguin Group (USA) Inc.

Chapter 8

Translations in this chapter are by B. Jowett: Aristotle, *Politics,* 1329b25, Modern Library (New York, 1943). Reprinted by permission of the publishers and the Loeb Classical Library from Diodorus Siculus, Vol. VIII, *The History,* 16.92.5–95.1, 17.41.3–45.5, translated by C. Bradford Welles, Cambridge, Mass.: Harvard University Press, 1963. The Loeb Classical Library® is a registered trademark of the President and Fellows of Harvard College. Ian Scott-Kilvert: Plutarch, *The Age of Alexander: Demetrius,* 38 (Penguin Classics, 1973). Translation © Ian Scott-Kilvert, 1973. L. Casson: Lucian, "A True Story, 1.9–11" from *Selected Satires of Lucian.* Copyright © 1962 by Lionel Casson. Reprinted by permission of the publisher, Doubleday, New York, N.Y. T. L. Heath, Archimedes, "The Sand Reckoner," from *The Works of Archimedes,* Dover Publications, 1958. Copyright © 1958. Used with permission. Reprinted by permission of the publishers and the Loeb Classical Library from Diodorus Siculus, Vol. X, *The History* 20.91–92, translated by Russel M. Geer, Cambridge, Mass.: Harvard University Press, 1954. The Loeb Classical Library® is a registered trademark of the President and Fellows of

Harvard College. R. J. H. Jenkins: Philon of Byzantium, *The Seven Wonders of the World,* in H. Maryon, "The Colossus of Rhodes," *Journal of Hellenic Studies,* 76, 1956, Vol. 69. Excerpts from C. Andrews: *The British Museum Book of the Rosetta Stone,* copyright © 1991 The British Museum, British Museum Press.

Appendix

Plato: *Timaeus and Critias. Criti.* 115c ff, translated by H. D. P. Lee (Penguin Classics 1971), copyright © H. D. P. Lee, 1965, 1971, 1977. Reprinted by permission of Penguin Books, Ltd.

Illustration Credits

All photos are by the author except as listed here and on the copyright page.

Figures

Chapter heading coin photo by Kathy Thomas

1.2 By permission of Equinox (Oxford) Ltd.

1.13 Paros Museum

2.3, 2.6 Deutsches Archäologisches Institut, Athens

2.5, 3.2, 3.11, 3.14, 5.1, 8.2, 8.16, 8.17 Photograph by Karen A. Peters; courtesy of Harlan J. Berk, Ltd.

3.9, 5.6 Photo by Kenneth W. Chapman

3.15 Attic Red-Figure Neck Amphora (84.AE.63). Artist: Euthymides, The J. Paul Getty Museum, Malibu, California

4.2 Museo Archeologico Nazionale Tarquiniense

5.2, 6.6 From J. Warry, *Warfare in the Classical World* (London: Salamander Books, Ltd.), 1980.

5.11, 5.16, 6.2, 6.8 American School of Classical Studies at Athens: Agora Excavations

5.14 The Metropolitan Museum of Art, Dodge Fund, 1930. (30.141.2)

7.5 From H. F. Mussche and P. Spitael, "Town and Country Homes of Attica in Classical Times," in *Miscellanea Graeca,* fasc. I: "Throkios and the Laurion in Archaic and Classical times," Ghent (1975). By permission of H. F. Mussche, P. Spitael, and J. E. Jones

7.6 The Metropolitan Museum of Art, Fletcher Fund, 1937. (37.11.19)

8.10 Reprinted by permission of The Bodleian Library, University of Oxford, MS Bodi. 264, fol. 50r.

8.18 Drawing by Ann Dallas from H. Maryon, "The Colossus of Rhodes," in *The Journal of Hellenic Studies,* 76 (1956)

8.19 From J. G. Landels, *Engineering in the Ancient World* (Berkeley and Los Angeles, University of California Press), 1981. Copyright © 1978 J. G. Landels.

Maps

Except as listed below, all maps are by Martha Gilman Roach.

8 From M. I. Finley and H. W. Pleket, *The Olympic Games: The First Thousand Years* (London: Chatto & Windus), 1976. By permission of H. W. Pleket and the estate of M. I. Finley and Chatto & Windus.

10, 17 American School of Classical Studies at Athens: Agora Excavations

13 Reprinted by permission of the publishers and the Trustees of the Loeb Classical Library from *Herodotus: The Persian Wars,* Vol. III, Loeb Classical Library® Vol. 119, translated by A. D. Godley, Cambridge, Mass.: Harvard University Press, 1922. The Loeb Classical Library® is a registered trademark of the President and Fellows of Harvard College.

Index